Judaism or Zionism?

Judaism or Zionism?

What Difference for the Middle East?

edited by
EAFORD & AJAZ

EAFORD

Zed Books Ltd.

Judaism or Zionism? was first published by The International Organization for the Elimination of All Forms of Racial Discrimination, Agriculture House, Knightsbridge, London SW1X 7NJ, and Zed Books Ltd., 57 Caledonian Road, London N1 9BU, in 1986.

Cover designed by Lee Robinson.
Printed by The Bath Press, Avon.

British Library Cataloguing in Publication Data

Judaism or Zionism: what difference for the
Middle East.
1. Zionism
I. International Organisation for the Elimination
of All Forms of Racial Discrimination II. AJAZ
956.94'001 DS149

ISBN 0-86232-475-0
ISBN 0-86232-476-9 Pbk

US Distributor
Biblio Distribution Center, 81 Adams Drive,
Totowa, New Jersey 07512, USA.

Contents

Preface

The papers published in this volume were all presented at a Symposium held in Washington, DC, on 6-7 May 1983, sponsored by AJAZ (American Jewish Alternatives to Zionism) and EAFORD (International Organization for the Elimination of All Forms of Racial Discrimination).

In agreeing to co-sponsor the Symposium, EAFORD's main objective was to encourage informed public debate on a question vital to world peace and to peoples whose national and human rights are being violated. By doing that, EAFORD, as a non-governmental organization with consultative status with the UN Economic and Social Council, was trying to give its support to, and fulfil its obligations under, the United Nations Charter and the various resolutions of the General Assembly and other organs of the United Nations, particularly the Commission on Human Rights.

No permanent peace can be secured through military superiority which, as history teaches, has never been and will never be the exclusive monopoly of one nation or one people. Likewise, no just peace or security can be guaranteed through the violation of the national and human rights of other peoples. Consequently, what is urgently needed in the explosive situation of the Palestinian-Zionist conflict is an objective understanding of the forces generating the conflict, particularly the ideologies involved. An informed public debate is certainly a better instrument for peace and understanding than accusations and counter-accusations.

Ideally, any debate should include the various protagonists, and EAFORD tried to respond in that manner when it was subjected to a campaign of accusations by some major Zionist organizations in Canada in July 1983. Regrettably, the Zionist organizations refused to participate in a public debate and thus deprived the Canadian public of the opportunity of deciding for itself, on the basis of a responsible debate, the rights and wrongs of the issues involved.

The second best is to try to bring together persons of recognized intellectual integrity who can present the issues and deliberate on them objectively and authoritatively. And that was what the Washington Symposium attempted to do. The co-sponsors invited a well-known Israeli scholar and activist who belonged to a group which had declared itself for peace and understanding. He expressed readiness to participate, he prepared his paper and arrived at Washington. However, his group vetoed his appearance and participation, and thus deprived the Symposium of the opportunity of listening to a point of view which would have enriched the debate. Out of respect for him and because he is not to blame for failure to participate, I refrain from mentioning his name.

We do not believe that is the way to further peace and understanding.

There is no denying the pivotal role of political ideologies in the promotion and sustenance of the rights of peoples, groups and individuals or in the denial and violation of such rights. No political ideology should enjoy immunity from scrutiny and evaluation, or has the right to claim such immunity. Fortunately, since the creation of the United Nations and through its numerous resolutions, declarations and the international conventions, we have an objective body of principles and criteria which have been voluntarily accepted by the vast majority of the international community for making such scrutiny and evaluation. Whereas the adoption of a resolution may suffer from pressures exercised by some members on others, ratification of international conventions is normally voluntarily undertaken by a state. And these international instruments should provide the reference points for the evaluation of political ideologies and practices in the field of national and human rights. For example, the International Convention on the Elimination of All Forms of Racial Discrimination (see Chapter 18, Appendix), which was adopted by the General Assembly on 21 December 1965 and entered into force on 4 January 1969, and has been ratified by more than 100 member-states, including Israel, should be used to measure the racist nature or otherwise of any ideology or policy; and my regret was that, in dismissing the UN resolution on Zionism, Dr Peretz, for whose integrity I have the highest respect, failed to take note of that Convention and the objective criteria it established ten years before the adoption of the resolution on Zionism.

Through a strenuous effort to strengthen the rule of law in international and human rights affairs, we can hope to confirm objectivity instead of subjectivity and thus build on solid foundations.

EAFORD is most happy to extend its sincere thanks and appreciation for the great wisdom and energy displayed by Rabbi Elmer Berger for the realization of the Symposium. At the grand age of 75, he has maintained an agility of mind and dedication to the truth which is inspired by the best in the Jewish traditions and the immortal messages of the prophets.

EAFORD is also more than happy to join him in the words of thanks he expressed in his Foreword to the galaxy of scholars who gave so much of their time and energy for the cause of peace and understanding.

Anis al-Qasem
Secretary General – EAFORD
London, England

Foreword

'What is a nice, intellectual Symposium on Zionism and Judaism doing in this capital city of rough-and-tumble politics. "pragmatic" policy-makers and orchestrated clamour of special pleading lobbyists?' In various forms, this question was put to me by a number of friends during the several months of preparing for the Washington Symposium on 'Judaism or Zionism: What Difference for the Middle East?'.

The question reflects an ignorance or misunderstanding of the phenomenon of Zionism and its relevance to American policy on the Middle East's central and most stubborn problem. It was precisely this that stimulated the idea of the Symposium. My colleagues in EAFORD readily agreed and provided indispensable advice and support.

The history of the diplomacy which, after nearly half a century, resulted in the Declaration of the Establishment of the State of Israel in 1947, provides ample 'pragmatic', legal and political evidence to support the decision to sponsor the Symposium. Contemporary pragmatic considerations recommended the capital of the United States, Washington, DC, as the place to convene the sessions.

For the past several decades the United States has aspired to the leading role in the search for an elusive Middle East peace. At least a temporary end to that leadership aspiration came with the disastrous end of the Reagan administration's misconceived intervention in Lebanon, the collapse of the Camp David 'process' and the short-lived 1982 Reagan proposals. Even the Secretary of State, George Shultz, admitted the loss of American 'credibility'.[1] There are many complex historical reasons for this mournful admission. But in virtually every critique of American policy and analysis of the reasons for a consistent record of failure, the Zionist/Israeli lobby and its impact upon 'domestic politics' plays a role. Its significance is variously described from important to decisive. A veteran American diplomat and Middle East expert, Alfred Atherton, Jr, offers his inside, personal assessment. He writes:

> In my experience domestic political considerations have probably carried more weight in determining American Middle East policy over a longer period of time than they have on any other major foreign policy issue since the days of the China lobby. I say this not as a

> criticism, but as a statement of fact. It is a fact which Israel has long recognized, but which Arab leaders – with the sole exception of Egyptian President Anwar Sadat – have tended to wring their hands about rather than including it in their own calculations.[2]

The Ambassador writes with habitual, diplomatic tact. His complete article leaves no doubt that, while there have been – and are – other domestic activists, the predominant influence shaping public opinion – and the decisive political pressures have been provided by organized Zionism. Other authoritative interpreters with credentials comparable to those of Atherton agree, often employing more specific language. Among them are Evan Wilson,[3] Seth P. Tillman[4] and Stephen Green.[5] Even President Truman, considered one of the Israeli state's most dedicated friends, complained about Zionist pressures upon him in 1947. His administration was in the process of formulating policy on the proposed partition of Palestine and on the recommendation to establish a 'Jewish state'. To his *Memoirs* he confided:

> The facts were that not only were there pressure movements around the United Nations unlike anything that had been seen there before but that the White House, too, was subjected to a constant barrage. I do not think I ever had as much pressure and propaganda aimed at the White House as I had in this instance. The persistence of a few of the extreme Zionist leaders – actuated by political motives and engaging in political threats – disturbed and annoyed me.[6]

The list could be extended. No Arabs are included here to avoid any charge of self-interest. Stephen D. Isaacs, an American Jewish Zionist and a senior journalist for the *Washington Post*, has added testimony on the perceived power of the Zionist lobby in Washington in a book entitled *Jews and American Politics*.[7]

This abridged inventory should suffice to indicate that a symposium focusing on the distinction between Zionism and Judaism was no mere esoteric, ideological exercise. The authors mentioned are all down-to-earth political observers, with specialized knowledge of the Middle East, particularly of the long, bitter controversy over Palestine. None of them is a fanatic. None is 'freaked out' in some witch-hunting backwater of American life. None denies the right of the Zionist lobby to petition the American decision-makers. None can be tarred with the ubiquitous Zionist smear of 'anti-Semitism'.

The anomaly therefore is not the existence of such scholarly works or the organization of the Symposium. The anomaly is the rarity with which Zionism is mentioned in the plethora of words written and spoken about Palestine and United States policy. All too frequently, when reference is made to what Ambassador Atherton calls 'domestic political considerations', they are inaccurately, or at least imprecisely, labelled the 'Jewish lobby'. Occasionally this is recognized as an awkward designation with far-reaching political implications. More responsible authors or speakers will identify it as the 'Israeli lobby'. Whatever nomenclature is used, admission of the pivotal role played by organized Zionism in the diplomatic history of the Palestine problem is generally infinitesimal, measured against the abundance of news and commentary devoted to the subject.

Consider the record:

(1) The organized Zionist movement was a party to the negotiations which produced the Balfour Declaration.
(2) It played a major role in drafting the Palestine Mandate.
(3) It was recognized by the League of Nations and the United Nations as the representative for 'Jewish' interests in Palestine.
(4) It was a party to the Declaration of the Establishment of the State of Israel.[8]
(5) In 1950, the Knesset enacted legislation entitled the 'World Zionist Organization/Jewish Agency for Israel (Status) Law'. (See Chapter 16, Appendix A.) It is one of the Zionist state's 'fundamental' or 'basic' laws. This legislation makes the World Zionist Organization either an agent of the Israeli government or, as some legal scholars hold, an actual part of the government. Whichever description is correct, the law makes operative, as a functioning policy of the government of the Zionist state, the claim that Israel is the state 'belonging to world Jewry'. That is Zionism.
(6) In 1952, the World Zionist Organization and the conventional Israeli government completed negotiations for, and signed, a Covenant, which implemented the 1950 Knesset legislation. (See Chapter 16, Appendix B.) The Covenant established a 'co-ordinating committee' to allocate state functions between the government and the organized Zionist movement.

These are a few of the salient actions and legislative enactments which place the organized Zionist movement prominently in the spectrum of Israeli domestic and international affairs. In both arenas, therefore, Zionism should be a substantive consideration determining United States policy, just as the formulations of Marxism-Leninism are taken into account in US relations with the Soviet Union, or as apartheid is a factor in US-South African relations.

There is nothing conspiratorial about this organic relationship of organized Zionism with the conventionally recognized government of the Zionist state. It is all inscribed in published Israeli/Zionist law, in Knesset (Israeli Parliament) debates, in the official records of the World Zionist Organization's congresses. If there is a conspiracy it is one of deliberate silence or cover-up, or the indefensible ignorance of legislators and executive branch decision-makers in Washington. The general silence of the information media about these matters, not only in the United States but throughout the Israeli-orientated Western democracies, is also attributable either to dereliction, to inadequate investigation of so important a party as the Zionist movement to all Israeli policies, or to deliberate muting of information which is of critical importance to public opinion. Consequently, the policy-making machinery of democratic states fails to cope adequately with the core of the Palestine problem.

The Symposium papers – all by recognized authorities – examine the impact of Zionism and/or its Middle East state on the generally recognized issues. For the Zionist character of the state of Israel, and the influence of the Zionist/Israel lobby in Washington and the United Nations, have direct and identifiable bearing on the displaced Palestinian people, on acceptance of the PLO (Palestine Liberation Organization) in political processes for resolving this central issue, on Israeli aggressions into territories generally recognized to be Arab lands, on the domestic Israeli problem of second-class citizenship status for its Palestinian minority, now approximately 16% of the total population. Official Washington's 'recognition' of the Zionist *apparat* as spokesman for something called 'the American Jewish community' creates a seriously distorted perception of the identity of Jews in American society. Washington's politicizing of American Jews as bloc voters to be delivered by the Zionist lobby ignores the fact that only a minority of American Jews are card-carrying Zionists. There is a long, historic tradition of rejection of political/national Zionism, not only in the United States, but in all democratic states. The political cynicism that ignores these salient facts, or the convenient ignorance which simply does not want to know the more complex truth, nourish popular questioning of the integrity of the nationality status of Jews and threaten corruption of the spiritual integrity of Judaism.

All of these were – and are – pragmatic, real-world reasons for convening a Symposium of scholars who, in some form and with varying reasons, could, in the front-yard of the official policy-makers, penetrate the myths about Zionism and help lift public discussion of the phenomenon out of the partisan, contrived, emotionalized 'sacred cow' status it has enjoyed for all but the knowledgeable and sophisticated. In fact, a Symposium where the 'virtues' commonly attributed to Zionism were subjected to public debate and critical analysis was, in itself, a bold stroke for free discussion of many of the issues thwarting progress towards settlement of the problems of Palestine and the Palestinians. For only when the 'sacred cow' image of organized Zionism is dissipated by such responsible, knowledgeable scrutiny will it be profitable to debate the issues in the Middle East's central problem free from the taboos usually associated with the sacred and the reverential.

In my introductory remarks, opening the Symposium, I said,

> We are all particularly grateful to the scholars and political authorities who have come to present the formal papers. Some have come from long distances and even from foreign lands. Their travel and preparation have required sacrifices of time and effort. The only compensation offered has been the sincere hope that in these two days, collectively, we may contribute some enlightenment about a factor in the protracted, central problem in the Middle East about which full and free discussion has been, with excessive delicacy, studiously muted and generally avoided.

The principal participants have not been asked – nor have they volunteered – to submit to any intellectual inquisition. They exemplify freedom of thought at its best and offer conclusions of conscientious thought, freely and independently pursued. The symposium was not conceived to offer any common political/territorial resolution of the historic Palestinian/Zionist confrontation, now approaching the seventh decade of its duration. The single element about which I feel confident to say there is broad agreement is that what is generally described as 'political' or 'national' Zionism – or by some as 'Jewish nationalism' – is an important ingredient for understanding the root-cause of the protracted conflict. The presence of both the principal participants and audience, I believe, suggests the American people – in fact all interested in a genuine Middle East peace – are entitled to, and indeed must have, a better understanding of this Zionist phenomenon than our governmental officials or the media have so far provided.

The initial announcement for the Symposium promised there would be no effort to homogenize the deliberations into any final, declaratory resolutions. A record will be made and, as soon as responsibly possible, will be published in a volume for distribution to wider audiences.

I have one, final word of introduction. I am unapologetically a declared anti-Zionist. That designation has substantive meaning only in the context of understanding the variety of Zionism which it rejects. Some who address this Symposium call themselves Zionists. They will explain why, nevertheless, they are here. One participant – and a long-time personal friend – in response to my invitation to provide one of the papers, wrote, 'I would not classify myself as an anti-Zionist, perhaps not even a "non", but I am happy to accept your invitation'. Perhaps one of the most important contributions of the Symposium will be to caution against employing clichés and labels as substitutes for substance in the continuation and almost certain expansion of debate about the issues of the Middle East problem. This, in itself, would be no small achievement.

Labels are not of themselves important. What is important is that free, responsible, substantive discussion and partisan views are now – and almost consistently have been – more visible and articulate in the Zionist state than here. The sponsors of this Symposium hope it will help correct this imbalance.

In this volume, I take the opportunity to thank the Symposium participants again. I hope, as with most scholars, they will feel that 'publication' is a small part of their reward for having contributed to this effort to put Zionism into the category of responsible political debate where it should long have been. Among others to whom I am grateful are my associates in EAFORD. They were unstintingly supportive. They demonstrated genuine intellectual and moral integrity by permitting an absolute freedom in programming the event. Dr Alfred Moleah, one of these associates and also a participant, was particularly helpful. He devoted several days to minor editing and preparing the papers for publication. Gratitude is also due to a number of scholars and eminent political personalities who were invited to the Symposium but because of other commitments were unable to accept but took the trouble to send encouraging and supportive messages.

The sponsors regretted that none of the American media saw fit to report the proceedings, either as general news or for any of its outstanding individual papers. We regret, too, that although invitations were delivered personally to all members of both Houses of the United States Congress, only two former members of the House of Representatives, the Honourable Paul McCloskey and the Honourable Paul Findley, accepted. Both had been defeated in the elections of 1982 and *post-mortem* election analyses in much of the same media that failed to cover the Symposium attributed their loss to massive intervention by Zionists, both belonging to and outside their electoral districts. Mr McCloskey's statement is included in this volume. It is an unusually candid, first-hand memoir, both of the tactics of Zionist interference in the political process and of the capitulations of his former colleagues.

The timidity of the American media is, at least partially, explained by Lawrence Mosher, a distinquished, veteran Washington journalist.

Two Israelis, a Christian and a Jew, are among the participants: Dr Riah Abu al-Assal, the Anglican Rector of Nazareth, and Dr Uri Davis. Both find the Zionist character of Israel contrary to accepted values of democracy and contemptuous of the rights of self-determination for what I call non-'Jewish people' nationals of Palestine, both inside pre-June 1967 Israel and in the occupied territories. Both have suffered for their persistence in advocating correctives for the Zionist flouting of these rights.

Although the Symposium's title featured 'Judaism and Zionism', there is at least as much theological confusion in Christian circles as there is among Jews about the endorsement of the Zionist state as the fulfilment of Scripture. But as with Jewish anti-Zionists, there is relatively little public exposure given to the explicit rejection of this idea compared with the gaudy blandishments of the Zionist state and of the former Prime Minister, Menachem Begin, by such as the Jerry Falwells and the Moral Majority. The Reverend Dr William A. Walmsley provides an eloquent, Bible-orientated refutation of such evangelism.

The segment of the Symposium dedicated to a critical examination of the religious/theological presumption of exclusivist, political/national Zionism and its Middle Eastern state, features an exponent of orthodox, traditional Judaism, Rabbi Yosef Becher, and an exponent of fundamental, traditional Islam, Dr Isma'il R. Al-Faruqi. Both examine the political phenomena, using the authority of their respective Holy Writs. These two papers are indispensable for all who wish to understand the Arab/Israeli/Zionist/Palestinian conflict as the *political*/territorial problem it is, lifting it out of the realm of objectionable controversy between genuine religionists, which it certainly is not.

Rabbi Becher, a sound scholar both of Scripture (the Torah) and of rabbinic (post-biblical) literature, finds the present state and the political Zionist movement totally incompatible with the divine promise of a redemption and the authentic hope for a messianic era.

Dr Al-Faruqi's paper has the added dimension of addressing forthrightly the Zionist campaign to 'religionize' the issues by misrepresenting Islam and campaigning pejoratively against Muslims (although the Zionist state has been a quiet, even if not very formidable, ally of the Ayatollah Khomeini).

Dr Herrmann addresses the subject of Zionism/Israel from the viewpoint of a liberal, Reform Jew. The two, he finds, are antithetical and his presentation fleshes out important details of the long history of rejection of Zionist nationalism among Jews of free, democratic societies. Liberal Judaism reached its fullest development in the United States where, today, in their political capitulation to Zionism and ethnic 'Jewishness', ironically the politicians find no time for consideration of devotees of this liberal tradition.

Dr Alan Taylor's paper addresses the deliberate, or inherent, ambiguity of Zionism. That theme is amplified by Dr Mezvinsky whose paper is an in-depth examination of the tortured and futile efforts of two humanitarians, Dr Judah Magnes and Dr Martin Buber, to lift Zionism above its inherent tribalism and exclusivism, and stretch its principles to accept the humanity of Palestine's non-'Jewish people' Palestinians. Both Dr Taylor and Dr Mezvinsky, either directly or indirectly, raise the basic question which cannot much longer be deferred by the world's policy-makers who profess dedication to democratic values. That question is whether or not the Zionism which campaigned for and built a state structured to be permanently dominated by Zionists can ever accommodate itself to embrace non-'Jewish people' citizens on a basis of full equality, regardless of religious preferences or ethnic derivation. The question is now raised in a political context by minority political parties in Israel which depart from the standard Zionism of both Labour and Likud. The issue is much clearer to Israeli Jews and more freely debated there than it is in the world's established democracies. This embarrassing fact is an indictment of the governmental and information establishments of the traditional democratic states.

Dr Peretz's paper is not unrelated to these deviant Israeli 'Zionists'. He addresses the semantics popularly used and often encouraged by orthodox Zionists to ward off critical and precise judgements of the national/political variety. Dr Peretz has enjoyed a long career as a Middle East scholar. He commands respect from many 'moderate' Israelis as well as Arabs, including some Palestinians. A bit of spice was added to the programme, when his negative criticism of the United Nations General Assembly resolution which called Zionism 'a form of racial discrimination' evoked a challenge from Dr Anis Al-Qasem, who defended the resolution. The exchange is illuminating and contributes to the clarification which the Symposium hoped to achieve.

The difference of opinion arose, essentially, because Dr Peretz talked about *Zionists* while Dr Al-Qasem's challenge focused on the *Zionism* which is operative in official Israeli domestic legislation and in much of the state's foreign policy. The distinction reflects the essence of the Zionist/Palestinian problem. It explains why many Palestinians found Magnes and Buber at least amenable to some formula which might, eventually, have led to peaceful coexistence for the two communities. It helps explain why even Yassir Arafat has said the PLO could talk to Zionists who believe in democracy. Although he does not overtly admit it, Peretz could be perceived as agreeing with Al-Qasem, or vice versa, because in the final analysis Peretz dissociates himself from the chauvinistic, exclusivist form of Zionism which, in fact, is the variety dominating the state of Israel.

Whatever the relative merits of Dr Peretz's or Dr Al-Qasem's arguments, Peretz makes a major contribution in his unqualified condemnation of the use of the smear 'anti-Semite' against all who criticize or reject Zionism and/or the Zionist policies of Israel. The reckless use of this usually unwarranted slander has served Zionism well as a potent intimidator of the free and open democratic debate to which the politics of organized Zionism should be subjected as an important ingredient in the policy-making process.

Dr Tekiner's contribution is that of an anthropologist examining whether or not the General Assembly resolution condemning state Zionism as 'racist' is valid. Using authoritative Zionist/Israeli sources – some from anthropologists who are considered Zionists themselves – her conclusions bring a valuable and different discipline to bear on the matter. The subject deserves expanded research. Interestingly, although Dr Tekiner relied almost exclusively on *Zionist* sources, her paper evoked the only public disturbance in the several audiences who attended the Symposium. At least one apparently Zionist partisan stomped out of the session, shouting, 'I've had all I can take of this.'

Dr Alfred Moleah, a political refugee from South Africa, presented a scholarly comparison of state Zionism and its treatment of non-'Jewish people' Palestinians, with the official apartheid policies of the South African government. His evidence must also be regarded as indispensable for any who have accepted the propaganda line that Zionism is a liberation movement and the vanguard of democratic forces in the Middle East.

Dr Espersen's presentation emanates a sense of pathos and disillusion which must today be shared by many people, from many walks of life, as they begin to face the hard political reality which Zionism and its state have established in the more than three decades since the state removed Zionism from the speculative realm of ideology and theory. As a former Minister of Justice in Denmark, his personal confession of disillusion is of absorbing interest.

The two Mallisons' paper applies the criteria of United States domestic and international law to much of the substance covered in the presentations of other participants. Both Dr and Mrs Mallison have devoted years to this important subject. Husband and wife, they work as a team. Dr Mallison broke new ground some 20 years ago when he identified the Zionist organization as a 'public body', not a voluntary charitable or cultural organization dedicated to 'do-gooding' work for unfortunate Jews. As a public body it should have been – but rarely was – required to conform to the norms of international law in its international activities and to domestic law in its operations in the United States. The Mallison studies find less than scrupulousness in this respect on the part of both the Zionist organization itself and of its two most powerful patrons – Britain during the years of the Mandate and the United States government – beginning with support of partition and United States 'recognition' of Israel in 1948. Those who wish to discuss the problem of Palestine with the least amount of political, religious or historical polemics will find the Mallison paper a store-house of little-known but critically important knowledge.

Dr Al-Qasem's presentation places EAFORD properly among the activist proponents of a just and equitable peace in Palestine. It focuses on problems of human rights, in which field Dr Al-Qasem has considerable expertise. A Palestinian himself, Dr Al-Qasem's presentation is factual, and his arguments are supported by abundant references to the numerous international agreements on human rights, to most of which Israel and the United States are signatories.

My own paper, probably too ambitiously, attempts to put something of all of these specialists into a comprehensive overview. I leave it to the tender mercies of the reader to judge how well or badly it discharges this function.

This Foreword is at least one responsible answer to the question with which this Foreword begins: 'What is this intellectual Symposium doing in the political jungle of Washington?' The published papers now recommend a different question: why, considering the central role of Zionism in one of the world's most dangerous trouble spots, has such a symposium never been organized before? And if not in Washington, where there has been so much dallying with superficial territorial and political bargains, all of which have failed because they glossed over the major source of hostility, where else?

But in the American democracy it is unlikely that the political savants will take the trouble to inform themselves of the wisdom to be found in these papers until enough of the American people inform themselves and outflank the purveyors of the myths and misrepresentations of Zionism as a movement consistent with either democratic values or United States interests in the Middle East.

I am reminded of an experience I had many years ago on the campus of Stanford University in California. I had been invited to address an audience of graduate students and their faculty advisers. In my lecture I had laid much the same emphasis on the critical role of Zionism in the Middle East as I have here. In the question period which followed, one faculty member who identified himself as an expert on the Soviet Union asked me why, in my opinion, there had been so little public awareness of the character and role of organized Zionism. As I remember now, some years afterwards, I listed for him some of the more prevalent restraints: the slanderous accusation of anti-Semitism which is levelled at anyone who offers a critical appraisal; the deliberate confusion of Zionism with Judaism; the propagandized image of Israel as a bastion of democracy and of Zionism as a laudable liberation force; the reluctance to treat Zionism as the ethnic-theocratic national movement it is because of the understandable sympathy with, and even sense of guilt generated by, the tragedy that the Nazi regime brought to the Jews of Europe. Then, I added, much of this protective screen which competent Zionist propaganda had erected about the movement could have been penetrated by a corps of expert 'Zionistologists' with a full grasp of the ideology and able to translate its language into plain English. For example, I said, could the questioner give me a definition of a 'Jewish democracy' (which Zionism claims Israel to be) that would be consistent with generally accepted criteria of democratic societies? My questioner thought for a moment and then said, 'I see what you mean, but you should not be discouraged in your efforts. Kremlinologists are now considered essential for understanding Soviet policies, but it took decades for Washington to realize that without the advice and expertise of expert Kremlinologists it was not possible intelligently to cope with problems between the United States and the Soviets.'

This volume will not, of itself, create the requisite number of 'Zionistologists' which the United States and the Western democracies need both in their electorates and among their policy-makers. But it is the sponsors' sincere hope that publication of these papers will be the beginning of a process which, sooner rather than later, will provide the knowledge which has been so disastrously missing from all the misguided efforts to resolve the persistent problem which is the major cause of international instability in the Levant, and the consequences of which proliferate throughout the Middle East. It is still axiomatic that it is the truth which will set men free. The sponsors of the Symposium believe that knowing the truth about political/national Zionism and providing authentic, democratic alternatives will free Western policy-makers, Jews who reject Zionism's 'Jewish national identity', the Palestinians who are the most egregiously wronged by Zionism, the Arab states victimized by Zionism's still unfulfilled territorial aspirations, and the free-thinkers of Israel itself from the incubus of this exclusionary, arrogant, often lawless and undemocratic force which, because of the inexcusable ignorance and the uncritical permissiveness of others, has been allowed to play a wholly disproportionate political, even imperialist/colonialist, role in the sorely troubled Middle East.

Elmer Berger
Longboat Key, Florida
July 1984

Notes

1. *The Wall Street Journal*, 2 April 1984, p. 2.
2. 'Arabs, Israelis – and Americans', *Foreign Affairs*, vol. 62, no. 5, Summer 1984, p. 1195.
3. *Decision on Palestine* (Hoover Institution Press, Stanford University, Stanford, Calif. 1979).

4. *The United States in the Middle East* (Indiana University Press, Bloomington, Ind. 1982).

5. *Taking Sides* (William Morrow & Co., New York, 1984).

6. *Memoirs by Harry S. Truman*, 'Years of Trial and Hope' (Double-day & Co., New York, 1956), vol. II, p. 158.

7. Doubleday & Co., New York, 1974.

8. This is the correct title for the proclamation of 14 May 1948 announcing the establishment of the state. It is *not*, accurately, a 'Declaration of Independence'. Meticulous scholars and legal authorities – among them some Israelis – argue that the selection of the title was deliberate and not the result of innocent ambiguity or an inaccurate translation from the Hebrew. So, for example, a brilliant, scholarly exile from Israel, Akiva Orr, in a book of compelling importance, *The UnJewish State* (Ithaca Press, London 1983):

> The Independence Declaration of the State of Israel, published on 14 May 1948 – the day Israel was declared independent – contains a number of peculiar formulations whose significance eludes anyone who is not intimately familiar with the contemporary crisis of Jewish civilization. One of these formulations is the key phrase, following the preamble, which asserts the independence of the state. This phrase ought to have read: 'We hereby proclaim the establishment of an independent state in Palestine'. This is what one expects from a declaration of independence. Instead, this phrase states: 'We hereby proclaim the establishment of the Jewish state in Palestine, to be called Medinat Israel (the state of Israel)'. So that Israel, instead of being proclaimed an independent state, is declared to be a Jewish state. It may seem to some that the difference between the two terms is insignificant and does not merit analysis. Yet declarations of independence are not drafted haphazardly. They are drafted only once in the life of a state, and every single word and phrase is carefully and meticulously selected, debated, and agreed upon by all the parties who struggled for the creation of that state. This was the case with the Israeli Declaration of Independence, which had to satisfy deeply conflicting secular and religious trends within contemporary Judaism. The Proclamation itself went through several drafts, each prepared by a different committee, yet even the final, approved, draft was an uneasy compromise. (p. 15)

Orr then explains by referring to a statement made by Ben-Gurion in 1970 at a time when the government and the Israeli courts were engaged in one of many controversies about the meaning of 'Jew' in Israeli law. 'Ben Gurion', Orr says,

> expresses the basic Zionist conviction that Israel must be a 'Jewish', rather than merely an 'independent', state, and that it is a state belonging to world Jewry rather than solely to the Israeli Jews, providing all Jews with a secular political identity, rather than merely a religious one. (p. 100)

That, of course, is the essence of Zionism. It was reaffirmed by the highest Israeli court in 1961 in the judgement handed down in *The Attorney-General of the Government of Israel v. Adolf, the son of Karl-Adolf Eichmann*,

Criminal Case No. 46/61 District Court of Jerusalem. The court held that '[Israel] is the sovereign State of the Jewish people' (paragraphs 33–35; 38) (emphasis supplied).

Translated into simple, non-legal language, this means the state of Israel – by its own definition – is *the* Zionist state. The more wonder that in assessing its policies and its relations with the United States – and other states – there is such a muting of the pragmatics of this fact and so little attention given to the substance of this ideological nationalism.

Part 1: What Did God Promise? A Look at the Scriptures

1. Introduction

Rev. L. Humphrey Walz

The declared, overarching objective of this conference is to generate peace with understanding. Such a goal is in keeping with the hopes carved into the wall facing United Nations Plaza from the west. Quoting Micah and Isaiah, the inscription there reads: 'They shall beat their swords into plowshares and their spears into pruning-hooks.'

Much has changed in the 27 centuries since those Hebrew prophets wrote. Technology has made pruning-hooks and ox-drawn ploughshares obsolete. Monstrous farm machinery, chemical sprays, blended fertilizers, genetic engineering and complex preservative and delivery systems have replaced them. And swords and spears have become quaintly irrelevant in our era of rocket-propelled, computer-guided, nuclear-warheaded intercontinental ballistic missiles and even more sophisticated and deadly weaponry.

Still, no modern words have yet surpassed that ancient scriptural expression of hope: that triumphant common sense will one day so dominate human behaviour that the energies and resources traditionally dedicated to destruction will be redirected to peaceful, productive pursuits. Even the Soviet Union, when it commissioned a peace statue for the UN gardens, could do no better than have it depict a broad-shouldered youth wielding a mighty sledgehammer to beat a gleaming sword literally into a ploughshare.

But if that vision is to be realized in practice, the Bible writers insisted, certain prior conditions must be established. People must first recognize that a righteous and compassionate God requires that they do justly, love mercy and walk humbly with Him (Micah 6:8). The prophets, therefore, vigorously and persistently challenged their fellow-citizens in Jerusalem and fellow-worshippers at Zion to do just that. In a community that rises to such heights, they promised, internal harmony would be so noticeable and external influence so beneficent as to startle and inspire others near and far to come and learn how they, too, might live as effectively under God (Isaiah 2:2–5, Micah 4:1–3). It was thus and only thus that the nations would be led to beat swords and spears into ploughshares and pruning-hooks.

The people of Judah and Israel, however, chose another course. They brushed aside the divine priorities. Instead, the narrow interests of self, tribe, race, nation and (most disturbingly) their religious institutions were uppermost in their minds. Covetousness of other people's lands, oppression of the powerless, scorn for the poor, disdain for the suffering, and contempt for justice and fair play characterized their self-serving planning. The results, the prophets warned, could only be calamitous. If Israel does not repent and change its ways, predicted Isaiah (1:20), it 'shall be devoured by the sword'. 'Zion', Micah (3:12) added, 'shall be ploughed as a field and Jerusalem become a heap.'

Such perceptions mark a peak in the ups and downs of the thousand years of spiritual development covered by the Hebrew Scriptures. The primitive beginnings and frequent backslidings recorded along the way often show a notably contrasting misunderstanding of the requirements of God. For instance, Exodus 32:26-9 reports Moses as believing that the Lord had commanded him to carry out a systematic pogrom of 3,000 Israelites who had been worshipping the golden calf. And, in the biblical book that bears his name, Israel's genocidal General Joshua credited God with ordering him to massacre every Palestinian man, woman and child in city after city of Canaan. Climbing past such low points in the biblical record of moral and ethical progress, however, makes us all the more appreciative of those high points of Hebrew Scripture in which the likes of Micah and Isaiah proclaim their clearer insights into the divine standards, warnings and promises.

The Protestant Reformed tradition to which I belong assumes, as did the pioneer American Reform Jews, that the Bible's most compelling charges and challenges to Israel, Jerusalem and Zion apply equally vigorously to us, our countries, our home towns and our religious institutions today. They also apply to the people who now live in the historic Middle Eastern setting where the prophets originally preached God's requirements to do justly, to love mercy and to walk humbly with Him.

It is with these requirements in mind that four competent scholars – an Orthodox Jewish rabbi, a Reform Jewish cantor and lay preacher, a Christian pastor and a Muslim professor – will now shine the light of Scripture on that too often obscured theme, 'Judaism or Zionism'. As they confront the modern Israeli scene with the Hebrew scriptural demand to choose ethical faith above ethnical nationalism, let us not be oblivious to the fact that Micah, Isaiah and their prophetic ilk are also sending each of us the same message very personally, loud and clear.

2. The Torah and Political Zionism

At the request of Rabbi Becher, his Symposium paper has been published separately by EAFORD. The editors of this volume have been happy to comply with his wishes. We believe a brief explanation of his reasons provides an important clarification of the important subject he addressed.

Rabbi Becher's paper reflects the purist, theological principles of the Neturei Karta, a segment of Jews who not only profess strict adherence to tradition, but who live by it, day to day. The entire question of Zion and the Holy Land, for them, is strictly a religious matter. The state of Israel, established through the mundane efforts and ordinary political activities of mortal men, is a secular matter, violating their vision of how Zion, as a sacrament, shall be redeemed. For Rabbi Becher and his colleagues, the true Zion will be restored by the Almighty God when the Holy One determines Jews have redeemed themselves by observing, to the letter, every one of the stipulated 613 commandments ordained by the Almighty God. Human usurpation of this divine judgement by regarding the state of Israel as sacred and central to Judaism cannot be countenanced as consistent with Judaism's tradition, according to the Neturei Karta. Therefore, in their view, the state of Israel exists contrary to the divine will.

The Neturei Karta are committed to the uniqueness of their faith. On principle, they reject even an apparent dilution of their conviction. To avoid any risk of transgressing this principle, Rabbi Becher asked for separation of his paper from those of other participants reflecting different theological views.

The editors willingly complied. We believe the separation dramatizes the dedication and piety of this group of traditionalists in Judaism and, accordingly, adds greater force to the authenticity of Rabbi Becher's rejection of national/political Zionism as a profanation of the 'divine promise'.

3. Politics and the 'Divine Promise'

Dr Klaus Herrmann

In the realm of the divine, reasoned argument is excluded. Religious faith and conviction cannot be tested in the crucible of laboratory experiment nor even with reference to the facts of historical evidence.

Presentation is submissible on relevant documentation and as to decisions, opinions and interpretations of acknowledged spiritual leadership. Religious spiritual authority must necessarily adhere to the particular faith community under discussion in order to apply or to counsel certain theological orientations.

The topic under consideration here is Almighty God's promise to that community which is known as the Jews or the Israelites or the Hebrews. Further elaboration of this promise may be found in that collection of sacred writ acknowledged as the Bible, more particularly the Hebrew Bible. This divine assurance and promise to the community of the Jews is concretely expressed and makes careful mention of certain prescribed, delimited and surveyed regions of the Near East. The area of this Promised Land is not merely Canaan ('land of the purple'), the ancient name for what subsequently became known as the land of the Philistines, i.e. Palestine. Original reference had actually been to the coastal area leading northwards from the city of Acre or Akko, but the name was applied far more generously to include appreciably larger geographic territories.[1] The 'Promised Land' as a term of reference was not to mean 'blessed land' (as in Deuteronomy 7:7–10), but rather a land assented to or assured. The precise biblical statement. 'And the Canaanite was then in the land, and the Lord appeared into Abram and said: "Unto thy seed will I give this land. . ." ' (Genesis 12:7), is the first of a great many. But this is the original one on which the Promised Land terminology appears to be predicated. In Genesis 15:18–21, a more detailed promise is cited:

> That very day, the Lord made a covenant with Abram and he said: 'To your descendents I give this land from the River of Egypt to the great River: the River Euphrates, the territory of the Kenites, Kenizzites, Kadmonites, Hittites, Perizzites, Raphaim, Amorites, Canannites, Girgashites, Hivites and Jebusites.

The Hebrew Bible's definitions of the Promised Land, as Basheer K. Nijim (a professional geographer) indicated,[2] do differ as to the particular time frame, the party to which the land was promised, and the general situation of the Hebrews/Israelites/Jews at various relevant periods. Thus, a very explicit and carefully delineated description of the promise is cited in Numbers 34:1–12. According to Nijim, the territory referred to would encompass the area from Mount Hor (some 40 miles north of Beirut) to Hazar Enon (some 100 miles to the east of Mount Hor), then due south and west to the Sea of Galilee's southern shore, following the Jordan River some 40 miles south of the Dead Sea, and then to the shores of the Mediterranean, some 70 miles south of Gaza.

However, the kingdom of David and of Solomon (10th centry BCE)* represented the maximum extension of the Promised Land; in territorial sweep it extended beyond the boundaries of Canaan. Certain methodological parameters of approach are indicated. Within this present context no attempt will be made to question the veracity of the Holy Scriptures. Scriptural sources are therefore accepted as they have been transmitted to posterity and as the acknowledged theologians in Judaism have interpreted them.[3]

While traditional (Orthodox) Judaism claims a monopoly on the Jewish religion, the progressive religious theology of Reform (Liberal) Judaism is included in this treatise, because it is conventionally recognized as one of the authentic expressions of that religion. There is, nevertheless, no endeavour to discriminate in favour of or against either grouping, or to assess relative merits, one against the other.

A particular vantage point, namely that of theologically dispensationalist Christianity, cannot here be assumed. Evangelistic or other forms of Christianity (whose theologians view the emergence of Zionism, as that term is conventionally understood, and the subsequent establishment of the Republic of Israel, as the fulfilment of the divine promise) remain outside the present discussion. The premise is that only Jewish religious assessments of the issue ought to be entertained here.

A further caveat: there is no intention whatever here of violating the religious sensitivities of any who are at variance with the arguments and conclusions of this presentation. Politically, Zionist Jewish believers in the liberal dispensational character of Holy Scriptures (the Hebrew Bible and the Talmud) act according to standards of behaviour and orthodox belief, as they and their rabbis interpret it. They are determined to commit themselves to an enterprise which they perceive to be divinely enjoined, and therefore reject the counter-arguments of other orthodox authorities. Secondly, with regard to Christian dispensationalist beliefs on the founding of the Israeli Republic and the extension of its dominion to those areas once part of the ancient kingdoms of Israel and Judah, it cannot reasonably

*BCE is the equivalent of the more common BC.

be a Jewish religious concern to enter into conversation with Christendom on the matter of expediting the second coming of the anointed one in Christian theology. Consequently, adherents of Judaism are not obliged to dissuade dispensationalist-minded Christians from their creed or course of action. Plans for the establishment of Jewish states or similar authorities predate Herzlian Zionism. Nearly all of the planners were non-Jewish. We challenge those who argue *on grounds of Jewish theology* for the occupation, liberation or annexation of ancient biblical lands: lands which are identifiable as the divinely ordained patrimony (subject to clearly stated conditions) of the house of Israel. Concomitantly, no case is made to challenge the state of Israel's geopolitical, military, foreign, economic or other non-theological activities. These considerations are outside the substantive purview of this presentation.

Utopianist Projects towards Biblical Fulfilment

The advent of the Christian Messiah was to be hastened, in the mind of Christians, by facilitating the establishment of a Jewish state in one form or another on those territories which are called the Promised Land. To be sure, not all of the non-Jewish planners of such projects responded to biblical motivations, although the literal reading of scriptural passages undoubtedly influenced them.

In 1695, the Danish merchant Aliger (Holger) Paulli submitted to King William III of England a plan for the re-establishment of a Jewish commonwealth in Palestine. His ideas influenced a number of his contemporaries who pursued the project. In 1714, the French adventurer, the Marquis de Langallerie, initiated negotiations with the Turkish envoy in The Hague towards the same goal, also applying to Jewish notables for financial assistance. Moses Mendelssohn in Berlin was approached in 1770 by one of his 'peers' about the re-establishment of the Jewish state in Palestine, but he refused to participate. Several German officers in 1781 suggested to the Jews of Livorno in Italy that they might be able to buy Jerusalem and large parts of Palestine for the 'Jewish nation'. These officers, apparently on duty in Livorno, had connections and influence with Ali Bey, a Turkish freebooter, who with his armed followers controlled these areas. When Ali Bey died, the negotiations came to naught. The Prince de Ligne in 1797 wrote a project for the founding of a Jewish state in Palestine, which he submitted to the Baroness Grotthus, daughter of a Jewish banker. A year later, an anonymous Jew of France published a call for such a re-establishment, soliciting the support of the revolutionary Directorate of France. Napoleon Bonaparte was influenced by this call and in April 1799 he issued a proclamation to all Jews in Asia and Africa in which he summoned them to battle under the flag of France to reconstitute Jerusalem. A certain impostor who claimed to be the representative of a non-existent King Siegfried Justus I appeared in Austria between 1832 and 1839. He published a proclamation to the Jews of the Austrian empire in which he nominated himself as the Liberator of Palestine, demanding that the Austrian Jews 'return' there under his leadership. The imperial Austrian police thought the matter sufficiently serious to obtain testimony of Jewish notables. One of these was Joseph Perl (1774-1839), patron of the arts and writer. Perl, who served as the leader of the Enlightenment (*haskala*) in Galicia, responded that Jewry had no ambitions whatever to return to Palestine. By 1839, the official newspaper of the British Foreign Office, the *Globe*, featured a series of articles on the establishment of a 'neutral' state in Syria and Palestine. The state was designed for the settlement of Jews from Czarist Russia, among others. It received the support of such leading British statesmen as Lord Shaftesbury who solicited Lord Palmerston to 'redress the historical injustice perpetrated on the Jewish people'. Christian mass meetings in England demanded of Queen Victoria that she restore (the community of) Israel in Palestine. The subject was even placed on the agenda of the Five Powers Conference, which was convened in London in 1840. This 'Restoration of the Jewish People' Movement among British Christians resulted in a project which Colonel John Churchill transmitted to Moses Montefiore (1784-1885). Colonel Churchill asked Montefiore, who was widely regarded as one of the most, if not the most, respected Jewish figures of his era, to establish a Jewish agency for the purpose of re-establishing the ancient Judaean state in Palestine. Montefiore actually submitted the proposal to the Board of Deputies of British Jews, which summarily refused to entertain the recommendation. In Switzerland, the Calvinist orientalist Samuel Preiswerk, in a series of essays which he published in the Basle journal *Morgenland* between 1839 and 1841, emphasized the necessity of the re-establishment of the Judean state in Palestine. His views were strongly rejected, in particular by the eminent Rabbi Ludwig Philippson, publisher of the leading German Jewish newspaper. Between 1850 and 1870 a number of prominent British and French statesmen spoke for such re-establishemnt, or at least for widespread Jewish colonization of Palestine. Benjamin Disraeli, Earl of Beaconsfield (an Anglican of Jewish origin), treated such plans in his Utopian books, *Tancred* and *David Alroy*. George Eliot (pseudonym of Mary Ann Evans, 1819-80), the famed British author and protégé of Carlyle and Thackeray, developed the method of psychological analysis in modern fiction. She published *Daniel Deronda* in 1876, a book with the same Utopian, Zionist theme. In a work entitled 'Tranquillizaton of Syria and the East', British Colonel George Gawler in 1845 stated that only the Jews would be able to rebuild all of these (!) territories, and in France one Monsieur Guers propagated much the same ideas in 1856.

Guers' ideas were advocated by Ernest Laharanne, private secretary to Emperor Napoleon III, in his 'The New Question of the Orient: Reconstitution of the Jewish Nationality' (1860). Jean Henri Dunant (1828-1910), who founded the International Red Cross, also spoke for the return of the Jews to Palestine and established the first Palestine Research Society in 1876. Numerous other Christians, G.J. Adams, Cresson Warder, Williams Newton and Edouard Cazalet Petavel among others, pursued identical objectives between 1850 and 1880. In 1876, the Earl of Shaftesbury, who was probably the most effective social reformer of 19th-century Britain, asked that Britain immediately facilitate the Jews' return to Syria and Palestine. Lord Shaftesbury, as the leader of the evangelistic movement in the Church of England, thus followed the general evangelistic message. Finally, in 1879, Sir Laurence Oliphant (1829–88), a British diplomat and author who in 1865 entered the House of Commons, drafted an ambitious project for Jewish colonization in Transjordan, the biblical Land of Gilead. (His 1880 book carried that title.) His research supporting the project received the highest British sponsorship, such as that of Lords Salisbury and Beaconsfield.

Theodor Herzl

It is doubtful that Dr Theodor Herzl had any acquaintance with dispensationalist Christianity before he wrote and published his *magnum opus*: *The Jewish State: An Attempt at a Modern Solution of the Jewish Question* in 1895; this is the English title of *Der Judenstaat*. In fact the correct meaning of *Der Judenstaat* is 'The Jews' State' (were it 'The Jewish State', it would have been entitled 'Der juedische Staat').[4] This book is correctly identified as the principal and definitive volume in which the plan for constituting a Jews' state was outlined lucidly and with great attention to detail. There was certainly no intention of re-establishing the ancient kingdom of Judah: the question which Herzl posed revolved on the decision as to whether Palestine or Argentina was to be the locale for this future Jews' state. Palestine is referred to as 'our unforgettable historical native home (*Heimat*)', but not in any biblical or theologically valid sense.[5] There can be no doubt that Herzl wrote the *Judenstaat* in a particularly highly strung frame of mind. He completed the manuscript during his last two months in Paris in 1895, before returning to Vienna. In his own words, he could not remember that he had ever been in a more exalted emotional spirit than when he wrote the book. He worked at the manuscript until he was totally exhausted. Interestingly, his relaxation in the evenings was attending the Paris Opera to listen to Richard Wagner's music. Herzl was especially enthralled by Wagner's *Tannhaüser*, to which he listened as often as it was featured.[6]

The *Judenstaat* specifically opposed theocracy. So did Herzl's historic address to the first Zionist Congress. His well-publicized remark that the return to Zion would be preceded by a return to Judaism 'seemed at the moment due rather to a sudden inspiration than to deep thought. . . .'[7]

The religious and messianic link between Theodor Herzl's *Judenstaat* and the biblical, conditionally assured Zion was actually established by one person: Rev. William Henry Hechler, Anglican chaplain to Her Britannic Majesty's Embassy in Vienna.

On 26 March 1896, this dispensationalist Anglican priest excitedly wrote to the Grand Duke Friedrich of Baden, to whom he had repeatedly spoken of 'the Return of the Jews to Palestine, foretold by the Hebrew Bible'.[8] His Royal Highness was not only sovereign of his grand duchy, but also one of Emperor Wilhelm II's uncles, a fact which subsequently proved to be of great importance in the furtherance of Rev. Hechler's mission.[9] 'I was wondering', he wrote to Friedrich, 'whether the Dr. was trying to fulfil prophecy. This would be wrong, for God will in His own good time and in His own way bring about His wonderful purposes.' This was not Dr Herzl's wish, however, for he knew nothing of the special prophecies on this subject. His book can therefore be summed up with his own words: 'der Judenstaat ist ein Weltbeduerfnis' (the Jews' state is a world requirement).

For the remainder of his eight-page letter to Grand Duke Friedrich, Rev. Hechler, in striking penmanship, elaborated on his central theme, namely that the 'last Return of the Jews to Palestine' had already begun; that 'Palestine belongs to them by right, for it is the only country in the whole world of which God has Himself said to whom it is to belong'; that Jesus said to his disciples in Luke 21:24 that the Jews 'shall be led away captive into all nations, and Jerusalem shall be trodden down of the Gentiles, until the times of the Gentiles shall be fulfilled'. Referring to the angel who said to St John the Divine in Revelations 11:2 that 'the holy city shall they [the Gentiles] tread under foot forty and two months', Hechler argued that these were 42 'prophetic' months. With the precision of an Einstein he submitted an amazing mathematical solution: the first week to which Revelations 11:2 alludes had commenced in AD 627 to 628 when the Caliph Omar, father-in-law of the prophet Muhammad, had taken possession of Jerusalem. 'If this is correct, then the 42 prophetic months come to an end in 1897 to 1898', Hechler wrote. It seemed to him therefore that within a year or two the angel's prophecy to St John would be fulfilled. The Land of Promise will then 'again belong to the people to whom God gave it about 1895 years Before Christ'. Dr Theodor Herzl, continued Hechler, offered the first 'serious and practical attempt to show the Jews how they can reunite and form a nation of their own in the Land of Promise given to them by God'.[10] Rev. Hechler's reception at Friedrich's court eventually resulted in significant political repercussions, including Emperor Wilhelm II's intervention. The emperor was also a Protestant Christian of inflexible commitment, as well as head of this Church by 'the Grace of God' in his kingdom of Prussia. On 29 September 1899 he responded to a letter which his uncle, Grand Duke Friedrich, had written him.

The emperor referred to the material on Zionism which his uncle had provided. He already regarded Zionism with sympathy and now saw it as of far-reaching significance and of serious, well-founded purpose. Emperor Wilhelm II was concerned not so much with the biblical and dispensationalist facets of the reconstitution in Asia Minor of the Jews' state, as with more immediate issues: the resettlement of Jews in the Ottoman empire would be of immediate financial advantage and would prevent Turkey's dismemberment, which Wilhelm greatly feared. Furthermore, as far as he was concerned, the Jews 'had killed the Saviour', and 'this the dear God knows better than we do and He has punished him accordingly'. There were still more tangible benefits to be gained from Dr Herzl's and Rev. Hechler's plans. In the mind of the German emperor there was somehow an unholy conspiracy between Jewish capitalists and socialists, although the latter were really no longer Jewish by religious persuasion. 'Moreover', the German emperor wrote to his uncle the Grand Duke of Baden, 'the energy, vigour and productive efficiency of the Tribe of Sem [sic] would be diverted to more dignified aims than on the draining of the Christians [sic].' There were, however, even more worthwhile reasons for establishing some Judaean kingdom in Palestine, a project to which Wilhelm II would lend his full support: 'Many a Semite who is stoking oppositional Social Democracy will take off for the East (the Orient), where he will devote himself to more worthwhile work, whose end is not, as in the above instance, maximum security penitentiary [*Zuchthaus*].'[11]

If the world Zionist movement were to fulfil its mission, reliance on Christians who viewed the Jews as divine pawns in the great chiliastic plan (whose crowning triumph would be the reappearance of Jesus the Christ) was insufficient. Obviously the essential precondition was the willingness of the Jews themselves to launch a *fin de siècle* exodus from new Egypts to God's Promised Land. Great expectations for such an endeavour could not be placed on the Jewish population of central and Western Europe who were economically secure and who believed they were also socially secure. Nor were there any illusions about the liberal-religious rabbinate, also known as the Reform rabbinate. With some exceptions they were fully committed to the social goal of secular integration. They had even formally renounced all chiliastic pretensions of Judaism towards a return to Zion and Jerusalem, much less a secular effort towards that end. It became necessary, therefore, for those intent on rallying the great masses in Jewish religious orthodoxy, to establish an acceptable connection between the sacra of Torah-true Judaism, its terminology and eschatological expectations, on the one hand, and the immediate requirements of the political settlement movement called Zionism, on the other.

Jewish Religion and Herzlian Zionism

Certain problems arise in defining the descriptive *orthodoxy* (Greek for *right opinion*) in so far as it applies to Judaism. The word is of ecclesiastical usage. It was applied to those (Christians) who adhered completely to creed and dogma and, regardless of criticism, believed the infallible truths therein expressed. The term was entirely unknown in Judaism until first employed by Abraham Furtado (1756–1817), a prominent member of the Napoleonic Sanhedrin of 1807 and chairman of its committee on resolutions. Several decades later it was adopted in Germany, actually for pejorative reasons by the reformist, liberalist element in Judaism. It was intended to stigmatize their co-religionists who insisted on retaining the old rites and traditions.

Jewish orthodoxy proclaims the unity and the incorporeality of a God Who revealed Himself both in written and in oral evidence. God's Torah or Doctrine is found in the books of the Hebrew Bible, particularly in the five books of Moses. More extensively, the orthodox Jews regard the Talmud (The Teaching) as equally divinely revealed. 'Talmud' is the name applied to works which are preserved to posterity as the product of the Palestinian and Babylonian schools during the 3rd and 5th centuries of the Common Era. The Talmud as interpreted by their rabbis and scholars remains the supreme religious authority for the great majority of the world's Jewish population.[12]

Jewish religious orthodoxy proclaims the eventual arrival of a human, but divinely appointed, *moshiach* (anointed) who will be a biological descendant of King David. This anointed one has not arrived yet. He will do so only in the 'end of Days'. His arrival on earth will be signified by the ingathering of the Jewish exiles from the symbolic four corners of the earth. With their ascent to Zion and Jerusalem, God's dominion will be established over all the world. The relevant biblical passages predicting this end are contained in Holy Writ: the Hebrew Bible and Talmud. They form part of the daily and holy day prayers of orthodox Jews, arranged in the Orders of Devotions for the year.[13]

These examples of divine prophecy and commitments might suggest that Judaism's traditional believers and practitioners would rally *en masse* to the emergent Zionist movement to reaffirm and redeem the promise. Such was not the case, however; not surprisingly the very opposite took place. Succinctly stated, orthodox Judaism proclaimed that the land of Israel was by *divine covenant* deeded to the Israelitic or Jewish religiously-defined people or community for eternity. God's metaphysical covenant with Israel, the 'holy people and congregation of priests', was entirely dependent on His bounty and protection for both fertility and safety from attacks by foes. The covenant was to be operative *only on specific conditions*. These conditions were that the Torah was to be observed and God's name sanctified. Judaism has been described as a divine pilot project, originally directed at the establishment of a model society within a circumscribed area of land and water as delimited by the Torah's definition of the frontiers of this Holy Land.[14] (In contemporary geopolitical terms the territory includes not only conventional Palestine but also the land beyond the Jordan River – i.e. parts of the present kingdom of Jordan – as well as significant territories in Lebanon and Syria, not forgetting the Sinai peninsula of Egypt.) But this eternally valid grant of title to the area of the Promised Land is inextricably linked to a theologically equally valid penalty of exile.

Such reasoning is forcefully brought home to all orthodox Jewish believers on the three pilgrimage festivals of Passover, Pentecost and Tabernacles, as part of the Additional (Mussaph) liturgy.[15] This exile, which God visited on the Israelites/Jews because of their transgressions against Him and His law, is very much part of the Israelitic and Judaean prophets' predictions of events to come, the foretelling of Israel's doom:

> Now these are the words of the LORD: . . . Your land shall be divided with a measuring rod, you yourself shall die in a heathen country, and Israel shall be deported far from its native land and go into Exile. (Amos 7:17)
>
> Do not rejoice, Israel, do not exult like other peoples; for like a wanton you have forsaken your God, you have loved an idol . . . They shall not dwell in the LORD's Land; Ephraim shall go back to Egypt, or in Assyria they shall eat unclean food. (Hosea 9:1 and 3)

For traditional Judaism, this banishment from the land which God had eternally promised Israel and Judah is conceived as a temporary punishment, a trial and a test of faith. But in rabbinic declarations, which have the weight of authentic, divine transmission from Sinai's heights, no voluntary emigration of Israelites from the Holy Land (voluntary exile) is permissible. It is regarded as a cardinal sin.[16]

Consequently, the orthodox books of prayer are replete with petitions for the anticipated return to Zion.

The realization of the return is foretold by the prophet Obadiah (17–21):

> But on Mount Zion there shall be those that escape, and it shall be holy, and Jacob shall dispossess those that dispossessed them.
> Then shall the House of Jacob be fire and the House of Joseph flame and the House of Esau shall be chaff.

In the light of such divine promises the religionists of orthodox and conservative Judaism could have been expected to rally to this nationalist movement that introduced itself as Zionism. The very term which became the hallmark and ensign of Jewish nationalism was itself one of sacred association and messianic assertion. The Zionides (songs of Zion), which sages such as Ibn Gabirol in the 11th century composed, were incorporated into the liturgy of Judaism. These Zionides expressed prayers for the restoration of what these composers perceived as the splendour of ancient Zion.

Nathan Birnbaum, the Polish Jew of Vienna who in 1886 had invented the word *Zionism*, or rather had plagiarized it from sacred Jewish liturgy, was infuriated by Dr Theodor Herzl's presumption in utilizing his term for the international movement's *nom de guerre*. Birnbaum, unlike Dr Herzl an anti-assimilationist theoretician, had created the word in the 1880s to apply to certain 'Lovers of Zion' whom time had passed by. In 1893 he wrote a sectarian tract with the impressive title, 'The National Rebirth of the Jewish People in its Own Country, as a Means to Resolve the Jewish Question: An Appeal to all Noble-Minded Men of Good Will'. Birnbaum thought Herzl would support his ideas. Birnbaum, who was desperately poor, characteristically immediately asked Dr Herzl to provide him with money. Herzl gave him 20 guilders.[17] In gratitude, Birnbaum accused Herzl of espousing Zionism for personal gain. The charge was an absurdity. Herzl had practically sacrificed his personal wealth to mobilize the world community on behalf of his vision. Birnbaum, the envious, vain and dogmatic miscreant,[18] eventually returned to orthodoxy whence he had originally appeared on the scene. He spent the rest of his days attempting to retrieve the word *Zionism* for purposes of Judaic orthodoxy. Yet, even among those rabbis who were in the vanguard of Liberal religious Judaism, and were instrumental in rejecting traditonalist Orthodox theology in favour of a reformed theology and ritual, Zionism meant something different from the movement which had appropriated the term.

Wrote Kaufmann Kohler (1843–1926), one of the leading intellectual forces in Reform Judaism,[19] convenor in 1885 of the famed Pittsburgh Conference of Reformed Rabbis: '. . . the true Zionism demands of the Jews to be martyrs in the cause of truth and justice and peace until the Lord is One and the world One'. This was not to say that Rabbi Kohler opposed colonization in then Ottoman Palestine by Jews who wished to settle there and develop the agricultural potential of the land. In fact he supported those efforts.[20] But such aspirations were not what the 'political Zionists'[21] had in mind. This then was the crux of the issue: a political, late 19th-century, secular interpretation of the longing for Zion of both the Orthodox and the Reformed Jew; the Orthodox who yearned for the physical restoration of the land of Israel under the supernatural command of a divinely decreed Messiah; and the Reform Jews who saw in Zion and Jerusalem the symbolism of the messianic period, but without either a personal Messiah or a physical restoration of the Jewish polity in Palestine and its environs.

Orthodoxy viewed God's promise and commitment to the Israelitic/Jewish community as being redeemable exclusively through the Messiah's personal instrumentality, not by those of secular-political leadership in either Christendom or Jewry. Therefore, once the World Zionist Organization had been formally established and the first Zionist Congress convened in 1897, a veritable hurricane of protest and outrage swept Jewish theological establishments. The reaction was observable in as widely disparate regions as Czarist Russia and Western or central Europe. Theodor Herzl had contemplated Bavaria's then royal capital city of Munich as the preferred location for the first Zionist Congress. On 16 July 1897, the executive of the Allgemeiner Rabbinerverband in Deutschland (General Rabbis' Union of Germany) published a declaration of 'protest' against Dr Herzl's call. Comprised of three Orthodox and two moderately Liberal (but not Reform in the American sense) rabbis, the manifesto

a) referred to *so-called* Zionists, thereby in effect denying the world Zionist movement a basic right of self-determination.
b) stated their aspirations for the establishment of a 'Jewish-national' state in Palestine to be contrary to the 'Messianic promises of Judaism, as contained in Holy Scriptures and subsequent religious sources'.
c) called on the 'confessors of Judaism' to serve the country to which they belonged (sic) with utmost devotion and to further its national interests in total commitment.

d) declared that these obligations do not contradict those 'noble endeavours' which are designed to enable Jewish field farmers to colonize Palestine, as such endeavours 'have no relationship to the establishment of a national state'.

e) asserted that religion and love of country place a charge on the rabbinate to request all in the interest of Judaism's well-being to remain away from Zionist endeavours, and especially from the projected Zionist congress.

Herzl's response was sharply sarcastic. He was able to summon the names of certain well-known rabbinical authorities (men like Grand Rabbi Zadok Kahn of Paris, Mohilewer of Bialystok and Ruelf of Memel) who were supportive of his position to 'redeem Zion' by secular and nationalist means since these were appropriate to modern diplomacy. While not willing to engage in theological argumentation (in which he was not competent), Herzl ironically commented on the rabbis' ability to twist everything to their requirements: 'When they speak of Zion, it can mean anything but not, Heaven forbid, Zion'.[22] An interesting retort also accompanied the fourth point on the manifesto, that of the Jewish farmers' efforts: 'We Zionists admittedly regard the settlement of farmers (in Palestine) as more foolish than noble, if it proceeds without the guarantees of international law'.[23] 'Protest Rabbis', a well-turned phrase which made short shrift of rabbinical opposition to political Zionism's purpose, became a household word in Zionism's public relations vocabulary.

The leadership of what became popularly known as Zionism, but should more properly be designated 'political' Zionism, could not pragmatically be faulted for using the vocabulary of Jewish scriptures and the prayer book for its own tactical and strategic purposes. It must be accused, though, of misusing religious terminology.

Political Zionism began as a revolutionary movement, though one in which all kinds of ideological inducements were being offered to a mixed clientele. Theodor Herzl and his immediate retinue were thoroughly assimilated and integrated into the upper-middle-class structure of central and Western Europe. A liberal and secular nation-state was their ideal for this new state of the Jews. Herzl certainly did not aspire to a *Jewish* state polity in which theocratic institutions would be restored. Had he been successful in implementing his own ambitions, the German language – not Hebrew – would have been introduced as the lingua franca.[24] But political Zionism was not, in the event, established by Herzlian national liberals, upper-middle-class adherents of the enlightened world of central and Western Europe. Rather, a somewhat odd coalition of East European folkishly-Jewish socialists and national-Orthodox religionists would do the real work of colonizing Palestine in their own image. Admittedly, those national-Orthodox Jews who accepted the political Zionist movement were much in the minority among the teeming masses of East European Jewry. In 1902 they formally founded the Mizrachi ('spiritual centre') organization within the Zionist movement under the banner: 'The land of Israel for the people of Israel on the basis of the Torah of Israel'.[25] From the very beginning therefore, even prior to the formal formation of Mizrachi, the Zionist leadership had an adequate collection of strictly Orthodox rabbinical talent, who interpreted biblical and talmudical statements on the Promised Land in precisely the secularist and non-religious manner which was useful to the Zionist endeavour.

But the Mizrachists did not represent genuine Orthodox Jewish theology. A large number of them actually left the World Zionist Organization after the tenth Zionist Congress in 1911 to start the anti-Zionist Agudath Israel, the world organization of Orthodoxy. This principled Orthodox-religious opposition to political Zionism continued during the formative period of the world Zionist movement.

In a book of the Babylonian Talmud entitled 'Kethuboth' (literally: marriage settlements) there is a significant passage about three sacred oaths which the community of Israel was supposed solemnly to have sworn 'at the beginning of the Exile'.[26]

These sacred affirmations were related to the words of certain talmudical sages who expressed their profound emotional yearning for the land of their ancestors, extolled the superiority of residence in the Holy Land as against living anywhere else and, once actually arrived there, 'kissed the stones and threw themselves in the dust of Palestine'.[27] Yet, with all of these religious prescriptions pertaining to the land of Israel, Orthodox Jews considered themselves to be bound strictly by those three solemn oaths. The community of Israel swore to: 1) refrain from 'forcing the end', i.e. attempting to hasten the divinely promised Restoration to their land through the instrumentality of the Messiah; 2) abjure any 'rebellion against the peoples of the world'; 3) abjure any attempt at regaining possession of the Holy Land.

Political Zionism was definitely considered to be in direct contravention of these three oaths. The talmudical sages also attached serious punitive measures against violators. 'Dire calamities' were to befall any who transgressed.[28] This attitude prevailed even though anti-Jewish hatred was the order of the day in Eastern Europe, particularly in the Czarist empire where imperial autocracy and the Church encouraged such virulent hatred. It held true also for the Galicean and Lodomerian areas of the Austro-Hungarian empire where the Roman Catholic Church trumpeted the charge of deicide. Despite these conditions, political Zionism met with condemnation in these territories. The overwhelming majority of the talmudic sages, pietists and moralists levelled threats of excommunication and banishment against it. Thus the Zadok Hakohen of Lublin (1823–1900) expressed this amalgamation of what might be called 'Zionidism', but which was anti-political Zionism (this is a term of reference which is deliberately coined, in order to differentiate the Orthodox Jewish yearning for a messianic Zion from pragmatic political Zionism).[29]

> Jerusalem is the loftiest of summits to which the hearts of Israel are directed, and our souls yearn for its holy air. . . . But I fear, lest my

> departure and ascent to Jerusalem might seem like a gesture of approval for Zionist activities. I hope unto the Lord . . . that the Day of Redemption will come. I wait and remain alert for the feet of His anointed. Yet, though three-hundred scourges of iron afflict me, I shall not budge from my place. I shall not ascend [to Jerusalem] for the sake of the Zionists.[30]

The spiritual leader of Poltava, Rabbi Elieser Akiba Rabinovich, who lived there between 1893 and 1917, organized a 'Black Cabinet' of Orthodox rabbis and laity to prevent the Zionists from opening libraries and information centres in the Czarist Pale of Settlement. In the Holy Land itself, protagonists of militant Jewish Orthodoxy in religion, notably the Rabbi of Brisk, Joseph Hayyim Sonnenfeldt (1848–1932), led the militant opposition to political Zionism. As early as 1898 he wrote from Jerusalem:

> As to the Zionists, what shall I say and what am I to speak? There is great dismay also in the Holy Land that these evil men [sic] who deny the Unique one of the world and His holy *Torah* have proclaimed with so much publicity that it is in their hands to hasten Redemption for the People of Israel and gather the dispersed from the ends of the Earth. They have also asserted their view, that the whole difference and distinction between Israel and the nations lies in nationalism, blood and race; and that the faith and the religion are superfluous.
>
> The chief of these ruffians [sic] in our holy land has uttered terrible words, full of denial of the Most High, promising that Doctor Herzl will neither rest nor be silent until the foot of Israel ceases from the lands of the Exile: mocking at the saying of the sages that the day of the Gathering of the exiles will be as great as the day on which heaven and earth were created. We in the Holy Land are distressed and our pain was not alleviated, when the chief of these evil men [sic] presented himself before the German Emperor whilst he was in our Holy Land and asked him to influence the Sultan – may his majesty be exalted – to restore the land to the people of Israel. And had I intended to describe to Your Honor the storm that was aroused among the masses of Arabs and Christians [sic] I would have had insufficient paper and been too weak to elaborate, since when he entered the Holy Land, Hell entered with him. We do not yet know what we have to do against the destroyers of the totality of Israel, may the Lord have mercy. For us in the Holy Land it is a sure sign, that Doctor Herzl comes not from the Lord but from the side of pollution, for we say: anyone who pleads in defense of Israel is exalted in the world by the Holy One – blessed be He –, while this evil man [sic] pleads in condemnation and multiplies accusations.[31]

Less stridently and more reasoned, in the language of European civilization and with scholarly vocabulary, Chief Rabbi Dr Moritz Guedemann of Vienna provided a more impressive comment. Guedemann (1835–1918) had made a name for himself, previous to his appointment in 1894, as one of the most inflexible opponents of reform in worship services. He had persuaded the leaders of Austrian Judaism in 1871 to desist from following their German co-religionists. In a sermon, later published, Guedemann emotionally defended the retention of those passages in the prayer services which referred to the Jews' restoration to Jerusalem and Zion, and the reinstitution of the sacrificial service on the Temple Mount in Jerusalem:

> Says the Prophet Isaiah (62,1): 'For Zion's sake I will not keep silence, for Jerusalem's sake I will speak out'. Why are they opposed to these prayers? They [the Reformers] say, that they do not square with patriotism, with the duties which are incumbent on us as citizens. . . All Jewish history proves that prayers for Jerusalem have not turned the Jews into poor citizens . . . Prayers for Jerusalem are entirely unrelated to citizenship, exile and political freedom . . . They represent the issue as if it were a political *coup d'etat* with cabinet intrigues and the like. The petition for Jerusalem is nothing less than the scaffolding of our Messianic aspirations which were not arbitrarily invented, but based on the presentiments of our people. . .[32]

Rabbi Guedemann had initially co-operated with Theodor Herzl. He even reviewed the *Judenstaat* manuscript before it was published and had no objection to it whatsoever. Then he obviously became deeply perturbed by the powerful repercussions the book produced. He recognized the irreconcilability between messianic Zionism (or 'Zionidism') and the very political, practical and this-world-orientated movement which the charismatic Herzl had created. Heinrich York-Steiner (1859–1932), one of Herzl's closest colleagues (in 1904 he had obtained the Vatican's promise that the Apostolic See would interpose no obstacles to the Jewish colonization of Palestine), wrote that Guedemann's vociferous opposition to the Zionist movement was Herzl's first great disappointment. This was not surprising because Herzl assumed the rabbis would be the very first of those who, flags aflying, would lead their congregations to Palestine.[33]

Guedemann added fuel to the fire by publishing his *National-Judenthum* ('National Judaism'). It was in direct contradiction to the ambitions, goals and programmes of the Zionist movement. The brochure's central thought was: true Zionism is not separable from the future of humanity. The Jewish future is not dependent on 'our national restoration in Palestine, with all the requirements of state sovereignty'. According to the 'true Zionism' such a Jewish future proceeds in closest connection with the ethical perfection and brotherhood of all mankind: 'Thus and not otherwise have our greatest past spirits understood and maintained Zionism. . . Zion counted and counts for the Jews as the symbol of its own future but also comprises all of mankind's future.'[34]

A half-century later, a Reform rabbi, Dr Ignaz Maybaum, was to echo some of these views. With incisive reflection on the distinction between God's perceived promise to the congregation of Israel and the republic by that name, Ignaz Maybaum stated:

> The Zionist crusade led Jewry from the holy dream to reality. Reality awakens all dreamers. The Jewish National Home is the reality, and it is *not* the Holy Land for which we have prayed for two thousand years . . . the Jewish people built a temple and proclaimed that God was not living in this building. The absolute monotheism of Judaism excludes every form of incarnation. . . Zionists do not descrate Palestine by living again on its soil and working on it. But they destroyed the conception of holiness which made Palestine appear more than any country in God's world a suitable place for the revelation of God. . . Palestine with its Jewish state will become as holy and unholy as William Blake's England is holy and unholy. . . In praying for Zion we cannot as faithful Jews mean the Mecca of the Jewish nationalists who set the State of Israel above all other congregations of the Jewish diaspora. In praying for Zion, we cannot as faithful Jews mean the Orthodox Jewish Rome to which the Jew living in the diaspora should surrender his religious independence.[35]

Is the political application of these Jewish *sancta* justifiable? There has been discussion of the intrinsic merits of the word 'Zionism' itself, and how this eschatologically valid term has been essentially transformed.

Of the same order of magnitude is the misleading designation of the state as 'Israel'. Israel is the biblical name which God assigned to one of the three patriarchs, Jacob: 'Your name shall no longer be Jacob, but Israel ("God strove"), because you strove with God and with men and prevailed' (Genesis 32:27, 28). 'Israel' in time became the name of the kingdom of the Israelites, i.e. the twelve biblical tribes who are also known as the 'Children of Israel', the 'House of Israel', or the 'House of Jacob'. The kingdom of Israel survived for about a century, from 1040 to 937 BCE. Eventually, 'Israel' became the name of the theological community or collectivity of Jews. 'Israelite' was the term commonly applied to Jews, especially during the 19th century. Regardless of particular sectarian preferences, i.e. Orthodox or Liberal, 'Israelitic' refers to the members of 'Israel', the covenanted religion-community. The central declaration of the Jewish or Israelitic faith is therefore: 'Hear oh Israel, the Lord [is] our God, the Lord is One'. With the identification of 'Medinath Yisrael' (state/republic of Israel), a very serious problem of semantic confusion was deliberately initiated, and it generated principled criticism. Furthermore, the definitive, descriptive terms 'state' or 'republic' have been (probably deliberately) abandoned. Official Israeli agencies declare themselves to be 'Embassy of Israel' and the like. The Israelitic religious communities in Europe are increasingly referred to as 'Israeli' communities, causing even more distortion. Consistently Orthodox Jews have therefore declared:

> The fact that the country which is the result and embodiment of Zionism has adopted the name of Israel, tends to spread utter con-

> fusion within the Jewish community and in the outside world: its policies and actions are carried out under the name of Israel which is the historic designation of the Jewish people. . .[36]

There are other words with some historic sanctity in Judaism that have been invested with secular identities: *aliyah* (ascent) is descriptive of the pilgrimage of Jews to Palestine as a religious duty in Orthodox Judaism ever since the (second) Judaean state's destruction. Even in biblical periods, the word was used to describe the obligatory attendance at the central Temple in the land of Judaea, as specifically prescribed in Exodus 34:24:

> Three times a year, all your men shall come into the presence of the LORD, the LORD the God of Israel; for after I have driven out the nations before you and extended your frontiers, there will be no danger from covetous neighbours when you go up these three times to enter the presence of the LORD your God.

Aliyah is used to describe the ascent of worshippers to the synagogal reading desk, to recite the prescribed benedictions over the Scroll of the Torah, i.e. the parchment scroll which contains the five books of Moses.

The Zionist movement appropriated the word for secular purposes, namely for the general immigration of Jews to Palestine, unrelated to specific religion-orientated goals.[37]

Keren Kayemeth (eternal fund) applies to one of the prayers in the daily litany and refers to an eternal fund in the world to come. The term was appropriated for the Jewish National Fund as the *Keren Kayemeth Leisrael*, established in 1901 at the fifth Zionist Congress. The fund's statutes declare that it was founded for the exclusive purpose of acquiring land in Palestine by purchase. Purchased land becomes the 'inalienable' property of the 'legal' entity described as 'the Jewish People'.[38]

Reform Judaism and the Divine Promise

A number of religious reforms ocurred towards the beginning of the 19th century. But one would probably have to specify 17 July 1810 as the verifiable beginning of Jewish Reformation. On that day, in Seesen, Israel Jacobson, the Royal Westphalian president of the Israelitic Consistory, formally inaugurated the first Reform Temple. Heralded as the Festival of the Jewish Reformation, the ritual reforms initiated were indeed revolutionary. An organ was introduced to the worship services as were a litany and sermon in the vernacular German language. There was a variety of other changes to the traditional manner of conducting worship services. Jacobson was a layman, but a number of Jewish theologians would subsequently reform substantially not only ritual and ceremony, style and mode of worship but the whole tapestry of Jewish theology.

Those who reformed and liberalized the Jewish religion substantially eliminated Zionidism as one of the cardinal principles of Judaism. The pioneers of this reformed Judaism essentially accepted David Friedlaender's (1750–1834) exhortation:

> As long as the Jews were, if not actually persecuted, at least regarded as strangers and treated as such, as long as they nowhere formed an integral part of the state, as long as they were not only made to feel – but were actually told that they were only tolerated and that they really belonged to Palestine, so long was there neither cause nor reason to change the contents and the language of prayers . . . it requires no special mental effort, only straightforwardness of soul, for the religious Israelite to say to himself: 'Here I stand before God. I pray for blessing and success for my king, for my fellow citizens, for myself and for my family, and not for a return to Jerusalem, not for a restoration of the Temple and the sacrifices. Such wishes I do not have in my heart. Their fulfillment would not make me happy. My mouth shall not utter them'.[39]

Friedlaender uttered these words in 1812. That year the Jews of Prussia were rather reluctantly granted citizenship, a right which was withheld in other German states for another 57 years.

This reform trend in Judaism was accompanied by significant changes in the theological interpretation of the divine promise. Rabbi Dr Abraham Geiger (1810–74), one of the most eminent of the Liberal-religious savants, saw Jerusalem and Zion as places from which holy instruction had at one time gone forth. He now wanted to see them as a 'spiritual idea' and no longer as a 'certain geographical locale' or one which was connected with a 'special divine Providence for all times'.[40] Abraham Geiger's opposition of 1868 became the standard of reformed Liberal Judaism. Petitions for the restoration of Zion and Jerusalem and for the ingathering of the (theologically) exiled Jews to Palestine were consistently eradicated from the liturgy of Liberal and, in one instance, even from American Conservative Judaism.[41]

The 1885 declaration of principles of American Reform Judaism, known as the Pittsburgh Platform, was primarily the thinking of Rabbi Kaufmann Kohler (1843–1926). It took special aim at the issue. 'We consider ourselves no longer a nation, but a religious community, and therefore expect neither a return to Palestine, nor a sacrificial worship under the sons of Aaron, nor the restoration of any of the laws concerning the Jewish state.'[42]

'It stood to reason that the theology of Reform Judaism would be deemed as incompatible with a movement like political Zionism.' There was a vital distinction between Reform Judaism as the interpreter of the universalistic outlook, on one side, and political Zionism, reincarnation of narrow nationalism, on the other.[43]

Rabbi Isaac Mayer Wise (1819–1900) more than anyone else may accurately be called the builder of an American Reform Judaism. Under his leadership, the Central Conference of American Rabbis resolved in 1898:

> That we totally disapprove of any attempt for the establishment of a Jewish state. Such attempts show a misunderstanding of Israel's mission, which from the narrow political and national field has been expanded to the promotion among the whole human race of the broad and universalistic religion first proclaimed by the Jewish prophets. . . We reaffirm that the object of Judaism is not political nor national, but spiritual, and addresses itself to the continuous growth of peace, justice and love in the human race, to a Messianic time when all men will recognize that they form one great brotherhood for the establishment of God's Kingdom on earth.[44]

The existential pressures created by the regime of Adolf Hitler influenced the Reform movement in Judaism to alter its theological position. In 1937, the Central Conference of American Rabbis replaced the Pittsburgh Platform with new 'Guiding Principles of Reform Judaism' (the Columbus Platform). The resolutions committee of six contained avowed Zionists, including Rabbi Abba Hillel Silver, one of the two most prominent spokesmen for Zionism in America. One member, Rabbi David Philipson (1862–1949), was the very incarnation of 'Classic Reform' and had vigorously opposed political Zionism and also Zionidism throughout his long life.

The Columbus Platform represented a decisive rupture with historic Reform Judaism. The salient passage on Zionism read:

> In the rehabilitation of Palestine, the land hallowed by memories and hopes, we behold the promise of renewed life for many of our brethren. We affirm the obligation of all Jewry to aid in its upbuilding as a Jewish homeland by endeavoring to make it not only a haven of refuge for the oppressed, but also a center of Jewish culture and spiritual life.[45]

This statement was in specific contradiction to the motivations of even many of the German Jews who had entered British Mandated Palestine to secure a refuge from the oppressions imposed upon them in Nazi Germany. They were refugees from their German homeland whose Nazi government had declared them alien and unwanted sojourners. Among these expatriated arrivals were some who had previously demanded the virtual surrender of Judaism as the price of total assimilation into the body politic of Germany. Some had also recommended the revocation of German citizenship from professing Zionists.[46]

The Columbus Platform would be only the beginning of surrender. There were continuing capitulations in response, first, to the Nazi murder of millions of European Jews, a number which Howard Morton Sachar estimates at between 4.2 and 4.6 million,[47] and secondly to the establishment of the republic of Israel in May 1948.

The World Union for Progressive Judaism became a member of the World Zionist Organization in 1975. In 1970, the independence day of the state of Israel was officially entered into Reform Judaism's calendar as a religious holiday. By 1976, the Union Prayer Book and the Union Passover Devotional (*hagada*) were replaced by what are virtually Zionist propaganda manuals.

All petitionary prayers for the (theological) ingathering of the exiles, the restoration of Zion and Jerusalem, and the return to Palestine were reinstated. The word 'reinstated' requires qualification because the terms of reference were entirely different from those of Orthodox Judaism. Traditionally these petitionary prayers refer to an eschatological event, and the traditionally Orthodox Jews recite them in this meaning. Their utilization by 'heretical' so-called Liberal or Reform Judaism is deeply resented by the Orthodox religionists who view such proceedings as blasphemy.

Even contemporary Reform Judaism, as a Zionist political conquest, has not accepted such Orthodox Jewish articles of faith as the belief in a personal messiah and his establishment in Zion of God's kingdom. Hence, the introduction of such petitions as: 'Next year in Jerusalem' are of a political character. They have been divested of any sacredness.

Rabbi David Polish, a foremost spokesman for political Zionism, put it well in stating that:

> When the Reform Movement began, it would have been inconceivable that it would ultimately strike root in the very land whose restoration it had rejected. In a profound sense, Reform Judaism today bears little resemblance to Reform of the first quarter of the 20th century. Philosophically, theologically, demographically and structurally it is a different entity.[48]

Reform Rabbi Ignaz Maybaum wrote in 1949:

> Zion is the mountain of the Lord with the house of prayer for all the nations of the world (Isaiah 56, 7). Zion is not yet. We must still pray for it to be established. The Messiah has not yet come, only a Jewish State has been established. The world is not yet redeemed. We must still wait, hope and pray. We are still in the *galuth* (exile); the citizens of the State of Israel as well. The Kingdom of God has still to come. . .
>
> There is no short cut to Zion whether the Jew is a citizen in the diaspora or whether he is a citizen of the Jewish State. Zion is not yet. The Mountain of the Lord is not yet established. We must still pray: 'Next year in Jerusalem'.
>
> May the citizens of the State of Israel learn from history and understand that Jerusalem is situated where what is beyond history enters history.[49]

Notes

1. There are other designations of biblical origin which apply to this area: Land of Israel (I Samuel 13:19), Land of the Children of Israel (Joshua 11:22), Land of the Hebrews (Genesis 40:15), Land of Judah (Haggai 1:1, 14) (Nehemiah 5: 14), Inheritance of Israel (Judges 20:6), a land flowing with milk and honey (Leviticus 20:24, *inter alia*).

2. Basheer K. Nijim, 'Biblical Zionism and Political Zionism', in *American Church Politics and the Middle East* (Association of Arab-American University Graduates, Inc., Belmont, Mass., 1982), pp. 22–5. Professor Nijim's well-researched article is deficient in the sense that he reads the Bible as one would a secular, historical account. Once the Bible is accepted as Holy Writ, as in fact it is not only by the Jews but also the Christians and the Muslims, it becomes logically impossible to change the premises of argument.

3. Reference is to the theologians of Orthodox, Conservative and Reform Judaism. Reform Judaism, in its wider sense, includes the Liberal Jews of continental Europe and the Neologue Jews of Hungary. In the United Kingdom, *Reform* is applied to the more conservative, and *Liberal* or *Progressive* to the more radical wing of non-Orthodox Judaism. No attempt has been made to include Reconstructionist and Humanist Judaism within the context of this discussion.

4. Leon Kellner, *Theodor Herzl's Zionistische Schriften* (Juedischer Verlag, Berlin, no date), p. 41. Herzl also refers to the 'Jews' land' (ibid., p. 127).

5. Ibid., p. 68.

6. Ibid., p. 18. Therefore Richard Wagner's musical compositions were absolutely indispensable for the *Judenstaat*. *Per contra*, his music is still not authorized in the state of Israel.

7. Ibid., pp. 122 and 222. Herzl's exact words for his inaugural address at the first Zionist Congress were: '[The] Zionism is the return to Judaism, even before the return of the Jews' Land.' See also Amos Elon, *Herzl* (Holt-Rinehart-Winston, New York, 1975), *passim*.

8. 'Herzl, Hechler, the Grand Duke of Baden and the German Emperor 1896–1904', documents found by Hermann and Bessi Ellern, reproduced in facsimile (Ellern's Bank Ltd, Tel Aviv, 1961), p. 1.

9. Herzl first heard of dispensationalist Christians when he addressed the 'Maccabean Club' (an elitist club of British Jews) in London in July 1896. He met several upper-class British supporters of Christian dispensationalism there. The Rev. William Hechler had originally served as a tutor with the grand duke and subsequently became an Anglican priest. Theodor Herzl actually rejected any kind of messianic intimation and told Hechler: 'I stand on realistic premises, and have got to find my successes in facts, which I have gained by work.' (Cf. Heinrich York-Steiner, *Die Kunst als Jude zu leben-Minderheit verpflichtet*, (M.W. Kaufmann, Leipzig, 1928), pp. 462–4).

10. 'Herzl, Hechler . . .', op. cit., pp. 2 and 6.

11. Ibid., pp. 48–53.

12. Emile Marmorstein, *Heaven at Bay: The Jewish Kulturkampf in the Holy Land* (Oxford University Press, 1969, Oxford) p. 8.

13. Genesis 28:15; 35:9–12; Exodus 3:8; 6:2–9; Joshua 24:13 and 18; Jeremiah 3:18 and 19–20; and 21:2–12; Amos 2:10; 9:14–15; Zechariah 2:16.

14. Marmorstein, op. cit., p.8.

15. Jakob J. Petuchowski, *Prayerbook Reform in Europe: The Liturgy of Liberal and Reform Judaism* (The World Union for Progressive Judaism, Inc., New York, 1968), pp. 252–4.

16. Kaufmann Kohler, 'Banishment', in the *Jewish Encyclopedia* (Funk & Wagnalls, New York, 1902), vol. 2 p. 490.

17. Elon, op. cit., *passim.*

18. Desmond Stewart, *Theodor Herzl: Artist and Politician* (Doubleday, Garden City, New York, 1974), p. 221.

19. This is, *inter alia*, Rabbi Samuel Schulman's characterization. See *The Universal Jewish Encyclopedia* (New York, 1942), vol. 6, p. 428.

20. David Philipson, 'Zionism', in the *Jewish Encyclopedia*, op. cit., vol. 12, p. 672.

21. *Inter alia*: Gerhard Holdheim, *Der Politische Zionismus: Werden, Wesen, Entwicklung. Schriftenreihe der Nidersaechsischen Landeszentrale fuer Politische Bildung.* (Hanover, 1964), p. 11.

22. 'Protestrabbiner' in Kellner, op. cit., pp. 211 ff.

23. Ibid., p. 215.

24. M. Berkowicz, 'Herzl and Hebrew', in Meyer W. Weisgal (ed.) *Theodor Herzl, a Memorial* (The New Palestine, New York, 1929), p. 74.

25. Marcus Cohn of Basle (in *Jüdisches Lexikon*, op. cit., vol. 4, p. 232) writes that Mizrachi emanates from the theological thinking of certain rabbis of the 19th century: Hirsch Kalischer, Elia Gutmacher, Mordechaj Eliasberg and Samuel Mohilewer (all of them strictly Orthodox), who quoted Nachmanides (Rabbi Moses ben Nachman, namely Bonastrung de Porta (1195–1270) of Gerona in Spain) in stressing the importance of settling in the Holy Land, that the spirit of the Torah could only be revivified in Palestine, and that only the Jews themselves could there prepare the final Redemption. However, according to Emile Marmorstein ('Theologian'): 'Zionist collectors quote Nachmanides on residence in the Holy Land. But this was excluded by Maimonides, who applied it only to the ancient Israelites' (*The Jewish Outlook*, London, May 1946, p. 10).

26. Jacob A. Lauterbach, 'Ketubot' in the *Jewish Encyclopedia*, op. cit., vol. 7, pp. 479–80. To this particular entry, 'Theologian' (see note 27) has further commented that Zionists are fond of quoting paragraphs 109b and 110a of the Tractate Ketubot in the Babylonian Talmud. But, 'They never mention Rav Jehuda, who forbade his students from leaving Babylon for Palestine.' As printed on the same page they would have been 'guilty of trespassing a positive commandment'. Rabbi Yehuda is also quoted to the effect that one who lives in Babylon is 'like one who lives in Palestine' (Ketubot par. 110a).

27. Marmorstein, *Heaven at Bay*, op. cit., p. 121, fn. 37.

28. Op. cit., Marmorstein, p. 121.

29. For an explanation of Zionides see: Schulum Ochser, '*Zionides*', op. cit., *Jewish Encyclopedia*, vol. 12, p. 666.

30. I. Domb, *The Transformation* (London 1958). Cf. Marmorstein, op. cit., p. 70.

31. Quoted in Marmorstein, 1969, op. cit., pp. 79–80.

32. Moritz Guedemann, *Jerusalem, die Opfer und die Orgel* (Sermon of the 18th March, 1871) (Harzfeld & Bauer, Vienna, 1871), pp. 5–8.

33. Kellner, op. cit., Herzl, *The Jewish State*, pp. 100 and 107.

34. Moritz Guedemann, *National-Judenthum* (M. Breitenstein, Vienna, 1897), pp. 40–1.

35. Ignaz Maybaum, *The Jewish Mission* (James Clarke & Co. Ltd, London, 1949), pp. 71–3.

36. *Jews, Not Zionists*, published by Friends of Jerusalem (American Neturei Karta), 545 Fifth Avenue, New York City, October 1978.

37. George Herlitz, *Aliya* in *Juedisches Lexikon*, op. cit., vol. 1, p. 216.

38. 'These are commandments which, when man performs he enjoys the interest in this world, and the principal remains for the World to come. They are: honouring father and mother, charitable deeds, early attendance at the House of Learning in the morning and evening, hospitality to strangers, visiting the sick, providing dowry for indigent brides, accompanying the dead to their graves, devoutness in prayer, establishing peace between man and his neighbour: but the study of the *Torah* is equivalent to all of these.' Said at the very beginning of each morning service of worship for Orthodox and Conservative Judaism. See also Hugo H. Schachtel, 'Keren Kajemeth Lejisrael', in *Juedisches Lexikon*, op. cit., vol. 3, p. 655.

39. Petuchowski, op. cit., pp. 277–8.

40. Ibid., pp. 278–9. See also Petuchowski, 'New Perspectives on Abraham Geiger', a Symposium of the Hebrew Union College – Jewish Institute of Religion (Hebrew Union College Press, 1975, distributed by Ktav Publishing House, New York), pp. 44–5.

41. Moshe Davis, *The Emergence of Conservative Judaism, the Historical School in 19th Century America* (The Jewish Publication Society of America, Philadelphia, 1965), p. 142. See also Petuchowski, 1975, op. cit., pp. 43–4.

42. David Philipson, *The Reform Movement in Judaism* (Macmillan, New York, 1907), p. 492.

43. Ibid., pp. 213, 441.

44. Ibid., pp. 496–7.

45. David Polish, *Renew Our Days, the Zionist Issue in Reform Judaism* (World Zionist Organization and World Union for Progressive Judaism, Jerusalem, 1976), pp. 199–200.

46. Dr Max Marcuse, 'Die Assimilation der Juden in Deutschland' in *Diskussion* (Hans Ostwald, Berlin, 1913), no. 4, pp. 3-14.

47. Howard Morton Sachar, *The Course of Modern Jewish History*, (Dell, New York, 1958), *passim*.

48. Polish, op. cit., p. 247.

49. Maybaum, op. cit., pp. 73–5.

4. The State of Israel: Biblical Prophecy or Biblical Fallacy?

Rev. Dr William A. Walmsley

One of the controversies raging through Christendom in recent years has been the matter of our Scriptures. The question being debated is whether they are inerrant, infallible and inspired, or merely the loftiest of literature. This is a germane question when one approaches the issue of 'peace and justice' in an area fraught with terrorism which is being opposed by the might of a modern military nation, nibbling away at the balance of that Middle East real estate known as Palestine. It is a germane question because everyone seeks some authoritative word, an utterance from God for the resolution of the most difficult and complex problems, especially the problem of the place of Israel and Palestine in the divine scheme of things. There are those who claim to have knowledge of such divine revelation. However, it comes only in their interpretation of this inerrant, infallible and inspired word.

While those who make these infallible claims do so with tremendous fervour and fever, they are of fairly recent origin. Not until after the middle of the 19th century did anyone regard that small trickle of Jews returning to Palestine as significant. After 1830 and continuing for several decades there was a tremendous dissatisfaction within the Church of England because of noticeable worldliness in the search for temporal security, and it was then that certain leaders began struggling with the issue of the Christian's proper place and plan in such a rigid but lifeless religious environment. Within this struggle came voices who wished to separate and identify themselves as Christian brothers, but to do so quite apart from the organized or institutional Church. They formed the 'assembly of believers', the cohesiveness of which came at least in part from a strong emphasis on prophecy and eschatology, the doctrine of future events. Their impact on the pool of Christian belief and thought left very few ripples until late in the 19th century.

Consideration on this occasion is germane for the Judaeo-Christian heritage because since late in the 19th century this movement has gained momentum and force, and the followers have become not only euphoric, but completely convinced that their prophetic exposition of Scripture has been and is completely correct: the evidence is that modern Israel was established as a nation in May 1948. At that time the leaders of this not insignificant segment of Christendom declared Christ would return to earth within a generation. This they rather loosely define as 40 years. If this scholarship and exposition of the Scriptures is correct and justifies their position, then the second advent or Christ's return will occur by 1988. Thus, it is important for us to consider whether modern Israel is the product of biblical prophecy or is merely an apparition of biblical fallacy.

In 1879 a young lawyer by the name of Cyrus Ingersoll Scofield was abruptly and convincingly converted to the Christian faith, becoming an ardent and faithful student of the Bible. He immediately began a fervent study of the prophetic passages and in so doing became cognizant of things in this world from a different perspective. He soon gained stature in this movement. In 1888 he was invited to address an important and formidable Bible conference in Rochester, New York, which he did with great enthusiasm, quickly becoming the darling of those in attendance because of the prophetic approach and eschatological appeal of his message. Early in the 20th century he published what is now known as the Scofield Reference Bible, in which the Scriptures are followed by a black line; below this line are found his thoughts and reflections on that portion of God's Word. From this publishing event in 1909 has developed a cult of those almost intoxicated with the concerns of prophecy as found in the Scofield Bible. Frequently they are unable to discern whether their understanding comes from above or below that heavy black line which divides divine inspiration from human enthusiasm.

It will surely not go unnoticed to anyone interested in the Palestine problem that this ringing address at the Rochester Bible Conference came less than ten years after the assassination of the Czar and the hideous persecution and pogrom of Jews in Russia. Possibly the single most significant force in turning American Christendom towards acceptance of modern Israel as part of Bible prophecy are the reflections, sermons and especially the commentary notes found in the Scofield Bible. It might seem uncharitable, but it would not be unfair, to say that these notes, even in the recent revised version of the Reference Bible, do not meet the standards of quality exegetical scholarship.

When Mr Scofield was reflecting on his commentary, he surely must have been reading in the newspapers about the return of Jews to Palestine. The first such wave began in 1881. It was a rather heady intoxicant to write and preach about what God had prophesied centuries before, and then hold up the newsprint before the audience and point to that moment as the one of fulfilment. Numerous sincere, devout and dedicated Christians have become intoxicated by drinking from that cup. However, as will be shown, this is biblical exposition of fallacy rather than prophecy.

To avoid pitfalls similar to those of Mr Scofield and his followers, certain guidelines and directions are imperative for any Christian interested in the study of God's Word. This is especially true for those interested in prophecy and eschatology. Christians have always recognized the Bible as inspired, a volume into which 'God has breathed'. This has been accomplished by His

Holy Spirit, which gives the Christian an infallible rule for faith and practice, or instruction on what to believe and how to live. To tidy away the cobwebs from that statement, let it be said that the Christian must always read, study and understand the Old Testament from what he reads, studies and understands about the New Testament. The Christian will, therefore, interpret the Old Testament in the light of New Testament revelation, that of Jesus Christ, His message and His mission for the world. It means that for the Christian, the Old Testament cannot be interpreted independently of what is known and understood about the New Testament. This is known as the hermeneutic principle, and when applied, the Christian must then conclude that the New Testament Church is the 'new Israel', the Israel of God. It might be said that the Christian Church is to the national Israel of the Old Testament, as the butterfly is to the chrysalis. It is part of God's own design, His plan and His continuing, tireless effort to reach the entire world with knowledge and understanding of His love and grace, as made known in the message and mission of Jesus Christ, who is the Christian's Saviour and Lord.

This is to say, therefore, that the Old Testament has been fulfilled in the New Testament, and what has not been fulfilled has been abrogated or set aside. It must be understood that this was the position of Christendom for at least 1,850 years. It was the position of such stalwart saints and scholars as Justin Martyr, as Origen, Iranaeus and Hippolytus; a position embraced by Martin Luther and John Calvin, the two towering figures of the Protestant Reformation.

It is not adequate for one to say this is so because members of the Christian's theological hall of fame say it is so. The concern here is that of 'Biblical Prophecy or Biblical Fallacy'. Therefore the focus must be on what the Bible says, following the rules and principles of exposition and exegesis. It must also be remembered that the whole is greater than the sum of its many parts, therefore the whole of the Bible and all that it says must be the concern of those interested in this timely subject. This obviously invokes the principles of theology.

This entire concern could be more readily addressed in regard to modern Israel, if the question could be readily answered of who is a Jew. The Knesset, or legislative body of modern Israel, continues to struggle with a definition; the American people are perplexed and confused, vacillating between racial and religious definitions. As recently as March 1983 the American Reform Jewish rabbis broadened their definition to include children of all mixed marriages. This is not modern Israel making a declaration, but a portion of those vitally interested in the future of modern Israel. For our purpose the definition of being a Jew takes as its reference the Old Testament, and not a quasi-religious-secular state definition, which takes as its reference the modern State of Israel.

The struggle for understanding begins with the matter of 'covenant'. God made a covenant with Abraham, the father of the Jewish people. Scholars today find little agreement as to the number of covenants made. However, for purposes here, the term 'covenant' is a singular, but refers to that which has been restated, redefined and regiven by God's grace through the centuries.

Caution should be taken immediately in regard to the meaning of this Hebrew word, *be-rith*, or 'covenant'. Common understanding equates this with 'agreement' or 'contract'. This is inadequate as a definition. A covenant is that which the greater gives to the lesser, and there cannot be any negotiating or bargaining over terms. In addition, it always had a spiritual or faith-like connotation. God offered a covenant to Abraham, which can be summarized by the declaration, 'I will be your God, if you will be my people', meaning, of course, that they would be His people and tied to Him by faith, or spiritual bonds. However, there were added incentives in the terms of promises. First, the seed; second, the land; third, the nation. At this point some scholars add the fourth promise which was the Messiah.

Briefly, these points must be considered. The 'seed' shall be numberless as the 'sands of the earth', or the 'stars of the heavens'. In numerous places in the Old Testament we find references to national Israel as 'stars', 'sand' and 'dust'. This was especially true during the golden age of the monarchy. It was Isaiah, perhaps the greatest of Israel's prophets, who first cautions about the 'remnant', that when looking to salvation or redemption, only the 'believing remnant will be saved'. The meaning of 'seed' will be discussed more fully in another place. Let it be said that some see here two seeds, which would indicate both the natural descendants and the spiritual descendants. The promise of the land was also fulfilled: fulfilled by the conquest of Canaan under Joshua and Caleb who prevailed when Moses' health failed. This precise piece of real estate was also held during portions of the reigns of both David and Solomon, for a period of about 26 years. The reference to 'nation' in the third place undoubtedly points to the hour Moses and Joshua emerged with a national people, free of the slave chains imposed by the Egyptians.

Several other remarks must be made concerning this covenant. As seen, these three promises of the covenant were fulfilled over an extended period of time. The land of Palestine, which is currently under contention, is claimed by the modern State of Israel on the ground that the Old Testament defines this part of the Middle East as Israel's territory 'forever'. It must be understood that the Hebrew word *ad olam* is more precisely defined as 'a long, long time'. This is not a term that would be equivalent to the English word 'perpetuity'. In addition, these promises of the covenant were conditional: the land, the posterity and the nation were all contingent upon 'obeying the law and keeping the statutes'.

The term 'spiritual' keeps wedging itself into our text and thoughts. Perhaps 'faith' would be more appropriate, as faith is that bond which transcends the old to the new: from Israel to the body of Christendom. In moving on through biblical history, we soon come to Isaac, the son of Abraham through whom all these promises were to be transmitted. Abraham stumbled in regard to his first born, lacking faith that his God would keep His promise regarding progeny. Ishmael was born out of wedlock, but within a perfectly legitimate custom of that time. Later, Sarah became pregnant and gave birth to this child of their advanced age. God then brought about the hour for Abraham to be tested, and he was taken to a rippling stone where, according to Abraham's understanding, God had requested a blood sacrifice. Abraham did not stumble at this juncture; he lifted the knife that would be plunged into the breast of this child who would continue his name, his posterity, who would inherit the promises and extend God's blessing to the world. However, Jehovah intervened, acknowledging Abraham's 'faith', or 'spiritual bond'. The Christian, when referring to the 'Holy Catholic Church', points to the example of Abraham and defines members in this 'Holy Catholic Church' as those who have united themselves to God by faith, since the time and in the manner of Abraham's uniting himself to God by faith in this heroic act described in the book of Genesis. This blind, unerring, unswerving, life-directing faith is that spiritual bond that qualified one as a citizen of Israel, and qualifies the Christian now as a part of this 'Holy Catholic', universal or indivisible Church; the Christian has the advantage of uniting himself to God by faith in Jesus Christ.

Following immediately on the heels of faith is that 'obedience' which is one of the covenant conditions. The heartbeat of Judaism, ancient Israel, and the Christian faith or the Kingdom of God is 'faith' and the pulse is 'obedience'. The first order for Abraham was to obey in the matter of circumcision; living, visible proof of his life-sustaining union by faith. Faith and obedience have been the two beats of God's plan to redeem humanity from the very beginning; this presupposes that there is a definite purpose and plan behind the goal of history.

The covenant with Abraham was never intended to be a purely Jewish covenant. From the beginning, it had universal scope, and both Judah and Israel were called upon to be the implements and tools in achieving that ultimate goal of redeeming lost humanity, which was to be accomplished through faith and obedience.

Abraham met these demands from the beginning. This is especially evidenced in that event which could have conceivably brought about the sacrifice of his son. This faith and obedience were counted to Abraham as 'righteousness', and God declared that all the nations of the earth would receive special blessing because, as the Scriptures declare, 'You, Abraham, obeyed my voice.' Later the covenant was confirmed to Isaac when its conditions were again stated, and the expectation of obedience repeated.

However, that is not the end of the story. Under Moses, Israel became a nation, some 640 years after Abraham's affirmation of faith as he stood alongside that stony altar. Later these people engaged in mass defection and went whoring after other gods. So. after some six centuries of living under the guiding presence of God's spirit within the individual conscience, their morale, conduct and deportment began to decay. God then gave His new leader, Moses, a set of laws for use as a guideline by which to live. The law demanded obedience; defection demanded repentance. However, pride and arrogance set in, and the concept of 'chosenness' became so cherished that it began to control these people as the centuries wore on. So God gave them a warning: 'If your heart turns away, and you will not hear, but are drawn away to worship other gods and serve them, I declare to you this day that you shall perish, you shall not live long in the land which you are going over the Jordan to enter and possess.' The warning was not heeded; penitence did not proceed out of their hearts, so a change was in order.

It has been said that Israel was a holy nation, the chosen people; and the failure of ancient Israel lay precisely in its mistaken interpretation of the word 'chosen'. Far too often the word was interpreted in terms of privilege. It was this concept of 'chosenness', implying privilege, that the prophets began to condemn. They wept and railed at what was happening to this nation of people they loved and served, but they were unable to acquaint them with what was so obvious. This chosenness was a chosenness for responsibility and for service, not for privilege; or rather, to focus the entire matter more precisely, the service was the privilege.

It must be recognized, however, that God was not through. As painful as it was for God, it was painful also to the faithful, the loyal, those walking in the steps of Abraham as men and women of faith. For history continues by recording the capitivity and exile of the just and unjust of these people alike, all together being taken into strange lands. Prophecy is occasionally called 'prewritten history', and here we learn that these prophets told how thousands would return from their exile, would rebuild the temple and the walls surrounding the temple, and would reinstate blood sacrifice. We need not wait for this to be fulfilled. It came to pass in about 516 BC and is recorded by some of those called 'minor prophets'.

God devised another phase and another means to nudge His people into the role of responsibility and privilege He had devised. Jeremiah, the gloomy prophet, became the mouthpiece of the Lord and foretold another approach, another way, a different tack that God would soon try. It would be a 'new covenant'. As with the first covenant, it was not limited to the Jews, or to national Israel, for means and methods had been provided for all of humankind to receive His salvation. Now, however, it would come through a new covenant.

The Christian faith for nearly 2,000 years has defined and defended the Christian or Holy Catholic Church as the fulfilment of that prophecy of Jeremiah which came with the advent of Christ and is now known as the new covenant. That part of the Church which might be called 'mainstream' Christianity would consider itself the legitimate and sole heir to the countless, exceedingly precious promises given by God to His people.

The new covenant is that which is spun from possibly the most familiar story, or historical event, known in our world's history. Mary was a special servant of the Lord, and uniquely chosen to bear that child to be called 'Christos' or 'the Anointed of God'. He had long been anticipated and awaited under the old covenant, and has been designated as the 'pre-existent Word of God'. This Jesus of Nazareth lived the humble life of an itinerant preacher, soon finding Himself in trouble with the religious authorities of that day. These religious leaders missed the countdown of the Messiah, because of their pride, lust for power and their single-mindedness in ridding their land of the Roman intruder. This rabbi preacher lived for about 33 years, was crucified by the Romans as they were manipulated and intimidated by the corrupt leaders of the Sanhedrin; later He was placed in a borrowed grave, from which He arose as a means of assuring humankind of God's grace, love and mercy both in this life and in the life to come. Quite simply, these are the events that established the new covenant which was not only predicted, but demanded by the failure of the old order, and foretold by the prophet Jeremiah, who was a voice of that order.

Within a few weeks of Christ's death and resurrection, a new form of the old order was organized. On that day the Church took form, and it is said that a large number 'were added unto', which means they were added to the organization, or the body of believers, that already existed. Christianity looks upon itself as a continuation of Judaism. The institution of Christianity, known as the Church, is not an addendum tacked on almost as an afterthought. It is clearly anchored in history by its identity with Judaism, with ancient Israel, and becomes the 'New Israel', or the 'Israel of God'. This is according to its most ardent and fervent spokesman, a Jewish rabbi by the name of Paul, who hailed from Tarsus. This means that the Christian Church, or body of believers, has not broken with the past, but rather is a development out of the past; it is a blossom which comes from time-honoured roots; it is the branch that must bear fruit. It would be impossible for the Christian Church to be cut adrift from the past without irreparable loss: 'the Christian church cannot forget the rock from which it has been hewn'.

It would be unfortunate to pass through the life and ministry of Christ, and fail to point out just one or two of the numerous ties and anchors in Judaism that He would have us maintain in the Church. First, there are the sacraments. The Protestant branch limits itself to two sacraments: baptism, the continuation of circumcision, that identifying mark for the Christian signifying what Jeremiah maintained was predicted and which would be 'circumcision of the heart'. Second, is the sacrament known as the Lord's Supper. This sacrament was initiated in the Upper Room where Jesus was celebrating the Passover feast of Judaism with His disciples. As part of our ritual, we remember His words when He said, 'This Cup is the New Covenant in my blood shed for the many unto the remission of sin.' During his ministry, Jesus' greatest emphasis in His preaching was on the Kingdom of God. This word 'kingdom' is *basileuo* in the Greek, and has nothing to do with borders, boundaries or limits of nation or state. Rather, it is that power or dominion which rules within the heart. It was Jesus' consuming effort to have that 'dominion' over the hearts of all His followers, over all the world, that they might feel the impact of His ministry and mission. This would be known as the 'fruits' provided within the new covenant community by His loyal and loving followers. From the branch comes blossoms; from blossoms, buds; from buds, fruit. This was Jesus' hope for God's kingdom.

For us to consider the plan of national Israel and move on into the early work of the Church without drawing attention to a significant parable Jesus taught during the last days of His ministry would indeed be derelict. It is the parable of the so-called 'Wicked Husbandman', which is found in several of the Gospels. The story is simple. The landowner went to a distant place and leased his vineyard, expecting some compensation probably in the form of a portion of the vineyard's harvest. His compensation didn't come; so he sent servants to enquire, but they were handled in a rough manner, being thrown out of the owner's vineyard. After this had occurred several times, he decided to send his own son, for surely, he thought, they would honour the request if made by the one who would inherit the property. For his trouble, he was not only beaten, but killed. The analogy is so obvious that Jesus didn't bother to explain. The vineyard was national Israel, God's chosen people, who had been chosen to bear fruit by taking his message of love, grace and mercy to the entire world. The servants seeking compensation were the prophets of Israel who taught and preached against the selfishness, the defection, the lack of loyalty and appreciation on the part of those who occupied the land. The son, obviously, was Jesus Himself, who was slain by those who leased and occupied the land. At the end of this parable, Jesus said softly and no doubt sadly to the Jewish leaders, 'I say to you, the Kingdom of God shall be taken away from you, and it shall be given to a nation bringing forth the fruits thereof.' The word 'nation' is *ethnos* in the Greek, which may be translated 'Gentiles'. Jesus here is saying that the new covenant will also have a new arrangement and it will be with the Gentiles. Then, referring to Himself, Jesus quoted from a prophet of the Old Testament: 'The stone which the builders rejected, the same will be made the cornerstone. The Kingdom of God will be taken from you and given to the Gentiles, who will bring forth fruit from the vines.'

Before considering that portion of the New Testament comprising letters addressed to the young and struggling churches, let us consider one or two other references where Jesus alluded to 'fruits' that were desired for the kingdom. Throughout the Old Testament the nation of Israel was likened to a fig tree. One day Jesus came by such a tree standing at the roadside, and even in proper season it lacked fruit. Jesus was obviously disturbed, but He paused for a moment, then He said, 'Let there be no fruit from thee henceforth forever'. We are told that the fig tree immediately withered. Any orchardist will confirm that when a tree has 'withered away' as described by the writer of this Gospel, it does not recover; life is gone, and its last service will be as kindling for the fire. Another time, early in His ministry, Jesus alluded to national Israel by speaking of Abraham, the father of that people and nation, saying, with some disgust no doubt, that God could raise up stones which would serve as better children than some found in national Israel. Then He concluded, 'Even now the axe lies at the root of the tree, for every tree that doesn't bring forth good fruit, is hewn down and cast into the fire.'

After Jesus spoke about national Israel, which was surely the first instrument God chose for ministering His message and mission for the world, it became obvious that this work was being carried on by only a few. These few became known as a 'remnant'. That term appears on numerous occasions throughout the Old Testament. Some twelve of their number were found in that Upper Room on the day of Pentecost, when the new covenant was affirmed, establishing the Church as the new Israel, or the Israel of God. This remnant is also the 'seed' to which reference was made earlier. There was always that one group that was recognized by God as being the 'seed of Abraham', the community with which God is in covenant relationship. That group was to be found even after the rejection of Jesus by the rulers and the majority of the old covenant Israel. It was the 'remnant', the faithful, the Abrahamic seed, the unswerving believers, who manifested faith in God in the same manner as Abraham when he was poised to sacrifice his son. When God's Son was sacrificed, God selected twelve to take the places of leadership in the new Israel. They were the apostles who were found huddled together on the day that marks the birthday of the Church, when the new covenant came into existence. These apostles became the heads of this new covenant people, the Israel of God.

No doubt Saul, the squatty rabbi from Tarsus, has gained most attention throughout the unwinding centuries of the new covenant's existence. He came from the tribe of Benjamin; trained under Gamabiel, the greatest mind of his day. He excelled first in the persecution of those embracing the new covenant; then with new light and understanding changed, and excelled above all others in advancing that message and mission of Christ. It was this man, Paul, who wrote some 13 letters to counsel and strengthen the churches which he established, then nurtured through his years of ministry. It is this man who addressed the church in Ephesus by speaking of the new Israel. This was a man steeped in the nationalism of Israel, the doctrines of Judaism, but he now refers to the followers of Christ as 'the New Israel'. Elsewhere he calls another group of following and worshipping Christians the 'Israel of God'. It must be remembered that the new covenant or new fellowship of Christians were worshipping on Sunday, or the Lord's Day, in the familiar synagogue, where they worshipped while part of Judaism. This was not done to accommodate the Jews and leave the synagogue vacant on Saturday, but because this was the day to be kept in honour of Christ's resurrection. However, this joint use of the synagogue didn't foster perfect relationships. All the early adherents of the new covenant were Jews who were part of that 'remnant' from the old covenant, from Judaism. They came into the new covenant clinging to many of their old beliefs, practices and ceremonies, insisting especially on making circumcision a prerequisite for membership in the new covenant. This was the first rift, and was caused by those called 'Judaizers', and was not settled until determined by James, the first leader of the struggling Church. It was the Jews of the first century who became the first Christians in new covenant membership, and of them, Paul said they were 'fellow heirs, fellow members of the body and fellow partakers of the promise in Christ through the Gospel'.

The allusions of Paul to the new Israel, or the new covenant, as the continuation of the old Israel or the old covenant, are too numerous to mention in this restricted time. However, one or two are of paramount importance and must be mentioned. When writing to the followers of Christ in Galatia, which was a hotbed of Judaizers, those demanding circumcision and old covenant ceremonies, he told them that if they were followers of Christ, then they were of 'Abraham's seed'. Whether or not they had been born into a Jewish household and practised the faith of their fathers, they were therefore 'heirs according to the promise'. He affirms the same thought elsewhere by saying, 'The blessings of Abraham come on the Gentiles through Jesus Christ.'

The greatest storehouse of new covenant treasure is that which came from the pen of Paul. He wrote the long, involved and penetrating letter to the church in Rome. This portion of God's Word is frequently used by those who claim modern Israel to be the same as national Israel of the Old Testament. It is essential therefore that a brief look be taken at this book, and those penetrating verses.

Paul earnestly affirms that Israel had obligations, but failed to keep the covenant it had accepted from God. He pointed out that Israel sought righteousness and justification not by faith, but by works of the law, which was never God's intention. He continues by assuring those Jews living in Rome that salvation is not gained by law; it is not gained by circumcision; it is not gained by ancestry. He then continues by explaining that this salvation is God's gift through faith and urges them to understand that every descendant of Abraham is not assured of salvation, only those who believe and accept the promises of God.

He then brings up the matter of Gentile inclusion in the plans of God, affirming that this is part of the prophecy, and makes the Gentile equal to the Jew. This brings us to that difficult section of Romans 9 to 11. It's unfortunate that time will not allow a thorough exposition of these passages, but permit me to point out briefly some of the errors many make by attempting to keep national Israel and faith Israel, or the remnant, all within the old covenant and as one and the same, but completely different from the new covenant, or what Paul terms the new Israel.

It is obvious that this body of believers in God was the remnant of the old covenant and one and the same as the Church of the new covenant. We might say that this Church was 'latent'. It was not completely explained and defined in the teachings of the prophets. Paul tidies this up in the Romans, Chapters 9-11. Again we have the symbolic tree, this time it is an olive tree, and through this Paul gives clear presentation of the relationship that exists between the Church and the old covenant. The Abrahamic or old covenant was that of which he had been a part most of his life; he grew up within its framework, the culture was in his blood, he had even persecuted this upstart

Church which he is now claiming is equal to Israel.

He begins by explaining that some of the branches were broken off, then a wild olive branch was grafted within the branches that remained, and this for the reason 'that they might partake of the root and fatness of the olive tree'. The new branches obviously represent the Gentile Christians, a new grafting on the tree of faith. It would be rather difficult to state more clearly in any manner that the Gentile members, who were just at that hour becoming part of the Christian Church, were members of that body, which had roots in the Abrahamic covenant, or the old covenant. It was to this covenant that all true descendants of Abraham belonged; however, membership was not by blood, but by belief. Belief or faith was what qualified the individual for membership in the holy remnant of Israel. This is the tree to which Paul now refers and it is faith that bonds or grafts branches within the trunk. Some of the natural branches were removed, because, like other vines and the tree to which we have referred, they didn't bear proper fruit. Where these natural branches were broken away, the new branches were grafted in and bonded or held together by faith, as were the natural or original branches. Paul makes is quite clear that it was the unbelief that caused the fruitlessness, and was the reason behind this pruning procedure. One point that should not be missed but must be stressed as heavily as possible is that there is but one tree. It is the tree of faith in God, and there are not two trees, not Jews and Gentiles, not national Israel and the new Israel, not Judaism and Christendom – but a single faith, which has united humankind with its creator since Abraham's courage stood him above Isaac with knife in hand, ready for the sacrifice.

It should be made quite clear and understood well that neither Paul nor any other New Testament writer shows any interest whatsoever in a national Israel, either then or prophesied for a later fulfilment. It never crossed their minds. The core issue of these writers was salvation of the immortal soul, not restoration of real estate for national pride and power. One of the hallmarks of the Scofield Bible, in its untoward emphasis on the restoration of Israel as the fulfilment of prophecy, is that which we find in this passage of Romans, where it says that 'all of Israel will be saved'. No one is allowed the luxury of interpreting a single passage of the Bible in a manner that is inconsistent with or contradicts every other reference to the same subject. When looking carefully at this passage, we find that it means 'all of remnant Israel', all truly united to God by faith since the time of Abraham, 'will be saved'. It could not possibly refer to a religious nation with boundaries and borders, armies and air forces, because there is no confirmation of that view anywhere else in the New Testament and it totally contradicts the concept of faith-relationship Israel that is strung through both the Old and New Testaments like a golden thread.

Paul is eager that both the natural and the grafted branches should receive the same blessings, which are secured by faith, and are the common possessions of all believers, both the Jew and the Gentile. He reiterates that he has little or no concern for the nationalistic pretensions of Israel, only that the citizens of that nation might be saved, and then together undertake the mission of the common creator to the needy of this world.

If it was within the mind of God to establish a nation for His people, we would have every right to expect that nation to be a theocracy. Modern Israel shows no signs whatsoever of being concerned about the will of God or His wishes for neighbouring nations. Modern Israel shows no signs whatsoever of being concerned about the will of God or His wishes for neighbouring nations. God's plans changed when His chosen people refused to accept and receive His grace and perform their assignments. He made another approach which was not through national boundaries. His plans are now to have a Commonwealth of faith, where His will and domain will rule within the boundaries of the individual heart. This is the new covenant.

We return to our question, 'The State of Israel: Biblical Prophecy or Biblical Fallacy?' It is not a fallacy that Israel exists. It is part of our world, and is creating much of its torment. It is not a theocracy. It is barely a democracy. It is surely more biblically fallacious than biblically prophetic. It follows few, if any, of the biblical injunctions; it is war-like, violent, vicious to the extreme; has little or no concern for the Semites displaced by waves of immigration over the last 100 years. God does not have His way with these people.

What then can be said in answer to our question? About 1,900 years ago an unknown writer picked up his pen and wrote to the Hebrews who were residing in Rome. He devoted much of his letter to explaining all the blood sacrifices, how they were now outdated by the single sacrifice of God's Son, and he applied all that he had learned as a student in Jewish school to what he had learned in the Christian faith concerning the old covenant and the new covenant. He continued by trying to convince his readers of how much better he found the new covenant than the old. The entire epistle is woven with the ribbons of faith, wrapped around great heroes of Judaism and Christianity, but in the middle he hesitates for a minute and says, 'When the second Covenant comes, the First is done away or abrogated.' We need not concern ourselves with the place of Israel in biblical prophecy, for it is fallacious, if it has been 'done away'.

5. Judaism, Zionism and Islam

Dr Isma'il R. Al-Faruqi

Whether we like it or not, we, the adherents of the Abrahamic faiths (Jews, Christians and Muslims), are doomed to coexist on this planet for long into the future. Moreover, we are doomed to do so as neighbours – nay, as neighbours so interdependent that our livelihood, our prosperity, our happiness and security are extremely difficult – if not impossible – without mutual co-operation. This truth is for us self-evident. To deny it on the level of theory may be considered academically, but it does not interest us. For any of the three communities to deny it on the level of action is certain to lead to disaster for all. Under the influence of modernity the world has surely shrunk, causing our activities and interests, our fears and hopes to criss-cross several times every day of our lives. The planet earth is bound to shrink still further in the future, and this is bound to intensify the criss-crossing traffic of our lives. All plans and measures to isolate one community from another are futile; interpenetration seems to be the law of the present and the future. If this criss-crossing of interests and activities on all fronts, of fears and hopes, is not to lead to conflict – a conflict which none can afford and only the morbid and insane can desire – a number of necessary prerequisites must be fulfilled.

Mutual Understanding and Recognition

Understanding the other faith is a *conditio sine qua non* of recognition of that faith and co-operation with it. Upon it depends the movement of the mind to drop previous prejudices about the other faith, and stereotyped images of its adherents. Elimination of bias, in turn, is a prerequisite to perception of the other faith as *de jure*, as a legitimate way of relating to God; and these are necessary conditions for the movement of the heart towards appreciation of and willingness to co-operate with the other faith community.

Islam's understanding of Judaism occurs on three distinctive levels: it sees members of that faith as humans, as heirs of the Semitic religious tradition, and specifically as Jews.

The Jews as Humans

Islam holds the Jews to be absolutely equal to its own adherents, the Muslims, all being the creatures of one and the same God. It holds them all absolutely equal in their creatureliness or their natural human figurization by God. This absolute equality extends to and covers their relationship to God and the totality of creation, namely, the carrying of the *amánah* or cosmic trust, the *khiláfah* or viceregency of God, the *taklíf* or standing under the law of God, the individual *mas'uliyyah* or ultimate personal responsibility on the Day of Judgement, and their absolutely equal entitlement to God's mercy which encompasses all. Islam's definition of man, therefore, is the same for all humans. It rejects all claims that human nature has altered since creation, or that there is or can ever be any variation in human creatureliness. This creatureliness Islam defines in the following terms. God created man in the best of forms, and breathed into him something of His spirit. He endowed man with his faculties of perception, communication, understanding, will and action, and thus prepared him for moral action. God created the world as a theatre for man's action, and he made it beautiful for man's enjoyment. He made the whole universe subservient to man, malleable enough to suffer change so as to yield to man's usufruct and benefit. All this God has done to enable man to prove his moral worth in his deeds, and thus to actualize the higher part of the divine will – the moral. For the moral is precisely that which is done deliberately for His sake, by a creature capable of fulfilling as well as violating the divine imperative.

All humans, Islam affirms, are created to serve God. It defines 'service' as the actualization of the divine patterns, or 'oughts', and conceives of these as affirmative of life and the world. Such service Islam regards as the justification of the whole of creation including man. Since man is the only creature capable of it, Islam regards him as God's *chef-d'oeuvre*, higher in status than the angels. The latter are lower because they are incapable of moral achievement. Being created sinless, they fulfil God's will necessarily; and their value to God is of a different order altogether from man's. To each and every human being, therefore, Islam assigns a cosmic function – that of realizing the higher part of the divine will in space and time. This cosmic function of man is his *raison d'être*. It is also the highest possible meaning and significance his life on earth can ever have. As human creatures of God, the Jews enjoy this significance and can achieve of the meaning of creation as much as any other humans.

Moreover, Islam holds the Jews equally endowed with *al fitrah*, or the religious capacity of nature, the innate faculty by which God, ultimate reality or the holy, is recognized; and His law, or the good, the absolutely valuable, is perceived or apprehended in experience as the moral imperative.

Therefore, Islam holds the Jews as capable by their human nature, and hence necessarily, of reaching the same conclusions as Muslims regarding the whence, why, how and whither of life on earth. Should they, like Muslims or any other humans, perceive otherwise, or fail to agree on the given of the senses, of the understanding and of reason; should they differ in judgement or the given of the moral sense, and the sense of the holy (the *sensus numinis*), Islam holds them endowed by nature with an alternative avenue leading to identically the same truth and apperception. This is the avenue of revelation, or prophecy. Islam holds all humans to be recipients of revelations from God, articulating one and the same 'what' or content, the values or first principles of religion and ethics; that this identical 'what' has indeed been repeatedly conveyed to all human groups through their own prophets and in their own tongues. Whether by the self-reliant avenue of intellection, or the immediate revelation of the divine will by the prophets, all humans must have had access to God's will. As humans, the Jews have such access by the sheer fact of existence, of creation as humans.

Under this view, Islam regards the Jews as fellows of Muslims, placed together on earth to the end of 'serving God', i.e. proving themselves in their deeds as worthy of His pleasure and reward, as unworthy of His wrath and punishment. This active service is Islam or submission to God in the present participial form, of suffering oneself to be determined by the ought – His divine commandment or will – and pursuing the real, existential *matériaux* concretizing the ought in space and time. Moreover, Islam perceives the content of the ought as the welfare and prosperity of all humans, and hence of Jews *a fortiori*. It perceives and defines the welfare and prosperity of all humans in terms of *a priori*, self-existent, absolute values which are so to all creatures, and hence as the desiderata of utility and morality universally applicable to all. Still more, Islam perceives these desiderata of utility and morality as rational – hence necessary – truths, demonstrable beyond the claims of sceptics, cynics and relativists. Islam thus provides us with a *Weltanschauung* which serves as a perfect base for the moral homogenization of the universe, for a world – and life-affirmative service to humankind promotive of the welfare and happiness of all humans. Whether as subjects of this service to God, or as its objects, the Jews are by necessity partakers of this human predicament, like all Muslims and non-Muslims.

The Jews as Heirs of the Semitic Legacy

The 'Semitic' legacy has been so-called by Old Testament scholars who were influenced by the biblical genealogy of nations, in the absence of direct evidence linking together the archaeological discoveries of the ancient Near East. The languages of the ancient Near East showed such affinity with one another that the assumption of their belonging to one and the same family of nations could not be avoided. Hence, the history of the ancient Near East (the Fertile Crescent) came to be regarded as the development of a common tradition of which the various 'Semitic' languages and literatures were the expression. This tradition certainly includes the whole history of the Hebrews and the greater part of that of their descendants, the Jews. Finally, the Semitic legacy includes the whole history and culture of Islam. The Jews therefore are integral constituents of Semitism, sharing in and determined by the Semitic legacy on a par with Muslims. This makes the Jews and Muslims not only partners in a common inheritance, but members of a single family, closely bound together by language, culture, common history and religious tradition.

Indeed, scholarship has revealed that there is much more to this common Semitic legacy than either Jews or Muslims have been willing to admit.

1. The Semitic languages stemmed from a single source called 'proto-Semitic' or *'Ur-Semitisch'*, which has not been identified. As the speakers of this original language migrated to new places within the Fertile Crescent, underwent new experiences and met new needs, they dropped some vocabulary, some of the compositional forms of words, and some rules of syntax and grammar. The losses seem to be either such as to make the language easier for strangers, or the consequence of mental laziness on the part of its own speakers. The gains, on the other hand, are not structural, but material, adding new words and usages to express new experiences. The Arabic language of today, having preserved its structure, forms and roots, its grammar, syntax and lexicography for at least two and a half millennia and probably much longer, still contains most of the roots, forms, grammar and syntax of all Semitic languages. Equally, the other Semitic literary forms are identical to those of the Arabic literary tradition. While it is certainly no piece of daring speculation to perceive Arabic as the postulated mother of the Semitic languages – i.e. the still undiscovered but postulated *'Ur-Semitisch'* – one must at least recognize that Arabic is indeed their twin sister. As further corroboration of the closeness of Arabic to the other Semitic languages, there is a tremendous amount of incontestable evidence from other fronts of scholarship.

2. Geographically speaking, the Fertile Crescent is merely the extension of the Arabian peninsula. Together, they constitute an indivisible unit, separated on all sides by mountains or seas which up to the beginning of the first millennium BC were impassable by the Semites who populated the region. All movements creative of culture and civilization prior to 1000 BC, therefore, must have been internal to the region. Thus the Akkadians, the Amorites, the Aramaeans, the whole array of peoples and tribes roaming the area (of whom the Hebrews were one), must have all derived from one and the same stock as the Arabians. After 1400 BC, Kassites, 'People of the Mountains', 'Sea People' from Caphtor (Crete?) and other Hellenic islands, Hittites from Asia Minor and Egyptians entered the Semitic 'theatre'. But history knows of none who has not been absorbed and assimilated by the 'Semitic stream'. As Sabatino Moscati once said, the Semitic stream celebrated its religio-cultural victory over the invaders even as it lay defeated under the hoofs of their chariot horses.

3. To suggest that the native population of lower Mesopotamia migrated thither from the Persian plateau to the east, or from East Africa to the west, or mixed with migrants from that area before 4000 BC is sheer speculation. What is known for certain is that Sumer or lower Mesopotamia began to blossom only when Semites arrived there to fertilize and acculturate the

natives. But the Semites could have come to Sumer only from the Fertile Crescent or the Arabian peninsula, travelling on the edge of the desert (the inner rim of the crescent) because their donkeys were incapable of crossing the northern Arabian desert. No non-Semitic intruded into the Semitic theatre before the 15th century BC; and when they did later, as we have mentioned earlier, all of them were 'Semiticized', i.e. converted to the Semitic language, culture and religion. The Semite, as anthropological type, remained the dominant feature of the theatre's demography. Hebrews and Arabs therefore are indeed just as their own legacy told them, namely, descendants from one and the same origin – Abraham, whether conceived as a person or as a name of a whole people.

4. All the Semitic civilizations share one and the same understanding of the beautiful. This is clearly evident in their persistent attempt to stylize, and thus to denaturalize, the images depicted, whether vegetal, animal or human. Their visual arts were never representational, never naturalistic or realistic. They were more arts of decoration than expression. They contrast radically with the visual arts of Egypt which were highly naturalistic (except for the image of Pharaoh), and those of Greece which pushed naturalism to its extreme, especially in its portrayal of its gods. The greatest of all arts for all Semites, however, is the art of the word. The varieties of literary form among the Semites remained the same throughout history. Every description of any tradition in any Semitic language is also true of all other Semitic languages or traditions. Essentially, Semitic literature is the opposite of the dramatic literature developed in Greece or India. It is non-developmental, concentrating all its strength on the fine chiselling of words, phrases and sentences in a narrative which seems to have neither beginning nor climactic end. The verse, sentence or tableau, as a constitutive unit of the composition, is the purveyor of literary beauty, not of an integral personality through its participation in a centralized – hence unified – series of unfolding events. The power of the proverb, common saying, aphorism, single tableau or *maqám* of the Semitic literary tradition to carry precepts of religious and moral truth has never been surpassed or paralleled anywhere. This has been the very stuff of which the Arabic literary tradition is made. Islam carried that same genius to heights hitherto unknown, and embodied its categories in non-Semitic languages spoken by hundreds of millions of non-Semitic but Islamized peoples. Muslims rejoice that the Jews share this literary heritage and recognize it as constitutive of a very significant segment of humanity's cultural legacy.

5. Finally and perhaps most importantly, the Semitic peoples betray a unique religious consciousness which sees reality as dual. Rather than the 'monophysitism' of the ancient Egyptian which sees the divine as nature and nature as divine, the Semite has always perceived the divine as other than nature. Creator and creature, in Semitic religiosity, are never one, but always ontologically disparate; the creature being of the making of the creator, and for the latter's service. Humans were created to serve in God's 'manor' (the earth), to fulfil His commandment (the law). For them

as well as for their descendants, obedience was the greatest virtue and the guarantor of success and prosperity; disobedience, the opposite. Whether in this world or in the next, judgement follows man's life, his career of service determines the pleasure of his creator. The pleasure of the divine master constitutes the meaning and ultimate goal of man's existence and life.

This religiosity is the Semitic people's greatest contribution to humanity. It received its finest expression in Islam which is understood by all Muslims as being the religion of Abraham, of the Patriarchs Ishaq, Isma'īl and their descendants; of Moses, David and Solomon; of all the Hebrew prophets; of Zechariah and Yahyá (John the Baptist); and finally, of Jesus and Muhammad. This demonstrable unity in the religious tradition of Jews and Muslims is incontestable – at least for the Muslim. Historical scholarship certainly corroborates this basic intuition of Islam; for the principles constitutive of it are certainly true of all great moments of the 6,000-year-long Semitic tradition. That after 1400 BC Semitic religiosity got mixed up with that of non-Semites (Aryans, Hittites, Philistines, Greeks and Egyptians) in the western arm of the Fertile Crescent (Syria, Lebanon, Jordan and Palestine), is not denied. But the foreign elements were never strong enough to dominate or to change the character of Semitic religiosity except in Pauline Christianity, which is readily acknowledged as being essentially unsemitic. Indeed, that is precisely why it had to emigrate from the Semitic theatre and find its people elsewhere. It is also the deeper reason why, even after it was imposed by the Byzantine empire on those territories for four centuries, it took little or no root and was swept away by Islam, in whose march the Semitic spirit reasserted itself just as clearly as it resisted the spiritual onslaught of Hellenism under Alexander and his successors, though this time more triumphantly. While Jews, Muslims and some Eastern Christians identify totally with this Semitic religiosity, Western Christians acknowledge it as the cradle in which their own religiosity was born, nursed and brought to flower.

The Jews as Jews

The identity between Jews and Muslims is further heightened by the common history of their faith. Islam regards Judaism as containing most of the important moments of the religious tradition to which it itself belongs. It regards Judaism and Islam as composing one integral tradition of prophecy or divine revelation and human achievement. The Quran affirms that the Torah is revelation from God; that the prophets of Judaism (Abraham and his two sons, Isma'il and Isháq), Ya'qúb, Yúnus and Zakariyyá are prophets of God. No Muslim may deny any of these prophets, or the divine source of the revelations which they conveyed, and remain a Muslim. By denying any of them, such a Muslim commits blasphemy and makes himself guilty of apostasy.

All this notwithstanding, Islam does indeed call the Jews to itself. But in doing so, it does not seek to convert them from their faith, which it holds to be from God and hence true. Rather, it seeks two goals. First, to convince them that the prophet Muhammad believed in and advocated their faith, and that the Quran is a restatement or crystallization of that same faith. Accordingly, what is needed by them is not a new faith, but an extension of the tradition of their faith so as to include the Islamic revelation as a natural sequel to, and indeed culmination of, the Semitic-Jewish tradition. In the perspective of Islam, it is not the religion of Judaism that is at fault. It is rather those Jews whose narrow understanding of their faith leaves no room for Islam, the rebirth and reaffirmation of Semitic religion in its utmost purity. Divine unity, ultimacy and transcendence, and the absolute verbatim status of the revealed word of God have never been as emphatically affirmed as in Islam. Neither has obedience to the divine word as commandment and law! The new religion called itself *islam*, i.e. 'submission', to God and His imperatives.

Secondly, Islam's appeal to Jews seeks to purge Judaism of the elements extraneous to the core of Semitic religiosity, which history, alien influences and the passion and forgetfulness of humans have superposed upon the Abrahamic faith. In so doing, Islam speaks from a stance internal to Judaism. Having already proclaimed the God of Judaism and the God of Islam to be one and the same God, the prophets of both to be the prophets of God, their revelations as issuing from the same source and containing the same divine truths and commandments, its criticism must therefore be internal, domestic to Judaism. In fact, Islam's criticism of Judaism does not go beyond what Jews have often addressed to their own faith. On the whole, the Islamic critique of Judaism has restricted itself to the core of religion, namely, the concept of God and the integrity of what is held to be His revelation.

Islam's Critique of Judaism

The content of Islam's critique of Judaism was not new. But its basing of that critique on Hebrew Scripture and its presentation of it as textual criticism of Holy Writ is. In this, Islam set a precedent for biblical scholarship of modern times. It is not far-fetched to assume that the fathers of biblical criticism – Wellhausen, von Graf and Kuhnel – who were the foremost Islamicists of their day, were moved by the Quran's textual criticism of the Bible to launch the new discipline. For their assumption was the Quran's basic charge, namely, that the extant text of Jewish Scripture has been tampered with by human hands and that human writ has been mixed with divine writ. This charge, made by the Quran repeatedly, and amplified in almost every Islamic treatise in comparative religion, might have moved the Orientalists to investigate the biblical text rationally in order to refute the Islamic claim. But a rational consideration of the biblical text, with minimum information about the points elaborated by Islamic literature (Quranic exegesis and world history, as well as comparative religion) is all that is necessary to expose the veracity of the charge, and to seek ways of explaining it away or justifying the multi-layer theory (J, E, D, P) of the formation of the biblical text. Just as on the Muslim side, the Quran has made possible for the first time the consideration of the biblical text with the eye of a critical historian, and enabled Muslim scholars to conduct critical analyses of the biblical text, on the Christian side, the same charge coupled with the rationalist, reforming and scientific tendencies of the Enlightenment might have laid the foundation of the modern discipline of biblical criticism through the works of the aforesaid three Islamicists.

The Quran merely mentioned the charge of human tampering in Holy Writ. The substantiation of the charge was made later by Muslim comparativists. They noted that God, Who is claimed by Jews to be the Author of the Torah, could not possibly have made a mistake of simple arithmetic when He informed about the ages of Noah and his descendants; or gave the ages of Jacob's descendants; or when He reported the number of Hebrews that entered and exited from Egypt, and enumerated their generations. They charged that the extant Torahic text ascribed to God numerous self-contradictions and erroneous geographical data.

Ibn Hazm, one of the most thorough Muslim biblical critics, gave a long list of these and other discrepancies, all of which one can read today in any book of biblical criticism. Muslim comparativists also noted the crimes attributed by the extant Torahic text to the prophets of God (Abraham, Jacob, Moses, etc.) and the moral turpitude of God's messengers implied or alleged by these narratives. For the conscientious believer, whether Jew or Muslim, such charges cannot be accepted. It is easier and better to give up the claim that the extant Torahic text is integral Holy Writ dictated by God, than it is to predicate moral turpitude to God's great prophets and thereby destroy the moral foundations of the faith.

Still more disturbing to Muslims are: the Torahic use of the plural form *Elohim* for God; the intermarriage of these 'gods' with the daughters of men and their begetting of offspring (Genesis 32:24-30); Jacob's theft of the gods of Laban, his uncle, which Rachel hid under her skirts when their owner burst into her tent looking for them (Genesis 31:30-6). This radical departure from monotheism and the constant description of the king of the Jews as 'Son of God' (e.g. Psalms 2:7; I Samuel 7:14; I Chronicles 17:13), as well as of the Jews themselves as 'sons of God' in a real sense not affected by their immoral – nay, even idolatrous – behaviour (Isaiah 9:6; 63:14-16; Hosea 1:10; etc.), overstrains the Jews' claim to adherence to the monotheistic faith of Abraham. Indeed, the Jews' claim for 'elect' or 'chosen' status, and their understanding of the 'covenant' as necessarily binding on God regardless of their performance, transforms the transcendent God of ethical monotheism into a single ethnocentric monolatrous deity of the Jewish people. There is much more in the extant Torah to support the racist thesis. The Hebrews' condemnation and slaughter of the Shechemites (Genesis 34:25-31) for the 'crime' of converting to Judaism and circumcising themselves, and their welcoming the landless nomadic Hebrews to intermarry and live with them in peace, expresses the Hebrews' deep-rooted opposition to universalism and their hatred of all goyim (non-Jews). Ethnocentrism is indeed the corollary of monolatry (idolatrous worship of a single god); both are incompatible with the absolute unity and transcendence of God.

Muslim-Jewish Relations

Despite the difference on the doctrinal level, the Quran proclaimed before and after the founding of the first Islamic state that the Jews were *Ahl al Kitáb* (people endowed with scripture, and hence with a divine religion whose Author is God). Muslim governments everywhere honoured the Torah as the law of God and enabled the rabbinic councils and/or courts to order the lives of the Jews in accordance with its precepts. Religious debates and dialogues, and comparative, medical and scientific studies were carried out by Jews and Muslims in co-operation and harmony, despite the differences separating their religious understandings. When the Jews were persecuted by Christians in Spain, the Muslim lands opened their doors and Muslims accommodated them as equals, kindred in faith. The two faith communities built together one of the greatest legacies of interreligious co-operation; a legacy so rich and powerful that in front of it all differences pale. All the greater therefore are the shock and consternation of Muslims all over the world that the Jews of today have rallied to the colonialists' side against them; that they subjected the Muslims to worse treatment than the Jews had received at the hands of their persecutors. Innocent Muslim blood has been shed by Jewish hands; Muslim property – lands, buildings and personal belongings – has been stolen at gunpoint; Muslim honour, dignity and the effects of their history have been systematically destroyed by the same Jewish hands which until very recently were either the beneficiaries of Muslim hospitality and friendship or victims of Europe's Holocaust.

The fact that the Jews have been subjected to all kinds of suffering during their stay in Europe commands the Muslims' sympathy. For the Muslims have been for the last two centuries victims of the same European forces. Anti-Jewish persecution and anti-Muslim colonialism were regrettable tragedies which teach the most clear lesson against European ethnocentrism. It is to be hoped that after Europe has paid most dearly for it in two world wars, it has begun to outgrow it and seek a *modus vivendi* which would give the peoples of Europe the desired level of prosperity with mutual respect, and dignity and freedom for all concerned. But apparently, the ethnocentric disease of the masters seems to have caught the victims at the very time that the masters are cleansing themselves of it. Zionism is little else besides a caricature of the *Volk*-romanticism, the violent racism of National Socialism. Its claim is that the Europeans are so hopelessly committed to anti-Semitism that the Jews must leave Europe. This is only partially true. The Europeans are not hopeless addicts; and to think so is a counsel of despair. The Europeans are not hopeless, nor is the Jews' exodus from Europe the only solution. To vent their anti-Christian resentment on the Muslims is very poor morality on the part of those who claim to uphold the faith of Abraham.

Any reader of the history of Judaism will notice, firstly, that the early roots of Judaism stemmed from the Semitic tradition. Secondly, the reader would have to note that all Talmudic thought developed in Palestine and Iraq, among people whose religious, legal, social and cultural institutions deeply influenced that development. Thirdly, the reader would have to note that all medieval Jewish thought arose out of a soil irrigated by Islam; that without Hayyuy bin Zakariyyá, there would be no Hebrew grammar, without Musa ibn Maymún there would be no Jewish philosophy or orthodoxy as a system of thought and ideas, indeed, no terms in which the Jews of the world today could define their religious identity; that without Ibn Ghabirol, there would be no Jewish mysticism, no Hasidic or cabbalistic thought or practice.

The Jews as Zionists

Zionism is a political programme born in the last decade of the 19th century concerning the Jews of Europe. These people had endured a great deal of suffering at the hands of Christian Europe. The victory of Christianity spelled disaster for those Jews who emigrated to or were forcibly brought to live in Europe. The Papacy gave a number of Roman Jews a place to live within the walls of the Vatican City, as specimens of Satan and his ways to be seen by all visiting Christians as a lesson against the forces and agents of the Antichrist. The princes of Europe extorted money and jewels from Jews, subjected Jewish girls to prostitution, regarded all Jews as outlaws if found outside the quarters assigned to them, treated them not as individuals but as a group, and pounced upon their ghettos whenever booty or a scapegoat was needed. The Jews led miserable lives in their crowded, unhealthy and isolated ghettos, with little or no communication with the outside world. The Crusaders fed and funded themselves throughout their long marches in Europe off any Jewish population that happened to live on their way. The Spanish inquisition killed those who resisted and converted the rest: and for centuries of European history, (in Norway down to World War II) to be a Jew was illegal, if not an outright crime. In modern times, the Enlightenment and its stepdaughter, the French Revolution, brought emancipation and consequent great benefits, prosperity, culture and prestige, to European Jews, but not without a price. The price was assimilation: the dilution of Judaism and its transformation into a likeness of Protestant Christianity and the transformation of Jews into hyphenated monstrosities (German-Jew, Dutch-Jew, French-Jew, etc.). The reaction of Europe against the Enlightenment, the French Revolution, *l'Empire* and their consequences was swift and furious. A romantic revolution conquered the newly industralized Europe and developed European nationalism and ethnocentrism to heights unparalleled before or since. Persecution of the Jews followed inevitably; and it was not always civilized as in the case of Captain Dreyfus in France. Anti-Jewish pogroms erupted in most cities of Europe, and they were especially cruel in Eastern Europe. Nazism or National Socialism, Fascism and Russian Communism were the outcome of this European romanticism. The Holocaust of World War II was *la fin qui couronne l'oeuvre*, the crowning development.

The Jews of Europe could easily read the writing on the wall. Theodor Herzl, the first Zionist, was a hyphenated Jew who witnessed the Dreyfus trial as a correspondent for a Viennese newspaper. It was in his mind that the Zionist idea was born. The Jew, he reasoned, had no place in Europe, where if he were to live safely, he must dilute and efface his Jewishness, and if he were to keep it, he would be fought and persecuted. Therefore, the Jews must get out of Europe and build for themselves somewhere a *Judenstaat*, or state for the Jews, not a Jewish state as is commonly held.

A 'Zionist Congress' was formed and a programme established to procure a land on which to found the 'state for the Jews'. At that stage, Palestine was not even contemplated. Rather, it was the newly conquered territories of Uganda, South America and Central Asia that were the choices when Zionism allied itself to England following the Franco-Prussian War. Later, the movement harmonized its purpose with that of British colonialism in the Near East. It was in the aftermath of World War I that Zionism focused its attention on Palestine and rallied Britain to endorse the Zionist plan by its infamous Balfour Declaration. In that declaration, Britain committed itself to create in Palestine a national home for the Jews.

From 1918 to 1948, Britain ruled Palestine with arms and terror. It confiscated land owned for millennia by native farmers, evicted them at bayonet point, and planted Jewish emigrants from Europe in their stead. It armed and equipped those immigrants, who lived isolated in fortresses of barbed wire, observation towers and underground shelters, protected by British guns. It granted powers to itself to uproot and destroy any Palestinian opposition, and power to the Jewish village and township councils to impose taxes upon and annex the lands of their neighbours. Finally, in 1948, the British handed their weapons to the Jews, whose numbers had grown from 10,000 in 1918 to 650,000, and left the Palestinians, whom the British had deliberately kept disorganized, untrained and ill-equipped during 28 years of occupation. The Zionists wiped out Palestinian resistance, terrorized the population with wholesale massacres as at Deir Yasin, induced them to flee for their lives and took possession of their lands, their homes and their personal belongings. In 1956, 1967, and 1973 the same aggression was repeated, first with the participation of Britain and France, and then with the support of the United States. Since the early 1960s clandestinely, and after 1967 openly, Israel has received the full backing of the US in military, intelligence, economic and diplomatic assistance, and has become an instrument of US foreign policy worldwide. Its function has been to do 'dirty work' on behalf of the master, serving the neo-colonialist purposes of the world's superpower in Africa, Asia and Latin America, as well as in the Muslim world. Selling arms, destabilizing local governments, training the rulers in how to terrorize their own subjects, engaging in all sorts of spying activities, and generally contributing to the economic and military ascendance of the United States –

these have been the objectives of the superpower and its client state. Israel's method in pursuing these objectives is absolutely Machiavellian and amoral. Anything is permissible – nay, desirable and obligatory – which contributes to that pursuit, however immoral, however contradictory to the ethical norms of civilized behaviour. While Israel ravaged Lebanon, bombarded it indiscriminately with the most lethal weapons, seized civilians and treated them worse than cattle, robbed homes and offices, shops and museums, destroyed hospitals and schools, and violated every principle of decency, the US fleet protected its forces against foreign interference, supplied all the weaponry, and bankrolled all the expenses. In the Palestinian territories occupied by Israel, military rule and 'emergency regulations' continue to terrorize the people. Lands are confiscated, and villages are literally erased. Shops, homes and properties are seized or destroyed, colleges and schools closed or subjected to control (of the calendar, curriculum, faculty appointments, student admissions, cultural activities), elected officers dismissed, banished or otherwise disposed of with bombs – all these have become commonplace occurrences since 1967. And yet, all this notwithstanding, Israel has known no peace and no security.

Zionism and Judaism

In order to justify itself, Zionism claims that it is the quintessence of Judaism. The truth is that Zionism is an interpretation of Judaism characterized by the strongest ethnocentrism human history has ever known. It cannot be denied that numerous texts in the Old Testament do lend themselves to ethnocentrism. But Christians as well as Jews who are moved by ethical considerations subject those passages to allegorical interpretation and thus make them ethically acceptable. The Zionists take the same passages in their naked, literal, material meanings. Indeed, they make those meanings the keys with which to understand the rest of scripture and religion. Zionism is therefore an unfortunate but thoroughly sectarian interpretation of Judaism. It is an interpretation which debases the ethical, monotheistic, universal religion of Abraham and Moses and the prophets to an immoral, idolatrous ethnic religion of a primitive tribe. From the standpoint of Islam, Zionism is apostasy against Judaism, the religion of God and revelation.

Zionism and the Jews

Whereas Herzl's decision, in the face of diluted 'Reform Judaism' and the pogroms against Orthodox Jews, may have been justified at its time, it cannot be justified after World War II and the cleansing of Europe of its Nazi and Fascist clients. Herzl's judgement was a counsel of despair. Europe did rise against its own aberration, and paid dearly for it. But it can proudly point to its cleanliness, its freedom from racism and anti-Jewishness since the war. Europe's Jews have contributed so much to Europe that they necessarily belong to it. To force them to leave, or to prevent those who left during the war from returning, is unjust aggression. For Israel as a government to accept European money as compensation for the properties of Jews seized or destroyed in Europe is another violation of the sacred rights of the Jew as individual. Indeed, it is collaboration with Europe's anti-Jewish desire to see the Jews expelled once and for all.

Few Jews are independent enough to make any choice in the matter. The majority are helpless victims of a ruthless organizer who sees them as soldiers for its dreams of conquest. Israel 'deals' with the lives of these unfortunate humans as if they were bricks. It gives them one choice: Zionism or continued statelessness and misery. Zionism has terrorized the Jews of the Arab world in order to get them to emigrate to Palestine to fill the homes vacated by the Palestinians. It has thus uprooted them from their lands and the environment in which they lived and prospered for centuries. Besides this robbery, Zionism has imposed upon the oriental Jews the mentality and ideology of Europe. Racism and ethnocentrism, nationalism and materialism, individualism and utilitarianism, sexual promiscuity and anarchism, nihilism and existentialism, scepticism in knowledge and religion: this is the legacy of Europe imposed upon the Jews of the Orient by Zionism in the name of 'Westernization' or 'progress'. It has destroyed their faith in God and His law. Strange as it may seem, Zionism was born to stop the assimilation of the Jews brought about by the Emancipation. It has become itself the very instrument of assimilation. No other time in Jewish history has witnessed as much loss of Jewish culture, mores and identity as Zionism has achieved in Israel during the last 35 years.

As far as security is concerned, Zionism has provided none. Rather, it has created hatred and antagonism between the Arab Jews and Muslim Arabs where mutual love, esteem and co-operation had existed. And it moved the European Jews from the frying pan which Europe was before and during World War II into the fire of a Near East caught in a death struggle with a neo-colonialist Europe and America. Israel has provided an alternative place for the Jews to live. But physically it is the security of a concentration camp at the 'frontiers' of Israel, where the settlers must sleep in bomb shelters, close to their guns; psychically, it is the precariousness of an artificial state planted in the midst of a billion or more anatagonized Muslims and supported by the flimsy coincidence of a temporary common purpose between the Zionist objectives and those of a colonialist West. From the standpoint of Islam, this is injustice against the Jews of the world which must be stopped and its consequences undone.

Zionism and Non-Jews

The grand-scale robbery which Zionism perpetrated and continues to perpetrate every morning against the Palestinians, Syrians, Lebanese and Jordanians is a horrible crime which Islam condemns. Indeed, Islam commands all Muslims of the world to rise to defend their fellow-Muslims and protect their lives, their lands and properties. Justice, whose balance has been violently shaken by Zionism, must be restored. The lands and properties must be returned to their legitimate owners, and their psychological and physical deprivation of their rights ought to be compensated. The fixation in human consciousness which a violated right creates does not simply go away. In the body of humanity, these violations are canker sores which continue to fester until the injustice is undone and the balance of justice redressed.

The evil of Zionism, however, has not only touched the Palestinians and their neighbours, the oriental Jews and the Jews of Europe, all of whom were its immediate victims. It has touched the whole world. By claiming the Jews to be a race, a chosen race, a race privileged by God to receive His favour even though it treads upon every one of His laws, and by living this claim impertinently and shamelessly in defiance of mankind and morality, Zionism has insulted and injured humanity. Even if Zionism set up its house on the other side of the moon or in another galaxy, Islam sees the task of its adherents as well as of humanity at large as being to challenge Zionism and bring it down. The world should not and cannot agree to live with a Sparta gone berserk, which thinks of itself as different from God's other creatures, destined to smash whom it pleases, and despising all humans.

Part II: Cultural Dimensions of Zionism

6. The Two Faces of Zionism

Dr Alan Taylor

The intense debate now going on in Israel over the country's direction, ethical values and relations with the Arab world is really a recapitulation of the disagreements about Zionism which became the focus of attention in Jewish circles a century ago. It is seldom remembered today that when Zionism was organized by Theodor Herzl in 1897, it was opposed by most Jews, and the movement itself was far from monolithic. Indeed, many of the problems Israelis are dealing with in the present situation stem from the attempts of a clique of 'political' Zionists to popularize their doctrines among Jews, and to control the policies and activities of the movement.

The negative response of Orthodox Jews to early Zionism is succinctly expressed in a letter written by Rabbi Joseph Hayyim Sonnenfeld of Brisk to a colleague in 1898:

> With regard to the Zionists, what shall I say and what am I to speak? There is dismay also in the Holy Land that these evil men who deny the Unique One of the world and His Holy Torah have proclaimed with so much publicity that it is in their power to hasten redemption for the people of Israel and gather the dispersed from the ends of the earth. They have also asserted their view that the distinction between Israel and the nations lies in nationalism, blood and race, and that faith and religion are superfluous. . . . Dr. Herzl comes not from the Lord, but from the side of pollution. . . .[1]

The oppositon of Reform Judaism was based on different premises, summed up in the position articulated by Reform rabbis in the Pittsburgh Platform of 1885:[2] 'We consider ourselves no longer a nation, but a religious community, and therefore expect neither a return to Palestine, nor a sacrificial worship under the administration of the sons of Aaron, nor the restoration of any of the laws concerning the Jewish state.' In 1897, the leading Reform rabbi, Isaac Mayer Wise, reiterated this attitude even more forcefully:

> We totally disapprove of any attempt for the establishment of a Jewish State. Such attempts show a misunderstanding of Israel's mission, which from the narrow political and national field has been expanded to the promotion among the whole human race of the broad and

> universalistic religion first proclaimed by the Jewish prophets. . . .We affirm that the object of Judaism is not political nor national, but spiritual, and addresses itself to the continuous growth of peace, justice, and love in the human race, to a Messianic time when all men will recognize that they form one great brotherhood for the establishment of God's kingdom on earth.[3]

A similar view was expressed in 1930 by the renowned Jewish scientist, Albert Einstein:

> Apart from practical considerations, my awareness of the essential nature of Judaism resists the idea of a Jewish state, with borders, an army, and a measure of temporal power, no matter how modest. I am afraid of the inner damage Judaism will sustain – especially from the development of a narrow nationalism within our own ranks, against which we have already had to fight strongly, even without a Jewish State. We are no longer the Jews of the Maccabee period. A return to a nation in the political sense of the word would be equivalent to turning away from the spiritualization of our community which we owe to the genius of our prophets.[4]

The political Zionist élite regarded such opinions as an obstacle to be overcome. At the second Zionist Congress in 1898, Herzl declared: 'It cannot continue much longer that in enlightened Jewish communities an agitation should be carried on against Zion. . . .We must once and for all put an end to it. . . . I place among our future aims the conquest of the communities.'[5] Herzl had earlier admitted in his diaries: 'I conduct the affairs of the Jews without their mandate, though I remain responsible to them for what I do.'[6] This concept of Zionism's relationship to world Jewry was shared by the élite group under Herzl's command and was passed on to future generations of Zionist and Israeli leaders. At the sixth Zionist Congress in 1903, Herzl's closest associate, Max Nordau, asserted that 'this Congress is the authorized legitimate representative of the Jewish people. It is its duty to make Jewish national policy.'[7]

The Zionist idea originated from a concern that the Jewish communities of Europe were being assimilated into the secular Gentile culture surrounding them. Actually, it only compounded this problem by drawing as heavily as it did on Western models and ideologies. But the issue which ultimately enabled it to become the dominant force in European and American Jewish circles was anti-Semitism. From the Kishinev pogrom in 1903 to the rise of the Hitler regime, most Jews in the West became so disturbed by the rising tide of anti-Semitism that they put aside all reservations they may have had about Zionism and became avid supporters of the quest for a Jewish state in Palestine. This brought the reinforced Zionist movement into a direct confrontation with the Palestinian Arabs, whose aspirations for sovereignty in the same homeland were equally strong. The unfortunate conflict of interests engendered by this circumstance automatically made the issue of Palestinian Arab rights the major problem facing the realization of Zionist aims.

But within the Zionist movement itself there were two schools of thought on how to deal with the Arab question. The political Zionist élite initially formed by Herzl sought to transform Palestine into a Jewish state through force, disregarding the interests of the indigenous Arab population. Herzl anticipated a systematic process of acquisition and expulsion:

> We must expropriate gently the private property on the estates assigned to us. We shall try to spirit the penniless population across the border by procuring employment for it in the transit countries, while denying it employment in our own country. The property-owners will come over to our side. Both the process of expropriation and the removal of the poor must be carried out discreetly and circumspectly. Let the owners of immovable property believe they are cheating us, selling things for more than they are worth. But we are not going to sell them anything back.[8]

Herzl's whole approach to Zionist political action was secretive and conspiratorial. He imagined secret agents operating under the auspices of a clandestine organization which he referred to as 'the company'. Jewish youth was to be recruited into military units, and special paramilitary cadres would carry out dangerous missions designed to facilitate the ultimate establishment of the Jewish state.

Later political Zionist leaders had similar attitudes towards the Arabs, sometimes more gently stated and sometimes virtually Arabophobic. Aaron David Gordon, perhaps the major champion of Zionist colonization, favoured an open economic competition between Jews and Arabs for the soil of Palestine, based on the premise that the Palestinians had forfeited their political title to the country when it came under Turkish rule and that, therefore, 'Whoever works harder, creates more, gives more of his spirit, will acquire a greater moral right and deeper vital interest in the land.'[9] Vladimir Jabotinsky, the founder of the militant revisionist faction within Zionism, never tried to conceal his utter contempt for the Palestinians, whom he once described as 'a yelling rabble dressed up in gaudy, savage rags'.[10] He agreed with Herzl that the Zionists should gradually expropriate the uncultivated lands of the Arab gentry, and entertained a scheme of inducing the masses to migrate to Iraq. He knew that the fulfilment of Zionism would necessarily involve the displacement of the indigenous population, and emphasized the importance of paramilitary activity in achieving this end.

At the eleven Zionist congresses prior to World War I, it was barely mentioned that an Arab population existed in Palestine or that this fact constituted an ethical problem to be resolved. Almost exclusive consideration was given to the establishment of a Jewish state, without any significant expression of concern among political Zionists for the rights and aspirations of the Arab populace. Chaim Arlosoroff, who was appointed head of the Jewish Agency's political department in 1931, was one of the few mainstream Zionists to recognize that Arab-Jewish co-operation was important at least as a way of protecting the interests of the Zionist immigrants. But while in the process of organizing talks between Arabs and Jews on the possibilities of a bi-national system, he was assassinated, probably by members of the extremist revisionist faction. His successor was David Ben-Gurion, who announced that he would pursue a policy of cordial relations with the Arabs. But as Aharon Cohen has noted:

> His statement, like so many other Jewish Agency statements, glossed over the most important element: the question of what basis for accord was proposed by the Jewish representatives. The only basis that provided any chance of reaching an agreement – political equality and parity in government among the two peoples, and the establishment of a bi-national framework – was never proposed to the Arabs.[11]

Exclusive Jewish control of Palestine became an obsession among the political Zionists, and eventually ruled out any consideration of bi-nationalism or other projects based on the idea of sharing the country. Because the very existence of the Arabs was a major obstacle to the creation of a purely Jewish Palestine, a strong tendency developed among the political Zionists to dehumanize the Palestinians and deny their existence as a community. A House of Commons delegation visiting Jerusalem after the 1967 war was told by the chairman of the Knesset's Foreign Affairs Committee that the Palestinians 'are not human beings, they are not people, they are Arabs'. The same sentiment was expressed two years later by Golda Meir in a *Sunday Times* interview: 'There was no such thing as Palestinians. . . . It was not as though there was a Palestinian people in Palestine considering itself as a Palestinian people and we came and threw them out and took their country away from them. They did not exist.'[12]

The political Zionists also denied that the displacement of the Palestinians constituted a moral problem, and refused to accept the validity of Arab nationalist aspirations. Professor Eliezer Schweid of the Hebrew University summarized this position in an article which appeared in 1970:

> The general policy of Zionism based itself upon the certainty and primacy of the right of the Jewish people to its homeland. From this point of view, the opposition of the Arabs was a practical stumbling block that must be overcome, not a moral problem that must be dealt with. We must emphasize again that one should not see in this approach a disregard for truth and righteousness. This approach had a factual and moral basis. Arab nationalism in the Land of Israel appeared from its beginning, not as a movement whose purpose is to realize or defend the right of an existing national entity, but rather as a movement that realizes its very being in defiance of Zionism.[13]

There were others in the Zionist movement who did not share the views of the political faction. Many of them were associated with Ahad Ha-Am's 'cultural' or 'spiritual' Zionism, which emphasized the culturally regenerative aspects of Jewish colonization in Palestine over the purely political statehood project. Ultimately, this group became the foundation of a humanistic Zionism which was very sensitive to the moral issue surrounding the Arab question.

In one of his earliest articles, written in 1891, Ahad Ha-Am remarked that the Jewish colonists 'treat the Arabs with hostility and cruelty, deprive them of their rights, offend them without cause, and even boast of these deeds; and nobody among us opposes this despicable and dangerous inclination.'[14] Much later, in one of his last letters, written in the 1920s, he commented bitterly on the Zionist recourse to violence:

> Is this the dream of a return to Zion which our people have dreamt for centuries: that we now come to Zion to stain its soil with innocent blood? . . . Are we really doing it only to add in an Oriental corner a small people of new Levantines who vie with other Levantines in shedding blood, in desire for vengeance, and in angry violence? If this be the 'Messiah,' then I do not wish to see his coming.[15]

Dr Yitzhak Epstein, one of the early Jewish settlers, was deeply disturbed by the widespread disregard for the Palestinians among the Zionists. In 1907, he wrote:

> Among the grave questions linked with the concept of our people's renaissance on its own soil, there is one question more weighty than all the others put together. This is the question of our relations with the Arabs. Our own national aspirations depend upon the correct solution of this question. . . .
>
> The regrettable fact that our attention could be diverted from such a fundamental question, and that after thirty years of settlement activity it is being talked about as if it is a new topic – all this proves that our movement is unreasonable. . . .
>
> At a time when we feel the love of our homeland. . . we forget that the people now living in this land also has a heart and a soul. Like all men, the Arab is bound to his homeland by strong ties. . . .
>
> We shall commit a grave sin against our people and our future if we throw away so lightly our principal weapons: righteousness and sincerity. . . .[16]

The moderate wing of Zionism initially formed the Brit Shalom (Covenant of Peace) organization in the 1920s. This was later reconstituted as the Ihud (Union) Group, which in the 1930s made a concerted effort to bring about an accord between the Arab and Jewish communities. But the Jewish Agency was more interested in the idea of partition, first proposed by the Royal Commission in 1937, because it implied an exclusively Jewish state in at least part of Palestine. Dr Judah Magnes, first president of the Hebrew University, continued to champion the bi-national idea until his death in 1948. His plea for Arab-Jewish co-operation expressed with particular lucidity the concern of the moderate camp that the unfolding policies of the Zionist movement had given rise to a profound moral crisis:

> Perhaps we have made mistakes. Let us look them in the face and learn from them. We seem to have thought of everything – except the Arabs. We have issued this and that publication and done other commendable things. But as to a consistent, clearly worked out, realistic, generous policy of political, social, economic, educational cooperation with the Arabs – the time never seems to be propitious.
>
> But the time has come for the Jews to take into account the Arab factor as the most important facing us. If we have a just cause, so have they. If promises were made to us, so were they to the Arabs. Even more realistic than the ugly realities of imperialism is the fact that the Arabs live here and in this part of the world, and will probably be here long after the collapse of one imperialism and the rise of another. If we too wish to live in this living space, we must live with the Arabs. . . .[17]

The attempts of moderate Zionists to encourage Arab-Jewish understanding were submerged in the climate of political agitation which dominated Palestine in the late 1930s and the intense animosity generated by the events leading to the emergence of Israel. The new Jewish state was run by political Zionists in the tradition of Herzl. But ultimately, the moral issue which had so concerned Ahad Ha-Am, Yitzhak Epstein, Judah Magnes and others caught up with the Israelis. The October 1973 war raised many perplexing questions, the most important of which was whether the whole thrust of the country's policies towards the Arabs had not been wrong from the start. In this context, Dr Nahum Goldmann, a prominent Zionist leader for many decades, posed many of the major questions confronting Israel's conscience. He held that 'The emergence of tendencies contrary to the soul of the Jewish people may have consequences disastrous to our future.'[18] Goldmann also considered Israel's reliance on military prowess to be short-sighted, and believed that the country would not survive if it did not make the necessary concessions to the Arabs. Professor Jacob Talmon had raised the same issue in 1969 when in an open letter to a cabinet minister he insisted that Israel had to come to terms with the problem of Palestinian rights:

> In the eyes of the world, and in my eyes too, the recognition or lack of recognition of the Palestinian Arabs as a community with the right of self-determination is the cardinal question at issue. It is the acid test that will determine whether we are bent on settlement and reconciliation or on expansion – on respect for the rights of others or on ignoring them. This is the measuring rod for determining the democratic character and moral qualities of our State.[19]

In the 1980s, Israeli society is divided over the Palestinian question. It is not an academic debate, but a crucial hour of decision in the history of Zionism. What hangs in the balance is not the redress of this or that transgression, but the future course of the Jewish state. Against the background of the Beirut massacre, the Israelis have been placed in a situation which forces them to make a choice between the humanistic and morally sensitive Zionism of Ahad Ha-Am and the self-centred and violent Zionism of Herzl. For 36 years of statehood, the latter has obstructed peace and compounded Israel's problems. The former remains an untried alternative, but it holds out the prospect of a much more rewarding kind of relationship with the surrounding nations and a far richer, less troubled way of life for the people of Israel.

Notes

1. Emile Marmorstein, *Heaven at Bay: The Jewish Kulturkampf in the Holy Land* (London: Oxford University Press, 1969), pp. 79–80.
2. Israel Knox, *Rabbi in America: The Story of Isaac M. Wise* (Boston: Little, Brown, 1957), p. 111.
3. Ibid, pp. 114–15.
4. Moshe Menuhin, *The Decadence of Judaism in Our Time* (New York: Exposition Press, 1965), p. 324.
5. *Jewish Chronicle*, 2 September 1898, Supplement, p. iii.
6. Raphael Patai (ed.) and Harry Zohn (trans.), *The Complete Diaries of Theodor Herzl* (New York: Herzl Press and Thomas Yoseloff, 1960), I, p. 42.
7. *Jewish Chronicle*, 28 August 1903, Supplement, p. xii.
8. *Complete Diaries of Theodor Herzl*, I, pp. 88–9.
9. Aaron David Gordon, *Selected Essays*, trans. by Frances Burnce (New York: League for Labor Palestine, 1938), p. 24.
10. Joseph Schechtman, *Rebel and Statesman: The Vladimir Jabotinsky Story, The Early Years* (New York: Thomas Yoseloff, 1956), p. 54.
11. Aharon Cohen, *Israel and the Arab World* (New York: Funk and Wagnalls, 1970), p. 255.
12. *Sunday Times*, 15 June 1969.
13. Eliezer Schweid, 'new Ideological Directions after the Six Day War', *Dispersion and Unity*, no. 10 (Jerusalem, 1970), p. 48.
14. Hans Kohn, *Reflections on Modern History* (Princeton, NJ: Van Nostrand, 1963), p. 196.
15. Ibid., pp. 203–204.
16. Cohen, op. cit., p. 67.
17. Norman Bentwich, *For Zion's Sake: A Biography of Judah L. Magnes* (Philadelphia: Jewish Publication Society of America, 1954), p. 199.
18. Alan R. Taylor, 'Talking to Nahum Goldmann,' *Middle East International*, June 1978, p. 15.
19. 'Self-determination for Palestinian Arabs: An Open Letter by Professor J.L. Talmon,' *Jewish Liberation Journal* (New York), November-December 1969, p. 4.

7. The Semantics of Zionism, Anti-Zionism and Anti-Semitism

Don Peretz

I am an American Jew who empathizes with the aspirations and dilemmas not only of other American Jews, but also of Jews beyond the United States, including those in Israel. Empathy by no means implies uncritical acceptance of Establishment views, policies or directives, but rather an attempt to understand whence they have come, where they might lead, and how they will affect the larger human condition. From my perspective, it requires an attempt to understand the Jewish condition in the context of the larger human condition. Failure to relate the situation, the goals, the aspirations of Jews to those among whom they live, whether in America, in Israel, or elsewhere, would only result in incomplete understanding, and eventually in a distorted vision, of the Jewish condition.

Although many have tried to bestow labels on me such as Zionist or anti-Zionist, I have refused to conform to the images associated with these labels, and at times have had intellectual and even spiritual communion with individuals who are perceived as one or the other. The labels themselves are often distortions of reality, just as similar labels such as pro- or anti-American, racist, or inhumane are often distortions of reality.

Because the themes of Zionism and anti-Zionism are so central to this conference, I think it essential that I offer briefly my own perception of Zionism before discussion of its 'anti' dimension.

I see in modern Zionism a sort of microcosm of the many products of Jewish thought and consciousness. It represents the diversity of Jewish tradition, the wide range of Jewish perspectives on the world, the traditional struggle in Jewish consciousness between particularism and universalism. Of course this struggle in Jewish consciousness extends beyond Zionism, but during the last century much of the tension between Jewish particularism and Jewish universalism has been incorporated within the wide-ranging debates among diverse trends in Zionism. In the larger context, we might say the struggle is between Masada and Yavneh, or in modern terms, between Jewish nationalism and Jewish universalism.

In many ways the dichotomy between universalism and particularism is reflected in the recent history of Israel and in the cross-currents of Jewish thought which attempt to define the role of the Jewish state in the life of modern Jews. At times there is tension and at times ambivalence between the poles of the two orientations. Frequently the diverse perceptions of the Jewish role in history clash in the ideas of a single individual who may simultaneously reflect both the particularism and the universalism of the Jews.

There were many instances of the most zealous nationalists who were simultaneously ardent universalists, seeing in the particular role of the Jew and in the special mission of Israel some connection of importance for all mankind. The Jewish state was not only to fill a national mission, but to become the fulfilment of messianic vision.

I believe that attempts to use labels like 'Zionist' and 'anti-Zionist' are distortions of reality; they are crude, unsatisfactory classifications that often explain the intent or purpose of the labeller more than the identity or outlook of the labelled.

Yet they have been important reference points – true, often deceptive reference points – in the history of the conflict. The meanings of Zionism and anti-Zionism have been far from constant, and have perpetually shifted during the past half-century. Associations or terms that were at one point in recent history acceptable to large numbers of Jews in the United States and the West have now acquired hateful connotations. And subtle shadings between the terms Zionist and anti-Zionist, like the once commonly used expression, non-Zionist, have all but disappeared from the lexicon of political labels. Despite the fact that these terms have been reference points in the debate on Jewish versus Arab nationalism, I believe my observations about the lack of consistency in their use and in their association with specific groups only prove my point that they obfuscate rather than clarify the real issues. I certainly feel that they do little if anything to further understanding and peace in the Middle East, to bridge the chasm between Arab and Jew, or to clarify issues in the Middle East conflict.

Yet both Arabs and Jews continue to use these terms with the same mindlessness protagonists in the East-West big-power conflict use terms such as Free World and Slave World, Communist and anti-Communist. (In this dialogue there is also no room for the term 'non-Communist'.) The terms more often than not are used to rally emotion rather than thought, to stimulate hatred rather than understanding, as stigmas in the propaganda war that has raged around the conflicts in the battlefields.

The United Nations General Assembly discussion in the 'Zionism is racism' debate during 1975 underscored the extent to which all parties to the conflict and their allies were willing to enter the propaganda game. The wording of General Assembly resolution 3379 which 'Determines that Zionism is a form of racism and racial discrimination' was fatuous; as fatuous as a resolution that would declare democracy, Communism, or socialism forms of racism because of the misdeeds of the Soviet Union in Afghanistan, the US in El Salvador, or the British in the Falklands. The debate surrounding discussion of the resolution displayed the ignorance of many, and the determination of others to use the issue as a prod for divisiveness and animosity rather than to seek peaceful resolution of the Arab-Israeli conflict.

While the debate underscored the pervasive ignorance about Zionism and Jewish thought among Assembly members, it also offered the Israeli delegate, Chaim Herzog, an opportunity to raise many of the old clichés and slogans about the Hilter era in Germany, about anti-Zionism and about Palestinian nationalism.

Since that resolution has faded into history and any political significance that it had has totally evaporated, it is hardly worthy of discussion at this point. Since 1975 even PLO chairman Yassir Arafat has established friendly contact with Israeli Zionists and paid homage to Dr Nahum Goldmann, one of the Zionist luminaries of the century, after his death. Of far more importance are the more recent misuses of history and terminology as they relate to Zionist and anti-Zionist.

Since 1977 and the accession to power of the Begin government in Israel, there has been a continuous and dangerous escalation of rhetoric in the Arab-Israel conflict and in use of the Zionist and anti-Zionist terminology. In a recent issue of the Mapam periodical, *Progressive Israel*, commentator Levi Morav stated that he believed the most important change in Israel since Begin became Prime Minister was in the Israeli style of speaking, writing, lecturing and speechmaking: 'The effect of our being constantly subject to this special style is catastrophic'. This style he described as:

> Pathos, or pathos blown up and without any real content. Its starting point is that nothing is simply just what it is – everything is gigantic, tremendous, colossal, one-of-a-kind, exceptional. A bridge dedicated over a creek leading muddy water is the bridge proving the eternity of the Jewish people, the final answer to the schemes of Haman, Chmielnitzky and Hitler. A new road crossing a densely-populated Arab community is an old-new road proving the eternity of the people of Israel's return to its historic and undivided homeland and a challenge to the genocidal schemes of Arafat and Company. The cornerstone of a new plant is an historic stone, the first after 2,000 years of exile, the ultimate answer to those desiring to destroy us.[1]

This style which is common among Begin's Likud associates has also infected other ordinary Israelis like the El-Al workers in their response to the government's decision to stop the airline's flights on Saturdays and holidays. The workers' committee published a press statement pleading: 'We will not allow ourselves to be led like sheep to the slaughter.' That, observes Morav,

> is not only desecrating the memory of the victims of the Holocaust but completely misunderstanding the nature and character of the Holocaust and a lack of understanding of what 'sheep to the slaughter' really means. However, if the heads of our political system and especially the Prime Minister, are incapable of doing anything without bringing up our children and grandchildren, and cannot say 'PLO' without mentioning the victims of the Holocaust, what wonder that the

employees of the national carrier are infected by the same mad style.

The author calls on Israeli journalists to defend their language against those who are making it

> inhuman, noncommunicative, bombastic and educating toward falsehood and lies. The danger to any people's spirit and soul lies first of all in the corruption of its language. A bridge over a stream has to ease traffic, a broad new road must cut the time needed to travel from one place to another, a new plant has to provide employment. Important and necessary plants have nothing to do with the eternity of Israel. Not every new drainage ditch is a singular historic event.

This rhetorical escalation, especially as it relates to the Holocaust, is all too often superimposed on political discussion related to one or another of the positions of the government of Israel. The theme is used by all parties to the conflict, not only by Begin's side. In summer 1982 Begin used it in response to a letter from President Reagan during Israel's siege of west Beirut, and many observers made use of Holocaust terminology in comparing Beirut to Lidice, or Beirut to the Warsaw ghetto, or in the use of Holocaust metaphors like 'genocide', 'final solution' and 'pogrom' in reporting the impact of Israel's invasion on Beirut's civilians.

Commenting on political use of the Holocaust in December 1982, Rabbi Harold Schulweis observed that the danger of misusing history is that 'catastrophic thinking, fixated on trauma, can only destroy the full memory of the past and the opportunity of our future. Use of the Holocaust as an instrument with which to deal with the Gentile world and as an instrument of international diplomacy has boomeranged.' The view that Jews continue to face destruction at all times and all places, that all roads lead to Auschwitz, 'is self-defeating and negates any plea to non-Jews to live in peace with the Jewish people'.

Not only is the Holocaust used to induce guilt in the new generation of both Jews and non-Jews, it is often used as a club against current political figures who may disagree with the policies of the government of Israel or the Jewish community. The employment of such false equations between past anti-Semites and current political figures is to indulge in a 'desperate fantasy'. Schulweis warned:

> It is a perilous mind-set to conduct diplomacy by false analogy. . .It is dangerous to our future to invent new enemies in the image of unreachable barbarians who burned our children. In fact, rational men and rational women know the cast of characters is not interchangeable. The fantasy of history relived, rewritten, refought and reversed can only confuse our goals; it tends to make foes out of friends, turns potential allies into implacable enemies; it twists the possibilities of the future into hopeless repetition of the past.

Parallel to misuse of the Holocaust terminology has been increased misuse of the Zionist-anti-Zionist dichotomy. As I mentioned above, the term non-Zionist has all but disappeared from the political lexicon, so that a few years ago Norman Podhoretz, editor of the American Jewish Committee's magazine *Commentary*, published by an organization that only recently claimed to be non-Zionist, could write an article in the *New York Times* called 'We are all Zionists now'. The assumption of the article was that all supporters of Israel were Zionists, although that was about as far as the author's definition of Zionism could go. The trend in the Jewish Establishment has been to assume that nearly all Jews are supporters of Israel, therefore nearly all Jews are Zionists. Until recently support for Israel has implied, if not insisted on, full support for the policies of the Israeli government. This formula 'Zionist means support for Israel, support for Israel means support for the policies of Israel's government' was often turned on its head: 'those opposed to policies of Israel's government do not support Israel, therefore are anti-Israel, consequently anti-Zionist'. In many cases another step or two led to the equation of anti-Zionist with anti-Jewish or anti-Semite.

This formulation was not explicitly stated but often implied. In effect, a number of leaders in the Jewish Establishments of Israel and the United States created a kind of Nicene Creed, a loyalty oath that was expected of all non-anti-Semites. Not one, but a group of Jewish 'popes' arrogated to themselves the divine right of defining not only who was a good Jew, but who could be considered a friend of the Jews. Non-acceptance of their creed with its new conception of Zionism, anti-Zionism and anti-Semitism relegated dissident Jews to the category of 'self-hating Jew', and non-Jewish critics to the category of 'new anti-Semite'. This situation prevailed until Israel's 'Peace for Galilee' operation in summer 1982, when a number of Establishment figures began to question the Jewish papal authority.

Prime Minister Begin clearly underscored the situation in a meeting with Rabbi Alexander Schindler, former president of the Conference of Presidents of American Jewish Organizations. Before Begin agreed to appointment of an Inquiry Commission following the Beirut massacres, Schindler was sent to discuss the matter and to prevail on Begin to agree that a commission be appointed. According to the Israeli newspaper *Yediot Aharonot* Schindler told the Prime Minister of the disquiet among American Jews about the situation, detailing a picture of growing resentment in the American Jewish community. After a bitter argument between the two, Begin said angrily:

> 'You must decide whether you are a Jew or an American. To be a Jew means to give full support to the government of Israel and to back the Prime Minister unequivocally on all issues, whether you agree with him or not.'
>
> Schindler, taken aback by these words, expressed disagreement with the Prime Minister on a number of points. Menachem Begin summed up: 'If you do not support what I say, you are an American and not a Jew.'[2]

From Begin's perspective, the meeting was counter-productive, for rather than consolidating Jewish opinion behind his policies, it apparently opened the fissures between Establishment leaders in their reactions to Begin's policies.

Not only Schindler but other Jewish Establishment figures in the United States began to question the dogma which placed any action of Israel's government above criticism or question, not only by Jews, but by Jews who were Zionists.

By December 1982 even Bertram Gold, former head of the American Jewish Committee, noted that events in Lebanon had 'raised some new questions'. Events of summer 1982 had 'increased dialogue between American Jews and Israelis in which more questions are being asked about the relationship from both sides'.

Schindler, in his role as president of the organization of Reform Jewish synagogues, the Union of American Hebrew Congregations, now called on American Jews to assert more independence from Israeli concerns. 'We have slipped into the sloppy equation which says that Judaism equals Zionism equals Israel', he observed in a radical departure from the Establishment perspective which until the end of 1982 had more or less accepted this 'sloppy equation'.

> For many American Jews, he continued, the state has become the synagogue and its prime minister their rabbi. Their opinions on domestic and international issues are too often determined by the standard – is it good or bad for Israel? . . .We do ourselves irreparable harm when we make Israel our surrogate synagogue, when we permit our Jewishness to consist almost entirely of a vicarious participation in the life of the state.[3]

In another statement during December 1982 Schindler also openly dissented from Begin's policy of absorbing the West Bank, saying that it would 'sow the seeds of endless conflict'. But more importantly, he now openly defended the right of Diaspora Jewry to dissent from official Israeli government policy: 'Dissent should never be equated with disloyalty. Let us once and for all reject the accusation that by seeking the truth as we see it, by giving Israelis our own perception of events, we are somehow treasonous.' He warned that: 'if either Israeli leaders or the institutions of American Judaism suppress honest dissent and smear the dissenter, I predict that the Jewish people will be spiritually impoverished and Israel's cause intolerably diminished.'[4]

Not only operation 'Peace for Galilee' but a variety of other Begin policies seemed to reopen the gates to independent interpretation among American Jews and cast into question the dogma of the sacrosanctity of Israeli government policy. Israeli policy in the West Bank, towards the Palestinians, and rejection of the Reagan Plan out of hand also provoked overt public criticism by loyal adherents of the national credo, including many respected members of the Establishment. Unusual platforms were used to proclaim dissidence, not expected platforms of forums like meetings of foreign-policy associations, or anti-Zionist or pro-Third World groups. In December 1982 at a meeting of the American Jewish Congress to honour two Jewish New Yorkers for their community service, those being honoured spoke out critically of Israel's policies. The two were Felix G. Rohatyn, chairman of the Municipal Assistance Corporation of the City of New York, and Victor H. Gotbaum, a leader of the American Federation of State, County and Municipal Employees. Rohatyn observed that:

> Many Jews critical of the Israeli Government have felt that it was somehow disloyal to express criticism publicly. . . . They were pressed into that position by explicit suggestions of Israeli officials and Jewish leaders that such criticism played into the hands of Israel's enemies and ultimately fostered anti-Semitism.

Both Rohatyn and Gotbaum had come to their new position after 'agonizing over our feelings on the issue', and after sending a joint letter to Begin criticizing Israeli actions. While the two declined to make their correspondence public, they felt that the time had come 'to say at least some of the things in public'.[5]

Although the gates of interpretation have been pushed ajar, and even Israeli officials have begun to take notice of the tremors of dissent, dissenters still have a long way to go before becoming exempt from the labelling game. Dissident Zionists will still be called anti-Zionists by Israeli officials seeking to keep the dogma pure, and by American Jewish Establishment leaders who fear their eventual loss of control over Jewish public opinion. In December 1982 Rabbi Joseph Sternstein, president of the American Zionist Federation, warned that American Jewish support for Israel 'had ebbed perilously', and that he saw 'dangerous elements that indicate the American Jewish community may be drifting away from Israel', leading to an inconceivable situation 'of a Jewish community without Israel'. The 'dangerous trend' aroused Rabbi Gilbert Klaperman, president of the Rabbinical Council of America (Orthodox), to warn that: 'American Jewry must be aroused to completely stand by the Jewish state, which with each passing day feels isolated and besieged by the world powers.'[6]

On the other side the danger still remains that ignorance of Zionism and its diversity leads many non-Zionist critics of Israel's policies to label Zionism with such broad-brush terms as racist or Fascist. If one recalls the history of the propaganda game in the Arab-Israeli dispute, one cannot escape the conclusion that such labels are indeed ridiculous, for it was only a third of a century ago that Arab propaganda was calling Zionism the dangerous ally of the Soviet Union, and Arab leaders who today are called tools of Soviet imperialism by Zionist propagandists were labelled Fascist and racist in the 1950s. I believe that it is not the terms that are important, but the audience for whom such propaganda is intended.

The efforts of those who have appointed themselves unilateral definers of such useless terms as Zionist, anti-Zionist, anti-Semite, racist, etc. have not abated. They still work assiduously to enlist this lexicon in their propaganda war against dissent. Every few years the Anti-Defamation League (ADL) of B'nai B'rith attempts to revive the battle of terminology with a new list of charges against both Jewish and non-Jewish dissenters.

In 1974 the ADL published a book called *The New Anti-Semitism*, and in 1982 the organization's national director published *The Real Anti-Semitism in America*. Although neither volume states overtly that criticism of Israel's domestic or foreign policies is automatic anti-Semitism, both link such criticism with anti-Semitism, or anti-Semitism by association. Since anti-Semites hate Israel and are therefore critical of its policies, those who are critical of its policies are anti-Semites. Since there are anti-Semites who support the Arab cause against Israel, supporters of the Arab cause are anti-Semites.

The New Anti-Semitism linked the American Friends Service Committee (Quakers) with anti-Semitism because of their 1970 publication, *Search for Peace in the Middle East*, which was labelled 'a pro-Arab document masquerading under repeated claims of objectivity by its authors', of whom I was one. The ADL report on the 'New Anti-Semitism' proceeded to extract a number of quotations which, out of context, could imply meanings opposite to those intended by the authors. It made charges of bias without offering evidence, attributed to the authors motives which were the opposite of their real motives, and omitted from its references any iota of the sympathy for Jews and Jewish aspirations that was a major theme of the Quaker report. The result was a statement that, if it did not make the Quakers sound anti-Semitic, certainly made them sound like vicious enemies of Israel, a perception that was the exact opposite of genuine Quaker feelings and orientations. Of course, a major difficulty for a group like the ADL is that Quakers are both pro-Arab and pro-Israel, a stance that it cannot comprehend. If one engages in the debate, one must choose sides between the pro-Arab 'anti-Semitic' side or the anti-Arab pro-Jewish, pro-Zionist, pro-Israeli, pro-freedom side. No half-way measures are acceptable. If one finds a gleam of righteousness in the enemy's eye, one has failed the test of truth and justice and must be relegated to the ranks of the 'anti-Semites'.

The Real Anti-Semitism in America follows a similar line of argument. It too castigates American Protestants for taking political positions in the Arab-Israel conflict contrary to those of the Israeli government. I must emphasize Israeli government, because many of these positions are also taken by Israelis not in government but in the opposition Labour party, and in other reputable Israeli organizations. They are positions supported in the Israeli media by some of its most respected columnists and editorial writers. The authors of this second ADL volume are worried about military aid to Arab nations, pressure on Israel to make concessions for peace, opposition to military spending and to American intervention abroad, détente with the Russians, and affirmative actions quotas. Although those who assume such positions are not automatically 'real anti-Semites', by implication or by association they aid and abet anti-Semitism in America.

The National Council of Churches is accused of calling on the United States government to establish contacts with the PLO. Even worse, the United Methodists have dared to favour a PLO state, by implication an even more heinous anti-Semitic stance.

The book makes a very large issue of American sale of AWAC planes to Saudi Arabia during 1981, and includes support for the sale under the rubric of 'the real anti-Semitism'. On the other hand, the authors have nothing to say about Begin's policies nor do they offer any proposals for a peaceful solution of the Arab-Israeli conflict. Rather, their intent seems to be to divide all political acts with which they are concerned into those that are pro-Jewish and pro-Israel versus those that are anti-Israel and therefore by implication anti-Semitic.

By far the greatest damage of such 'labelling' is that it discredits anti-anti-Semitism. By attempting to force silence on critics of Israeli government policies through use of the anti-Semitic label, the authors have obscured the real issues of anti-Semitism, and driven many who would otherwise have joined the fight against anti-Semitism from the field of battle. Furthermore, they have done a disservice to the cause of peace in the Middle East by attempting to silence discussion on some of the more controversial issues; or if not to silence discussion, they have attempted to force it into a pattern they have established as the only legitimate one.

Discussion of these questions – Zionism, anti-Zionism, and anti-Semitism – becomes more intense as the ideology of Israel itself goes through a process of transition. Many Israelis, many Zionists and many Jewish Establishment figures are disturbed by the direction the transition is taking. Schindler, for example, has warned that American Jews must recognize that they are more than just a part of Israel:

> We must also affirm our own identity and integrity, even as we deepen our solidarity with Israel. . . .It is difficult to explain this to American Jews, who for too long have been plugged into Israel as if it were a kidney machine – a scientific marvel that keeps them alive as Jews. How can we teach two apparently contradictory lessons: that we have a worth as Jews independent of Israel, and that we must continue to love and support Israel? If we make too much of the first lesson, some will take it as an excuse to cut themselves off from Israel. And if we make too much of the second, we will never know who we are, for we have slipped into the sloppy equation that says Judaism equals Zionism equals Israel.[7]

The policies of any government in any country including Israel could bring the country to ruin.

Indeed, history has taught us that all political states are transitory. Some pass away in decades, others in centuries or millennia, but none has been eternal. The volatile shifting of international alliances, the rapid decline and fall of empires, the sudden ascent and descent of superpowers, has made the stability and security of small nation-states even more perilous today than in the past. To point out that Israel is a modern state like others in the Western world is not to denigrate it but to belabour the obvious. As a modern state there are many ways in which it might be transformed into a political entity far different from the one envisaged by most Jews who call themselves Zionists.

First, world and local conditions could force changes in Israel, transforming it into a state that would not be recognized as Jewish. Because of the circumstances of its creation and its situation in a hostile environment, because, too, of its shifting relations with the great powers, Israel must perforce carry out actions for its security and survival which are in their essence antithetical to many aspects of traditional Jewish teachings. As the recent elections showed, Menachem Begin or another similar zealot could create a militantly nationalist state.

Second, if Israel retains the 1.5 million Arabs now under its jurisdiction, within a century it could become orientalized – with internal peace but little national drive or distinctiveness. Other unpredictable political and social forces could easily transform Israel into a Levantine country far different from the socially advanced, culturally progressive, Western-type democracy that most of its supporters now perceive it to be.

The question is not whether Israel must implement the amoral policies of the modern nation-state to survive (it must) or whether it will be transformed into a Levantine outpost (it may be), but the effect of these actions on world Jewry. Will the diverse forms of world Jewry also be transformed? Would they be able to continue their existence at all if there were no Israel, or a transformed Israel?

These anxieties are fomented by the belief of some that all forms of Judaism have acquired mystical, life-sustaining ties with the establishment of a Jewish political state. They are based on the assumption that the present country called Israel is isomorphic with the Israel – the Jewish people – which sustained Judaism during its long Diaspora. With such a viewpoint, one sees the establishment of the state in 1948 as the apex of Jewish attainment, the fulfilment of Jewish prophecy and a long step towards realization of the Jewish role in history.

The state, however, is a national entity with its own distinctive and particular interests, frequently separate and apart from many vital interests of Diaspora Jews. In certain circumstances the claims made upon citizens of the state could contradict not only the vital interests of Diaspora Jews, but the fundamental moral foundations of traditional Judaism. Therefore, to confuse the modern political state of Israel with the Israel that has sustained Judaism endangers not only Judaism, but the very existence of the Jews as a people which has been a moral force in Western civilization.

True, visions of ethics and universal peace are rooted in the land and the people of Israel, and draw their inspiration from its mountains and hills, from its rivers and deserts, from its capital city of Jerusalem and from its ancient centres of learning. This land was central to Judaism as a religion and as a civilization. Yet no state was necessary for the Jews, either as an ethnic group or as successors to prophetic tradition, to continue their love affair with the land of Israel throughout the millennium of the dispersion. Neither was a state required to sustain and continue the existence of the Jewish people, or for it to develop as a moral and social force second to none in Western civilization. While Judaism has undeniably had an inseparable bond with the land of Israel, the Jewish people survived and flourished not because of its generals, but because of its scholars; not through its memories of ancient monarchs and their governments, but through memories of its prophets; not because of Masada, but because of Yavneh.

It is true that since the 1967 and 1973 wars there has been a revival of Jewish identity; a return of many Jews who had strayed from the community; a stiffening of Jewish pride and a momentous increase in non-Jewish respect for Jews. But this was the result of an ethnic rather than a religious revival, akin to the rebirth of Irish, Armenian or Arab nationalism.

Orientalization of modern Israel would certainly traumatize the Diaspora. Such a retrogressive change would be devastating to those whose Jewish ethnic pride was fortified by vicarious identity with the prevailing Western image of the Jewish state. Many such individuals might in their shock or disappointment turn away from Judaism. The least we can expect from an evolving process of orientalization would be the gradual loss of identity among those Jews who have only an ethnic identity. For the community structures built upon reverence for and association with Israeli military heroes and diplomats, fund-raising and other secular rituals would surely disintegrate.

It is ironic that Jewish identity and even sympathy for Jews have increasingly come to be equated with uncritical acceptance of the state of Israel and support for its political positions, especially for its international policies. This engenders the philosophic error of confusing all aspects of Judaism with Jewish ethnicity. Although Jewish ethnicity may be identical with Jewish nationalism expressed in support for the new Jewish state, other forms of Judaism are no more identical with the nation-state than Presbyterianism is with Ulsterism, or Islam with Arabism.

Implicit in the current dogma suggesting that world Jewry cannot survive without the state of Israel is the confusion of several different concepts of Jewishness and an attempt to homogenize them within the single matrix of the Jewish political state. The confusion results from attempts to superimpose Jewish nationalism or ethnicity on all forms of Jewish identity.

Jews need to begin asking themselves: can ethnic Judaism outlast the modern nation-state in its present form? Is ethnicity the most meaningful or the most vital source of Jewish group consciousness today? Has traditional Judaism with its emphasis on justice and right in preference to armed might become an anachronism, to be replaced by ethnic group loyalty centred on the Jewish state? Must Jews not rather assert that, though Judaism depends on the existence of the Jewish people, it can either live in the modern world with the sort of Jewish ethnicity which expresses itself in unqualified support for the state of Israel, or if need be it can live without the existence of a Jewish state?

Questions that non-Zionists, anti-Zionists, or those who have no positive reference point with Israel must begin to ask themselves, if they are genuinely interested in peaceful resolution of the Arab–Israeli conflict, are: in what way, if any, do these terms contribute to the dialogue necessary for diminishing the tension between contending parties? Does usage of terms such as racist, or do political propaganda acts like the United Nations resolution 'Zionism is racism', help to bridge the gap between Jewish and Arab nationalisms? In what way were the Zionists Martin Buber, Judah Magnes, Ahad Ha Am and Natan Hofshi 'racist'? When PLO chairman Yassir Arafat invited Israeli Zionists to confer with him in Tunis, was he conferring with 'racists' or 'Fascists'? Were his accolades to Nahum Goldmann after the latter's death accolades to 'racism' and 'Fascism'? Perhaps it would be useful to rethink and to redefine some of these terms which have been so freely distributed in the propaganda war, or perhaps the time has come to discard many of them.

Notes

1. *Progressive Israel*, vol. 8, no. 10, June 1982.
2. *Yediot Aharonot*, 17 October 1982.
3. *New York Times*, 5 December 1982.
4. *Jewish Reporter*, 16 December 1982.
5. *New York Times*, 6 December 1982.
6. Ibid., 5 December 1982.
7. Ibid., 3 January 1982.

8. Zionist Revival of the 'Jewish Race' Concept

Dr Roselle Tekiner

At the annual meeting of the American Anthropological Association in Washington, DC, in December 1982, a motion was passed condemning the systematic and deliberate destruction of the Lebanese and Palestinian peoples and cultures by Israeli and Lebanese militias, and calling for the American government to withdraw assistance from any government playing a role in that destruction.

The belief that the Jewish people constitute a homogeneous racial group fosters popular support in Israel for an aggressive military posture. A sense of identity as Jews gives the Israeli people the feeling of being the persecuted group the Jews long have been, still requiring protection against hostile outsiders. In reality, however, Israel is a strong nation with military power far superior to the enemies that are said to aim to destroy it. In this paper I shall point out the ways in which the fallacious race concept can be used to incite one group of people against another in order to further expansionist aims of the kind apparent in Israel today.

To my knowledge, the American Anthropological Association resolution is the strongest official condemnation of Israeli military actions in Lebanon by any national organization of social scientists. The very nature of their work – recording and comparing human communities around the world – draws anthropologists into involvement in issues that threaten the existence of any group of people. The motion condemns cultural destruction as well as human destruction because, to an anthropologist, it is just as heinous a crime to exterminate the culture of a population as it is to extinguish the population by mass killing. Culture gives a group its distinctiveness and sets it apart from other populations. The language spoken, the set of religious beliefs, the nation to which people pledge allegiance, their unique ways of expression through artwork, dress and food preparation, the specific rules regarding relationships between men and women, the marriage customs, child-rearing practices and attitudes towards relatives: these are just a few examples of the many elements that comprise a culture. Culture consists of customs and behaviour that are learned, not biologically inherited; culture provides a shared value system and gives people a feeling of solidarity and defence against outsiders.

The significance of ethnic identity is apparent even in America. Although adherence to ancestral customs diminishes and eventually disappears in this huge melting-pot after a number of generations, the children of immigrants, and even their grandchildren and greatgrandchildren, often retain remnants of Old World customs that enrich their lives. These may be likings for food the way grandmother prepared it, or the persistence of culture if represented by the retention of the religion of one's ancestors. Even if much of one's cultural heritage is lost, there may still exist pride in being Irish or German or Puerto Rican on days of ethnic celebrations. People may just enjoy belonging to a club of their ethnic origin. There is often a tendency to vote along ethnic lines.

Here, in America, the eventual loss of cultural identity comes as a matter of course. In most cases, newcomers voluntarily choose a new and different way of life. They endure the hardships of assimilation in order to see their children easily take on a new identity in their adopted land. The choice has no effect on the continuity of the native culture the immigrants left behind. Culture persists and changes gradually whoever the individual participants are.

But the loss of culture is not always voluntary. Throughout recorded history attempts have been made by one population to exterminate another by force. The world knows well about systematic assaults aimed at a particular group of people from the history of Jews; or today, from the plight of the Palestinians. Jews, we know, were often expelled forcefully from their homes and countries, and went into exile, looking for refuge in all directions. They endured pogroms in their native countries, persecutions in the Diaspora, and the horrors of the Holocaust. They survived mainly through group solidarity. No matter where in the world they were forced to flee and how distantly they were dispersed, identity as Jews was maintained, an identity that provided the cohesiveness necessary to resist brutal attempts to destroy them. The Holocaust took countless lives – lives of Jews, Gypsies, Poles and other people that Nazi political doctrine did not include in their mythical superior 'Aryan race'. A new word seemed necessary to describe the executions that were carried out with bureaucratic efficiency. The word 'genocide' was coined and first used by Raphael Lemkin in his 1944 study entitled *Axis Rule in Occupied Europe*.[1] He believed it to be as harmful to the existence of a group to take away its cultural foundations as to kill its members. He therefore designated physical extermination and cultural extermination by the same term. The first formal, legal use of the term 'genocide' was at the Nuremberg trials in 1945. Then, the word was used as defined by Lemkin. However, at the Genocide Convention debates at the United Nations, conflicting views among participant nations about the definition of genocide resulted in the elimination of acts of cultural destruction from the definition in the final text of the convention in 1948.

The anthropological view is that of Lemkin but, in recognition of the coventional definition of genocide, we use the word 'ethnocide' instead to refer to acts of cultural destruction. Acts of ethnocide are less likely than those of genocide to cause people to recoil in horror, which is one reason why ethnocide is a more insidious and potentially more successful form of mass extermination than outright massacre. Examples of blatant acts of ethnocide are confisications of homes and lands, terrorizing populations to force them to flee for refuge, and setting up obstacles to prevent their return. People who insist on remaining may be harassed to the extent of being prevented from earning a living, and thus eventually forced to leave. It is also culturally destructive to persecute people for practising their religion or carrying on other traditions. Books, papers and art objects may be destroyed that could be used to help rejuvenate a dying culture. If the aim is to expel a group of people from a particular piece of land, policies of systematic extermination of culture are more likely to be successful than slaughter. When a culture is dead, no one is left with any incentive to revive land claims. Calculated mass murder, on the other hand, seldom can destroy an entire people, especially when the group is as large as the Jews or Palestinians. Survivors unite with reinforced determination to right the wrongs inflicted on their people.

In the aftermath of the revelations of the barbaric atrocities that constituted part of the Nazi scheme to purify the human race, anthropologists and other scientists published essays and studies to expose the fallacies of racism. 'Racism' refers to the claim that some races are superior to others. Racism lays foundations for hatred, bigotry, prejudice, discrimination and persecution against particular groups of people simply through authoritative-sounding assertions that they have fewer innate good qualities than those who are proclaimed to be superior. The process of promoting racism begins with bestowing a name on a group of people that purports to indicate that they are united by ties of blood. Names such as Aryan, Anglo-Saxon, Jew, Semite, Arab and Palestinian have all been used in this way, although none of these constitutes a race. A race refers to a group of people that have inherited characteristics in common, sufficient to distinguish them as a specific physical type when compared with other groups of people. None of the alleged 'racial' names just mentioned refers to a race. All denote either religious, linguistic or national groups. If, however, any of these groups lived together in the same or adjacent territory for many generations, racial similarities would develop. People must be in constant contact to exchange genes and contribute to race formation.

After so-called 'racial' appellations are designated, the next step in the development of racism is to spread through various means of propaganda that a particular race is superior in intelligence, temperament and/or abilities to another race. When the superiority of one race compared with another is accepted, the superior race is often seen as deserving special privileges that are not deserved by the others. The indoctrination is successful when society accepts the proclaimed genetic inferiority, even believing the stereotype and accepting it as truth. If the incentive should arise for the self-proclaimed superior race to get rid of the inferior ones, hatred and discrimination can easily be encouraged. This can result in an express form of racism, i.e. acts of ethnocide and genocide.

Scientific attempts to expose racism were supported by the General Conference of UNESCO which passed a resolution in 1950 entrusting the secretariat with the responsibility of collecting scientific material concerning the race question and giving it the widest possible diffusion. The result was a volume authored primarily by anthropologists entitled *Race and Science.*[2] Because of the widespread and long-standing hatred of Jews which led to the loss of many lives under Hitler's regime, anti-Semitism was particularly attacked by the anthropologist contributors to the volume. Harry Shapiro, in his lengthy essay *The Jewish People: A Biological History*,[3] points out that according to archaeological, skeletal, linguistic and literary references, the early Hebrews were not racially different from the surrounding population. People interbred and in the process mixed their physical characteristics. There were taboos against intermixture, but the very need for a taboo suggests that miscegenation with non-Jews occurred throughout their history. Instances of intermarriage are mentioned in the Bible and the taking of captured women as wives as part of the spoils of war is sanctioned. After the destruction of Jerusalem by the Romans in AD 70, the Jewish population became widely dispersed. Settled among strangers, they were held together by traditional customs that set them apart as Jews. But this separation did not totally segregate them or prevent intermixture. Analysing the situation in the Diaspora, Shapiro concludes that Jews absorbed biological characteristics from the groups with whom they settled either through marriage, illicit sexual contact or rape.

At the time of these writings, it was important to combat anti-Semitism, a widespread attitude that encouraged dislike and even hatred of Jews, and purported to justify discrimination against them. A number of contributors to the volume emphasized that the false assumption rooted in anti-Semitism is that Jews constitute a race. However, to be a Jew really means to be a member of a religious group. Another theme that was stressed is that achievement is not a matter of race but of culture or learned behaviour. There is no scientific support for the belief that racial groups differ in intellectual ability. Nor are personality or temperament determined by biologically linked racial differences.

These were not new ideas. As early as 1924, Franz Boas, a renowned anthropologist who is regarded as the father of modern American anthropology, stated:

> Even in antiquity, while the Jews still formed an independent state, they represented a thorough mixture of divergent racial types. . . . The dispersion of the Jews all over the world has tended to increase considerably the intermixture. . . . The Jews of North Africa are, in their essential traits, North Africans. The Jews of Europe are in their essential traits Europeans, and the black Jews of the East are in their essential traits members of a dark pigmented race.[4]

Ernest Hooton, a famed Harvard anthropologist, expressed the same idea as Boas, i.e. 'To refer to the "Jewish race" is to differentiate race on the basis of religion'.[5] Ashley Montagu summed up:

> The fact is that there is not now nor was there ever a Jewish race. The Jewish religion is not a mark of any race whatsoever since any member of any race may belong to it. As for people who are identified with 'the' Jews, they are drawn from probably more heterogeneous sources than any other identifiable people in the world. The ethnic ingredients entering into the formation of the group called 'Jews' have not undergone mixture in a common melting pot but remain very various. Clearly then, the Jews are not anything approaching a homogeneous biological entity, nor are they a race or an ethnic group.[6]

Despite the unanimity of sound scientific opinion that Jews are not a racial group, information that they are is fed to the average person through the popular media. Two such articles are quoted below. One, dated 9 August 1981, is anonymous. The other, dated 9 November 1981, is credited to Aaron Meged, an influential Israeli writer and journalist.

> *Lesser genetic differences between the Jewish communities than between Jews and Gentiles*
>
> Genetic research done in Israel during the past ten years shows that the genetic differences between Jews of various communities are usually smaller than differences between Jews and non-Jews from the same country. For example, Jews who originated in Poland are like Jews who originated in Yemen from a genetic point of view much more than they are like Christian Poles. Among Ashkenazi Jews the 'foreign' genes constitute less than 10%. It is impossible to determine the exact parallel percentage for Oriental Jews, lacking comparative research with the Muslims from their countries of origin. The external physical differences that can be seen between Jews of various communities, such as hair color, develop mainly because of environmental influence (climatic factors such as the sun) and not the hereditary balance.[7]
>
> *With tears and sweat we shall build our race*
>
> In our bitter fight against the race theories of H.S. Chamberlin and the Nazi, Alfred Rosenberg, the theories that brought terrible disasters to us, that allocated to all of us the possible evil characteristics and being 'naturally' inherited ones, so that no Jew could escape them, we tended to disregard totally the existence of biological characteristics that are common to all Jews.
>
> The Hebrew Encyclopedia, while dealing with the term, 'the people of Israel', dwells lengthily on this problem, whether the Jews are a 'race', and claims that mixed marriages, conversions, rape, etc., over generations in which Jews have been living among other peoples, have eroded their biological characteristics and eliminated the 'unity of the

> race'. But just as archaeology is not a precise science so it is with the science of genetics. Findings change; conclusions change. In a few days an international genetics congress will convene in Jerusalem and Prof. Arie Shinberg from Tel Aviv University will say that 'genetic research done in this country by various scientists proved that there is a great genetic bond within the Jewish people among all its communities: Ashkenazi, North African and other'. He will add that the results of this research are astonishing because for years we accepted the idea that among the various communities of Jewish people there are different genes as a result of assimilation in other nations.[8]

Such writings represent the first step in the process of promoting racism, i.e. asserting with authority that a group of people are united by blood ties.

The question that may arise at this point is, 'Why, if the Jews do not constitute a race, can Jews often be identified as Jews?' Raphael Patai addressed this question in a chapter entitled 'Looking Jewish' from his book, *The Myth of the Jewish Race.* Summing up his observations, he quotes Ashley Montagu, who stated in 1945:

> There undoubtedly exists a certain quality of looking Jewish, but this quality is not due so much to any inherited characters of the persons in question as to certain culturally acquired habits of expression, facial, vocal, muscular and mental. . . . It is possible to distinguish many Jews from members of other cultural groups for the same reason that it is possible to distinguish Englishmen from such groups, or Americans or Frenchmen, Italians and Germans. . . . Members of one cultural group do not readily fit into the pattern of another.[10]

Patai points out that 'looking Jewish' is diminishing, especially in America. In Israel it is also disappearing.

> The experience of living in their own country, of being the dominant majority and the masters of their own fate for the first time in almost two thousand years has wrought a most remarkable transformation. The heirs of those earlier ethnologists who had found people or tribes 'looking Jewish' in all parts of the world now come to Israel and find that the young Israelis do not 'look Jewish' at all. It is as yet too early to say how they do or will look. But whatever the emerging Israeli look will be, one thing is certain; it will bear little if any relation to what in the past was so often, and with remarkable unanimity, described as 'looking Jewish'.[11]

We may not know what the Israelis of the future will be like or how they will look, but we do know from Georges Tamarin's *The Israeli Dilemma: Essays on a Warfare State* quite a lot about how Zionist ideology influences what the Israelis of today think of themselves.[12]

Tamarin is a psychologist associated with hospitals in Israel and France.

He was a lecturer at Tel Aviv University and the director of more than 60 studies of Israelis aimed at learning the origins, functions and dysfunctions of Israeli political ideology. Because of his conclusion that there are symptoms of a ghetto mentality in Israeli, Dr Tamarin was forced to leave his chair at the university on grounds of 'non-integration'. Ghettoism is defined by Tamarin as mutually reinforcing processes of cultural and political isolation. He found that the Israeli belief that theirs is a democratic, egalitarian, progressive and enlightened society is contradicted by theocratic, racist laws, and that the educational system imparts intolerant and ethnocentric concepts. Tamarin stated that 'the most sinister aspect of any ghetto is that one may not feel its abnormality nor conceive that the world on the other side of the sacred walls is not necessarily one of hatred, impurity and abject customs. It is patriotic not to be interested in it.'

One of Tamarin's most interesting studies was based on a technique of story completion that he gave to 512 Sabras or native-born Israelis. There was a consistent evaluation of themselves as 'typical' Sabra by virtue of light-coloured eyes and hair. Tamarin points out that this blatantly contradicted reality and is reminiscent of the ideal of the 'nordic' or 'Aryan' type that prevailed during Hitler's regime. Other traits said to be typical of Sabra women were that they are tall, strong, tanned, clothed with negligent simplicity, for example in sandals or slacks. Female personality traits were: dynamic, aggressive, ill-mannered, arrogant, patriotic, impudent, well-liked, kind-hearted, clever, free-spirited, sincere, pioneering and cynical.

Male personality traits according to the Sabra study were: dynamic, well-liked, arrogant and boastful, aggressive, sincere and self-reliant; they are also good-looking, slender, blond, tall, freckled and simply clothed. Some Israeli men may well be good-looking, slender, blond and tall, but those we see regularly on television do not embody these characteristics. Menachem Begin and Ariel Sharon are as much a departure from the ideal Israeli type as Adolf Hitler and Heinrich Himmler were from the Aryan.

In contrast, these are the characteristics of the Diaspora Jew, according to the Sabra mentality. (The Diaspora Jew is any Jew not living in Israel.) Non-Sabra women have black hair, sad eyes and a strange pronunciation. They wear long, modest dresses with a kerchief or a wig on their heads and their clothes are worn. They have a strange and closed personality and are frightened and distrustful. They are religious, quiet, modest, lonely, narrow-minded, conservative, obedient and polite, and are old in spirit.

Diaspora men are believed to have many of the same personality traits as women, and are pictured with sideburns or a beard and wearing traditional European clothes with a hat or a skull-cap and dark worn-out suits.

Tamarin points out that Diaspora Jews are depicted as sad because they experienced persecution in all cases, even those who never did or could not have experienced it either because they were too young or did not live in countries where Jews were persecuted. Sabra beliefs about the dress of Diaspora Jews are true of only the very small fraction of contemporary Jews who do wear typically religious garb. The descriptions have no regard for time, place or critical judgement, as the Sabras live in an unrealistic world.[13]

The positive attitude of the Sabras towards impoliteness and impertinence, and their negative attitude towards good manners and obedience, conflict with standards that are socially acceptable in other countries. They themselves may not be aware that there is a problem. There is national encouragement of their behaviour. Jay Gonen, an Israeli admirer of the Israeli state and more kindly disposed to it than Tamarin, in his *Psychohistory of Zionism*[14] characterizes typical Sabra behaviour and attitudes as a cute form of *chutzpa.*[15] To illustrate his points he gives the following examples of jokes that he regards as indicative of the cleverness and humour of the Sabras. He calls the humour,

> fresh but smart, direct and charming, naive yet clever and bold and daring.
>
> 'Mum, how did I come into this world?' 'The stork brought you.' 'So it's true what the neighbours say about Daddy's being impotent?'
>
> Another: Teacher: 'There is so much noise in this classroom I can't hear my own voice.' Sabra: 'Don't worry. You're not missing much.'[16]
>
> Or: Teacher: 'I can't understand how one person can make so many mistakes in one composition.' Pupil: 'Teacher, it was not one person. My Daddy helped me.'
>
> Another: An employee in a factory invites his boss to dinner in his home. At the dinner table the employee's son asks, 'Mother, is that ass meat?' The mother responds, 'Why do you think of something like that?' Her son replies, 'Because this morning Daddy said that he was going to bring an ass home for dinner.'

Returning to Tamarin's studies, he found the Sabras to have virtually no knowledge of Jewry outside Israel and concluded that their views represent ideological fanaticism. As a result, they have no feeling of solidarity with world Jewry. There is even a feeling of contempt towards those Jews of the Holocaust who, the Sabras assert, went to their death like sheep.

Although he excuses the Sabras' lack of sensitivity, Jay Gonen exhibits sympathy towards the passivity of the Jews during the Holocaust, an attitude that is in stark contrast to that of the Sabras. He says that in an attempt to change the native Israelis' image of the cowardly Jew, the Israeli government inaugurated official celebrations of Holocaust and heroism, and Holocaust and rebellion. Gonen does not say how successful these attempts have been.

One need not wonder why Tamarin was removed from his post at Tel Aviv University when one reads his summation of his studies: 'The originators and propagators of the national mythology who are responsible for the creation of the stereotype of the Diaspora Jew are guilty of involuntarily injecting moral insanity in the youth toward the greatest tragedy of their people.'

To close this paper I wish to point out ways in which stories from the Bible have been distorted and misinterpreted to contribute to the formation of prejudice among Israeli youths. 'The chosen people', an expression from the Bible describing the nation of the Jews, can be taken as meaning that the Jews are special, that they are superior to people of other nations, according to the word of God. This reinforces feelings that Jews deserve special privileges simply by virtue of being Jewish. Also, there are biblical heroes whose acts of genocide are lauded, acts such as the elimination of another group of people: for example, the story of Joshua's conquest of Canaan: 'The people utterly destroyed all that was in the city, men and women, young and old and ox and sheep and ass, with the edge of the sword.'

It is likely that the uncritical telling of these stories encourages prejudice and feelings of superiority, and seemingly justifies massacres of Palestinians, if such acts are perpetrated by 'the chosen people', as opposed to others. Palestinians are regarded by many Israelis as unfit, inferior to themselves and deserving annihilation in order to fulfil a primary goal of Zionism – a Jewish state for Jewish people.

Zionist ideology that says Jews are a special race of 'chosen people' has contributed to the current situation in which the children of the Holocaust victims are the hapless perpetrators of genocide. Acts of genocide and ethnocide, such as bulldozing Palestinian homes, villages and lands, are permissible when done by the 'chosen people' of Israel. 'The chosen people' seem to have the special privilege of terrorizing Palestinian civilians, forcing them to flee for refuge and preventing their return home. Palestinians are sanctimoniously killed, even those still in the bellies of their mothers. And, as if it were not enough to destroy the people and their culture, documents are also destroyed which could some day help to rejuvenate the remnants of Palestinian culture that the Israelis have not succeeded in eliminating. The persecuted have become self-righteous persecutors.

Notes

1. Raphael Lemkin, *Axis Rule in Occupied Europe* (Carnegie Endowment for International Peace, Washington, 1941).
2. United Nations Educational, Scientific and Cultural Organization, *Race and Science* (Columbia University Press, New York, 1961).
3. Harry Shapiro, *The Jewish People: A Biological History* (UNESCO, New York, 1960).
4. Franz Boas, 'Are the Jews a Race?', *Race and a Democratic Society* (Augustine, New York, 1945).
5. Ernest Hooton, 'Methods of Racial Analysis', *Science* (Washington, DC, 1926).
6. Ashley Montagu, *Statement on Race* (Schumann, New York, 1951).
7. *Davar*, 9 August 1981.
8. Aaron Meged, *Davar*, 9 November 1981.

9. Raphael Patai and Jennifer Patai Wing, *The Myth of the Jewish Race* (Charles Scribner Sons, New York, 1975).

10. Ibid.

11. Ibid.

12. Georges Tamarin, *The Israeli Dilemma: Essays on a Warfare State* (Rotterdam University Press, 1973).

13. Anthropologist Melford Spiro, in his detailed case study, *Children of the Kibbutz* (Schocken Books, New York, 1965) says,

> Many students, ideologically in favor of immigration, are hostile to the immigrants from the Middle East, whom they view as inferiors – they call them shchorim, 'black ones'. They are the constant butts of verbal aggression, taunting, and teasing. European immigrants may also be the objects of hostility. The Mosad authorities decided that, instead of remaining as a group apart, the Polish immigrant students should be integrated with the other children. But these refused to live with the kibbutz children (because of their aggression) and threatened to leave the Mosad if the proposed integration were pushed through. The immigrant children feel like pariahs as a result of this treatment.
>
> Some of the students refused to eat at the same table with adult immigrants. A girl in the seventh grade stood up and walked away when one of them sat at her table. It made her ill, she said, to sit at the same table with 'them' – they didn't know any Hebrew, and besides they were the 'new immigration'.

14. Jay Gonen, *A Psychohistory of Zionism* (New American Library, New York, 1975).

15. Spiro, op. cit., also calls Israeli children's insolence *chutzpa*.

16. Spiro, ibid., says

> Teachers are the primary adult victims of aggression. That the disorder is an expression of aggression is indubitable. The students know that the teacher desires order, yet they refuse to comply with his request. . . After writing their answers to a history questionnaire, the ninth grade students are called upon by the teacher (male) to read their answers aloud. They say whatever comes to mind without waiting for the teacher to call on them, interrupting another speaker if necessary. . . . A boy does not want to answer a question and walks out of the class . . . . a boy is reading a paper, another is drawing a map, a girl is eating sunflower seeds.

9. Humanitarian Dissent in Zionism: Martin Buber and Judah Magnes

Dr Norton Mezvinsky

Those of you who are primarily interested in the present and who may believe that too many historians too often emphasize too much the historical antecedents of any specific topic, may already – from merely scanning the title – be dubious about what value may exist in my paper. I am not one of those who argue that what we think we learn from the past can necessarily help us shape the present and/or the future. On the other hand, I would suggest that the past – as we can achieve an understanding of it – may sometimes in varying degrees contain relevance for the present and the future. Indeed, I do believe that the ideas, the advocacies, of Martin Buber and Judah Magnes – and the ultimate defeat of those advocacies within the Zionist movement – do contain some such relevance and do significantly fit into the substantive context of this conference.

Martin Buber and Judah Magnes were both Zionist theoreticians and activists. They were also greatly concerned with Judaism and with the attempt to reconcile it with Zionism in a universally humanitarian framework. Being activists, these two Zionist leaders sought to reshape major aspects of the Zionist movement's thrust and goals. What Buber and Magnes advocated is important for us to comprehend in order to gain an understanding of Zionism's many-sided development. Why they failed is important for us to assess so as to determine and then perhaps judge what became the dominant essence of Zionism and the central feature in the character of the state of Israel.

The lives of Buber and Magnes spanned much of the same time period: Buber's from 1878 to 1965, Magnes's from 1877 to 1948. These two men came from different environments: Buber from Germany, Magnes from California. Their beliefs and Zionist activities, nevertheless, coalesced with one another. Both went to live in Palestine – Magnes in 1922, Buber in 1938. Both were at the Hebrew University – Magnes as one of its founders and long-time president, Buber as a professor of social philosophy. Buber and Magnes became two of the outstanding Zionist theoreticians and activists who opposed the political mainstream of developing Zionism in the 20th century.

Martin Buber, who became a noted philosopher and teacher in Germany before going to Palestine, was considered by many of his contemporaries a 'political radical' and a 'humanist socialist'. His great political passions were the reconstruction of society and the promotion of international peace. Buber's political passions were equal in importance to and clearly related to his religious and philosophical teachings. Politics for Buber was essential to life and was connected to God. Politics provided Buber with the required test of, and ultimately gave reality and truth to, religion and ethical teachings.[1]

In this sense Zionism for Buber was a political test of Judaism. It was a philosophy designed to liberate Jewry from the fractured or incomplete existence of the Diaspora or exile. Zionism, for him, politically challenged national life. The Arab question, the fact that Palestine was the ancestral home of an indigenous Arab population who had their own national aspirations, was for Buber the pre-eminent challenge of both Zionism and Judaism. As a touchstone of Judaism and of Zionism the Arab question for him became the innermost Jewish question.[2] In this sense Buber's approach was humanitarian.

Other Zionist theoreticians also keyed themselves to this Arab question. Ahad Ha-Am (Asher Zvi Ginsberg), acknowledged as the founder of what is often termed 'cultural Zionism' and a positive, substantive, albeit secular, influence upon Buber, registered early concern over the Arab question in 1891 when he returned from a visit to Palestine. Throughout the remainder of his life, Ahad Ha-Am continued to emphasize the importance of this question. Others, who were unlike Buber in orientation and advocacy, also displayed awareness of the Arab question. Even Vladimir (Zeev) Jabotinsky (1880–1940), the founder of the Revisionist Zionist Party and the political mentor of Menachem Begin, perceived, understood and acknowledged the moral problems herein involved but believed and argued that none of this could or should affect the Jewish people in so far as their Zionist political priorities were concerned.[3] For Jabotinsky and those who won the fray internally in the Zionist movement the correct approach had always to be based upon the consideration of what was best for Jews – regardless of the consequences for Palestinian Arabs. Zionist priorities could not be compromised. As Yitzhak Wilansky, one of the leaders of the Yish'uv Socialist Zionist movement, stated in a protocol of a conclave held in December 1918: 'If it would achieve the urgent goals of Zionism, I would commit an injustice against the Arabs.'[4] There was a great difference in kind between the Buber position and that of Jabotinsky, Wilansky and other political Zionists.

Buber knew that Palestine was overwhelmingly Arab. According to the British census of 1922, there were 660,641 Arabs then in Palestine, as compared to 83,790 Jews.[5] Buber worried about the prevailing view in the Zionist movement that a Jewish infrastructure should be established and that Jews should obtain more land, thus creating a *fait accompli* in Palestine. Chaim Weizmann rationalized this position in 1930 by asserting that Jews and Arabs had equal rights to Palestine but that Arabs were ahead of Jews: Jews therefore must attempt to catch up regardless of Arab feelings on the matter.[6] Buber was never convinced of the moral validity of the Weizmann rationalization, and he categorically rejected the tragic view, held by many Zionists, that continuing conflict between Jews and Arabs in Palestine was inevitable.[7]

Buber could not be satisfied by the Zionist movement's mere acknowledgement of the Arab problem and/or of existent conflict between Arabs and Jews. The Zionist movement, he argued, must become conscience-stricken and must find a morally equitable solution. This, he maintained, must become the central focus of the movement's political imagination and must be prominently placed on the top of the Zionist agenda. Buber's consistent logic led him to become a proponent of one bi-national state in which Jews and Arabs would enjoy political parity.[8] Buber criticized the majority of the Zionist leadership for not sharing this view. He continually emphasized the seriousness and the moral challenge to Zionist leadership posed by the Arab question. He argued that compromise and accommodation were needed. This meant Arab trust and Jewish trust were both necessary. Arab trust, Buber suggested, could only be nurtured by Zionist gestures indicating Zionism's willingness for mutual accommodation, respect and fraternity.[9]

The policy of creating a Jewish majority in Palestine was at the heart of political Zionism.[10] Buber opposed this policy; he allied himself to a minority grouping of self-proclaimed Zionists within the pacifist camp who – for the sake of accommodation with the Arabs – were prepared to limit *aliyah*. This was an extremely radical position that seemed to run counter to the fundamental principles of Zionism. *Aliyah*, immigration without restriction of Jews to Palestine, was for most Zionists the major requisite for the realization of the movement's supreme purpose.[11] In other words, *aliyah* was the proposed Zionist solution for the Jewish problem. The underlying assumption here was that persecution of Jews by non-Jews was endemic in nation-states wherein Jews constituted a minority. Buber did not categorically accept or reject this assumption, but he realized the sensitivities involved and accurately predicted an eruption of antagonism to his position on *aliyah*.

Buber neither believed that a politically sovereign Jewish commonwealth would solve the Jewish problem nor that world Jewry, unless severely oppressed everywhere else, would heed the call for *aliyah*. He called for large quotas for Jewish immigration to Palestine. He preferred that immigration be voluntarily regulated by the Zionist movement and be sufficient to provide a haven for Jews who needed to escape persecution. This in his view did not necessitate a Jewish majority in Palestine. To demand a Jewish majority was, he believed, unrealistic and potentially reckless, for it would exacerbate Arab fears and intensify tensions in Palestine.[12]

The Nazi Holocaust did not cause Buber to change his views. After the establishment of the state of Israel in 1948, he remained convinced that the pursuit of Jewish political sovereignty was wrong, and that the war which witnessed the birth of the Jewish state should have been foreseen. For Buber, the war was a consequence of the state of Israel's Declaration of Independence, which asserted that Israel was the state for all the Jews of the world, although only a small percentage were then in the Jewish state. As Buber viewed the situation, the 1948 war was unavoidable. Buber considered himself a citizen of the state of Israel, but he continued to criticize moral and political errors of his government and remained resolute that a solution to the Arab-Israeli conflict could be found.

Buber's distinctive approach to politics had its roots in the movement of religious socialism after World War I. According to the precepts of religious socialism, the true challenge of religious faith is to affirm life in the broken world of the everyday. Religious socialism for Buber was consistent with and at the heart of Judaism.[13] The ultimate intent of Zionism for Buber was to herald a renewal of what he termed Hebrew humanism, which would – he hoped – heal the division between morality and politics.[14] Implicit in Buber's conception of the task of Hebrew humanism was the debate over the relation of ethics to politics, a recurrent theme in German philosophical thought dating back to Johann Gottfried Herder (1744-1803).

Buber often emphasized the famous saying of Isaiah: 'Zion will be redeemed with justice.'[15] He worried, especially after 1932, that the building of the Jewish national home in Palestine was antagonistic to this concept. Many of Buber's followers and colleagues, including Judah Magnes and the eminent philosopher Hans Kohn, also worried greatly about this. From their worry and concern these people developed a philosophy of ethical action to deal with what they considered to be the moral ambiguities of Zionism. Kohn, however, as a type of purist, left Palestine in quiet moral outrage shortly before Buber went to live there. Buber believed and advocated that political activity needed to be directed to a particular situation in its locale. Hence, Buber decided to settle in Palestine in March 1938. As he wrote a few months after receiving Kohn's letter: 'If work is to be done in public life, it must be accomplished not above the fray but in it.'[16]

Buber remained firm in his support of his people's return to the land of Israel. Buber was certain that the Jewish claim need not negate the rights and aspirations of the Arabs of Palestine. His conviction was based to a large extent on religious trust rather than rational analysis. He wrote to Gandhi 'that it must be possible to find some compromise' between the Jewish and Arab claims to the land of Palestine: 'Where there is faith and love, a solution may be found even to what appears to be a tragic opposition.'[17]

In the ensuing conflict between Arabs and Jews, Buber believed that peace and justice would not be achieved by negating either the Jewish or the Arab claim. From this perspective, he opposed the *realpolitik* approach within Zionism, which centred upon creating and maintaining a Jewish majority. The *realpolitik* approach, he said, would lead to further injustices and commission of sins. Arab-Jewish *rapprochement* ultimately depended upon Jews and Arabs surmounting their mistrust of one another by empathy and effective dialogue. Buber believed God would help in achieving *rapprochement*. As indicated above, Buber's belief was a simple religious faith. He endorsed the neo-Kantian motto dear to and often repeated by his close friend and political mentor Gustav Landauer: 'Peace is possible because it is morally necessary.' Inspired by this motto, Buber insisted: 'Politics is the art of the impossible.'[18]

The combination of Jewish nationalism and humanism in Buber's thought appeared early. On 5 September 1921, at the twelfth Zionist Congress held in Karlsbad, Czechoslovakia, for example, Buber spoke formally and asserted:

> Our national desire to renew the life of the people of Israel in their ancient homeland is not aimed against any other people. . . . We do not aspire to return to the Land of Israel with which we have inseparable historical and spiritual ties in order to suppress another people or to dominate them. . . .
>
> Our return to the Land of Israel, which will come about through increasing immigration and constant growth, will not be achieved at the expense of another people's rights. . . . Our settlement [in the Land of Israel] which is exclusively devoted to the rescue of our people and their renewal is not aimed at the capitalistic exploitation of the region – nor does it serve any imperialistic aims whatsoever.[19]

Buber became aware that his 1921 assessment was largely incorrect. In its determination to further Jewish immigration to Palestine and to create a Jewish state, the Zionist movement demonstrated repeatedly that it had little regard for another people's rights. Buber continually worked to change from the inside the movement of which he was a part. His work in establishing the League of Jewish-Arab Rapprochement and Co-operation in 1942 is but one example of this. The platform of the League, of which Buber was one of twelve signatories, was first presented as an alternative both to the proposed creation of an Arab state of Palestine, implied in the British White Paper of 1939, and to the Zionist demand for a Jewish state, which seemed destined by the time of the Biltmore Conference in May 1942, if not earlier, to become official Zionist policy. The League's platform called for a bi-national state with equal rights for Arabs and Jews. The platform was adopted by a number of small Zionist parties, including Ha-shomer Ha-Tzair, a Marxist-Zionist grouping of considerable strength and prestige. These small parties finally joined the League officially and at a political gathering on 11 August 1942 established Ihud (Union) as a separate political party. Together with Judah Magnes and others, Buber was a prime mover of this happening.[20]

In June 1947, when the issue of Palestine was on the United Nations agenda, Buber was invited by Dutch radio to present his views. In a brilliant 50-minute presentation he stressed Arab-Jewish co-operation and the concept of a bi-national state. He stated:

> The Arab population does not need an Arab state in order to develop its potential freely, nor does the Jewish population need a Jewish state to accomplish this purpose. Its realization on both sides can be guaranteed within the framework of a joint bi-national socio-political entity,

> in which each side will be responsible for the particular matters pertaining to it, and both together will participate in the ordering of their common concerns.[21]

After the creation of the Jewish state, Buber and his friends, individually and jointly as members of Ihud, strongly criticized the government of the state of Israel for expropriating Arab lands and denying basic human rights to Palestinian Arabs. Throughout the remainder of his life, Buber remained consistent in this criticism. Even within the context of expressed concern over the security of the state of Israel, he continued to criticize the Israeli government for its treatment of the Palestinian minority. In January 1962, for example, at a Tel Aviv mass rally of Jews and Arabs protesting against the institution of the military government, Buber, unable to attend, sent a recorded speech. He said therein:

> We are obliged to grant that minority truly equal rights to the degree permitted to us by the conditions of our security. No more, but also no less. The main point here is to determine with extreme precision and at frequent intervals what is the positive and constructive maximum that we can offer at any time and to offer it. In my opinion we have not acted in that manner.[22]

As Buber grew older, he worried increasingly about the horrendous potential of the Arab-Israeli conflict. He emphasized the great need for peaceful reconciliation between Arabs and Jews along the lines he had advocated for many decades. As he wrote in his last published essay in *New Outlook*, in February 1965, shortly before his death on 13 June 1965: 'Undoubtedly the fate of the Near East depends on the question whether Israel and the Arab peoples will reach a mutual understanding before it is too late. We do not know how much time is given us to try.'[23]

As he grew up in the San Francisco bay area at the end of the 19th century, Judah Magnes was exposed to both the traditional and reform religious traditions in Judaism. From his father, David, who came from an orthodox background and was active in Oakland's First Hebrew Congregation, he acquired both understanding and feeling for one Judaic heritage. From his mother, Sophie, who came from one of Oakland's most prominent reform, German Jewish families and from Rabbi Jacob Voorsanger, spiritual leader of Temple Emanu-El in San Francisco, he grasped well another Judaic heritage. Rabbi Voorsanger, who tutored him in the Bible and the Talmud, also influenced Judah Magnes to enrol at the age of 17 at Hebrew Union College in Cincinnati to study for the rabbinate. Later, the young man became the college's first graduate from west of the Mississipi River.[24]

As a student at Hebrew Union College, Judah Magnes displayed great independence of mind. In his second year at the college when he was not yet 20, he wrote what became his first published essay, entitled 'Palestine – or Death'. Rabbi Jacob Voorsanger published it in his Temple's weekly newsletter, *Emanu-El.* In this essay Magnes maintained that American Jewry faced assimilation into the general society and that a 'return to the land of our fathers' and the 'establishment of a Jewish church and state' were necessary to assure the permanency of Judaism. He did not elaborate the totality of the Zionist theme nor did he yet seem to accept Zionism *per se.* Yet in a daring, if not profound, manner the college sophomore advanced a theory of Jewish nationalism, noted the defection of many reform Jews from Judaism, and mocked the classical reform position 'that says America is our Palestine, Washington our Jerusalem'. To formulate such views in the then anti-Zionist atmosphere of Hebrew Union College and have them accepted for publication in the journal of his strongly anti-Zionist mentor was a striking achievement.[25]

It was after finishing at Hebrew Union College in 1900, and while doing postgraduate study in Semitics and philosophy in Germany at the universities of Berlin and Heidelberg, that Magnes became a fully avowed partisan of Zionism. As he wrote to his parents from Germany:

> It [Zionism] is now my whole philosophy. It is my 'Lebensprogramm'. . . . Since I have become a Zionist my view of life has changed. . . . The questions concerning the Jewish people – and the Jewish religion is but one of these questions – are the questions that are consuming my days and nights. . . . My Zionism makes me more than a preacher or community leader. It makes me a worker for the preservation of the Jewish people as a whole and for their greater glory and better life in their own land.[26]

After acquiring his doctorate and returning to the United States, first to teach at Hebrew Union College and then to be a practising rabbi, Magnes continued to espouse his Zionism. Although he continually tried to put his Zionism within what he understood to be the theological and cultural context of Judaism, he repeatedly stated that he accepted the essence, if not the total, absolute truth, of Herzlian political Zionism. He continued to express great concern about the cultural and spiritual predicament of the Jews; assimilation continued in his estimation to imperil the American Jewish community.

Magnes credited many of his teachers in Germany with helping him develop his Zionist ideas. He was most influenced by Ahad Ha-Am, who emphasized the spiritual rather than the political problems facing Jews. Ahad Ha-Am's vision of Palestine as a necessary spiritual centre to re-invigorate and sustain Diaspora Jewry fitted Magnes's perception of what American Jewry needed. Although Ahad Ha-Am's nationalism was basically secular, it appealed to Magnes because of its recognition of the important position therein of religion. Magnes utilized the ideas of Ahad Ha-Am when he, while still a graduate student in Germany, began his own attempt to reconcile the reform emphasis upon universal ideals with the Jewish particularism inherent in and the ethnic allegiance demanded by Zionism. Being able to observe at close proximity the ongoing debate in the 1900–2 period between the Herzlian political Zionists and the Ahad Ha-Am-influenced cultural Zionists, the young Magnes achieved maturity in his own thinking.[27]

Upon his return to the United States and during the brief period he served as a Bible instructor and librarian at Hebrew Union College, Magnes expanded and expounded his Zionist ideas. In an article that appeared in the *Hebrew Union College Annual* of 1904, in which he discussed the poetry of Chaim Nachman Bialik, Magnes argued a number of Zionist themes. For readers of the *Annual*, nearly all reform rabbis, Magnes's most provocative argument was:

> The ideas of a universal religion in the keeping of a given nation and the idea of a national culture are not mutually exclusive. For a national culture may have developed a universal religion. National culture is thus the broader term in that it may have expressed itself in numberless other forms, as well as in terms of universal religion.[28]

Shortly after accepting his first rabbinical post at Temple Israel in Brooklyn, New York, in September 1904, Magnes found himself embroiled in difficulty with most of his congregation because of his Zionism. As he explained when he resigned this post two years later, he was too 'conservative in Judaism' and 'too active in Zionism' for the majority of them. Fortunately for his career, Magnes was thereafter appointed associate rabbi at Temple Emanu-El in New York City, regarded as the cathedral of reform Judaism in the United States. While at Temple Emanu-El, he became fully entrenched in Zionist activity. Working with a number of other distinguished rabbis and scholars, many of whom were on the faculty of the Conservative Jewish Theological Seminary, Magnes rose quickly to the peak of his influence in American Zionist circles and remained there until 1915. During these years he became the leading orator-preacher among rabbis in New York City, even surpassing in this regard Stephen Wise, who founded the Free Synagogue. Repeatedly Magnes emphasized Zionist themes in his sermons. Yet, he developed perceptions of Zion, exile and the centrality of Palestine that differed radically from those held by most European Zionists including Ahad Ha-Am. Far more than Ahad Ha-Am, Magnes put his Hebrew humanism within the context of religious belief. In a sermon delivered in 1909, for example, he declared: 'For the Jew there cannot, I think, be a permanent Jewish religion without Jewish nationality, nor can there be, I think, a permanent Jewish nationality without Jewish religion.'[29]

Being a Zionist for Magnes was equivalent to being a more earnest Jew committed to the support of the Jewish people's will to survive. In a 1910 formal address entitled 'Zionism and the Jewish Religion', he declared:

> Nor can there be any question that Zionism is doing more than anything else to strengthen the Jewish national consciousness or feeling of peoplehood wherever Jews live throughout the world. Whatever be our interpretation of Jewish history, the basic element of every theory of Jewish life is the continued existence of the Jews, and it is

> Zionism alone of all Jewish movements which can give a guarantee of the uninterrupted continuance of the Eternal People.[30]

For Magnes, the preservation of the Jews as a people was a requisite for all particularistic conceptions of Jews and Judaism.

Because of his impeccable credentials, knowledge, sincerity, imposing stature and emphasis upon what he termed spiritual Zionism, Magnes did not unduly antagonize the wealthy and powerful members of Temple Emanu-El who were hostile towards political Zionism. Magnes, moreover, combined his Zionist and Jewish communal activities in the turbulent arena of New York City. He successfully appealed to many of his congregation for their financial and personal help in these activities. Magnes did yeoman work and accomplished positive results in bridging the gap and tempering conflicts between Jews of German and Eastern European backgrounds in New York City. Perhaps the most significant aspect of his community activity was his attempt to create a structure that would encompass Jewish communal life. Central to this attempt was the Magnes proposal to establish a European-type Kehillah in New York City, not only to produce positive results there but also to become a model for Jews to follow in other cities. Funded almost entirely by two of his rich former Temple Emanu-El congregants, Jacob H. Schiff and Felix M. Warburg, and centred primarily on improving Jewish religious education, the New York Kehillah was founded in 1909 with Magnes as chairman. By 1922 this ambitious, creative experiment was moribund; apathy and dissension within ranks had exerted their toll. The Kehillah experiment did produce limited results, however, and did raise hopes about the progress that could be made in Jewish communal work. The Kehillah incorporated some Zionist ideas, but at most this community experiment was tangential to the developing Zionism of Judah Magnes.[31]

Beginning in autumn 1914 Magnes became embroiled in internal Zionist and Jewish organizational controversies. He opposed the creation of a new organization, the American Jewish Congress, to represent all of American Jewry in international and Zionist affairs. Instead, he chose to back the American Jewish Committee, of which the Kehillah served as the New York City division, in its more independent stance.[32] Magnes became even more irritated when American Zionists chose as their chief Louis D. Brandeis, the eminent Supreme Court justice who had risen in meteoric fashion to the top echelon of the American Jewish leadership even though he had previously been largely indifferent to Jewish problems and needs. By the time of the 1915 Zionist convention Magnes had accused Brandeis and his Zionist followers of fomenting disunity among American Jews and of deviating from the movement's primary concern over Palestine. This dual accusation turned many of the rank and file in the Zionist movement against Magnes.[33]

It was at this same point in time that Magnes publicly disagreed with the Zionist diplomatic policy and goal of Jews gaining 'special' political status in Palestine. 'I want equal rights for the Jews, no more and no less, in all parts of the world, including Palestine', Magnes wrote to Brandeis in September 1915. Magnes went on to argue in the letter and elsewhere that

Jews only had a right 'to ask for the opportunity to migrate to, settle in and develop their Jewish economic and cultural life in Palestine freely, just as other peoples of the [Ottoman] Empire have the same right.' Jews, Magnes concluded, should not enjoy any special political treatment or group preferment.[34] This constituted a foretaste of what Magnes would propound in expanded fashion a few years later, and would continue to emphasize for the rest of his life.

From 1915 to 1917 Magnes continued to play a significant role in American Jewish affairs, although his influence declined. In 1917 he plunged more heavily than ever before into general American political affairs. To the dismay and consternation of many of his friends, he became an active pacifist, an ardent upholder of civil liberties and an anti-imperialist advocate. For five years, until he sailed for Palestine in 1922, Magnes alienated friends, suffered indignities, and seriously jeopardized his position in the American Jewish community by his commitment to these general causes.[35]

In keeping with his general political views at the time, Magnes regarded the British Balfour Declaration in 1917, advocating the establishment of a Jewish national home in Palestine, as a move to help Britain achieve imperialistic goals. Magnes did not trust British promises; he regarded the San Remo Conference in 1920, at which the Allied powers assigned to Britain the mandate for Palestine, as a minor catastrophe. As he wrote to a friend:

> I mistrust the mandate, the government that is to exercise it, the peace conference that gave it, and the League of Nations that is to sanction it. I mistrust the motives that prompted the giving of it. . . . But whatever the conditions, the present state of the world, the dominance of economic imperialism, the precarious position of the Jews of Eastern and Central Europe, the bewildering problems of the Eastern and Mohammedan worlds – all make me fear that the mandate has no reality to it, that Palestine and the Jews are a kind of plaything in the hands of dark, unscrupulous forces. . . . I am afraid the exile of a people does not end by political fiat and that redemption does not begin with political favoritism. . . .
>
> That Jerusalem the Holy City of three great religions should have been conquered by force of arms is a paradox worthy of a smile of derision. As for the Jews, I am convinced that they have never gained anything from militarism. . . .
>
> As to Palestine, the principle of self-determination was disregarded. If self-determination is a just answer to other disputed problems, why not for Palestine and for the Jews? The fact is that Palestine has five or six times as many Arab inhabitants as Jews. You speak of the 'historic rights' of the Jews to offset the claim of the present-day Arab majority. I am aware of the way in which historic rights and strategic rights and economic rights have made short shrift of the principle of self-determination whenever this suited the needs of the conquerors. Yet I too believe in the historic right of the Jewish people to the Land of Israel, meaning thereby the right to make their historic

> land their own not by major force but, if they can, by labor, by work of brain and hand, by collaboration with and education of the present majority. Historic right means that the Jews should be given the free and unimpeded opportunity to come into the land, to bring there their workers, their peasants, their wealth of money, of brain, of human material; and to become in the course of time, if they can, the preponderant element of the population. In other words, 'historic right' means for me: equal opportunities for Jews, Arabs, Syrians, Moslems, Christians to live their lives freely and in proportion to their labor of hand and brain, to achieve power and the direction of affairs.
>
> Political favoritism is not to be depended upon for long. The one practical way and the one decent way towards permanence is through labor, through sound economic development, and through inner spiritual freedom and not through political patronage. What the Balfour Declaration means or does not mean is that Jews and Arabs, Moslems and Christians have a free and unhindered opportunity to develop Palestine through honest labor of hand and brain.[36]

Magnes decided to go to Europe and then to Palestine in 1920 but did not leave until 1922. His ultimate decision to settle in Palestine was not fully in keeping with the concept of *aliyah* in the classical Zionist sense, for it was neither a premeditated decision to move permanently nor a negation of Jewish life in the Diaspora.[37] Magnes actually defended the Diaspora in a major, public address, delivered shortly after his arrival in Jerusalem in 1923. He concluded that address by stating:

> Everyone who lives here in Eretz Israel [land of Israel] and works is helping the Jewish people create spiritual values and thus aiding the Jewish people to carry out its work in the world. The same is true of those who live and work in the Galut [Diaspora]. Where a man can do best for his people is an individual and private matter.[38]

Overcoming strong pulls to return to the United States during the first few years of the family stay in Palestine, Magnes involved himself deeply and seriously in efforts to establish and open the Hebrew University. He joined an *ad hoc* committee, made up of leading scholars and Zionists including Ahad Ha-Am. Magnes became a major fund-raiser for this project, utilizing his previous contacts, friendship and influence to acquire money from some wealthy New York Jews. He convinced Felix Warburg, for example, to contribute half a million dollars for an endowment for the proposed Institute of Jewish Studies. (Previous to Magnes's fund-raising Weizmann, representing the Zionist Organization, had been the sole sponsor of the university.) In September 1925, the Hebrew University Board of Governors chose Weizmann as president of the board, Magnes as chancellor, or executive officer of the university, and Albert Einstein, already a world-famous scientist, as chairman of the academic council.[39]

For Magnes the ideal of the Hebrew University derived from the essence of Eretz Israel, constituted an integral part of the Jewish people's mission to the world, represented the best features of Judaism, humanism and internationalism, and thus would become a realization of Ahad Ha-Am's spiritual Zionism. Magnes believed that the university, blending together the best features of universalism and Jewish particularism, would present Jews and Judaism with fresh values.[40]

Magnes and Weizmann differed sharply in their views about the development of the Hebrew University. In keeping with his belief that the university would combine universal and Jewish values, Magnes emphasized the school of 'Geisteswissenschaften' (humanities), in which Judaism would occupy a prominent position. Weizmann had different priorities: he felt primary emphasis should be put upon the natural sciences and the development of a medical school. He wanted to establish specialized scientific research institutes as the centre of the university. These institutes would be dedicated to 'pure science' in order to serve best what he considered to be the development needs of the *yishuv*, or Zionist settlement in Palestine. In the years immediately preceding and following World War I, Weizmann had devoted much time to preparing the groundwork for university development along the lines he favoured. He had convinced the Zionist Organization to purchase land on Mount Scopus for establishment of the university, and had converted Einstein to his point of view. In 1921, Weizmann and Einstein, who together undertook the first serious fund-raising effort, collected a sizeable amount of money for the university. Weizmann's dedication to his ideal of the Hebrew University was thus deep rooted.

Inspired by his spiritual Zionism, Magnes, between 1925 and 1935, assumed direct responsibility for the university. He served as administrator, fund-raiser, planner and academic head. Facing mounting pressures to enlarge research facilities and absorb qualified senior and junior scientists, especially after Hitler's rise to power, Magnes also had to deal with expanding teaching facilities, increasing student enrolment, and developing degree-granting programmes. The university's modestly increasing income, nearly 70% of which came from American donors, allowed for steady, if modest, growth in the first few years. The widespread economic depression of the 1930s, however, slowed expansion.[41] The absence of a university tradition and the problematic nature of scholars coming from different places with different academic standards and approaches made Magnes's job even more difficult. He nevertheless was still able to contribute mightily to the university's becoming a symbol of national renewal and an intellecutal and spiritual centre of the Jewish people in these early years when the *yishuv's* growth was slow.[42]

Magnes intensified his political involvements in 1929. By then, he had already broken with Weizmann and official Zionism. This was in part due to the influence of his major supporters, who were American non-Zionists, e.g. Marshall and Warburg. These supporters predicated their general support and direct financial help to the university upon Magnes's keeping the university free of Zionist domination. Obviously responding to his supporters,

Magnes opposed the election of Weizmann, who then headed the Zionist organization, as president of the university's board of governors. 'Zionist control', Magnes wrote to a friend in November 1925, 'would make the university something partisan and sectarian whereas it ought to be the university of all sections of the Jewish people.'[43]

Weizmann responded angrily to Magnes's opposition. He regarded the argument against Zionist control as specious, since he considered Zionism the movement of Jewish national revival. The antagonism between the two men grew increasingly bitter. Weizmann, however, maintained an uneasy partnership with Magnes, because he desired to bring those wealthy non-Zionist supporters of the university's chief executive into the enlarged Jewish Agency, the Zionist body designated to represent the Jewish people in building their national home.[44] Weizmann actually regarded Magnes as a dilettante rather than a serious thinker or scholar. He told his friends that Magnes was best qualified to head the university. Magnes, on the other hand, did not hide his negative feelings about Weizmann's moral character.[45]

In the ten-year period that he headed the Hebrew University, Magnes almost continually experienced great difficulties. Numerous academics on the scene were disgruntled about his refusal to attempt to build the kind of science faculty they believed was necessary and possible. Einstein, who barely knew Magnes personally and never visited the university, also criticized him on this ground. Einstein insisted that Magnes was a theologian, not a scientist, and that he wanted to turn the university into a 'diploma factory'. Nevertheless, Magnes built both the science and humanities faculties, responding – as he put it – to the needs of the *yishuv*. He brought renowned scholars in many disciplines to the university as faculty and contributed mightily to its reputation as a forum for uninhibited intellectual discussion and debate.[46]

The armed conflicts that erupted in parts of Palestine in August 1929 between Arabs and Jews, following eight years of relative quiet, greatly affected Magnes. By the time the university opened in November, he had decided to re-enter active political life. For the first time since his arrival in Palestine, he publicly addressed himself in the university's convocation to a political issue. In his brief address he stressed the themes that he would pursue diligently for the rest of his life. He maintained that Palestine was neither Arab nor Jewish, but was the 'Holy Land of two peoples. . . and three religions'. He argued that this fact should be the guideline for the Zionist leadership, which should seek accommodation with Arabs rather than relying upon force and British arms. Magnes called for concessions by both Arabs and Jews; he asked that both sides overcome their rage; he proposed a pacifist policy for Zionism and called for a politics of morality even if it meant that Zionism would not be able to achieve all its political aims:

> If we cannot find ways of peace and understanding, if the only way of establishing the Jewish National Home is upon the bayonets of some Empire, our whole enterprise is not worthwhile, and it is better

> that the eternal people that has outlived many a mighty empire should possess its soul in patience and plan and wait. It is in one of the great civilizing tasks before the Jewish people to try to enter the promised land, not in the Joshua way, but bringing peace and culture, hard work and sacrifice and love, and a determination to do nothing that cannot be justified before the conscience of the world.[47]

The above address propelled Magnes into political controversy that intensified in the following weeks. The *New York Times* of 24 November 1929 carried a long statement by Magnes, in which he advocated a binational government for Palestine with certain guarantees and obligations for both Arabs and Jews. So long as the Jewish people were in Palestine as a matter of right, not of sufferance, Magnes explained in his statement, they could create a home there that, as Ahad Ha-Am had stipulated, could become a spiritual and intellectual centre for Judaism and the Jewish people. The Jews, moreover, would be able to build agriculture and industry, and engage in all kinds of labour. As opposed to the position of political Zionism, and in agreement with the Palestinian Arab position, Magnes favoured establishing a legislative assembly.[48]

In his booklet, *Like All the Nations?*, published in December 1929, Magnes added specifications to his advocacy. He wrote again that the concepts of 'Jewish state' and 'Jewish majority' should be replaced by guarantees to Jews of immigration, settlement on the land, and the right to establish for themselves Hebrew life and culture. The guarantees, he reasoned, could only be forthcoming in a democratic regime in which rights would be specified, and tranquillity and mutual understanding would thus be secured.[49] Realizing that immigration was the key consideration, Magnes presented a demographic analysis. He opined that under optimal conditions Palestine by the next generation could not achieve the total population of three million, considered by many to be the maximum absorptive capacity in the foreseeable future. The number of Jews in Palestine then totalled only 160,000. Magnes suggested that at most the number of Jews could grow only to one million, or one-third of the maximum absorptive capacity, in 30 to 40 years. He therefore concluded that advocacies of a Jewish majority were anyway unrealistic.[50]

In the following years Magnes became the most vocal advocate of a binational state. He saw in such a state the only possibility for Arab-Jewish reconciliation. He stressed the strategic need of emphasizing interim agreements that would not unduly conflict with the national aspirations of Arabs or Jews. In his talks with Arabs and in his efforts to mediate between Arab and Zionist leaders, he proposed as a first step a ten-year agreement. During that ten-year period Jewish immigration would be allowed, he proposed, at a rate that would not endanger the Arab majority. At the end of the ten years, he calculated, Jews would at most constitute 40% of the population. In 1936 Magnes, in reaching a tentative understanding with the Arab leader, Musa Al-Alami, agreed upon an annual Jewish immigration quota of 30,000.

The specific plan he proposed as part of this tentative understanding assigned roles to Arabs and Jews in policy-making, governmental administration, and sharing of responsibility.[51] The plan then called for a federation of bi-national Palestine, Transjordan, Syria and Lebanon. The establishment of the federation, he believed, might induce the Arabs to agree to unlimited Jewish immigration to Palestine. Even for Magnes the refugee problem had become an urgent matter by the mid-1930s.[52]

Believing that his plan would lead to a permanent political solution, Magnes understood that agreement with the Arabs was necessary before the whole matter could be taken to the British. Although he did not fully trust the British, he maintained excellent rapport with the colonial secretaries and high commissioners. He was fairly confident that the British could be prevailed upon to agree to a joint Arab-Jewish proposal, and then to provide the needed governmental framework and authority to help substantially in the long process of conciliation and negotiation leading to final settlement.[53]

The impact of World War II influenced Magnes to revise some of his views. In his most important wartime statement, which appeared in *Foreign Affairs* in January 1943, he expressed some scepticism about whether Jews and Arabs could themselves agree upon a compromise. He pointed to the intransigence of leaders on both sides and suggested that the United States and Great Britain, in order to prevent Palestine from becoming 'a menace to the world's peace', might have to impose a compromise. Magnes also reconsidered immigration. Having lost some confidence in the possibility of an Arab federation, Magnes stated that the principle of political parity of the two peoples in the bi-national state should be applied, and that as large a Jewish immigration as possible should be admitted in the shortest possible time in order to help the thousands of remaining refugees.[54]

Although he continued to be politically active and thus to work in many ways with numerous people during the last two decades of his life, Magnes retained a personal political independence. He had clearly established himself as an independent in 1925 when he participated with but did not join the Brit Shalom (Covenant of Peace) society, founded to promote understanding between Arabs and Jews on the basis of absolute political autonomy of two culturally autonomous people. Seventeen years later in 1942, Magnes did join with Buber and a host of others in establishing the Ihud (Union) association, which was dedicated to advancing the bi-national programme. Magnes even became chairman for a while, but he continually maintained, sometimes to the chagrin of his colleagues, his freedom of action.[55]

After re-entering politics in 1929, Magnes began to involve himself in personal diplomacy in order to advance his bi-national programme. He talked with a large variety of people and in so doing antagonized political Zionist leaders who believed he was undermining their attempts to establish first a Jewish national home and then a Jewish state. Weizmann, for example, bitterly criticized Magnes for meeting and talking in 1929 with H. St. John Philby, an adviser to King Ibn Saud of Saudi Arabia who himself was in contact with Palestinian leaders.[56] Magnes was not stymied by Zionist criticism in this regard, however, and seemed both to enjoy and to consider worthwhile his discussions – both public and private – with Arab leaders. Some of the new, emerging political Zionist leaders in Palestine in the 1930s at times attempted to utilize Magnes's contacts and good offices to talk with Arab leaders themselves in attempting to promote their cause.[57] Magnes at times was even commissioned by these political Zionist leaders to speak to Arab leaders on behalf of the Jewish Agency. Too much distrust existed on both the Arab and Zionist sides, however, and mishandling of situations almost became the norm. Ben-Gurion, for example, wrote reproachfully to Magnes in 1938 after the latter, with the assent of the Jewish Agency, had met and discussed certain matters in Beirut with Nuri Al-Sa'id, the Iraqi Prime Minister:

> While we do not resort to strategems ourselves, we will not fall victims to those of the other side. We will examine seven times every plan and every proposal that is supported by these deadly enemies of ours. We are not afraid and we do not refuse to meet with them, but we will not rush to fall into their trap. In this entire matter you acted out of good intentions, of that I have no doubt. But intention alone is not enough. It is clear to me that your honest striving for peace is being exploited in order to undermine our position.[58]

Except for some revisions, cited above, Magnes did not waver in his bi-national advocacy. He steadfastly rejected both the conclusion reached and the recommendation made by the Palestine Royal Commission (Peel Commission) in its July 1937 report, issued after hearings had been conducted. The Peel Commission concluded that the national aspirations of Jews and Arabs were irreconcilable, and recommended partition of Palestine. Magnes argued instead that only the bi-national plan was viable.[59] He continued to seek political and financial support for the bi-national approach from his non-Zionist friends in the United States, and he unsuccessfully fought against the Jewish Agency's acceptance of the partition plan in 1937.[60]

By 1938 partition was generally rejected. In 1939 the Zionists were incensed by the British White Paper which was largely intended to appease the Arabs. The White Paper stipulated that 75,000 Jewish immigrants be allowed to enter Palestine over a five-year period, that further immigration could occur only with Arab consent, and that a time-limit of ten years should be set for establishing an Arab state in Palestine. At this point in time, to the dismay of Magnes, the single goal of Jewish sovereignty was revived. In 1942 Ben-Gurion proclaimed Jewish statehood to be the goal of the Zionist movement. At the historic Zionist meeting at the Biltmore Hotel in New York that year, over 500 Zionist delegates, representing nearly all factions in the movement, demanded 'that the gates of Palestine be opened. . . and that Palestine be established as a Jewish commonwealth.'[61]

Magnes led the opposition in Palestine to the Biltmore Declaration. 'The slogan Jewish state or commonwealth', he wrote, 'is equivalent, in effect, to a declaration of war by the Jews on the Arabs.' A few others, including some fringe Zionist groups, also remained loyal to bi-nationalism and opposed the Biltmore Declaration.[62] Magnes worked with these individuals and groups, who altogether constituted a small minority of the Jews in Palestine. Magnes also continued to seek support in the United States. After Warburg's death in October 1937, Magnes increasingly sought and received support from leading figures in the American Jewish Committee. He also took the opportunity to publish pronouncements in the *New York Times*. Yet he never achieved anything like the amount of support that he sought or needed. In 1942 he could acquire only enough funding in the United States to subsidize publication of the Ihud journal, *Be'ayot*. He came to the United States on a fund-raising tour in 1946 and stayed through the summer and autumn but could only raise $20,000 of the $100,000 he wanted. Discussions with State Department officials in Washington, however, encouraged Magnes to believe that the United States government would adopt the bi-national formula.[63] This inspired him to work even more diligently with his colleagues of Ihud when he returned to Palestine. He did so even though Ihud members were regarded as disloyal to the Jewish national cause by most Jews in Palestine at the end of World War II.

Judah Magnes could be classified as a religious social radical. He himself may have provided the best definition for this terminology. In 1939 he invited a group of friends, including Martin Buber, Hugo Bergman, Ernst Simon and Gershon Scholem, to join with him in a new religious society, named Ha'ol (the Yoke). The full title was the 'Yoke of the Coming Kingdom of God'. Magnes wrote the following description:

> We are united in the feeling of responsibility toward the life of society in general, and the life of Israel in its land and in the dispersion in particular. This sense of responsibility stems from faith in eternal values whose source is God. We believe in a life of faith which carries a commitment to social action and practical political work, and we reject any attempt to separate the two dominions, which are one in theory and practice.

The above creed of the religious social radical is the guide to an understanding of Magnes's thinking and behaviour. The creed, wherein the religious and the political are intermeshed, pervades his public addresses and writings. Magnes may have considered himself to be a modern version of the ancient Hebrew prophet who, in the name of the God of Israel, intervened in the political life of the nation. Resembling the ancient prophet, Magnes's political-religious rhetoric made him appear at times to be a self-righteous, rigid person who believed he was possessed of a higher authority. Through it all, however, shone his religious fervour, sincerity, courage and candour. He also displayed a kind of disarming innocence. His authority seemed to stem from his integrity. Buber observed that when watching Magnes challenge the Zionist *realpolitik* one was obliged to lend a hand.[64]

In April 1948, seven months before his death and one month before the state of Israel was proclaimed, Magnes received a message asking him to come to the United States. Some State Department officials and an *ad hoc* committee of some prominent Jews,[65] all of whom opposed the United Nations resolution of 1947 recommending partition of Palestine into Jewish and Arab states, believed Magnes could be helpful in maintaining American support for a United Nations trusteeship over Palestine that could prevent war and would postpone indefinitely the establishment of a Jewish state. (Support for the United Nations trusteeship constituted a retreat from the previous United States position backing partition.) Although in poor health Magnes came to the United States and worked diligently for this cause that meant so much to him. But it was too late. On 15 May 1948, the proclamation of the state of Israel was issued, and fighting erupted. The United States government backed the creation of the Jewish state. Magnes's long advocacy of bi-nationalism came to an end.[66]

Until his death in October of that same year Magnes busied himself with attempting to develop a confederation of Arab and Jewish states with Jerusalem as the capital. He also concerned himself with Arab as well as Jewish refugees and tried to convince Jews in Palestine and in the United States to help the refugees on a purely humanitarian basis. Before he died on 27 October 1948, he sent a message for the opening of the new academic year of the Hebrew University. In his message he, who had so strongly opposed Jewish statehood, accepted the reality and asked that the challenge of the new state be directed towards humane and peaceful ends. The message read in part:

> The people of Israel now confronts such problems as subjects and not merely as objects. In the eyes of many among us the chief value of an independent state is, that we ourselves bear the responsibility for our own decisions and that we do not just have to accept the consequences of decisions made for us by others.[67]

The humanitarian Zionism of Buber and Magnes may have influenced a significant number of people, but from its beginning it was doomed to failure. Before the 1930s most Zionist theoreticians and advocates believed and emphasized that a Jewish state, in which Jews would constitute the majority and maintain control, was an absolute necessity. Only the existence of such a state, they argued, would solve the Jewish problem. After the Holocaust large segments of the remaining world-wide Jewish population and impressive numbers of non-Jews, who had either rejected or had not previously concerned themselves with Zionism, accepted the idea of a Jewish state and aided the Zionist movement.

The demographically Jewish state, which emanated from Zionism, became upon inception a Jewish exclusivist state that by definition and by its developing public policy oppressed the non-Jewish indigenous Arab population of historic Palestine. Perhaps the mere historic existence of a thread of humanitarian Zionist thought has allowed some advocates to argue that Zionism has not been monolithic, but actually embodies humanistic, democratic ideals. Palestinian Arabs, however, primarily affected not by the words of differing Zionist advocacies but by oppressive acts of the Zionist movement and Jewish exclusivist state, cannot be expected to be greatly impressed by the historic, humanitarian emphases of Buber, Magnes and others.

Perhaps the major importance of the Buber and Magnes emphases within the Zionist context is that the fate of such advocacy shows not what Zionism is but rather what it is not. The ultimate, near-total defeat of humanitarian Zionism, the probability that it never had a chance of success within the Zionist movement, underline the anti-democratic orientation of Zionism. It is this Zionist orientation that became and has remained the central feature of the Arab-Israeli conflict.

Notes

1. The most comprehensive discussion of Buber's political thought is the Hebrew monograph: Ernst A. Simon, *The Line of Demarcation, Nationalism, Zionism and the Arab-Israeli Conflict in the Thought of Martin Buber* (The Center for Arab Studies, Givat Haviva, 1973).

2. Ibid., pp. 14ff.

3. See Z. Jabotinsky, 'The Role of the (Jewish) Legion: The Prevention of Violence', in *Speeches: 1905–1926* (in Hebrew), (Eri Jabotinsky, Jerusalem 1947).

4. Neil Caplan, *Palestinian Jewry and the Arab Question, 1917–1925* (Frank Cass, London, 1978), p. 29.

5. Dov Friedlander and Calvin Goldscheider, *The Population of Israel* (Columbia University Press, New York, 1979), pp. 53–82.

6. Letter from Weizmann to James Marshall, 17 January 1930, in *The Letters and Papers of Chaim Weizmann*, vol. 14, ed. Camillo Dresner (Rutgers and Israel University Press, New Brunswick, NJ, 1979), pp. 208–11.

7. Buber's writings and speeches, extending over many decades, clearly and specifically reveal this.

8. Among the many sources for this are:

(a) 'Judisches Nationalheim und Nationale Politik in Palastina', lecture held in Berlin Chapter of Brit Shalom, 31 October 1929, unpublished manuscript, *Martin Buber Archive*, MS varia 350, vav 14, trans. Gabrielle H. Schalit;

(b) Declaration of the Association 'Union' (Ihud) in English-language supplement to *Be'ayot Ha-Yom*, vol. 3, no. 1 (September 1942), p. 12.

(c) 'Rov O Rabbim? Beshulei Neum Ehad', *Be'ayot*, vol. 1, no. 2 (May 1944), pp. 52–4, trans. Deborah Goldman.

9. Ibid. Also see: 'Buber's Testimony before the Anglo-American Inquiry Commission', 14 March 1946, in Judah L. Magnes and Martin Buber, *Anglo-Jewish Unity: Testimony before the Anglo-American Inquiry Commission for the Ihud (Union) Association* (V. Gollancz, London, 1947), pp. 44–8.

10. See Ben Halpern, *The Idea of the Jewish State* (Harvard, Cambridge, Mass., 1961), pp. 20–51.

11. Caplan, op. cit., pp. 5–7, 200ff.

12. Those who, like Buber, favoured the pacifist approach of promoting Arab-Jewish understanding were split on *aliyah*. See Israel Kolatt, 'The Zionist Movement and the Arabs', in Shmuel Ettinger (ed.), *Zionism and the Arab Question: Collected Historical Studies* (in Hebrew), (The Zalaman Shazar Centre, Jerusalem, 1979), p. 10.

13. On Buber's religious socialism, see his 'Three Theses for a Religious Socialism', in Martin Buber, *Pointing the Way, Collected Essays*, ed. and trans. Maurice Friedman (Schoken, New York,)1974, pp. 112ff. Also see: Richard Falk, *Martin Buber and Paul Tillich: Radical Politics and Religion* (National Council of Protestant Episcopal Churches, New York, 1961).

14. Martin Buber, 'Hebrew Humanism' (1941), trans. Olga Marx, in Buber, *Israel and the Arab World: Essays in a Time of Crisis*, 2nd ed. (Schoken, New York, 1963), pp. 245–82.

15. Isaiah 1:27.

16. Buber, 'Gandhi, Politics and Us', in Buber, 1974, op. cit., p. 137.

17. *Two Letters to Gandhi: From Martin Buber and Judah L. Magnes*, pamphlets of the Bond (Rubin Mass, Jerusalem, 1939), pamphlet no. 1, pp. 1–22.

18. Cited in Stephen Poppel, 'Martin Buber: The Art of the Unpolitical', in *Midstream* (May 1974), p. 61.

19. 'Rede aif dem XII. Zionisten Kongress in Karlsbad, 2 September, 1921', in Martin Buber, *Kampf um Israel: Reden und Schriften* (Schocken, Berlin, 1933), pp. 225–42.

20. See: 'Declaration of the Association "Union" (Ihud)', in English-language supplement to *Be'ayot Ha-Yom*, vol. 3, no. 1, September 1942, p. 12.

21. 'Shenei Amim Be-Eretz Yisrael', *Be'ayot*, nos. 3–4. February 1948, pp. 200–8, trans. Deborah Grenimann. (Lecture originally delivered in German on Dutch radio, June 1947.)

22. 'Yesh Latet Le-Miut Shivyon Zekhuyot Amiti', *Ner*, no. 5–6 (February 1962), pp. 7, 13, trans. Jeffrey M. Green.

23. 'The Time to Try', *New Outlook*, vol. 8, no. 1, January-February 1965, pp. 13–14.

24. The most complete biography of Judah Magnes is Norman Bentwich, *For Zion's Sake: A Biography of Judah L. Magnes* (Jewish Publication Society, Philadelphia, 1974); see pp. 15–18.

25. *Emanu-El*, 6 January 1896, p. 13; Yohai Goell, 'Aliyah in the Zionism of an American Oleh: Judah L. Magnes', *American Jewish Historical Quarterly*, 65, December 1975, pp. 100–1.

26. Letter from Judah L. Magnes to his family, 9 October 1901, quoted in Goell, op. cit., p. 103.

27. Magnes diligently read *Ha'shiloah*, the Hebrew literary journal edited by Ahad Ha-Am. See Bentwich, op. cit., pp. 27, 30, 35.

28. Judah L. Magnes, 'Some Poems of H.N. Bialik', *Hebrew Union College Annual*, I (1904), pp. 177, 186.

29. *The Emanu-El Pulpit*, 2, 1909, p. 8.

30. Judah L. Magnes, *Zionism and Jewish Religion: Address Delivered Before the Philadelphia Section, Council of Jewish Women*, 12 April 1910 (pamphlet), p.5.

31. See Arthur A. Goren, *New York Jews and the Quest for Community: The Kehillah Experiment* (Columbia University, New York, 1970) for the

best overall discussion of Kehillah. For what is mentioned in this paper, see especially pp. 34–9, 47–8, 57–66, 94–6, 117–23, 207–8, 245–52, 276.

32. See ibid., pp. 44–56, 218–26.

33. Ibid., pp. 219, 307. See also Yonathan Shapiro, *Leadership of the American Zionist Organization, 1897–1930* (University of Illinois, Urbana, Ill., 1971), pp. 82–5, 88–92.

34. Letters from Judah L. Magnes to Louis Brandeis, 30 June 1915, and 2 September 1915, as cited in Arthur A. Goren, *Dissenter In Zion* (Harvard University, Cambridge, Mass., 1982), pp. 144–5, 149–52; Melvin I. Urofsky, *American Zionism from Herzl to the Holocaust* (Anchor, Garden City, New York, 1975), pp. 175–9.

35. See: Goren, 1970, op. cit., pp. 215–18, 231; Zosa Szajkowski, 'The Pacifism of Judah Magnes', *Conservative Judaism*, 22, Spring 1968, p. 37; C. Roland Marchand, *The American Peace Movement and Social Reform, 1898–1918* (Princeton University, Princeton, NJ, 1972), pp. 231–5, 249–59, 263–4, 303–6, 309–22, 334–5; *Minutes of Conference of Members of Various Peace Groups*, 5 April 1917, Emergency Peace Federation Papers, Swarthmore College, Swarthmore, Penn. Bentwich, op. cit., pp. 102–7.

36. Letter from Judah L. Magnes to a 'Dear Friend', May 1920, as cited in Goren, 1982, op. cit., pp. 183–90.

37. See Goell, op. cit., pp. 108, 112.

38. Judah L. Magnes, 'Eretz Israel and the Galut', English version of address delivered in Hebrew in Jerusalem, 22 May 1923, as reprinted in Goren, 1982, op. cit., pp. 208–14. For published Hebrew version see: *Hapoal Hatsair*, 8 June 1923, pp. 9–11. Magnes originally wrote the speech in English and then translated it into Hebrew.

39. Goell, op. cit., pp. 113–14; Herbert Parzen, *The Hebrew University 1925–1935* (Ktav, New York, 1974), pp. 2–3.

40. Judah L. Magnes, *Addresses by the Chancellor of the Hebrew University* (Hebrew University, Jerusalem, 1936), pp. 6–7, 16–18, 181–8.

41. Ibid., pp. 20–5, 212–14, 284–5.

42. Bentwich, op. cit., pp. 160–71; Parzen, op. cit., pp. 7–8, 13–21, 43–57.

43. Letter from Judah L. Magnes to Julian W. Mack, 4 November 1925, as reprinted in Goren, 1982, op. cit., pp. 242–52.

44. See letter from Chaim Weizmann to Judah L. Magnes, 15 December 1925, in *Letters and Papers of Chaim Weizmann*, ed. Joshua Freudlich, vol. 12 (1977), p. 456.

45. See: Parzen, op. cit., pp. 102–9; letters from Chaim Weizmann to Albert Einstein, 19 May 1926, 19 July 1926, 13 May 1928, in *Letters and Papers of Chaim Weizmann*, ed. Pinhas Ofer, vol. 13 (1978), pp. 16–17, 67, 399–400; Judah L. Magnes, *Journal*, 13 February 1928, as reprinted in Goren, 1982, op. cit., pp. 265–7.

46. See: letter from Judah L. Magnes to 'Dear Friend', 28 April 1929, as reprinted in Goren, 1982, op. cit., pp. 272–5; Parzen, op. cit., pp. 16–20.

47. Judah L. Magnes, 1936, op. cit., p. 62.

48. *New York Times*, 24 November 1929, p. 12, and section 2, p. 1.

49. Judah L. Magnes, *Like All the Nations?* (Hebrew University, Jerusalem, 1930), p. 6.

50. Ibid., p. 7.

51. Ibid., p. 8; see also Susan Lee Hattis, *The Bi-National Idea in Palestine*

during Mandatory Times (Haifa University, Haifa, 1970), pp. 146–8.

52. Judah L. Magnes, 'Palestine Peace Seen in Arab-Jewish Agreements', *New York Times*, 19 July 1937, part 4, p. 9.

53. See letter from Judah L. Magnes to Nuri Al-Sa'id, 23 February 1938, as cited in Goren, 1982, op. cit., pp. 346–7.

54. Judah L. Magnes, 'Toward Peace in Palestine', *Foreign Affairs*, January 1943, pp. 239–49.

55. See Hattis, op. cit., pp. 38–58.

56. Letter from Chaim Weizmann to Robert Weltsch, 19 November 1929, as cited in *Letters and Papers of Chaim Weizmann*, vol. 14, pp. 120–1; Hattis, op. cit., pp. 66–70; Magnes, 1930, op. cit., pp. 34–41.

57. David Ben-Gurion, *My Talks with Arab Leaders* (Tel Aviv University, Tel Aviv, 1972), pp. 33–5, 42–76; Hattis, op. cit. pp. 139, 148–54.

58. Ben-Gurion, op. cit., p. 194.

59. Walter Lacqueur, *A History of Zionism* (Holt, Rinehart, Winston, New York, 1976), pp. 514–18; letter from Judah L. Magnes to Reginald Coupland, 7 January 1937, as cited in Goren, 1982, op. cit., pp. 315–19.

60. Lacqueur, op. cit., pp. 518–20; Hattis, op. cit., pp. 167–71; Bentwich, op. cit., pp. 193–4; letter from Judah L. Magnes to Felix Warburg, 11 January 1937, as cited in Goren, 1982, op. cit., pp. 320–1.

61. Lacqueur, op. cit., pp. 521–36; 544–9.

62. Hattis, op. cit., pp. 212–31, 249–58.

63. Bentwich, op. cit., pp. 257–63; letter from Judah L. Magnes to Maurice Hexter, as cited in Goren, 1982, op. cit., 14 February 1947, pp. 447–8.

64. *Be'ayot*, July 1947, pp. 189–90.

65. The initial members of the *ad hoc* committee were Lessing J. Rosenwald, Edward Greenbaum, Jerome Frank, Lewis Straus and Maurice Hexter. James Marshall, David Sher, and Alan Stroock later joined the committee. All were members of the anti-partition minority of the American Jewish Committee.

66. Zvi Ganin, *Truman, American Jewry and Israel, 1945–1948* (Holmes & Meier, New York, 1979), pp. 175–7; letters from Loy Henderson to Acting Secretary of State, 9 April 1948, Henderson to Thomas C. Wasson, 10 April 1948, as cited in *Foreign Relations of the United States, 1948*, vol. 5, part 2 (US Government, Washington, DC, 1976), pp. 804–5, 811.

67. Letter from Judah L. Magnes to Simcha Assaf, 7 September 1948, as cited in Goren, 1982, op. cit., pp. 56–7.

Part III: International Aspects of Zionism

10. Introductory Speeches

by Abdulla Sharafeddin

In holding this Symposium, at this date and here in Washington, to discuss the subject before you, the International Organisation for the Elimination of All Forms of Racial Discrimination (EAFORD) had in mind the dialectical relationship between three elements: the subject of the Symposium and its connection with the time and place at which it is being held.

The members of EAFORD and probably many of the distinguished scholars who will present their studies at this Symposium believe that the problem under discussion will probably not be solved on the shores of the Mediterranean, the place of the conflict, since it was not originally born there, but rather that it will be solved in the West. As it was born in the West and was fed by Western contradictions and moral weaknesses, it can only be solved there, and through the West's moral strength.

This is as to the place. As to the time, probably this is the appropriate time for decision and resolution. Any delay will lead to further calamities. The tragic events of summer 1982 which shocked the conscience of the world and moved 400,000 people to protest in Tel Aviv are only minor indications of the devastating calamity which during the next few years will engulf both those who created the problem and those who are its victims.

The subject of this Symposium is: 'Judaism or Zionism: What Difference for the Middle East?' To be more accurate, we should say 'what difference to world peace?'.

We, in our organization, draw a definite and decisive distinction between Judaism and political Zionism. Judaism is the divine message of Moses which unified the creator with the created and which is recognized by Christians and Muslims as much as by the Jews, these people who lived for centuries around the city of Jerusalem in tranquillity, co-operation and peace. Zionism, on the other hand, is a racist political movement which lives on the complexes and memories of the past and the reactions to those sufferings and tragedies.

In our view, the difference between the two is very great and very important. As has been said by Rabbi Neuberger, 'A sincere Jew cannot be a

Zionist, and a Zionist can never be a sincere Jew.'

Judaism is the child of the East with all its philosophies, spirituality and meditation. Political Zionism is the child of the West, with all its conflicts, wars and thirst for domination. Political Zionism was not born in China, India or the land of the Two Rivers, but it was born in Russia, Poland, Romania, Germany and France. And it carries in its seed and its evolution all the contradictions prevailing in those countries during the 18th and 19th centuries.

There is no doubt that Zionism does not differ as to its aims, means and justifications from the well-known settler-colonialist ideologies. Zionism aims at gathering all the Jews in a ghetto which it calls the Promised Land and at establishing its hegemony over neighbouring lands, states and peoples.

The means to achieve this are wars, massacres, assassinations and terrorism. And the examples of this are plentiful: the destruction of the King David Hotel, the massacres at Deir Yassin, Sabra and Chatilla; the continuous wars and invasions to annex more territory under the pretext of Israeli security; the pursuit of the leaders and members of the Palestinian resistance in order to exterminate them; the attempt to prevent any Arab scientific or technological progress, for example through the murder of Arab scientists and the attack on the Iraqi nuclear reactor.

And all this is accompanied by great pressure on world Jewry to force them to leave their countries and emigrate to the large ghettos. Supporting all these means is the Zionist lobby which, in the view of many, has considerable control over the Western media and which is accredited with decisive influence over the decisions of the main superpower in the world, with the result that tax-payers' money and the most sophisticated weaponry of that particular superpower are put at the service of those aims and dreams.

The psychological and ideological justification for this attitude which has bred hatred, bloodshed and evil has often been given as the experience of the Jews in Europe during certain periods of history, coupled with misinterpretations of the Holy Books as to the meaning of the 'chosen people' and the 'Promised Land'. But unfortunately, the result of this was an ideology whose basis and consequences, for example as to the purity of the race, and distinctiveness from other people, seems to bear close resemblance to other dangerous purist ideologies.

Time does not permit me to go into any details. However, I have no doubt that the distinguished speakers who kindly agreed to participate in this Symposium will give the subject the depth of analysis it deserves. Nevertheless, I cannot but say that human tragedies throughout history, of which the tragedy of the Jews is one of the gravest and most influential, do not beset us arbitrarily or from outside ourselves. These tragedies have always been the result of our own mistakes and our own selfishness.

They are, firstly, the result of failure to comprehend the depth and vision of the great religions adopted by the large majority of mankind, and the consequent deviation from those religions and their aim of unifying humanity with the creator.

They are, secondly, the result of failure to appreciate the element of time in human life, so that many, in our own times, think with the mentality of 2,000 years ago. Our world has truly become a small world. Modern inventions have reduced distances, and forced the inhabitants of this planet to meet, to know each other and to co-operate. It has become impossible to live in a ghetto, even if that ghetto becomes a state.

Thirdly, we should admit that political Zionism is the fault of all of us. It is the result of all the mistakes and atrocities committed by man against man. Those people who raise the flag of hate and tragedy, and threaten the world with atomic catastrophe through the representation of the false as the true, those people are offering the world the sourness and pain they feel as a result of a long, long sojourn with humiliation and disrespect.

I would like to repeat what I said on a previous occasion: it is time for mankind to understand its long journey through history, and to learn from its experience which confirms that to fight evil with evil will only multiply evil, and that what the parents sow will be reaped by the sons and grandsons. This old story has become clear to those prepared to think and heed the lessons of history.

Therefore, we call upon all our brothers in humanity, the oppressed and the oppressor, the Black who has been subjected by the White, the Semite who suffered under the Aryan, the poor who has been exploited by the rich – we call upon them all to come to a world of justice. The story of action and reaction should end here and now, if we have minds with which to think and if man is truly the viceroy of God on this earth.

We are all from Adam, and Adam is from the earth. No two should differ in this whether they give a literal interpretation of sacred books or whether they adopt the theory of evolution. In any case, both lead to the same conclusion: the unity of origin and the oneness of human brotherhood.

Finally, I would like to ask our Jewish brothers in whose name the Zionists act, those living in every part of the world and particularly in the United States – I would like to ask them this: is it the message of those who were the first to raise the banner of the oneness of God to disperse two million Palestinians, Muslims and Christians, to evict them by force of arms from their homes, country and fields, and make them live, as they have for the last 40 years or so, in many different foreign lands, instead of leaving them in peace in their own homes and their own country?

In the name of everything that is sacred, I ask again, should this tragedy continue with daily shedding of the blood of children, women and the elderly? And until when? At least don't we fear the consequences for coming generations?

Finally, I should like to ask a precise question: does Zionism have right on its side? Were Abraham Lincoln, Einstein, Gandhi, Martin Luther King and the Universal Declaration of Human Rights – were all these wrong and false? Did the massacres we saw and read about in summer 1982 truly represent the message of Abraham and the laws of Moses? The various television channels present to us every day a picture of what befell the Jews at the hands of Hitlerism. Do we accept that others, even the sons and grandsons of Hitler, should be subjected to the same treatment?

The answer to this is known in the conscience of each one of us. It cries in the depth of our souls. Shall we have the courage and self-denial to declare openly what our conscience is harbouring?

We should not deceive ourselves or bury our heads in the sand, ignoring the glaring fact which confirms that there is no solution to this tragedy other than the establishment of a democratic non-sectarian state in which Jews, Christians and Muslims will co-operate and which will be the foundation of peace in the world blessed equally by the creator and His creatures.

My friends always tell me that I am sentimental and optimistic. They say this by way of criticism, not praise. I do not deny it, and I still look for the day when those who led the world towards oneness can drop the feeling of superiority and sourness, and participate in leading it to peace and freedom.

by Bruce Chasan

Dr Elmer Berger invited me to speak to you on behalf of American Jewish Alternatives to Zionism. I will give you five minutes of my personal philosophy with the assurance that it resembles the programme of AJAZ.

If today you visit the Nazi concentration camp at Dachau, just outside Munich, West Germany, as I did nine years ago, you will find it has been converted into a museum and memorial. There is a long barracks-like building containing a collection of photographs depicting the history of Dachau and the Nazi regime. Narrative material appears in several languages. In visiting this museum, I was struck by one historical fact even more strongly than all the gruesome and horrible pictures of tortured people; and that was the fact that Dachau was set up in April or May 1933 as a place of incarceration for opponents of the government.

Now Hitler came to power on 30 January 1933, and barely three months later he had in place a concentration camp for his enemies. It is easy to understand why those who were bent on the destruction of the Jews partially succeeded. The opponents of Nazism had only three choices: exile, Dachau and silence.

One might well consider how different the course of history might have been if in 1933 Germany had had many of the institutions of Anglo-American democracy, including for example: an independent judiciary; the writ of habeas corpus; and a bill of rights enforceable in the courts, including notably the right to be free from arrest unless a warrant is made out stating grounds for suspicion that a crime has been committed. Certainly Dachau could not and would not have existed.

If one goes back in history another 50 years, to 1883, the great migration of Eastern European Jews to American and other Western countries had already begun. They came here by the million, including all four of my own grandparents. Why did so many come to the United States? It is difficult to generalize or conclude that so many people came here for the same reasons, but I have to believe that the principal attractions included the achievements of Anglo-American democracy. These achievements, which insured the success of a pluralistic society, included the following: the notion that government derives its limited powers from the consent of the governed; the due process and equal protection clauses of the 5th and 14th Amendments to the Constitution; and all other rights, privileges, and guarantees embedded in the Constitution, not the least of which is the Amendment providing that Congress shall make no law respecting an establishment of religion or prohibiting the free exercise thereof.

There is no doubt in my mind that the separation of Church and state is more highly developed in the United States than in any other country in the world, and that this guarantee of liberty influenced millions of Jews and non-Jews to immigrate to America.

I do not mean to imply that the American experience with democracy has been free of trouble. The American Indians were brutally conquered. Slavery existed on these shores for more than 200 years. Even today there is a legacy of racial bigotry which detracts from the fabric of our society. Nevertheless, we Americans can take pride that discrimination is not the law of the land; indeed, the laws enacted by Congress prohibit discrimination in all its forms.

Now what does all this have to do with the Middle East? I think it underscores the fundamental defect of political Zionism. I will first define political Zionism so that you all know what I mean. As I use the term, it means the advocacy of a nation-state for Jews in Palestine, and the migration of Jews to Palestine for that purpose. Now back to the fundamental defect. At the beginning of this century, the population of Palestine was more than 90% Arab, and had been for hundreds of years. The programme to create a Jewish state in Palestine was undemocratic by all the standards of Anglo-American democracy. It denied the Palestinian people the right of government by the consent of the governed. Eventually it denied them the most basic civil and human rights, including the right to live in their own homeland. Those Arabs who still live in Israel today are second- and third-class citizens in every respect. The resources of the government are committed to the needs of immigrant Jews while native-born Palestinians continue to suffer deprivation.

American Jews present a great paradox. By a wide margin, they are supporters of the Jewish state, and yet they are non-Zionists. They will not emigrate from America to go to Israel in any great numbers. They are content to live in a country where they are a small minority. Why? Because the civil and human rights of all American citizens are guaranteed by law, and those rights are enforceable in court.

To me, the concept of a pluralistic society was best summarized in one sentence by Dr Martin Luther King, Jr, in a speech he delivered here in Washington 20 years ago at the Lincoln Memorial. He said on that occasion: 'One day my four little children will live in a country where they will be judged not by color of their skin but by the content of their character.'

I know the great majority of American Jews share the dream of Martin Luther King, Jr, for a pluralistic society – a society based on equality, liberty and law. And yet, when it comes to the Palestinians, the same majority of American Jews are not committed to equality, liberty and law.

These are discouraging times for Palestinians. Despite what seems to be an interminable flow of bad news for them, their struggle to obtain equal rights and equal status in their own homeland is not going to disappear. Their longing for justice is not going to subside. Already history has shown that each new generation of Palestinians shares the aspirations of the generation which preceded it.

I hope and believe that more and more Jews will recognize that while it is a grave misfortune to be a victim of persecution, it is morally unacceptable for Jews to victimize another people. I have some cause for optimism. Last month in Philadelphia, I attended a Passover Seder [ceremony or dinner on first night of Passover] sponsored by the Philadelphia chapter of the New Jewish Agenda. A Haggadah [order of prayer for the Seder ceremonial dinner] was specially written for the occasion, and it was entitled 'The Seder of the Children of Abraham'. The cover declared that it was 'Dedicated to the Fulfillment of the Dual Promise of the Land to Abraham's Children Isaac and Ishmael'. The theme for the evening was reconciliation, brotherhood and living together in peace.

Let us hope that more and more Jews will come to realize that it is a worthy calling to work to establish a society which does not grant privilege to one group, or burden another group solely on the basis of race or religion. It may take 50 years; it may take 500 years. But the day will come when the children of Isaac and the children of Ishmael will live together with equal rights under law.

Introducing Elmer Berger by John Reddaway

It is now some 15 years since I first met Elmer Berger. It was a disembodied meeting, a paper encounter, but one that made a lasting impression on me. I had just returned to London after some nine years in the Middle East working with the United Nations for the Palestinian refugees. It was a couple of years after the 1967 war, and in London I soon became associated with a group of people who had set themselves the task of trying to promote a better understanding in Britain of the Palestinian case and, in general, of Arab views and policies. One of the first steps they had taken was to publish three basic pamphlets about the Palestine problem. One was written by Sir Anthony Nutting who, you may recall, was the Minister in the Foreign Office who resigned in protest against the Suez aggression. The second was by a distinguished Palestinian lawyer. The third was by Elmer Berger. I recall thinking at first that it was a bit odd for a British organization to be relying on a paper by an American rabbi to put its case across to a British audience. Such was my ignorance at that time! Of course as soon as I read the paper and felt the impact of the eloquence, scholarship and patent honesty which are the hallmark of all that Elmer writes, I saw the light.

Shortly afterwards I met Elmer in the flesh and it has been my good fortune since then to enjoy and benefit from his friendship, abundant kindness and unfailing help. The simple fact is that he commands the affection, respect and admiration of all who know him.

We owe him special thanks on the present occasion. For it is he who is the author and architect of this conference with all its present importance and potential value for the future, its 'onlie begetter', to borrow Shakespeare's description of his enigmatic patron. It is a measure of Elmer's influence and of the respect he commands that he has been able to bring together such a wealth of talent and breadth of scholarship and experience for this conference.

I've often thought that Horace must have had some Roman prototype of Elmer Berger in mind when he wrote his ode beginning 'Integer vitae scelerisque purus' - a man who lives a life of integrity, innocent of wrongdoing, need fear no ill. In a long and politically active life Elmer has, we know, been subjected to not a little misrepresentation, not to say vilification, on account of his brave criticism of militant Zionism. The integrity of his adherence to right principle, his innocence of wrongdoing, the unquestionable honesty of his intentions and conduct, have served to turn aside all such malicious attacks, indeed often to turn them back on the heads of his detractors.

In concluding an address which he gave here in Washington in December 1982 he made an appeal which, to my mind, exemplifies the moral strength and integrity of his whole position on the antithesis between Judaism and Zionism. He said we should remember - and I quote his words - 'that God, whether different men call his prophet Moses or Jesus or Mohammed, is the God of all men and not some tribalistic deity lusting after the patrimony of men of different faith or ethnic origin'. He went on; 'This, I hope, will be the message which will go forth from this conference. To add my voice to this message is why I am here, to add perhaps one small stone to rebuild the true Zion of the true prophets of old as a "house of prayer for all people".

by Ole Espersen

May I – by way of introduction – underline the relationship between my country, Denmark, and the state of Israel?

During the 1930s we witnessed the massacre of the Jews in our neighbour country, Nazi Germany. We helped, as far as possible, those Jews who lived in our own country, which was occupied by Germany. The Danish population was shocked by the Holocaust. The shock has certainly not vanished. And it is a sound expression of human feelings.

This shock meant that we had very positive feelings about the creation of the state of Israel, and that we have been critical of those who attacked the very existence of that state. It also means that we have been very generous for many years in condoning measures undertaken by the Israeli government and the Knesset which we would in other cases condemn. We have accepted discriminatory practices to a certain degree, because the very existence of a Jewish state could make them necessary. We never criticized the state of Israel for its close collaboration with, for example, the apartheid regime of South Africa or with the cruel regime of Somoza in Nicaragua. I have been involved in the promotion of human rights for many years, and I did not voice any protest. I felt obliged to close my eyes, because I felt that the very existence of the state of Israel could be at stake and explain acts of this nature.

Let me continue by quoting what the Danish Foreign Minister said to his Israeli colleague during a luncheon speech in November 1982:

> Your very observant and well-informed Ambassador to Copenhagen will have reported that Danish public opinion has been painfully divided over the recent events in the Middle East. Even some who normally side with Israel in every dispute have voiced their reservations this time and are now turning a more critical eye towards the activities of your government, especially the continuing programme of settlements in the West Bank and Gaza and the continued presence of your troops in Southern Lebanon.

This is a very correct, but also diplomatic, way of expressing the deep anger and concern felt by many people – including myself who has visited Israel on several occasions, both officially and privately.

The great concern which I feel leads to the questions: am I and are we responsible for the developments? Have we condoned too much? In any event the Begin government has abused our previous support and feelings for the Jews. And we now ask ourselves: have we sacrificed the Palestinian people because of our trauma in World War II? I think that the answer is yes.

In his critique of the Department of State's 1981 country report on human rights practices in Israel, Rabbi Elmer Berger clearly proves that acts of discrimination against non-Jewish people have been taking place over a long period of time – and that they are an inherent element of Israeli legislation.

In my opinion, however, this does not represent a violation of the Convention on the Elimination of All Forms of Racial Discrimination. And, I might add, it is of course not possible to create a Jewish state without some special status for Jews. However, reports indicate that specific violations do take place within the 1967 borders: suppression of freedom of expression, torture or degrading treatment of citizens. But what has frightened me much more – as a lawyer in the field of human rights – are acts in the occupied territories and in Lebanon.

It follows from what I have said, that I do not consider – from a purely legal point of view – that Zionism is racism, although I fully understand that Palestinians might think so. But as Zionism has developed, I must conclude that the practical consequences of this policy are no longer compatible with human rights and international law in general.

The occupation of the West Bank and the Gaza Strip is in itself a violation of the laws of war. What might be justified for a certain period of time can, however, under no circumstances be justified for the length of time for which it has been continuing. But it is not only the very presence of Israeli authorities which is a violation of international law.

It is the obligation of any occupying power to do its utmost to respect the inhabitants, their culture, their administrative authorities, etc. This respect is not shown by the Israeli occupying force. The continuous building of settlements in these areas is of course a clear indication of the fact that the government of Israel does not have any intention of withdrawing. For every day in which this policy continues, the withdrawal of the Israeli forces and authorities becomes more and more difficult. Maybe by now it could be argued to be impossible. The policy of occupation means a policy of expansion, which people now rightly associate with Zionism. And it may lead to a policy of apartheid.

But what was decisive in my attitude towards the state of Israel was the invasion of Lebanon and the behaviour of the Israeli army and authorities during the invasion. There are certain rules which have to be followed under all circumstances even in a situation of war; rules which are based on respect for humanity, rules which do not in themselves prevent a war, but are intended to avoid unnecessary sufferings and atrocities. A country which does not adhere to these rules is violating the most basic human rights.

From information collected in Europe and elsewhere, I have been able to follow quite closely the experiences of people in Lebanon. It has been proved to me that Israeli forces prevented doctors and nurses from working to save lives in war. Doctors were arrested, medicine was prevented from reaching hospitals, even nurses were arrested. Weapons which are prohibited according to the rules of war were used – weapons which hurt at random in a terrible manner. The Palestinian Research Centre of Beirut had all its valuable books, antiquities, etc. taken away. The building was destroyed. It has been said in Israeli's defence that the Centre also contained plans for terrorism and even weapons. I cannot deny this. But that is no excuse for not safeguarding important historical items belonging to a people in a desperate situation. The Israeli authorities have so far refused to do anything to rectify this situation.

The Palestinian people feel, and I understand them, that attempts are being made to deprive them of their cultural background.

These acts – and others could be mentioned – have made me give up any illusions about Israel as a peace-loving and democratic country. It has been an extremely sad experience. It has made me regret the years of silence, silence which expressed the hope that the government of Israel would finally be reasonable, and be satisfied with the present state of Israel within legal boundaries.

But that experience has not changed my mind as to the very existence of the state of Israel. It may well be that politicians in the 1920s, 1930s and 1940s committed grave errors in planning a new state at the expense of the Palestinian people But now, many years later, a new, grave error would be committed if we did not support the right of Israel to exist within its 1967 boundaries. But Israel itself has certainly put us in a difficult situation.

It is my sincere hope that a conference like this – as one of many efforts within the United States and similar efforts in Europe – will clearly show the Israeli government that we do respect the Jews, the Jewish religion, the state of Israel – but not Zionism as it has manifested itself during recent years. The European countries, and especially the EEC countries, have clearly warned Israel and condemned its actions. Similar warnings must also be given by the government of the United States. Sometimes it is difficult in Europe to be sure what the position of the American government is, and to interpret statements made in especially controversial situations.

It is our hope that the peace-loving and democratic forces which certainly do exist in Israel shall become stronger and stronger, particularly because they have support in the outside world. This I believe is the only possible solution of this vital problem.

It means that we all bear responsibility. But let us not commit new mistakes! (I am addressing myself now!) Let us not make those who are now living peacefully in Israel feel that they are once more in the Diaspora. Let us not, in our desire to do justice to the Palestinians, create a new situation in which people who certainly also desire security are forced to live in insecurity. The present leadership of the state of Israel is taking a great risk. It has behaved in a manner which is detrimental to the Jews in Israel and maybe even to those outside Israel.

That is why it is so terribly important that we look to the interests of the ordinary people – be they Palestinians, be they Jews – and not to political dogma. Zionism reached what might be its *legitimate* goals long ago. It should not be permitted to jeopardize the future of human beings whose sole desire is to live and practise their religion peacefully.

11. The Unauthenticity of 'Jewish People' Zionism

Dr Elmer Berger

Israel is an ideological state. Step by step, it was built by Zionists. It is governed by Zionists. Zionism dictates the substance of its so-called 'basic' or 'fundamental' laws. Zionism dominates the objectives of its foreign policy. Zionism controls the pattern of its domestic, social, economic and political life.

Many Jews and probably more people of other religious or ethnic origins gave Israel their support at government or private level without full comprehension of the Zionism which built the state. For the most part they were recruited in the democracies of the West. One of the most imaginative propaganda apparatuses the modern world has known used a brilliant galaxy of disguises to bewilder well-intentioned, generous and often guilt-ridden people.

The pattern is not unique. Ideological states have often rationalized their ideological objectives by investing them with plausible concerns such as threats to national security, or idealistic aspirations to liberate humans from the real or fabricated disabilities attributed to other societal systems.

'Pragmatists' Take Note

Since the Israeli invasion of Lebanon in June 1982 a sufficient number of Western sophisticated and informed commentators on international affairs have pointedly – and sometimes eloquently – called attention to the internal conflict in the Zionist state. They have contrasted the Israeli government's policies of *fait accompli* annexations of Arab territories, its aggressive policy of settlements and repressions on the West Bank and Gaza, its complicity in the Chatilla and Sabra camp massacres with what, in one way or another, these political observers identify as 'the moral voice' of the Jewish tradition, something of which they find reflected in the report of the Kahan Commission which investigated the murderous assault on the two camps.[1] Meron Benvenisti, as an Israeli, was even more explicit. The war in Lebanon, he said, faced the Israelis with

> the choice between their humanist values and their nationalism. Mr. Sharon's demise will not significantly change the situation. He was only a catalyst; the forces he helped to unleash will outlive him, as will the forces mobilized to oppose him.[2]

It is important that Benvenisti identifies the repugnant force as the 'nationalism' of the state and despairs of any quick solution. Georgie Anne Geyer observed, in a similar spirit, 'the real struggle is just beginning'.[3]

The list could be extended. But these are perhaps enough to demonstrate that for these two days we are not fantasizing about abstractions. This Symposium has elected to identify the core of the conflict: these media personalities have reported by drawing attention to the distinction between Judaism – or what some prefer to call the 'Jewish ethic' – on the one hand, and what I define as 'Jewish people'-state Zionism, on the other hand. And it is important that the conflict between the two – though not always identified with these labels – extends into the lives and thinking of Jews in virtually every free, democratic nation.

The crisis of conscience, whether among Jews in the Zionist state or Jews, and even Christians and Muslims, in other countries, has one common characteristic. The voices of the protesters are lifted in general against the movers and shakers in the governments which, in one way or another, are parties to the 60-year-old conflict over the political destiny of Palestine and the Palestinian people.

'Great-Power' Derelictions

For 1982–83 is not the first historic opportunity the so-called great powers have had to choose between what Benvenisti identifies as humanism, on the one hand, and what I have called 'Jewish people'-state Zionism, on the other hand. There have always been those who called themselves Zionists but who were practitioners of what Ms Geyer and *Newsweek* and Anthony Lewis and Benvenisti refer to as 'Jewish morality'. There has been no masterfully contrived conspiracy about the intentions or aspirations of the orthodox Zionist ideologues. If there has been a conspiracy it has been by the several governments of the patron great powers, notably the British and, more recently, the United States. They have played a cynical, secretive and even cowardly game with skilful Zionist lobbies making extravagant claims about so-called Jewish votes and campaign contributions. Or they have supported Zionist nationalism to the detriment of self-determination for the Palestinian people in order to advance imperial or colonial objectives in the Middle East. In the process of pursuing either special-interest politics or camouflaging imperial ambitions with cynical, usually uninformed sentimentalities about 'the Jews', the political potentates have regarded Zionism as an omnibus word and Jews as a monolith with perhaps a few quixotic dissenters. The consequence has been that the rigid ideologies of organized Zionism have, with the help of the world's powerful, suffocated the humanists and dominated both the organized political movement and its product, the Zionist state. Neither Jewish need nor Judaism's moral imperatives required a Menachem Begin or an Ariel Sharon. But they are not Darwinian sports in Zionism. As much as anything they are 'gifts' to the world of great-power political chicanery, indulgence and derelictions. The frequency and candour with which former Presidents Ford and Carter have recently revised positions they took as politicians testifies to the corruption of the democratic process in the context of the search for a resolution of the Middle East's most dramatized problem.

Among the more notable advocates of humanistic Zionism were Ahad Ha-Am, the architect of what is called 'cultural Zionism', Martin Buber and Judah Magnes. More spectacularly, in recent months, there is Jacobo Timerman. And of those described by the distinguished Israeli journalist Amnon Kapeliuk as 'casting a vote of no confidence in Zionism' by emigration, we do not know what percentage was motivated by first-hand disillusion with Zionist ideology. While it served their purposes, the doctrinaire ideologues of the movement and later the state raised no exportable objections to these humanists. But at times when classical Zionist ideology came into conflict with conventional ideas of territorial sovereignty of other nations or the human rights of Palestine's non-'Jewish people' nationals, these humanitarians were at best ignored or, like Magnes, ruthlessly defamed and cast aside. The future must still determine whether the protesters in the Zionist state after the massacres at Chatilla and Sabra will suffer the same fate, or whether, as some are saying, summer 1982 marked a watershed.

The Zion of Redemption

There is another category of believers in Zion which requires clarification. Some Jews – and some Christians (and to a somewhat lesser degree theologically most devout Muslims) – regard the biblical Zion as a religious sacrament. Allowing for some theological differences, they believe that their conception of a universal, messianic era of redemption from varying conceptions of sinfulness will be realized by restoration of what the Bible calls 'the children of Israel' to a Zion from which there would go forth the law, 'and the word of the Lord' – not legislation by the Knesset – would resound 'from Jerusalem'. It would be an injustice to the scholars who address this spiritual vision of Zionism to try to reproduce their arguments here. I will simply state rather categorically that the usual Zionist political exploitation of this theological concept (repetitiously and sanctimoniously invoked by Mr Begin as 'the promise') is, in a most charitable characterization, a half-truth. Any half-way respectable theologian knows that a moral God makes no promises of mundane benefits without exacting stringent obligations of a high moral order. The authentic biblical so-called 'promise' is, in fact, a demanding contract.[4]

Judaism is a covenant religion. God promised the land to the people *only* if they strictly fulfilled specified moral obligations. The moral content of the obligations evolved over the centuries. The primitive nature of the first promise-covenant is stated to Abraham in the book of Genesis. The 'seed' of Abraham was to have only the one God, and was to circumcise every male child.[5] Perhaps seven centuries later, Jeremiah proclaimed in the name of the Lord, 'I will make a new covenant. . . not according to the covenant I made with their fathers. . . .' Unlike the original tribal prescriptions, this one raised moral conduct to the level of individual responsibility: 'In those days they shall say no more "the fathers have eaten sour grapes and the children's teeth are set on edge". But everyone shall die for his own iniquity.'[6]

Little emphasis and no exaggeration are needed to mark the chasm between that elevated principle and the obscenity reportedly spoken by the Israeli Chief of Staff defending Israeli military conduct in the occupied West Bank. His policy 'of collective punishment of relatives' of protesters, General Eitan said, 'works very well with Arabs'.[7]

But *ad hominem* evidence is not essential to differentiate the Zion of the biblical covenant from the Zionism of the government of Israel and the World Zionist Organization. The representatives of the mundane pretenders to the fulfilment of the prophetic Zion never cite the half of the promise which exacted meticulous observance of the divine commands in any given version of the covenant. Their counterfeit versions never recall Micah's apocalyptic admonition (4:9ff.):

> Hear this, I pray you, ye heads of the house of Jacob, and rulers of the house of Israel, that abhor justice and pervert all equity; that build up Zion with blood, and Jerusalem with iniquity. . . Yet will they lean upon the Lord and say: 'Is not the Lord in the midst of us? No evil shall come upon us.' Therefore shall Zion for your sake be ploughed as a field, and Jerusalem shall become heaps, and the mountain of the Lord as the high places of a forest.

It could not have been otherwise. It was not for men to make the judgement that the state of moral acceptability had been attained. That was the divine prerogative. Only if it was achieved, with unmistakable signs and wonders, would the anointed be recognized to lead the return.

It is a sacrilege and obscenity that many of the very people who assert that their Zionized Palestine is consistent with the absolutes of the biblical covenant are the same who defend some of the Zionist state's least appealing policies with the moral relativism that their state is no worse than other states and should not be expected to be better. Most reasonable men would probably agree in large part to that reasoning. But they would also agree that the state and its people cannot have it both ways.

Deliberate Obfuscation

The propaganda apparatus of the national state-building Zionist movement has brainwashed much of the world – including the policy-makers of nations whose decisions are crucial in determining the fate of Palestine – that all of these disparate threads are inextricably woven into a single pattern which is an authentic and even sacred commitment of all Jews. They have, in other words, insisted that Judaism, or even a non-theistic tradition of the Jewish ethic, is identical with a whole system of Zionist national rights and obligations pertaining to the Israeli state. This artificially forced fusing of religion and politics into an apparently seamless whole has produced an undemocratic climate. Those who reject, or raise serious reservations about, the 'Jewish people'-state Zionism are labelled 'traitors', or to use the more venomous term, 'anti-Semites', whether they be Jews, Christians or Muslims. Add to this political tactic one of Theodor Herzl's fundamental dogmas – that the entire world is incurably anti-Semitic – and the conclusion is that Jews are in a state of constant crisis. Therefore any rejection of the Zionist formula for a 'Jewish people' state acting as surrogate for what are called 'Jewish', rather than human, rights, is treason. Free, responsible, informed political debate about the policies of the Zionist state is impossible unless the debaters are liberated from the intimidation engendered by this Zionist-invented fabrication.

Prelude to Political Debate

These refinements are essential to any sophisticated examination and debate of the basic assumptions of the Zionism now codified in law and made sovereign in the state of Israel. Some of those now morally outraged at Israeli conduct in Lebanon may have neglected earlier to examine the basic assumptions of this Zionism. Others long ago made that examination. We were, therefore, less than astonished at these recent events. Whether or not the encouraging, visible protest demonstrations in Israel will mark a watershed will depend on the extent to which the protesters make such an examination. And whether they do or not may depend in turn and to a large extent on whether world opinion and particularly American policy-makers join in such an examination.

This Symposium was conceived in this contructive spirit. In this same spirit I invite you now to examine those basic assumptions. The examination will respect three criteria: (1) it will not employ single, personalized cases where non-'Jewish people' nationals of Israel or the occupied territories have suffered disadvantages and worse; (2) it will avoid magnifying the actions or speeches of so-called hard-line Zionist representatives as if, *ipso facto*, they reflect basic propositions of the Zionist state; (3) it will rely entirely upon codified, publicly proclaimed and properly deliberated Israeli law and patterns of administering this law which are extensive enough in space and time to be identified as official policy. I will add only a few references to the classic handbook of state Zionism, Theodor Herzl's *Das Judenstaat*, or 'the state of the Jews'. These references are important to verify the organic development of Israel's Zionist nationality criteria. Herzl simply decreed, without supporting evidence, that Jews are 'a people – one people'.[8] What he had in mind was not some amorphous collectivity. He naturally dominated the first Zionist Congress in 1897 where the Basle

Programme was formulated. This platform illuminated what Herzl really meant by the euphemism, 'people'. The vaguely named entity was to be granted in international law 'a publicly and legally secured home in Palestine for the Jewish people'.[9] Herzl conceived the Zionist Organization which was born at that first Congress as 'the Parliament' of this 'people'. In the style of the 1800s, he ordered the delegates to wear frock coats and striped trousers. The organization, Herzl declared, 'will be recognized as, to put it in terminology of international law, a State-creating power. And the recognition will, in effect, mean the creation of the State.'[10]

The assumption of a recognized 'Jewish' political nationality for all Jews was false, as Herzl was soon to discover. With but few exceptions, he found no support among the recognized leadership of Jews in Western Europe. They rejected, lock, stock and barrel, the idea that Jews possessed a common, so-called 'Jewish' nationality. They were willing to help disadvantaged Jews in countries where anti-Semitism was endemic, and one way to provide this assistance – but by no means the only way in their minds – was to help build a support structure in Palestine to absorb such disadvantaged Jews. It was not until a quarter of a century later that Chaim Weizmann cynically bridged the gap with what is probably state Zionism's most profitable deception. He seduced naive and uninformed American Jews into helping construct the Enlarged Jewish Agency. The action gave rise to such obscure terms as synthetic Zionism, practical Zionism and non-Zionism. Weizmann by that time had come to dominate Zionism. He reserved his hard-ball political dealings for secretive sessions with a wavering British government and periodically denied that a Zionist state was essential to the fulfilment of Zionist humanitarian and cultural aspirations. With this hydra-headed programme he extracted moral and financial support from Jews who insisted no 'Jewish' nationality existed and who relied upon England, as the Mandatory Power, to require Zionist compliance with the clauses of the Balfour Declaration which promised to safeguard Palestinian rights and to respect the single-nationality status of anti-Zionist Jews in countries other than Palestine. Of his new American associates, Weizmann later admitted in his autobiography, they 'were prepared to dispense a sort of left-handed generosity, on condition that their right hand did not know what their left hand was doing'. What they gave, he added, they considered 'philanthropy, which did not compromise them; to us it was nationalist renaissance. They would give – with disclaimers; we would accept – with reservations.'[11]

This was neither the first nor the last time Weizmann and his Zionist movement temporarily took half a loaf, counting upon Zionist single-mindedness and great-power derelictions or susceptibility to Zionist threats of political reprisals eventually to make possible acquisition of the other half. It is a certainty that neither then nor now does the majority of Jews throughout the world know much about the wheels within wheels in the Zionist movement which claims to represent them. This alleged 'Jewish people' had participated in no representative elections. The overwhelming majority of the alleged constituency does not know anything about any Zionist constitution, nor could they identify Zionism's officials, even those at the top. The Zionist claim to representation of a 'Jewish' political nation was – and is – a raw assertion of authority. It has been made more scandalous because presumably responsible governments of democratic states have given a kind of legitimacy to the pretenders by dealing with them, or their agents, on substantive political problems.

Early on, Weizmann exploited to the full the acquiescence and/or derelictions of the great powers and the ignorance of Jews about Zionism. Reporting in the early 1920s to some of his loyalists who were disappointed that the Mandate did not establish a Zionist state outright, he confessed, 'the Jews were against us'.[12] But he perceived that international recognition of the so-called 'Jewish people' was acceptance of Zionism's central assumption. The rest, he assured his audience, would follow.

> The value of the Mandate, apart from being a great success of Zionism, consists in the recognition of the Jewish people. This is of immense value, which will bear fruit and will open up new perspectives as yet hidden from our weak eyes, while we are engaged in our daily tasks.[13]

It is either supreme cynicism or supreme hypocrisy or unforgivable ignorance when governments of great powers meticulously split hairs, questioning the authenticity of the PLO's representation of a displaced Palestinian nation while they meet and frequently invite representatives of the Zionist Establishment which claims to represent a polity fabricated by Zionism and called 'the Jewish people'.

Zionist Statehood via Others' Derelictions

The apple does not fall far from the tree. There is little need to wonder why the state which Zionism established has consistently displayed such insensitivity to the consensus of a world which the Zionist ideologues have been conditioned to believe is ineradicably 'anti-Semitic'. That exaggeration amounted to paranoia. It was combined with the obfuscating casuistry for which Weizmann set a pattern, and added to deft exploitation of the ignorance and/or naivety of most Jews, then mixed with the non-feasance or craven indulgence of the great powers who determined the political fate of Palestine; all of which was well served by the inability of 'the Arabs' to communicate adequately with the power brokers. In a different context the end-product would have been recognized as a spoiled child. But in more than three decades, none of the would-be peacemakers has – at least publicly – diagnosed the cause of the state's errant behaviour. Instead, they have all pursued the Zionist blandishments which attribute the state's insecurity to an irrational and universal prejudice against Jews rather than to the parenthood which failed consistently, at every step from conception, to birth, to maturity, to require of the Zionist state-builders conformity with appropriate restraints.[14]

For, not surprisingly with this genetic history, when in a unilateral action in 1948 the Zionist movement declared the establishment of the state, it was as a 'Jewish people' state. The circumstances which made it possible for Zionism to create such a state and still claim the mantle of a democracy are not to be found in the 1947 General Assembly recommendation for partition. Months before the scheduled expiration of the Mandate, Menachem Begin's Zionist Irgun terrorists attacked Deir Yassin on 10 April 1948 and Jaffa on 27 April. Begin later identified the Zionist conquest of Jaffa 'as an event of first-rate importance in the struggle for Hebrew independence'.[15]

In the neighbourhood of 650,000 non-'Jewish people' Palestinians were displaced. The Zionist apparatus, represented by the Jewish Agency, publicly disclaimed responsibility for the Zionist Irgun and Zionist Stern terrorists. But in 1949, Weizmann called the displacement of so large a number of non-'Jewish people' Palestinians over the border 'a miraculous simplification of Israel's tasks'.[16] Rid of the impediment of a nearly numerically equal Arab population, the 'Jewish people'-state building process began.

'Jewish People' Legislation

The 'Jewish people'-state exists to this day. It is codified in a body of legislation known as 'fundamental' or 'basic' laws. A more illuminating title would be 'Jewish people' legislation. Distinct from domestic, statutory legislation, this body of laws conveys to 'the Jewish people' rights in the Zionist state, and, although without legislative power of enforcement for most Jews, it delineates 'Jewish people' obligations to the Zionist state.

Some of these laws are well known and need only brief mention here. The 'Law of Return' grants to every Jew the *right* to immigrate – unless the Minister of Immigration finds he or she 'is engaged in an activity directed against the Jewish people'.[17]

This is a nationality *right* decreed for all Jews, even though they are citizens of another state, but to no other classification of people. The 'Law of Return' was followed by the 'Law of Nationality'.[18] It stipulates that a 'Jewish people' immigrant automatically acquires Israeli citizenship unless he or she renounces such citizenship within a stipulated period of time after acquiring the immigration certificate or entry to the country. These two laws provide 'the Jewish people' with what Dr W.T. Mallison describes as a 'functional second nationality'. The critical criteria for possession of these extraterritorial rights are profession of Judaism or descent from a Jewish mother. The legislation, therefore, is predicated upon either theocratic or racial qualifications. It is prima-facie evidence that the state of Israel regards all Jews – 'the Jewish people' – as the 'one people' of Herzl and as the nationality constituency of the Zionist state.[19] The point is not whether individual Jews accept this system of rights and obligations. Nor is the point whether the Zionist state has the competence to apply this legislation to all Jews. The point is that, without specified disclaimers, recognition of the state implies recognition of this body of unconventional basic legislation. And a further point, crucial to any genuine peace, is that this extraterritorial nationality legislation provides foreign nationals with rights in the state which even its resident non-'Jewish people' nationals do not possess, let alone the displaced Palestinians.

But there is still another, less-known, law in this category. It is called 'The World Zionist Organization/Jewish Agency for Israel (Status) Law',[20] enacted by the Knesset in 1952. It codifies, with great precision, the Zionist concept of 'Jewish people' nationality as part and parcel of the national interests and prerogatives of the Zionist state. It designates the World Zionist Organization as '*the* authorized agency' to develop and settle the country, and to absorb immigrants. It states that the recruiting of Jewish immigrants is 'the central task of the State of Israel and the Zionist Movement'. The Zionist movement is consequently juridically a partner in the performance of the most vital services of the state. The law declares that the state of Israel 'expects' all Jews to co-operate in this endeavour and regards as 'necessary' the 'unity of all sections of Jewry. . . for this purpose'. It specifies that the state 'expects' the World Zionist Organization to devote itself to 'achieving this unity'.

During the Knesset debate of this law, the then Prime Minister, David Ben-Gurion, said, 'The sovereign authority of the state is confined to its own borders and applies only to its own citizens. But 80% of the Jewish people are still. . . outside the borders of the State.' He continued, with unmistakable clarity, 'It is the Zionist Organization. . .which is able to achieve what is beyond the power and competence of the State, and that is the advantage of the Zionist Organization over the State.'[21]

So the state of Israel stands four-square on the foundations which Theodor Herzl structured. In the famous trial of Adolf Eichmann its highest courts asserted it to be 'the sovereign state of "the Jewish People" '. It has had more subtle leadership than that of Menachem Begin and Ariel Sharon. But it has not transformed – and while committed to 'Jewish people'-state Zionism it cannot transform – its fundamental character. Its Zionist institutions, bound to the conventional government by a 'basic' law, serve only its 'Jewish people' citizens. This duality of governing explains the wide disparity between what are called 'Jewish' land, 'Jewish' housing, 'Jewish' education and 'Jewish' industry, on the one hand, and economic, educational and social institutions of the same categories for Israel's disadvantaged non-'Jewish people' citizens, on the other hand. The state's commitment to this discrimination is so profound that in

> the early and mid-60s, when financial contributions from world Jewry were at a low ebb, the Israeli government effected unilateral transfers of public monies into the treasuries of the national institutions. Between 1959 and 1967, for example, the Israeli government donated over $100 million to the Jewish Agency.[22]

'National institutions' is Zionist-talk for 'Jewish people' (or Zionist) institutions.

So, the supposedly free, autonomous Zionist organization is neither free nor autonomous. It is by law and function a servant of the state. And one of its functions, vital to the 'Jewish people' Zionist state, is to deepen and perpetuate Zionism's discriminatory nationalism to the detriment of the quality of life and the institutions of non-'Jewish people' citizens.

The 'Jewish People' Territorial Imperative

In addition to this 'Jewish people' nationality imperative a territorial imperative is very much alive in the policies of the Zionist state. Menachem Begin and his fanatic friends, members of the religious Gush Emunim organization and other proponents of 'Greater Israel' claim the Bible as the authority for this imperative. But it is not necessary to go so far back into misty history. At the Paris Peace Conference of 1919 the representatives of the World Zionist Organization presented a memorandum. Among other details was a proposal for the boundaries of a Palestine which, it was assumed, would eventually be a Zionist state. Those recommended boundaries included territory up to what is now Sidon, in Lebanon, with an arrangement to participate in control of the Litani River water, and territory stretching beyond the present West Bank into what is now Jordan as far as the old Hejaz railroad.[23] It is interesting that the original Zionist proposal to incorporate these territories had nothing to do with security or God. The 1919 memorandum is quite earthy. It candidly states, 'The geographical area of Palestine should be as large as possible. . . [and also] to secure all water resources already feeding the country, but also to be able to conserve and control them at their source.'[24] All these territories are related either to the water available to Israel or to control of the sources of this water.

Knowledge of this 1919 Zionist plan might have suggested to the present Secretary of State of the United States a better comment than he offered about the difficulties of persuading the Israelis to withdraw from Lebanon. 'There is a pretty wide gap', he said, 'between the conditions Israel feels she needs' for security and what Lebanon 'feels are consistent with the emergence of a new Lebanon, sovereign and in control of its territory'. There followed the usual platitudes about the difficulties of finding a balance between 'not only Israel's security, but the legitimate concerns and rights of the Palestinians'.[25] The same 1919 map would explain why the paranoid Begin rejected the Reagan proposal 'to take all necessary measures to guarantee the security of Israel's northern borders'.[26]

Both Mr Shamir and Mr Begin rejected the *principle* of such an American guarantee less than 24 hours after it was offered.[27] The Israeli reaction is reminiscent of a 1955 scenario. At that time, Ben-Gurion proposed taking over Gaza to provide security in the south. The United States offered Israel a security pact. Moshe Dayan rejected the proposal, explaining, 'it would put handcuffs on our military freedom of action'.[28]

The Dayan assessment surfaced only recently in the explosive Sharett 'Diaries'. The same source suggests that it is not security which accounts for the protracted negotiations over withdrawal from Lebanon. The Zionist state is attempting to implement a strategy which was proposed at the highest levels 30 years ago.

> To find an officer, even just a major (who could be persuaded or bought) to declare himself the savior of the Maronite population. Then the Israeli army will enter Lebanon, will occupy the necessary territory, and will create a Christian regime which will ally itself with Israel. The territory from the Litani southward will be totally annexed to Israel.[29]

The *Zionist* state has never been reconciled to any of the borders, proposed or accepted *de facto*, in any of the abortive peace formulas. In the Zionist lexicon a clear distinction is still maintained between *Medinah Yisroel*, whatever part of Palestine Israel has occupied at any time, on the one hand, and *Eretz Yisroel*, at least the territorial expanse of the 1919 map, if not all of Mandated Palestine before the establishment of the Hashemite throne in 1922, on the other hand. As long as United States extravagance sustains this Zionist dream, there is validity in Arab apprehension, in Palestinian moral indignation and bellicosity, and therefore little hope for realization of the liturgical 'just and enduring peace'.

The old Santayana maxim comes to mind: 'Those who cannot remember the past are condemned to repeat it.'

As long as presidents and secretaries of state – not to ignore the reactions of the Congress – continue to assure Israel of such support, it is simply a rhetorical question to ask why Mr Begin, Mr Sharon, and now the talk-alike-but-look-different version of Sharon, Mr Ahrens, the new Minister of Defence, should not have their cake as well as eat it.

Look to the Peacemakers

It is appropriate, I think, to conclude this examination of Zionist history and ideology with supporting evidence from two distinguished Israelis.

In October 1982, Amos Kenan, an Israeli journalist and writer, made a judgement of what he calls 'the Jewish community of America'. He likens it to what he calls 'a good Jewish mother'. What she 'doesn't know, and doesn't *want* to know or even hear about, is that she is smothering her child with love, drowning him in tears of joy and pity, killing him at her maternal breast'. 'The Jewish lobby', Kenan says, is 'like all good Jewish fathers'. It 'covers up every peccadillo and crime'. 'Israel', he continues, 'should long ago have separated from father and mother. Israel should be an orphan – like any normal, independent state.' And in a kind of peroration he pleads,

> As long as you Americans help us to stand up, we Israelis have no chance to stand on our own feet. We have no chance to have peace as

> long as you support us in war. We have no chance to straighten out our relationships with our neighbors as long as you help us forget that they too are legitimate children of humanity and that they, too, have legitimate rights.[30]

What Kenan said applies with equal cogency to the totality of American people and particularly to the United States government.

General Matityahu Peled is a former member of the Israeli General Staff and now an emissary for the views of a sector of the Israeli people which ought to be cultivated by the United States government. In a plea publicized in the *New York Times* Peled cautioned particularly about American military assistance.

> America's lavish aid is. . .having disastrous effects on Israel's army and its political constitution. . . .The military establishment has grown out of all proportion to our security needs. . . .I, for one, would like to ask the American taxpayer, 'why are you giving us the rope to hang ourselves?'[31]

Those earnestly concerned with a genuine peace in the Middle East, with enduring stability for the *people* of Israel, for authentic self-determination for the Palestinian people, for respect for the integrity of territory which has long been recognized as sovereign for one or another Arab state, would do well to heed these two Israelis. They see and warn that threats to peace objectives are being nourished by United States support for area-hegemony now exercised by 'Jewish people'-state Zionism. Recognizing the impropriety of the United States intervention in internal Israeli policies, an informed American government could at least withhold extravagant subsidies from the classical, Herzlian, hard-line ideologues. General Peled's plea can be translated to mean reducing the temptations for further Israeli attempts to pursue security by encroaching more and more on Arab national consciousness and destroying any territorial base for Palestinian self-determination. Ultimately, probably only the Israeli people can liberate themselves from the constrictive, racist/theocratic ideology of a nationalism predicated on a 'Jewish people' state concept. But the Amos Kenans, the Peleds, the present disaffected, humanitarian Zionists of Israel deserve assistance. We can help by refusing to encourage the rigid ideologues who, with American support based upon superficial knowledge, have controlled the Zionist state.

In his 1 September 1982 statement outlining American policy, Mr Reagan said that the United States 'must move to resolve the root cause of conflict between Arabs and Israelis'. He added: 'Some clearer sense of America's position on the key issues is necessary to encourage wider support for the peace process.'[32]

Nowhere in a rather lengthy and detailed address did the President indicate he knew, or had been advised, of *the* root-cause. Discovery of what Dr Uri Davis, one of the principal participants in this Symposium, once described as 'the original sin' will follow any reasonably diligent examination of history.

The 'root-cause' is not *only* the forceful imposition upon the indigenous Palestinians of a foreign political structure. The seedling from which this root-cause sprouted nearly three-quarters of a century ago was also, by definition, designed to advantage only the 'Jewish people' beneficiaries of this imposed system of political rights and responsibilities. And it followed, inexorably, that the non-'Jewish people' nationals of Palestine were disadvantaged. More than one commission, either British or American or a combination of both, and numerous investigative bodies of the United Nations and private organizations, have discovered this genetic fault of withholding elemental human rights from the majority of Palestinians. But the prescriptions of most of the doctor-diplomats have merely masked symptoms, moving boundaries a bit here or there, offering the deprived Palestinians placebos instead of the tried and proven cures of respect for the dignity and humanity of politically self-conscious peoples.

Introducing his 1 September statement, the United States President said American 'involvement in the search for Mideast peace. . .is a moral imperative'.

It is probably too late, there has been too much history, to eradicate completely the havoc wrought, the crippled national and individual lives which are the deformed progeny of this 'original sin'. But in all the three great religious faiths with spiritual roots and future hopes related to memories and ethical values which emanated from this troubled area of the world, there are provisions for atonement and rectification of injustice. In Judaism, all of the prophets offered explicit formulas for atonement even as they predicted divine punishment and banishment from Zion for a sinful people. One of my favourites is from Jeremiah advising an arrogant and erring nation that it was not the brick and mortar of the ancient temple, or the political alliances made for strategic reasons, or the numbers or sophistication of weaponry which made for the health and security of a nation. Standing in and pointing to the gates of the temple which was symbol of the inflated sense of glory adored by king, priest and people, the divinely inspired messenger spoke words which can profitably be heeded by the would-be peacemakers of today.

> Trust ye not in lying words,
> saying, 'the temple of the Lord,
> the temple of the Lord, the
> temple of the Lord are these.'
> Nay, but if ye thoroughly
> amend your ways and your
> doings; if ye thoroughly
> execute justice between
> a man and his neighbour;
> if ye oppress not the
> stranger, the fatherless
> and the widow, and

shed not innocent blood
in this place, neither walk
after other gods to your hurt;
then will I cause you to
dwell in this place, in
the land that I gave to
our fathers, for
ever and ever.[33]

To this reminder of the covenant, the Second Isaiah's description of the true Zion restored might be added: 'Thou shall not hurt nor destroy in all My holy mountain, saith the Lord.'[34]

Notes

1. See Georgie Anne Geyer, *Sarasota Herald-Tribune*, 13 February 1983, p. 3E; *Newsweek*, 21 February 1983, pp. 30ff; Philip Geylin, *Sarasota Herald-Tribune*, 11 February 1983, p. 14-A.
2. *New York Times*, 3 February 1983, p. E17.
3. Geyer, op. cit.
4. For a more detailed exposition of this subject, see: Elmer Berger, 'Prophecy, Zionism and the State of Israel' (a lecture to the Theological Faculty of the University of Leiden, Holland), (American Jewish Alternatives to Zionism, Inc., 1968); Elmer Berger, 'An Examination of the Claim of Zionism to Divine Authorization for Establishing Settlements', *Arab Perspectives*, May 1980 (Arab Information Center, 747 Third Avenue, New York, 10017).
5. Genesis 17.
6. Jeremiah 31:29ff.
7. UPI, *Sarasota Herald-Tribune*, 19 February 1983, p. 3-A.
8. 'The Jewish State', in Ludwig Lewisohn, *Theodor Herzl* (The World Publishing Co., Cleveland and New York, 1955), p. 238.
9. This translation from 'the original German' is found in Walid Khalidi (ed.), *From Haven to Conquest* (The Institute for Palestine Studies, Beirut, 1971), note on p. 89. It differs from the version in Nahum Sokolow's *History of Zionism* where the English version reads 'The object of Zionism is to establish for the Jewish people a home in Palestine secured by public law'. Whatever the minor differences, it is clear what Herzl had in mind was international recognition of Jews as a nation with national/political rights for a state in Palestine.
10. Lewisohn, op. cit., p. 253.
11. Chaim Weizmann, *Trial and Error: The Autobiography of Chaim Weizmann*, illustrated edn (Harper & Bros, UK, 1949), p. 100.
12. Paul Goodman (ed.), *Chaim Weizmann, A Tribute on His Seventieth Birthday* (Gollancz, London, 1945), p. 199.
13. Ibid., p. 179.
14. For a superb, detailed and documented history of the inherent expansionism and disregard for Arab rights in Zionist ideology, transferred

to Israeli policy, see Alan R. Taylor, *The Zionist Mind* (The Institute for Palestine Studies, Beirut, 1974).

15. Menachem Begin, *The Revolt*, revised ed. (Nash Publishing, New York, 1977), p. 348.

16. *Arabs in the Jewish State*, Ian Lustick (University of Texas Press, Austen, Texas, 1980), p. 28.

17. Joseph Badi (ed.), *Fundamental Laws of the State of Israel* (Twayne Publishers, New York, 1961), p. 156.

18. Ibid., p. 254.

19. The claim is specifically advanced in the Eichmann trial judgement, *The Attorney-General of the Government of Israel v. Adolf, the Son of Karl Adolf Eichmann*, Criminal Case No. 40/61, District Court of Jerusalem, 11–12 December 1961, affirmed, 29 May 1962, by the Supreme Court of Israel. For a detailed, legal analysis of the 'Jewish people' claim, see W.T. Mallison, Jr, 'The Zionist-Israel Juridical Claims to Constitute "The Jewish People" Nationality Entity and to Confer Membership in It', *The George Washington Law Review*, vol. 32, no. 5, June 1964, pp. 983–1075. The Eichmann trial judgement reads, 'Israel is the sovereign state of the Jewish people'.

20. Badi, op. cit., p. 285. (For a detailed analysis of the legal and political implications of this (Status) law, see W.T. Mallison, Jr, 'The Legal Problems Concerning the Juridical Status and Political Activities of the Zionist Organization/Jewish Agency', *William and Mary Law Review*, vol. 9, no. 3, Spring 1968, pp. 558–629.)

21. *The Jewish Agency's Digest of Press and Events*, Information Department of the Jewish Agency and World Zionist Organization, Jerusalem, 16 May 1952, pp. 1067–70.

22. Lustick, op. cit., p. 109.

23. J.C. Hurwitz, *Diplomacy in the Near and Middle East* (D. Van Nostrand Co., Inc., Princeton, NJ, 1956), vol. II, pp. 45ff.; see also map in Khalidi, op. cit., p. 193.

24. Hurwitz, op. cit., p. 48.

25. *New York Times*, 31 January 1983, p. 6.

26. *New York Times*, 23 February 1983, p. 1.

27. Ibid., p. 6, and UPI, *The Sarasota Herald-Tribune*, 24 February 1983, p. 5-A.

28. Livia Rokach, *Israel's Sacred Terrorism*, based on Moshe Sharett's personal diary (Association of Arab-American University Graduates, Inc., Belmont, Mass., 1981), p. 44.

29. Ibid., p. 28.

30. *New York Times*, 26 October 1982, p. 31.

31. *New York Times*, 30 December 1982, p. 2.

32. *New York Times*, 2 September 1982.

33. Jeremiah 7: 4–7.

34. Isaiah 65:25.

12. Zionism and Apartheid: An Unlikely Alliance?

Dr Alfred Moleah

Among the most ominous developments on a world scale are the ever-increasing and intensifying alliance between Israel and South Africa, and their links to right-wing forces throughout the world, particularly in the United States. South Africa and, particularly, Israel embody the very dangerous notion that there are transcendent ends and values which are their own justification. These two states and their world-wide ideological right-wing allies, or co-religionists, are bent on remaking the world in their own higher and self-righteous image. In pursuit of this higher calling, they brook no opposition or interference, and are self-assured and undaunted by any compunctions or doubts. This is a grotesque modern-day version of manifest destiny, which is imbued with a jaundiced, Manichaean view of the world the immediate historical antecedent of which is Hitlerite Nazism.

The secular interpretation of this higher calling is Western civilization, unsullied by liberalism and freed of the threat of Communism – its antithesis. They view their mission as a crusade, a divine calling, and are impelled to hasten their Armageddon. The language of Israeli and South African leaders is forever laced with apocalyptic terms, and Reagan increasingly speaks of the evil and amorality of Communism; and Jeane J. Kirkpatrick perceives a moral imperative in the United States foreign policy in El Salvador and elsewhere. All anti-Communists are welcomed into the crusade since all shortcomings pale beside the evil of Communism, and nothing, absolutely nothing, can be worse than Communism, *qua* threat to Western civilization.

In pursuit of this higher end: rights of people do not matter, sovereignty of states does not matter. Death and destruction in El Salvador are but a small price paid to prevent 'Soviet expansionism'; death, destruction and needless suffering in Namibia must continue until the higher end of preventing 'Soviet expansionism' is achieved by the removal of Cuban troops from Angola; and if apartheid is the price of protecting the strategically vital Cape sea route and minerals, then so be it. This logic led to the invasion of Lebanon and the siege and destruction of Beirut – the end justifies the means. Israel and South Africa are the point-man of this most dangerous thrust; but it is world-wide Zionism which is the real point-man.

Therefore, Israel as a Zionist entity and South Africa as an apartheid entity are an idea - an idea that has become a material force. The alliance between Israel and South Africa is the coming together of the two strands of the same idea; this is the manifestation of a shared ideology, a common world-view. Both Israel and South Africa believe in their divine calling; both see themselves as Western outposts in a sea of barbarism and/or Communist ungodliness, actual or potential. They both see their states and their political perspective as the unfolding of a divine drama - the work of a higher authority - and themselves as mere agents of this divine will. Their settler-colonial reality assumes the character of a mission, in the case of Israel, a restorative and fulfilment mission.

The Ideologies of Zionism and Apartheid[1]

Apartheid is a logical consequence of White settler colonialism which was initiated by the Dutch East India Company in 1652. The White settlers sent out by the Dutch East India Company were the first Whites to settle in the southern tip of Africa. These Dutch settlers were later augmented by German and Huguenot (French) settlers, and together, they came to constitute a White tribe which developed its own identity of language and culture, and appropriated the identity of the land by calling itself the Afrikaners, the Dutch word for Africans. Black African possessions and land were expropriated through unequal exchanges, chicanery and force. To rationalize and justify this wholesale plunder and dehumanization, the ideology of apartheid was incrementally developed. Apartheid, as an ideology, postulates the inherent superiority of Whites by reason of their Christianity and Western European culture. But others can also acquire Christianity and even Western European culture: this difficulty was obviated by simply declaring a White skin to be coterminous with Christianity and Western European culture. The equation of a White skin with Christianity/Western European civilization was made possible, in fact made inevitable, by Calvinism to which the White settlers adhered.

The tenets of the orthodox Calvinism of the settlers were in the main

> a belief in the sovereign God, sole creator and ruler through his Providence of the universe; the inborn sinfulness of both man and the world as a result of the Fall; the election by predestination of the few through grace to glorify God in building his kingdom on earth; and the damnation of the rest of mankind, also to the glory of God.[2]

Another significant characteristic of Calvinism is the central place it gives to the Bible. This induces 'a thoroughgoing fundamentalism, a literal interpretation of the Bible, not only as the revealed Word but also as the final source of all knowledge.'[3] These tenets have social implications that inexorably led to apartheid in the south African context.

First, the two-class distinction between the elect and the damned gave to the elect a special responsibility to implement the will of God in the world, and consequently a right to rule.[4] Second, in situations where Calvinists were confronted with a large population of different cultural background and different physical attributes, defined as less civilized, there was a strong tendency to categorize these people as belonging to the non-elect.[5] The dichotomy referred to individuals, but in the South African context it was transmuted into racial categories, whereby all Whites belonged to the elect and all Africans and non-Whites belonged to the damned. Third, a fundamentalist and literal acceptance of the Bible resulted in the Afrikaners' definition of their situation, their conceptions of themselves, of others, and of the world, being derived from the symbolism and mythology of the Bible, especially the Old Testament:

> The meaning of their being in the new land found expression in the symbols of the Chosen People, the Promised Land, the Children of Ham and the Philistines. They were called and led by Jehovah, their King, Ruler, and Judge, to glorify him by establishing his kingdom on the dark continent among the heathen. The Calvinists' doctrines of predestination and election provided justification of their position as defined by these constitutive symbols.[6]

Fourth, the Afrikaner/Calvinist conception of God as sovereign and intensely active, busy at every turning-point in the affairs of nations and men, allows them to shirk responsibility for their acts. All is preordained and they are mere agents of a divine will. This has pernicious and dangerous possibilities.

Afrikaners see themselves as true to their faith in promulgating and upholding apartheid. The authority of the Bible is constantly invoked. For example Psalm 105, which tells them that 'He brought forth his people with joy, and his chosen with gladness: and gave them the lands of the heathen; and they inherited the labour of the people', is cited to justify African expropriation. Segregation and discrimination find their justification in the advice given to the Corinthians which reads: 'Be ye not unequally yoked together with the unbelievers: for what fellowship hath righteousness with unrighteousness? Wherefore come out from among them and be ye separate, saith the Lord, and touch not the unclean thing and I will receive you.'[7]

Within the realities of South Africa, skin colour increasingly became the index, and with time, the only index. D.F. Malan, who became Prime Minister when the Afrikaner National Party came to power in 1948, and, therefore, the principal helmsman of apartheid, brought out the meaning and significance of colour thus:

> Difference in colour indicates a simple but highly significant fact, i.e. that Whites and Non-whites are not of the same kind. They are different. . . . The difference in colour is merely the physical manifestation of the contrast between two irreconcilable ways of life, between barbarism and civilization, between heathenism and Christianity, and finally between overwhelming numerical odds on

the one hand and insignificant numbers on the other.[8]

Malan, who was also a minister of the Dutch Reformed Church - the spiritual guide of Afrikanerdom - was in full accord with the teachings of the Afrikaner Church on this score. Similar views are expressed in a report, *Human Relations in South Africa*, adopted by the General Synod of the Dutch Reformed Church (1966). The report stated, among others, that:

> God created everything including the different races, peoples and nations on the earth. Had He wished to create all men the same He would have done so. . . . God mercifully decreed that man should have many languages and that he should be diversified and spread to all parts of the earth. This resulted in the formation of many different races, peoples, languages and nations. This can be seen from His anger at the sinful attempt at unity, manifest in the attempted construction of the Tower of Babel.[9]

Afrikaners see themselves, apartheid and their state, as well as all their acts, as a part of the fulfilment of a divine scheme. To them, God is the architect of all history, and imbues it with ultimate meaning. The Afrikaners' settlement in South Africa was divinely ordained and their history of survival and triumph a miracle. D.F. Malan spoke for Afrikanerdom when he observed:

> Our history is the greatest masterpiece of the centuries. We hold this nationhood as our due for it was given us by the Architect of the Universe. His aim was the formation of a new nation among the nations of the world. . . . The last hundred years have witnessed a miracle behind which must lie a divine plan. Indeed, the history of the Afrikaner reveals a will and a determination which makes one feel that Afrikanerdom is not the work of men but the creation of God.[10]

He further elaborated on this theme:

> It is through the will of God that the Afrikaner People exists at all. In his wisdom He determined that on the southern point of Africa, the dark continent, a People should be born who would be the bearer of Christian culture and civilization. In His wisdom He surrounded this People by great dangers. He set the People down upon unfruitful soil so that they had to toil and sweat to exist upon the soil. From time to time he visited them with droughts and other plagues.
>
> But this was only one of the problems. God also willed that the Afrikaans People should be continually threatened by other Peoples. There was the ferocious barbarian who resisted the intruding Christian civilization and caused the Afrikaner's blood to flow in streams. There were times when as a result of this the Afrikaner was deeply despairing, but God at the same time prevented the swamping of the young Afrikaner People in the sea of barbarianism.[11]

This, in sum, is the ideological foundation of apartheid. In the name of their Calvinist God are crimes against Africans daily committed and this is the rationalization and justification for the gross and blatant violations of human rights that apartheid has come to represent. This is what justifies White privilege and explains away African dispossession, exploitation, repression and discrimination. Laws have been passed to accord with this divine scheme and to fulfil this divine plan. To maintain and jealously protect the purity of the elect of God, there is the Population Registration Act of 1950 which, with absurd meticulosity, classifies each person into the racial pigeon-holes of White, coloured (people of mixed descent), Asian (mostly of Indian or Pakistani extraction) and Black. This Act, undaunted by the failure of geneticists and anthropologists to compile a complete and perfect grouping of people along racial lines, has constructed a racial classification scheme based on the criteria of descent, appearance and general acceptance.[12] In spite of this serious difficulty, this Act remains the cornerstone of the whole system of apartheid. Further guarantees of White purity are offered by the Immorality Act of 1927, which prohibits any carnal intercourse between Europeans (Whites) and Africans. In 1950, an Amendment to this Act extended this prohibition to all classes of non-Europeans, namely, Africans, Asians and Coloureds.[13] There is also the Prohibition of Mixed Marriages Act of 1949, which forbids marriage of a European to a non-European, and provides that any union in contravention of this law 'shall be void and of no effect'.

Zionism

Zionism presents a much more difficult scenario because it lacks the candour and forthrightness of apartheid. Indicative of the problem is a qualification that needs to be made from the outset: we are here referring exclusively to political Zionism, and not to its religious or cultural variants. This problem is compounded by the skilful manipulation of the religious and cultural variants by political Zionists. This skilful manipulation even succeeds in confusing Jews, not to mention the utter confusion or even bewilderment of non-Jews. To unravel this sedulously cultivated confusion let us turn to the elucidation of Rabbi Elmer Berger:

> Undeniably, 'Zion' (and not necessarily Zionism) is one of the sancta of traditional or orthodox Judaism. This Zion, in its authentic, orthodox meaning, is a theological – not a political/nationalistic – concept. In God's wisdom, when 'the people' morally merited it, God would usher in the millennium by sending the messiah to lead 'the children of Israel' back to Zion. Distilling this 'future hope' out of a correct interpretation of relevant Old Testament texts, these orthodox Jews understood the ancient Israelites and Judeans lost the Holy Land because they had sinned. They had gone 'whoring' after other gods and engaged in a long list of injustices towards fellow humans. Judaism is a 'covenant' religion. The covenant changed from age to age, but it was always a contract between 'the people' and God. God 'promised'

them the land and would prosper them in it if 'the people' rigorously fulfilled the precise moral and ethical stipulations of the covenant as it was interpreted by 'God's prophets' in any particular age. Micah spoke for all the prophets when he warned (III:9–10, 12) 'Zion will be plowed' and 'Jerusalem shall become a heap' because the people 'abhor justice and pervert all equity'. Only God – not men or any combination of men – could make the judgement of whether or not the conduct of the people had reached the point of moral excellence to repair the covenant and so clear the way for God to restore them to the land.

Interpreted in this accurate sense, not even the enormous tragedy of the holocaust could authenticate 'the return'. The Zionist exploitation of the tragedy perpetrated by Nazism is a better-than-average expedient to explain the establishment of the Zionist state. But it is a human explanation, not the fulfillment of Divine purpose. And the established state is anything but 'a house of prayer for all people'. (Isaiah LXVI:7). It is crucial to recognize that the decisive, definite factor distinguishing this religious/messianic Zionism from the political/territorial Zionism which built the Israeli state is the austere, stringent morality which is embraced in the unquestionable authority of God. God – not men – will determine the time and appoint the leader for 'the return' as it is conceived as a sacrament for some Jews.[14]

Another element of Judaism, which has been skilfully manipulated by Zionists, is the idea of chosenness. Jewish religious tradition has a rich vocabulary referring to the Jewish people variously as the chosen people, the holy people, the spiritual people – a people set apart from the rest of mankind by having a special relationship with a transcendent God. This derives from the Bible which, as a holy book, is linked in a supernatural way with the people of Israel who produced it, and with the land of Israel which nurtured it.[15]

Political Zionism, which claims to be a nationalist movement, masquerades in a religious garb. It freely misuses names and symbols sacred to Judaism. A prime example is the name Israel for the Zionist state. The Zionist land acquistion fund's name in Hebrew is *Keren Kayemeth Leisrael*; *Keren Kayemeth*, meaning permanent fund or lasting reward, is taken from the Jewish daily morning prayers. Even more cynically, this term traditionally implies the reward for piety, good deeds and charitable work. The state symbol of Israel is the *menorah* (candelabrum). This is extremely cynical. The Israeli army fights under an emblem that means 'not with armed force and not with power, but in My spirit says the Lord of Hosts'.[16] Even the special relation between God and the children of Israel, so predominant in the Old Testament, has been cynically transmuted. The idea of chosenness as regards the Jewish people in Judaism is a religious one, signifying a community of true believers who put faith in one true God, and whose membership in that community is conditional on their obeying God's commands. Zionist leaders reject this, except in its totally prostituted form.

For instance, Micah Berdichevsky, the Russian Zionist writer, declared emphatically that the Jews should 'cease to be Jews by virtue of an abstract Judaism and become Jews in their own right, as a living and developing nationality'.[17] Max Nordau, the Zionist leader and close friend of Herzl, declared that 'we do not want to be a mere religious community; we want to be a nation like all other nations.'[18] But these same Zionist leaders had no qualms whatsoever about investing a secular phenomenon with a religious idiom. The sanctity attached to the Jewish people in the religious sense is transferred to the Jewish people in the ethnic sense and, accordingly, to the people's history, to their land, and, finally and more importantly, to their state. A Jew, therefore, can only attest to his/her Jewishness by being a nationalist, i.e. an unwavering and uncritical supporter of the state of Israel. The Lord and the *Volk* have become indentical.

This Zionist transmutation of the religious into the political has invited rebuke and even attacks from representatives of religious Judaism because it leads to the worship of the state or the worship of collective human power. It has led to a religio-national pantheism which made it possible for Vladimir Jabotinsky, the mentor of Menachem Begin, to speak of himself as 'one of the masons building a new temple for my God – whose name is Jewish People';[19] and for General Ariel Sharon to declare 'the first and the most supreme value is the good of the State. The State is the supreme value';[20] and for the substitution of the state for God, for example by Rabbi Isaac Kook, who described nationalism or religion 'as merely elements of the spirit of Israel', and stated that a 'a Jewish nationalist, no matter how secularist his intention may be, must despite himself, affirm the divine.'[21]

This transmutation of the religious into the political is a most dangerous process in a settler-colonialist situation, with all its attendant problems. As Arnold Toynbee so rightly observes:

> The prevalence of this worship of collective human power is a calamity. It is a bad religion because it is the worship of a false god. It is a form of idolatry which has led its adherents to commit innumerable crimes and follies. Unhappily, the prevalence of this idolatrous religion is one of the tragic facts of contemporary life.[22]

Leaders of religious Judaism have been rightly alive to this danger, so much so that the venue of the first Zionist Congress (1897) was changed from Munich to Basle, Switzerland, mainly because of the strong anti-Zionist reaction of the German Rabbinic Executive and local Jewish community leaders. Exemplifying this position was the attitude of Rabbi Joseph Hayyim Sonnenfeld, of the Jerusalem separatist community, as expressed in a letter to a friend in Hungary (February 1898):

> With regard to the Zionists what shall I say and what am I to speak? There is great dismay also in the Holy Land that these evil men who deny the Unique One of the world and His Holy Torah have proclaimed their power to hasten redemption for the people of Israel and gather

> the dispersed from all the ends of the earth. They have also asserted the view that the whole difference and distinction between Israel and the nations lies in nationalism, blood and race, and that the faith and the religion are superfluous. . . . For us in the Holy Land it is a sure sign that Dr. Herzl comes not from the Lord but from 'the side of pollution'.[23]

Settler Colonialism

That South Africa is a settler-colonial state is self-evident. Even the racist rulers of South Africa do not deny this; they, instead, argue that, through their 'homelands' policy, Africans will be given back their traditional areas (which constitute 13% of South Africa) and Whites will retain what they found unoccupied upon their arrival (87% of South Africa). We need not waste time exposing this obviously spurious argument and not-so-clever rationalization. Zionists, on the other hand, vehemently deny that the state of Israel is settler colony, arguing, instead, that Jews have eternal and exclusive title to the land of Israel - a title conferred by God to Abraham and his seed, and that it is unassailably stated in Genesis 12:

> Now the Lord had said unto Abraham, get thee out of thy country, and from thy kind and from thy father's house, unto a land that I will show thee: and I will make thee a great nation and I will bless thee, and make thy name great – and Abraham passed through the land unto the place of Sechem, unto the plain of Moreh – and the Lord appeared unto Abraham, and said, unto thy seed will I give this land.

This specious argument notwithstanding, Israel, like South Africa, is a settler-colonial state. Political Zionism is a 19th-century colonial movement of some European Jews to found an exclusive Jewish colony, preferably in Palestine. This was European settler colonialism with the outlook and objectives reflective of other European colonial and imperialist ventures of the period. Zionist founders were quite unabashed in spelling out their settler-colonial scheme and intentions. Jabotinsky, for example, wrote of this in an essay entitled 'The Iron Law' (1925):

> If you wish to colonize a land in which people are already living, you must provide a garrison for the land, or find a benefactor who will maintain the garrison on your behalf. . . . Zionism is a colonizing adventure and, therefore, it stands or falls on the question of armed forces.[24]

All colonialisms have a racist predicate but settler colonialism has a virulent racist predicate. To enable ruthless exploitation, brutal repression, extermination or expulsion of the natives, their humanity is denied by the simple act of negation. The settler colonialist declares, one way or another, that 'the native is not human' or, worse, 'the native does not exist'. It is this mind-set that prompted Levi Eshkol, a former Israeli Prime Minister, to ask:

'What are Palestinians?' and for Golda Meir, another former Israeli Prime Minister, to declare: 'There is no such thing as Palestinians. . . they do not exist', and for the first Israeli Prime Minister, Ben-Gurion, to elaborate: 'In a "historical and moral sense" Palestine, the Holy Land, is a country, "without inhabitants"'.[25] Neither do Africans exist in South Africa. Denying the humanity of the natives is the *sine qua non* of settler colonialism. Yet an equally important aspect is the assertion of special superiority over the native. The most pernicious claim to specialness is the one that invokes God. This invocation is the total and ultimate justification. People become agents of God's will; human acts are attributed to a divine calling, and responsibility is avoided. Actions, and the consequences of those actions, become unquestionable and unassailable. This is the claim of Zionists and that of Afrikaner nationalists: they claim to be chosen peoples, the elect of God put into this world to fulfil a divine mission. These claims also have a virulent racist component.

To reduce the African majority to helotry, their lands and goods were expropriated, and they were left with only their labour power to subsist on; it was ruthlessly exploited. The same fate has befallen the Palestinians.[26] South Africa is a White man's country and all Africans are declared temporary sojourners, admitted only to minister to the needs of Whites.

Even more so, Israel is a state of Jews, not for Jews. In South Africa, the question of whiteness is of paramount importance; in Israel, the question of who is Jewish is even more important. Where one can live or work, even the opportunity to play in the Israeli basketball league, depends on the decision of the Orthodox rabbinate as to who is a Jew according to the criteria that they have established, which require either conversion or a proper genealogy going back four generations. Israel is, according to its Supreme Court, a 'sovereign state of the Jewish people'.[27] In both states, discrimination is inherent. An official Israeli government booklet published in 1950 regards the return of Arab refugees as inconceivable. It brazenly states:

> As a result of the war and the flight of the Arabs, Israel has become a State with an ethnically almost homogeneous population. The whole economic and social life of the State is centered on the problem of absorbing new immigrants. The culture of the State is Jewish, the government administration, the army and all its important institutions are almost exclusively Jewish. It would be folly to resurrect artificially a minority problem which has been almost eliminated by the war.[28]

Laws were passed to sanction this *de facto* situation, and help realize the impossible Zionist dream of 'a land without people for people without land'. On this, Lustick observes:

> The *raison d'être* of the State of Israel in Zionist ideology is the 'in-gathering of the exiles' (*Kibbutz Galluiot*) – to make it possible for most if not all the Jews of the diaspora to settle in the 'Land of Israel.'

> The first act of the Provisional State Council on May 14, 1948, was to abolish all restrictions on Jewish immigration and land sales to Jews. The Law of Return, passed by the Knesset in 1950, and the Citizenship Law of 1952 granted every Jew the right to immediate citizenship upon his arrival in Israel. Between May 1948, and December 1951, over 684,000 Jews entered the country as new immigrants, thereby more than doubling the Jewish population in two and a half years.[29]

Both Israel and South Africa stand in clear violation of Article 1 of the Universal Declaration of Human Rights which states: 'All human beings are born free and equal in dignity and rights. They are endowed with reason and conscience and should act towards one another in a spirit of brotherhood.'

Whereas South Africa finds itself universally vilified for its racist policies, the state of Israel is vaunted as an oasis of democracy and decency. Given the world-wide, awesome power of Zionism, the Israelis can act quite brazenly and arrogantly: they answer to no one. In full view of the world, they daily expropriate Palestinian lands and impertinently deny that these Palestinian lands are being stolen and expropriated. Likud Cabinet Secretary Arieh Naor asserted that: 'It would be an act of anti-Semitism to say that a Jew could not live in Judea and Samaria'.[30] The charge of anti-Semitism is the ever-pervasive weapon that Zionists wield with deadly abandon to silence all dissent and achieve absolute immunity from scrutiny and criticism. Among Jews, the charge of self-hatred has the same effect and results. The quintessential Zionist, Menachem Begin, took this to its logical conclusion in declaring: 'there is no difference between anti-Israelism, anti-Zionism and anti-Semitism'.[31]

It is this immunity that Zionism has extracted from world public opinion, especially in the United States, that has unleashed Israeli state terrorism and caused the horror of Lebanon and Beirut. Unbelievably, this immunity still prevails.

Foundations of the Israel-South Africa Alliance

As Dr Richard P. Stevens so insightfully and comprehensively chronicled,[32] Chaim Weizmann and Jan C. Smuts, South African leader, immediately recognized their similarities and common interests. The two men initiated the alliance between Israel and South Africa, but they did not create it: that was done by the objective conditions of their situation and goals.

Smuts as a South African leader was a great believer in the advance of civilization, by which he meant the expansion and domination of White Western European civilization throughout the world, and saw the British empire as an appropriate vehicle for this mission. He became a great supporter of the British empire, earning the sobriquet of 'Handyman of Empire'. For non-Europeans, especially Africans, Smuts had nothing but contempt and condescension. He called for a 'Christian' approach 'to the natives of Africa', warning that the 'natives have the simplest minds, understand only the simplest ideas or ideals, and are almost animal-like in the simplicity of their minds and ways'.[33] Smuts was also a great believer in White unity to achieve this great mission, and he included Jews among Whites.

His racist outlook and its predicates predisposed him favourably to anything like Zionism as it fitted neatly into his scheme of things. The real catalyst and link to his support for the Zionist venture in Palestine was the Jewish community in South Africa. While Smuts lay sick in bed at his home in 1916, Mr Nathan Levi brought him the resolutions passed by the Zionist Federation, and asked for his assistance in having the claim of the Jewish people to Palestine recognized at the peace settlement at the end of the war. Smuts promised to do all he could. So, when he was approached for help by Weizmann in 1917, he was already committed. He was even more convinced by the arguments of Theodor Herzl and Weizmann which linked the Zionist programme with British imperial interests.[34]

In Smuts, Weizmann found his staunchest support for Zionist goals within the corridors of power of the British empire. He had occasion to call on him repeatedly, assured of a sympathetic ear and a willingness to render assistance. Smuts, in typical Afrikaner Calvinist tradition, saw a close affinity between Afrikaners and Jews, between Afrikaner nationalism and Zionism. This he brought out in a meeting of the South African Board of Deputies and the Zionist federation, on 3 November 1919. He stated:

> I need not remind you that the white people of South Africa, and especially the older Dutch population, has been brought up almost entirely on Jewish tradition. The Old Testament, the most wonderful literature ever thought out by the brain of man, the Old Testament has been the very matrix of Dutch culture here in South Africa . . . .
>
> That is the basis of our culture in South Africa, that is the basis of our white culture, and it is the basis of your Jewish culture; and therefore we are standing together on a common platform, the greatest spiritual platform the world has ever seen. On that platform I want us to build the future South Africa.[35]

Even at this early stage, Zionists were in no way discomforted by South Africa's and Smuts's racism and inhuman policies. Such scruples were simply not allowed to stand in the way of achieving the higher goal of a Zionist homeland for the Jewish people. The end justifies the means.

The ties between Israel and South Africa are based on an identity of position and goals. These are basic and fundamental, and, therefore, totally unaffected by the vicissitudes of politics in both countries. Changes of government and political alignments and realignments have no bearing on this commonality of position and interest. Both Israel and South Africa are settler-colonial entities: both have expropriated the lands of other peoples; both see themselves as fulfilling a divine mission and are, therefore, supra-rational and supra-natural; both practise, as policy, harsh and extreme discrimination on the basis of the superiority and purity of their race against the dispossessed indigenous peoples; for these and other reasons both are beleaguered and garrison states.

After General J.B.M. Hertzog, then a bitter political enemy of Smuts and the British empire, and a rabid racist to boot, defeated Smuts in the election of 1924, and formed his Nationalist-Labour parties coalition government, he fully supported the creation of a 'Jewish homeland' in Palestine and adopted a resolution to that effect in 1926. The resolution also promised to support the Zionist aims before the League of Nations. The same year and month that the state of Israel was declared, the Afrikaners gained political power in South Africa under the leadership of Dr D.F. Malan, a political enemy of both Smuts and Hertzog, who became Prime Minister and was the architect of apartheid. Malan fully understood the significance of the declaration of Israeli statehood and quickly offered *de jure* recognition of the new state. Malan also became the first Prime Minister in the British Commonwealth to pay a courtesy visit to Israel. The symbolism of this visit was important. Malan permitted South African Jewish Reserve officers to serve in Israel and approved the transfer of funds and goods to Israel despite South Africa's financial difficulties at the time. The now ruling National Party also reversed its policy towards the Jewish community, which had hitherto been one of rabid anti-Semitism. Jews were now allowed into the Nationalist Party and prominent Jews were appointed to important governmental positions.[36]

The South African Jewish community served as an important link between the two countries. The South African Jewish community is a highly organized community; it is chiefly organized under the South African Zionist Federation and the South African Jewish Board of Deputies, and these two encompass a host of allied organizations. Because of this, they are the most Zionist Jewish community in the world. They established themselves as a financial power by the end of the last century, are overwhelmingly Lithuanian, and by 1945 constituted the wealthiest Jewish community in the world on a per capita basis. They are also the highest per capita contributors to the state of Israel in the world, and their pace of *aliyah* has been at least five times greater than that from the United States. Their number is only about 120,000, but due to superior Zionist organization, they are quite cohesive and, therefore, powerful. They have organized chapters of Christian Action for Israel among White and Black 'Gentile Zionist' groups as well as record-breaking Jewish and non-Jewish (White) tourism to Israel. For good measure, there are between 25,000 and 30,000 Israeli expatriates in South Africa. So, in response to Malan's new policy, the Jewish associations toned down their previously outspoken criticism of racial discrimination and followed the South African Board of Deputies in taking the position that, as non-political bodies, they would 'refrain from taking any position on party political issues' and would not 'express views on the various race policies being advocated.'[37] This position was elaborated upon by Rabbi M.C. Weiler at the eighth International Conference of the World Union for Progressive Judaism in London in 1953:

> The Jews as a community had decided to take no stand on the native question, because they were involved with the problem of assisting Jewry in other lands. South African Jewry was doing more to help Israel than any other group. The community could not ask for the Government's permission to export funds and goods and, at the same time, object to the Government.[38]

When African states gained independence in the 1960s, Israel, in courting these states, found it necessary to put some distance between itself and the abhorred apartheid regime of South Africa. When Israel, in keeping with this political expediency, voted in the United Nations General Assembly (1961) in support of a resolution which deprecated South Africa's policy of apartheid 'as being reprehensible and repugnant to the dignity and rights of peoples and individuals', South Africa felt betrayed. Dr Hendrik Verwoerd, Prime Minister and prophet/ideologue of apartheid, caustically observed that:

> They [the Jews] took Israel away from the Arabs after the Arabs had lived there for a thousand years. In that, I agree with them. Israel is an apartheid state. People are beginning to ask why, if Israel and its rabbis feel impelled to attack the policy of separate development, the policy of separate development in Israel is not wrong in their eyes as well. . . It may be said that they wish to differentiate in separate states because of religious and not racial differences, but if differentiation is wrong on one score, it is also wrong on another . . . We believe in the separate state of Israel, but now begin to wonder whether that support should be withdrawn, if, according to their own convictions, the idea of separate development is wrong.[39]

The government rescinded the special concessions in foreign currency regulations which allowed Jewish organizations to transfer money and goods to Israel despite the restrictions in effect since the Sharpeville massacre (1960), in which the South African police force fired shots into a crowd of African demonstrators, killing 69 and wounding 180. The Zionist organizations and press in South Africa were equally dismayed by this latest Israeli switch which they correctly saw as hypocrisy; according to Mr Katzew, many wondered whether there were 'any circumstances at present imaginable in which the Jews of Israel would consent to share power with an Arab majority' any more than Afrikaners would with Africans. The South African Jewish Board of Deputies and Zionist organizations intensified their efforts to deflect criticism abroad of South Africa by other Jewish bodies. Prominent Jewish figures travelled abroad to emphasize this message and succeeded in getting Zionist organizations to heed their plea at the United Nations and other forums.

In addition to the political expediency of wooing the newly independent African states, the contradiction between Jewish traditional and religious values and support for apartheid racism had become troublesome: a people historically victim of racism and discrimination just could not comfortably sleep in the same bed as racist South Africa. At least the pretence of opposition and protest had to be maintained to assuage the Jewish conscience.

Reaction from South Africa and its Jewish community forced a pained debate in the Israeli Knesset. The Herut Party, led by Menachem Begin, had no problem in supporting South Africa; it moved a motion critical of the Israeli government's stand in the United Nations vote of November 1961 which not only condemned South Africa for its racist policies but called for sanctions against the regime.

Others were less secure on the issue. Ben-Gurion remarked in response to a question during the Knesset debate:

> That was the reason for our votes at the UN [to avoid difficulties for South African Jews]. After 1960 we changed because we didn't want to alienate the new African countries. We knew the Jews there wouldn't suffer very much. The South African Government was angry but not against the Jews there – against Israel.
>
> If there would have been *pogroms* – if the lives were in danger – then we would have abstained, but we would not have voted in favor, certainly not. *A Jew can't be for discrimination.* (emphasis added)[40]

This was the first serious discussion of apartheid in the Israeli Knesset and it pitted principle against expediency and pragmatism. At that moment there was a majority that argued that Israel just could not afford to negate Jewish history, experience and values by supporting apartheid; and there was a minority which argued that the welfare of the Jewish community in South Africa and the survival needs of the Jewish state overrode all other considerations since they constituted the highest values. Troubled South African Jews were told that Israel could not abandon Jewish moral principles, and that to do so would bring contempt from the rest of the world. Ben-Gurion had explained the Israeli vote in the UN General Assembly, November 1961, as based on three considerations: first, that Israel speaks only for Israelis, but has to be sensitive to the position of Jews elsewhere; second, Israel could not ignore the feelings of Asian and African peoples; third, it was a matter of conscience: 'moral imperatives of Judaism were involved. . . . Was it possible for Israel . . . to remain indifferent to the deplorable regime of racial discrimination that reigns in South Africa?'[41]

Before 1960, states could be 'principled' in debates about South Africa at the UN on the cheap, i.e. they could engage in polite condemnation and empty, pious posturing. Resolutions resulting from these debates were innocuous, turning the whole exercise into a farce. South Africa did not very much mind this periodic ritual. Things changed dramatically in 1960 and after as African states attained independence and became part of the UN; 18 entered the UN in autumn 1960. From here on UN debates of apartheid became quite serious and were coupled with calls for action including sanctions. Those willing to condemn South Africa in the past now began to show extreme reluctance, even opposition to such condemnatory resolutions.

South Africa, in retaliation for the Israeli vote in the General Assembly, froze funds raised for Israel by the South African Jewish community. The South African Jewish Board of Deputies and other Zionist organizations went out of their way to distance themselves from the Israeli action at the UN and dispatched emissaries abroad to urge restraint on Jewish critics of apartheid. Meanwhile, relations between the two states became cooler, though they never approached estrangement.

This was not a break but merely a tactical hold. The ties between Israel and South Africa were just too real to disappear suddenly. In addition to factors already mentioned, there were also many personal ties, for example the large South African Jewish emigrant group in Israel, many of whom held prominent positions such as Mr Eban, and Mr Pincus who in 1966 was elected chairman of the Jewish Agency in Jerusalem, the controlling body of the World Zionist Organization. In South Africa, many Jews were quite influential in the governmental and National Party structure. Even more importantly, the litmus test of devotion and service to the state of Israel was bound to win out. The relationship between the two states therefore continued on many different levels, albeit with some rancour and less fanfare.

Despite the apparent rancour of the early and middle 1960s, when Israel unleashed its aggression in the 1967 war, South Africa escalated its support. Special regulations to allow free transfer of funds to Israel were quickly reinstated and other forms of material aid were made available. The war reaffirmed the basic similarity of the two countries and re-emphasized the need to co-operate. *Die Burger*, an organ of the National Party in the Cape Province, explained this commonality of interest, albeit in more mundane terms:

> Israel and South Africa have a common lot. Both are engaged in a struggle for existence, and both are in constant clash with the decisive majorities in the United Nations. Both are reliable foci of strength within the region, which would, without them, fall into anti-Western anarchy. It is in South Africa's interest that Israel is successful in containing her enemies, who are among our own most vicious enemies; and Israel would have all the world against it if the navigation route around the Cape of Good Hope should be out of operation because South Africa's control is undermined. The anti-Western powers have driven Israel and South Africa into a community of interests which had better be utilized than denied.[42]

The same sentiment was reiterated by *Jewish Affairs*, the official organ of the South African Jewish Board of Deputies:

> The argument that Israel and South Africa have a basic community of interest in the Middle East and further south has more than a grain of truth in it. There is nothing secret or sinister about it. The strong ties between the two countries, closer than ever since the 1967 war,

> are inseparable from their geographical and stragegic position, from their anti-communist outlook, and from all the realities of their national existence. . . . In short, the destinies of the two countries, so different in many ways, but so alike in the fundamental conditions of their survival, are interwoven in a much more meaningful sense than any enemy propagandist could conceive, or, for that matter, would be happy to see.[43]

The October 1973 war was a major milestone in the process of growing identification between the two countries. After this war, which led most African countries to break off relations with Jerusalem, Israel buried its pretence, especially at the United Nations, of being opposed to apartheid. South Africa openly expressed its support for Israel during the war. Mr P.W. Botha, then Minister of Defence and now Prime Minister, declared his full support. The then Prime Minister Vorster stated that if Israel lost the war, its defeat would have important consequences for South Africa. South Africa gave full support, including military support, both in men and *materiel.*

From Alliance to Organic Links

After the 1967 war, Israel and South Africa ironed out their differences, sort of forgot the past, and embarked on preparing for the future. Of significance in this regard was the founding in 1967 of the Israel-South Africa Friendship League at the initiative of Eliezer Shostak, a member of the Free Centre Party in the Knesset. Menachem Begin was made president of the Israel-South Africa Friendship League, in recognition of his consistent advocacy of an alliance between Israel and South Africa. In April 1968, the Man-to-Man Committee participated in the 'millionaires' conference held in Jerusalem to stimulate trade with Israel. On their return to South Africa, delegates to the 'millionaires' conference set up the Israel–South Africa Trade Assocation (ISATA), which was to play a key role in subsequent development of trade between the two countries.[44]

Trade between the two countries expanded rapidly, and both governments were fully and actively involved in these schemes. It must be noted that this increase in trade and other ties was taking place just as other countries were being increasingly embarrassed and condemned for their ties with South Africa, and were therefore loosening them.

There has also been a great deal of investment by Israel in South Africa and South African investment in Israel. The two countries are also increasingly involved in joint-investment ventures. By these arrangements, South Africa is able to use Israel as a base from which to evade boycott of her trade and commerce. This is simply done by the stratagem of shipping semi-finished South African goods to Israel to be finished there and qualify for an Israeli certificate of origin. This has the added advantage that South African goods benefit from Israel's free trade agreements with the European

Economic Community and the United States. Airline and shipping ties have increased; so have cultural, sports and scientific/technological ties. These joint-investment projects and the finishing of South African goods in Israel create special difficulties for the growing world-wide movement calling for sanctions against South Africa.[45]

The culmination of this greatly strengthened and invigorated relationship, which also casts light on its cynicism and amorality, was the visit to Israel in April 1976 by the then South African Prime Minister, John Balthazar Vorster. Yitzhak Rabin was the host. The visit was at first kept quiet and was then described as a 'private visit'. One of Israel's liberal dailies, *Ha'aretz*, reported that there was no opposition to the visit among cabinet members, and cynically described the visit as a pilgrimage by a deeply religious man.[46] This 'deeply religious man' was a former general of the *Ossewa Brandwag*, a pro-Nazi group; he had declared in 1942: 'We stand for Christian Nationalism which is an ally of National Socialism. You can call this anti-democratic principle dictatorship if you wish. In Italy it is called Fascism, in Germany German National Socialism, and in South Africa Christian Nationalism.'[47] He was interned by the British during World War II for his pro-Nazi activities.

This 'deeply religious man' had also been South Africa's Minister of Justice, Prisons and Police – the one directly responsible for the massacres of Africans, their brutalization and their repression. He was also the author of some of the most draconian laws in South Africa's history, and had shown a truly callous disregard for the rights, or even the humanity, of his victims. All this was simply overlooked and *Ha'aretz* in a welcoming editorial stated: 'This visit should be hailed as an expression of the improving quality of relations between Israel and South Africa.'[48] Other Israeli papers were even more glowing and enthusiastic.

Throughout Vorster's visit, the official Israeli line was to play up his religiosity. This was, indeed, appalling cynicism. He was shown visiting Christian holy places, declaring that this was the fulfilment of his childhood dreams, and emphasizing how important the Bible was in his life. The depths of this cynical spectacle were reached when Vorster placed a wreath at the *Yad Vashem* Holocaust Memorial.

> Israeli television viewers were treated to the amazing scene of the uncomfortable Vorster. . . being lectured about the evils of Nazi horrors by his obviously tactless hosts. The official press releases reported that Mr. Vorster, with characteristic good humor, expressed his shock at the extent of Nazi atrocities and added that Israel was a befitting answer to Nazi designs. The high point of the Jerusalem tour was a state dinner at the Knesset where Rabin toasted 'the ideals shared by Israel and South Africa – the hopes for justice and peaceful coexistence'.[49]

Reasons of state produce strange bedfellows, indeed!

In the wake of Vorster's visit wide-ranging agreements on economic, scientific and industrial collaboration were concluded. The military aspect was central to this new arrangement. The economic and military agreements that Vorster signed during his visit centred on South Africa's willingness to finance some of Israel's costlier military projects. Israel was to reciprocate by supplying weapon systems and training.[50]

After a mandatory arms embargo was imposed on South Africa by the United Nations Security Council in 1977, Israel, while pledging adherence to the embargo, stepped in as South Africa's arms supplier. Israel is now South Africa's principal supplier of arms; it also provides training, and its military personnel are active in the South African Defence Force, including its genocidal war in Namibia and its aggression against Angola. Israel's number one arms customer is South Africa, followed by Argentina.

The most ominous aspect of this military alliance between the two countries is their nuclear collaboration. The fact of this nuclear collaboration is no longer questioned; it is the details that are being debated. On 22 September 1979 a United States orbiting Vela satellite picked up what is believed to be a nuclear explosion off the South African coast. There is strong suspicion that this was an Israeli - South African nuclear explosion, probably a neutron bomb. CBS television news on 21 February 1980 broadcast a story sent from Rome by their Tel Aviv correspondent, Dan Raviv, quoting details of Israeli - South African nuclear collaboration from a book subsequently banned by Israeli censors. Other reports on this nuclear collaboration have followed, the latest being the book *Two Minutes over Baghdad* (1982) by three authors (Amos Perlmutter, Michael Handel, and Uri Bar-Joseph) all pro-Zionists with close ties to the Israeli Establishment.

The United States has aided and abetted this unholy alliance between Zionism and apartheid. When resistance in the US Congress prevented the administration from having a free hand in aiding pro-Western elements in the Angolan struggle for power as the Portuguese were leaving, the US got South Africa involved in the conflict. Kissinger then secretly, in early 1975, asked the Israeli government to send troops to Angola to help South Africa. The Israelis complied and sent South Africa military instructors specializing in anti-guerrilla warfare, plus equipment designed for the same purpose.[51] Israel is what the US administration, then and now, relies upon to thwart and subvert the will of Congress and US law to carry on its crusade of anti-Communism and anti-terrorism. Terrorists are what others accept as legitimate resistance forces and liberation movements. What the US administration cannot do, legally, politically and morally, Israel can do. Israel now fully plays the role of a US surrogate of sub-imperialism, not only with South Africa but throughout the world, particularly with the corrupt and brutal dictatorships of Latin America.

Conclusion

The alliance between Israel and South Africa is qualitatively different from other states' relations with South Africa. In just about every part of the world, every country, there is abhorrence of apartheid and a significant resistance to dealing with the racist regime of South Africa. Governments undertaking such dealings argue expediency and necessity, and offer rationalizations and excuses. These governments are condemned and called to account by their own citizens and the international community. This is not the case with Israel. Unlike in the past, the alliance is openly admitted and conceded as major. Nobody makes any fuss over it. South Africa is a part of everyday life in Israel.

> Since 1977, South Africa has clearly loomed larger than ever before in the consciousness of most Israelis. South Africa would be mentioned in conversation among 'beautiful Israelis' as a place they have visited, or plan to visit, as a place where acquaintances are having a good time, and especially making a lot of money.[52]

A good number of Israelis who have been to South Africa find it a congenial place.

The alliance between Israel and South Africa 'is a matter of true national consensus'. There is never a debate on the substance of the alliance, only on visibility and public image. Among the Israeli public there is virtually no opposition to the alliance with South Africa. In fact, the White minority in South Africa enjoys overwhelming and open support.

> The impression formed out of checking the Israeli consciousness, collective and individual, vis-a-vis South Africa and Southern Africa, is unmistakable. One notices a certain posture of empathy, a perception of similarity and closeness, and a recognition of identical interests.[53]

As the two countries draw closer and their links become organic, South Africa comes more and more under the protective cover of international Zionism, especially in the US. Criticism of South Africa and attacks on apartheid increasingly become criticism of Israel and attacks on Zionism, thus prompting the knee-jerk reaction of Zionists to deny and counter-attack, since the sacred state of Israel cannot be faulted on any account. Both South Africa and Israel are aware of this; in fact, Israel has developed the new enterprise of peddling its influence in the US – with Congress, the Executive and the public – as the case of Zaire illustrates.

What has brought this to pass is the internal logic of Zionism which fosters worship of the state of Israel. It is, indeed, sad that the victims of the past have become the callous victimizers of today. Israel has become a partner in the brutalization and oppression of the African majority in Namibia and South Africa.

Notes

1. This is excerpted from Alfred T. Moleah, *Zionism and Apartheid: The*

Negation of Human Rights (International Organization for the Elimination of All Forms of Racial Discrimination (EAFORD), London 1981), pp. 4–11.

2. Jan J. Loubser, 'Calvinism, Equality, and Inclusion: The Case of Afrikaner Calvinism', in S.N. Eisenstadt (ed.), *The Protestant Ethic and Modernization* (Basic Books, Inc., New York, 1968), p. 371.

3. Ibid.

4. Ibid., p. 368.

5. Ibid., p. 369.

6. Ibid.

7. Quoted in John Fisher, *The Afrikaners* (Cassel and Company, London, 1969), p. 302.

8. Quoted in Hermann Giliomee, 'The Development of the Afrikaner's Self-concept', in A. Paul Hare, Gerd Weindieck and Max H. von Broembsen (eds.), *South Africa: Sociological Analyses* (Oxford University Press, Cape Town, 1979), p. 58.

9. Robert P.D. Buis, 'The Relationship between the Dogmatic Teachings and Attitude towards Race Relations of Two South African Religious Denominations', in ibid., pp. 105–6.

10. Quoted in T. Dunbar Moodie, *The Rise of Afrikanerdom* (University of California Press, Berkeley, 1975), p.1.

11. *Die Tranvaler*, 16 December 1942, quoted in ibid., p. 248.

12. John Dugar, *Human Rights and the South African Legal Order* (Princeton University Press, Princeton, 1978), pp. 53–4.

13. *South Africa and the Rule of Law* (International Commission of Jurists, Geneva, 1960), p. 56.

14. Elmer Berger, *Zionist Ideology – Obstacle to Peace* (EAFORD, London, 1981), p. 2.

15. Fedynand Zweig, *Israel: The Sword and the Harp* (Heinemann, London, 1969), pp. 70–1.

16. G. Neuburger, 'The Difference between Judaism and Zionism', in *Zionism and Racism* (EAFORD, London, 1976), p. 189.

17. Quoted in Abdelwahab M. Elmessiri, *The Land of Promise: A Critique of Political Zionism* (North American, New Brunswick, 1977), p. 14.

18. Quoted in ibid.

19. Quoted in ibid., p. 15.

20. Quoted in ibid., p. 12.

21. Quoted in ibid., p. 15.

22. Quoted in Alfred M. Lilienthal, *The Zionist Connection: What Price Peace?* (Dodd, Mead & Co., New York, 1978) p. 3.

23. Gary V. Smith (ed.), *Zionism, the Dream and the Reality: A Jewish Critique* (Barnes and Noble Books, New York, 1974), pp. 13–14.

24. The Shahak Papers No. 31, 'Collection on Jabotinsky: His Life and Excerpts from his Writings', p. 16, quoted in James Zogby, 'Palestinian Human Rights in Context of the Historical Development of the Zionist Movement' (undated).

25. Elmessiri, op. cit., p. 120.

26. For a fuller discussion of the parallels and similarities, see Alfred T. Moleah, 'Violations of Palestinian Human Rights: South African Parallels', *Journal of Palestine Studies*, 38, vol. x, no. 2, Winter 1981, pp. 14–36.

27. Noam Chomsky, 'Introduction' to Sabri Jiryis, *The Arabs in Israel* (Monthly Review Press, New York, 1976), p. viii.
28. Quoted in Ian Lustick, 'Zionism and the State of Israel: Regime Objectives and the Arab Minority in the First Years of Statehood', *Middle Eastern Studies*, 16, no. 1, January 1980, p. 135.
29. Ibid., p. 129.
30. National Lawyers Guild, *Treatment of the Palestinians in Israeli-Occupied West Bank and Gaza: Report of the National Lawyers Guild 1977 Middle East Delegation* (National Lawyers Guild, New York, 1978), p. 12.
31. *Philadelphia Inquirer*, 26 October 1980.
32. Richard P. Stevens, *Weizmann and Smuts: A Study in Zionist-South African Cooperation* (The Institute for Palestine Studies, Beirut, 1975).
33. Jan C. Smuts, *War-Time Speeches* (London, 1917), p. 85, quoted in ibid., p. 5.
34. Ibid., pp. 7–11.
35. *South African Jewish Chronicle*, 22 September 1950, quoted in ibid., p. 33.
36. Richard P. Stevens, *The Paradoxical Triangle: Zionism, South Africa and Apartheid* (The Institute for Palestine Studies, Beirut, 1975).
37. Henry Katzew, 'Jews in the Land of Apartheid', *Midstream*, vol. 8, December 1962.
38. Quoted in Stevens, op. cit., p. 18.
39. *Rand Daily Mail*, 24 November 1961.
40. Quoted in Michael Brecher, *The Foreign Policy System of Israel* (Yale University Press, New Haven, 1972), p. 234.
41. Ibid., p. 235.
42. *Die Burger*, 29 May 1968.
43. *Jewish Affairs*, November 1970.
44. Rosalynde Ainslee, *Israel and South Africa: An Unlikely Alliance?* (UN Notes and Documents, New York, July 1981), p. 3.
45. Alfred T. Moleah, 'Israel and South Africa: The Special Relationship', *Africa Report*, November-December 1980, p. 17.
46. Benjamin Beit-Hallahmi, 'South Africa and Israel's Strategy of Survival', *New Outlook*, April-May 1977, p. 55.
47. Brian Bunting, *The Rise of the South African Reich* (Penguin Books, Baltimore, 1964), p. 88.
48. Quoted in Beit-Hallahmi, op. cit., p. 55.
49. Ibid.
50. *The Economist*, 5 November 1977, p. 90.
51. Ibid.
52. Benjamin Beit-Hallahmi, 'Israel and South Africa 1977–1982: Business as Usual and More', *New Outlook*, March-April 1983, pp. 31–5.
53. Beit-Hallahmi, 1977, op. cit., p. 56.

13. Zionism: As It Is in Israel for an Arab

Dr Riah Abu Al-Assal

First, I want to say how grateful I am to AJAZ and EAFORD for inviting me to participate in this conference in search of peace and understanding in the Middle East.

Second, I want to say how embarrassed I am, as a minister of a church and often described as a man of religion, that so much harm has been done in the name of religion. I am sorry to say that. To be honest, I am a little disappointed that so much emphasis has been laid on the religious aspect of the conflict in the Middle East, though I can understand and appreciate the religious background of part of this conflict.

I am reminded of a story about a Sikh from North India travelling on a train in England. He was being watched by an English person sitting opposite him to whom he wanted to introduce himself. He said, 'I am Sikh', and the Englishman said, 'Well, if you're sick, go and see a doctor.'

He said, 'No, I am Sikh in religion', to which the Englishman said, 'I am sick too.'

The Jewish question, a dilemma for Palestinians. I hope I will be able to touch ground, as it were, as I want to relate to what has been happening in that part of the world, Palestine, Israel, *Terra Sancta*, call it what you will, since the establishment of the state of Israel.

Most dictionaries define the word dilemma as a situation requiring a choice between equally undesirable alternatives and, therefore, undesirable consequences. In other words, where the choice is not only between two answers, but also between two solutions, both of which are bad and difficult. I want to discuss 'the Jewish question', as we Arab Palestinians in Israel understand it. I'm talking about the overwhelming majority of Arab people within Israel now, the simple folk, not the highly sophisticated, scholarly people. 'The Jewish question', Israel, the state of Israel, the dream realized by Zionists or Jews after so many generations of Diaspora, the achievement of modern Zionism, in the fullest understanding of the term, is a dilemma for me, an Arab Palestinian.

I see the dilemma as a triangle. The first side is the question of the land. Some call it the Promised Land, some Palestine, some Israel, and many, especially in the US, call it the Holy Land. In my opinion it is no longer holy, though I dare say it continues to be the land of the Holy One. Regardless of what we call it, the Jewish question is a dilemma because of its relation to this land. Somebody said that if the achievement of Israel had been made in a vacuum, it might command the admiration of the whole world, including the Palestinians. No wonder those committed admirers find it the most significant event in the 20th century. But the problem is that it was not born in a vacuum. It came into being in a land where others, we, the Palestinians, were; and not just since yesterday. But this is the kind of thing people say to me: 'Trespassers. You have all the Middle East'. They say, 'What do you have there in Palestine?' But we, the Palestinians, were not there only since yesterday but from pre-Joshua to post-Ottoman times. Israel was founded, perhaps I should say partly founded, on the remains of others – the Palestinians. It also belonged to us and we dearly love the land.

Love of Palestine by Palestinians did not begin with Israeli occupation of the land, nor was it a response or a reaction to the occupation by the Zionists. Love of Palestine by Palestinians was always the natural response to the land itself.

Next, the Zionists are in Jerusalem. It is no longer – and for centuries has not been – exclusively Jewish. It is in the hearts and minds and on the lips of every Palestinian insidc Israel as well as outside the Zionist state. The land is one of the causes of the dilemma. It is also one of the root-causes of the conflict, the hostilities, the lack of security and, to a great extent, the absence of understanding and, therefore, absence of peace in the area.

I don't know whether I should share with you another story which I had from the ex-chairman of the CCIA, the Church Commission on International Affairs of the World Council of Churches. He said, 'This whole conflict of the Middle East goes back to a divine mistake.' He tried to illustrate it by saying that at one time Almighty God approached Moses and asked him, 'What land would you like me to give to you and to your people?' We all know that Moses couldn't speak well. He stammered, and he said, 'Well I would like to have the land of Ca-ca-ca', and Almighty God said, 'Yes, I understand you want the land of Canaan.' But Almighty God didn't realize he was asking for the land of Canada.

The question of the land, the Promised Land, is one of the root-causes and we have to face the issue of how to tackle it. The second side of the triangle is the character of the state, the Zionist state, Israel, as envisaged by the fathers of Zionism and as it is today: namely, exclusively Jewish. The founders of modern Zionism and present-day Israel, including Chaim Weizmann, coined the slogan 'the land without people'. The leader of the Jewish National Fund, Joseph Weitz, in 1940 stated the following:

> It must be clear to us that there is no room for two peoples in this country. The only solution lies in the creation of Eretz Yisroel without Arabs, *at least* west of Jordan. This can only be done by *transferring the Arabs*, all the Arabs to neighboring countries. There is no alternative. (my emphasis)

This is not only the opinion of Zionists in days gone by. It is also the attitude of present-day Zionists, leaders and advocates, within Israel.

Israel Yeshaayahu Ben Porat says:

> It is the duty of Israel's leaders to explain to the public with clarity and courage a number of facts, the first of which is that there is no Zionism, no settlements or Jewish state without the eviction of the Arabs and the expropriation of their lands.

Zionism aspired to more than a large majority in what became Israel, a goal obviously impossible without drastic disturbance of existing demography.

An Arab exodus was, therefore, inherent in the entire enterprise of Zionism. Different means were employed and the Deir Yassin massacre was one in a chain of massacres that aimed at evacuating the people from their land. I don't want to use the Israeli term *Chavai Yisroel*, the residents.

To safeguard the exclusively Jewish character of the state, much has been done to further the cause of *aliyah*, immigration, into Israel while the Palestinians have been discouraged from staying. Those who did remain are the faithful remnant of the land, the Arab minority.

Immediately after 1948, Israel made it a policy to discourage any emergence of even Palestinianism as a national state-seeking state-making reality. Attempts were aimed at not only keeping Arabs out but also at de-Arabizing the Arabs within Israel. When officials refer to the population in Israel, they often describe the population as being composed of Jews and non-Jews. When we ask, 'Would you kindly define the non-Jews?', they say, 'They are the Christians, the Muslims, or the Druse' (a Muslim sect). They often describe the Arab minority as being composed of Arabs and Christians, as if Christians, the Christian Arabs of Israel, were not Arabs. They forget that Arab Christianity goes back to the time of Christ.

No wonder – and this is part of the effect of Zionism on the Arabs within Israel – that Arab Christians have become more Arab than the rest of the Arab world; and the Arab Palestinians within Israel have become more Palestinian and more conscious of their Palestinianism than all the rest of the Palestinians throughout the world.

The third side of the triangle is the question of power. Peoplehood, land, the exclusively Jewish nature of the community have already been achieved. The Zionist search can never be real or secure, however, without territory plus independence, insured with power. For Zionism to be concretized in actuality, in soil and soul together, power is essential. The frontiers for Israel stand wherever the arm reaches. Power justifies the 'liberation' of the occupied or administered territories of the West Bank and Gaza strip.

The *Shalom Hagalil*, 'Peace for Galilee Operation', is but one of a chain of operations where power was used, but not to secure peace or security, for neither peace nor security was obtained by that operation. Israel is trapped in its own might. As a result, the fact of survival by force puts at risk the quality of survival itself. The basic right of survival in its precious inward validity is incriminated and becomes a *de facto* wrong. The oppressed of yesterday have become the oppressors of today. No wonder a war for peace became a variant of tragedy.

One point must be made clear. The war is unfinished. This is not yet recognized. But the call for peace and understanding is unheeded.

The majority of Palestinians who later became known as the Palestinian refugees have been denied the right to come back to their homeland. But those who remained in what became the state of Israel, who were supposed to be treated equally in accordance with the Israeli Declaration of Independence, which states that all citizens of the new state are to be treated equally regardless of their ethnic or religious background, have suffered and continue to suffer because of an official policy of discrimination.

Perhaps most of you are well informed of the situation, but let me give you a few figures. In 1948 the Arabs numbered 156,000 in the new state of Israel. Today there are 650,000 of us. We have become a nightmare for people like the late Golda Meir, but we say: 'When they beat us on the borders, we beat them in our bedrooms.'

What happened to this community which, by remaining in the land despite all the harassments imposed on us, has won the war that had been lost by the majority? Our villages were ruined. Between 1948 and 1950, 374 villages were completely destroyed. Recently, where the Israelis went into Lebanon, they declared that part of their mission was to protect the Christian community of Lebanon. You should ask the Christian community, the Maronites of the two Arab villages in the north of Israel, Ikrit and Biram, what kind of protection they received after they had been promised during the hostilities of 1948 that in a matter of a week or two they would be able to go back to their villages. They had to sue the government in the high court. They won their case on Christmas Eve 1949. The army went in and levelled those villages. Millions of dunams – a dunam is one-quarter of an acre – were expropriated with the object of Zionizing the Arab-inhabited areas. In 1948, 16.5 dunams were allowed per capita for the Arab minority. Today about 0.5 dunam is allowed. We have no more space to bury our dead in that oasis of Middle East democracy. I am not exaggerating. I live in a town called Nazareth which has become the most crowded town in the country. Sometimes they compare it with the Rhine Valley. But I have been to the Rhine Valley where there is enough space. In the Greek Orthodox Cemetery in Nazareth – and the Greek Orthodox community numbers over 11,000 people – they dig up the graves of those who died ten years ago to bury the newly dead.

This lack of space has effected a change in the life of the community as a whole. Our villages have become rather like underdeveloped hotels. We've changed from being farmers into labourers doing menial jobs. This was also in the mind of those who established the state: any of the *goyim* who stayed were destined to become servants. In 1967, I still remember, a Zionist lady wrote that if the war solved any of her problems, it solved the problem of servants. We are a community greatly discriminated against.

As regards the question of identity, you are not what you are. To say that you are a Palestinian means committing the unpardonable sin. Today this is beginning to change: the word 'Palestine' lives again, through our own efforts.

As for the question of expropriation of land, when we demonstrated against further expropriation in 1976, six of our young people were killed by the army, by the Israel Defence Forces. And we are supposed to be citizens of the state of Israel!

On the question of education a UNESCO report of 1980 says the Palestinians in the world, i.e. outside Israel, rank second only to the Americans in the percentage of university graduates. However, in Israel where we make up 16% of the total population, we represent less than 4% of the university intake. I will use Nazareth, where I come from, as an example. If it were not for the church schools, 7,000 pupils and students would be on the streets, although national legislation says education is compulsory for all below the age of 14, or parents are liable to prosecution.[1] You might think we are subsidized like Aguda-Israel, or private schools in the Jewish sector. We are not.

The same may be said about the medical and other services. Our people live under great pressure and tension. We rank first for deaths from heart problems: 64.6% of all deaths registered in the Nazareth area are caused by heart trouble. These are official statistics.

Regarding primary schools for Arabs, Nazareth is fortunate because it has the church institution in the Arab village. The Minister for Education said in September 1981 that as many as 3,000 more classrooms were needed in the Arab sector – we know the figure should be higher – and that some of the rooms used as classrooms were not good enough for cattle.

We even tried to start a little Arab university or college in Galilee. We were denied this very right. But in 1923 the Jewish community in Palestine, numbering 56,000 people, started the Hebrew University in Jerusalem. Today we number 650,000 and, in 1983, we continue to be denied this very right. We see such a university as a way to equip our people, our young people, for some kind of life which is not mere coexistence, but co-living with our Jewish brothers and sisters.

I would like to elaborate a little on the questions of industrialization and job opportunities. But as I know time is limited, I will merely say that no industrialization has been carried out in any Arab village or town. But in Surat Elite, built on land expropriated from the Arab community of Nazareth, there are already over 100 industries, four of which are among the largest in the country. With regard to jobs, we are last hired but first fired. Hope is becoming hopeless.

The occupied territories present another situation which demands the attention of all peace-loving, concerned people in the world. The human rights of the Arab Palestinians are violated almost daily. Land is confiscated to allow the building of Jewish settlements. Gush Emunim groups are allowed to carry weapons, and sometimes use them against Palestinians demonstrating in defence of their rights to the land, including their mere presence on the land.

Universities are often closed and studies disturbed.

Some 250,000 people have been either detained, arrested or imprisoned since the day of occupation in 1967. The occupied West Bank is referred to as 'Liberated Judaea and Samaria'. Thousands of homes have been demolished, sometimes simply because one member of the family has something to do with, or happened to be a member of, a Palestinian organization.

Mayors have been expelled from office. Some have even been deported. When you visit the occupied territories, it seems as if occupation started only yesterday. Tension is great. The struggle against occupation is unending, human life is continuously endangered. People are shot during strikes, holy places are desecrated. The Camp David Autonomy Plan continues to be completely rejected. Arab labourers are not only exploited but also humiliated.

In conclusion, I submit that avoiding the issue will never solve the problem. It often simply complicates it. Some of our people say that time alone will solve it. In my opinion, this will never bring an end to hostilities. To resort continually to force and violence, as we know, allows violence to breed violence. Additionally, it prevents other means, namely, peaceful means, from having any chance of success. It is not tolerable that there should be no opportunity even to try peaceful means.

Israel must understand that the ultimate security of frontiers lies not in defeated foes but in reconciled neighbours. The dilemma, as we Arab Palestinians see it, raises many questions. What are we to do? Must one people go to outer space? Must one people try to annihilate the other in order to realize its objectives? Is there any way in which both peoples can live together?

I think there is a way to peace. There is a way to peace provided that realities of the conflict and not Israeli-imposed *de facto* situations are recognized by both parties involved in the conflict. The Palestinians' national rights are as much a reality as Israel is a reality.

Peace cannot come through treaties with Egypt, Jordon, Lebanon or Syria. Neither cessation of hostilities, nor a peace treaty with any one Arab country or with all the Arab countries will bring peace to Palestine. It must be realized by all that *the crux of the question is the Palestinian question*. We have the right to self-determination and the right to establish a state on Palestinian soil.

Solving the question at the expense of Jordan, as Mr Sharon would like to do, will never bring peace or understanding. A comprehensive peace in the Middle East demands changes including a change in several laws, by both the Arabs and the Israelis. 'No' to a complete withdrawal from the occupied territories must be changed to 'yes', if those concerned about peace and human life are really sincere. The Zionist 'no' to the right to self-determination for the Palestinians and the right to choose their legitimate representation must be changed to agreement to these elemental human rights.

I do not claim to be speaking on behalf of either party, but I am of the opinion that the day should come when the two communities will realize that they can supplement and complement each other. We have both lived in peace and in harmony for many generations.

I don't want to reflect on the involvement of the superpowers in the area. We all know about it. But I dare dream, as Martin Luther King used to dream, of a day when the two states become some kind of confederation. Today people speak of a confederation between Palestine-to-be and Jordan. I am of the opinion that there are better chances for a confederation between Israel and Palestine. There are 650,000 Palestinians in Israel, and 1.2 million Palestinians in the occupied territories. The ultimate outcome could be what many people have spoken of and continue to advocate, and perhaps we should promote, a bi-national state within the geographic boundaries of geographic Palestine.

It was Jesus of Nazareth who said, 'Blessed are the peacemakers for they shall be called the children of God.' Vice versa, only the children of God can make peace. The children of men may be able to talk peace, perhaps love peace, like Mr Begin. He loves another piece of land somewhere in the Middle East.

Notes

1. Dr Sami Khalil Mar'i, *Education, Culture and Identity among Palestinians in Israel* (EAFORD, London, 1984).

14. Israel's Zionist Society: Consequences for Internal Opposition and the Necessity for External Intervention

Dr Uri Davis

Israeli Jewish society identifies itself, and is correctly recognized, as a Zionist society, morally, politically and technically.

• Morally, in that the body of the Israeli Jewish society is predicated upon the preposterous claim that anti-Semitism is not a socially and politically manufactured phenomenon to be understood and combated historically, but, rather, that anti-Semitism is an essential aspect of non-Jewish human nature, and in consequence, Jews can never hope to achieve equality of rights as religious or cultural minorities in Gentile societies.

In the framework of Zionist moral perceptions, every Gentile must be classified, cannot but be classified, as a covert or overt anti-Semite. An enlightened Gentile is a Gentile who is aware of his or her irreducible anti-Semitism, and is thus led to assist the Zionist political organization in the achievement of the Zionist solution to the problem of anti-Semitism on a principled basis. As Hannah Arendt documents in her classic report *Eichmann in Jerusalem*, Adolf Eichmann, for instance, viewed himself as such a principled Gentile supporter of Zionism.[1]

• Politically, in that the Zionist political solution to the problem of anti-Semitism is predicated upon two correlative elements: 1) the mobilization of Jewish communities throughout the world towards immigration to Palestine; 2) the establishment of a Jewish state in Palestine, namely the state of Israel, and the mobilization of moral and material support in Jewish communities throughout the world for the continued existence of the state of Israel as a Jewish state.

The Zionist movement since its establishment as a political organization, the World Zionist Organization, at the first Zionist Congress in Basle in 1897, has been historically divided. The three mainstream Zionist political divisions inside the World Zionist Organization and, since 1948, in parallel inside the state of Israel, are Labour Zionism, Revisionist Zionism and Religious Zionism. In the course of Zionist history profound differences of opinion and judgement developed among those three mainstream Zionist divisions as to the desired scope of the Zionist project in Palestine at any given period of time; the desired strategy for colonization of Palestine and, since 1948, the desired boundaries for the Jewish state; the desired form of social organization for Jewish society in Palestine and the desired nature of the political regime of the state of Israel. But underpinning all mainstream Zionist divisions and political parties, there has been throughout Zionist history a shared political principle formalized above in its two correlative elements. It is this principle that defines the boundary of the Zionist political domain and underpins all World Zionist Organization political programmes.

Every Jewish citizen of the state of Israel is fully aware and completely informed of the basic realities underpinning his or her political existence as a Jewish citizen of the Jewish state and the nature of the Palestinian Arab resistance. To quote one of Israel's leading citizens, the late Moshe Dayan:

> Let us not today fling accusations at the [Palestinian Arab] murderers. Who are we that we should argue against their hatred? For eight years now they sit in their refugee camps in Gaza, and before their very eyes, we turn into our homestead the land and the villages in which they and their forefathers have lived. We are a generation of settlers, and without the steel helmet and the cannon we cannot plant a tree and build a home. Let us not shrink back when we see the hatred fermenting and filling the lives of hundreds of thousands of Arabs, who sit all around us. Let us not avert our gaze, so that our hand shall not slip. This is the fate of our generation, the choice of our life – to be prepared and armed, strong and tough – or otherwise, the sword will slip from our fist, and our life will be snuffed out.[2]

And again:

> Jewish villages were built in the place of Arab villages. You do not even know the names of these Arab villages, and I don't blame you, because these geography books no longer exist; not only do the books not exist, the Arab villages are not there either. Nahalal [Dayan's own village] arose in the place of Mahalul, Kibbutz Gevat – in the place of Jibta, Kibbutz Sarid – in the place of Haneifs and Kefar Yehoshua – in the place of Tell Shaman. There is not one single place built in this country that did not have a former Arab population.[3]

• It is a Zionist society technically, in that the legal structure and the routine of everyday life of Israeli Jewish society are determined in every domain by the apartheid distinction of 'Jew' versus 'non-Jew', both through the constitutional framework of the World Zionist Organization and its various executive bodies such as the Jewish Agency for the Land of Israel (JA) and the Jewish National Fund (JNF), and, since 1948, through the legislation of the Israeli Knesset, which in the key areas of immigration and settlement is directed to give legal garb in Israel to the constitutional principles of the World Zionist Organization.

Thus Article 3(d) and (e) of the constitution of the Jewish Agency stipulate:

> Land is to be acquired as Jewish property and . . . the title of the lands acquired is to be taken in the name of the JNF to the end that the same

> shall be held the inalienable property of the Jewish people. The Agency shall promote agricultural colonization based on Jewish Labour, and in all works or undertaking carried out or furthered by the Agency, it shall be deemed to be a matter of principle that Jewish labour shall be employed.

Similarly, Article 3, Subclause 1 of the Memorandum of Association of the Keren Kayemeth Leisrael (JNF) Ltd, as incorporated in the United Kingdom in 1907, defines the primary object of the company:

> To purchase, take on lease or in exchange, or otherwise acquire any lands, forests, rights of possession and other rights, easements and other immovable property in the prescribed region (which expression shall in this Memorandum mean Palestine, Syria, and other parts of Turkey in Asia and the Peninsula of Sinai) or any part thereof, for the purpose of settling Jews on such lands.

In parallel, since 1948, these constitutional Zionist principles have been legislated into Israeli law. Thus, for instance, Article 3(a) of the Memorandum of Association of the Keren Kayemeth Leisrael (JNF) as incorporated in Israel in 1954, following the passage in the Knesset of the Keren Kayemeth Leisrael (JNF) Law 1953, similarly defines the primary object of the Israeli company:

> To purchase, acquire on lease or in exchange [etc. . . .] in the prescribed region (which expression shall in this Memorandum mean the State of Israel in any area within the jurisdiction of the Government of Israel) or any part thereof for the purpose of settling Jews on such lands and properties.

Israeli legislation directed to institutionalize in terms of Israeli law the constitutional principles of the World Zionist Organization was begun immediately after the 1948 war and the conclusion of armistice agreements between the newly established state of Israel and its neighbouring Arab countries in 1949. The key pieces of legislation in this regard are listed below. Particular attention will be given in this paper to the first two pieces of legislation, the Law of Return and the Absentees' Property Law both passed by the Knesset in 1950, the first year after the 1948–49 war.

1950	Law of Return
	Absentees' Property Law
	Development Authority Law
1952	World Zionist Organization-Jewish Agency Status Law
1953	Keren Kayemeth Leisrael (Jewish National Fund) Law
	Land Acquisition (Validations of Acts and Compensation) Law
1954	Covenant between the Government of Israel and the Zionist Executive, also known as the Executive of the Jewish Agency for the Land of Israel
1958	Prescription Law

1960	Basic Law: Israel Lands Israel Lands Law Israel Lands Administration Law
1961	Covenant between the Government of Israel and the National Fund
1967	Agricultural Settlement (Restriction on Use of Agricultural Land and Water) Law
1980	Lands (Allocation of Rights to Foreigners) Law

The laws listed above were legislated *in addition* to the unlimited powers of requisition of lands and property which are vested with the Israeli authorities under the various Defence (Emergency) Regulations 1945 and Ordinances which have been in force throughout, from 1948-49 to the present. These are, *inter alia*: Defence (Emergency) Regulations, 1945; Emergency (Security Zones) Regulations, 1949; Requisitioning of Property in Times of Emergency Law, 1949; Emergency Regulations (Cultivation of Waste Lands) Ordinance, 1949.

It is through these mechanisms that an all-encompassing apartheid system was legislated in Israel, although the Israeli legislator did face one major legal-technical difficulty. Note, for instance, the introductory comments of Mr Zerah Wahrhaftig, then Minister of Religious Affairs and chairman of the Knesset Constitution, Law and Justice Committee, when presenting the Basic Law: Israel Lands to the Knesset:

> What is it that we want? We want something that is difficult to define. We want to make clear that the Land of Israel belongs to the people of Israel. The 'people of Israel' is a concept that is broader than that of the 'people resident in Zion', because the people of Israel live throughout the world. On the other hand, every law that is passed is for the benefit of all the residents of the State and all the residents of the state also include people who do not belong to the people of Israel. . .. [Knesset member] Meridor was wrong when he said that there is no legal innovation in the law. There is therein a very significant legal innovation; we are giving legal garb to the Memorandum of Association of the JNF. . . . As for the JNF, the legal innovation is enormous: it gives legal garb to a matter that thus far was incorporated only in the JNF Memorandum.[4]

And thus, through this 'enormous legal innovation', it was made possible in the state of Israel to prohibit non-Jews, and in the first instance the Palestinian Arab native population of the country, from purchase or lease of 92.4% of pre-1967 Israeli territory.[5] The same legal structures of apartheid obtain in the domain of access to water resources, and, in fact, in all domains of everyday life under Israeli rule. At all key junctions that determine everyday life and circumstances of living for the body of the inhabitants under Israeli rule, the Israeli legislature follows the same pattern of passing and contracting covenants that codify as Israeli law enforced by the legislative, police and military machinery of the state of Israel, the constitutional principles of the World Zionist Organization.

In order to understand in full the consequences of all this for Israel's internal opposition it is important to understand that under Israeli law, in so far as property rights are concerned, the Palestinian Arab does not exist. He or she is defined out of existence as an 'absentee'. As noted above, in 1950, immediately following the 1948–49 war, the Knesset legislated the two most important laws in the state of Israel to date: the Law of Return and the Absentees' Property Law. Through the Law of Return the state of Israel guarantees for any Jew throughout the world the right of immigration and settlement.[6] Through the Absentees' Property Law the state of Israel guarantees that the overwhelming majority of the Palestinian Arab residents of the territories which fell under Israeli sovereignty in consequence of the 1948–49 war, both refugees outside the pre-1967 borders of the state or citizens inside its pre-1967 borders, are denied their rights to property in Israel. In other words: in order to create the physical space for the Jew the property rights of the Arab must be denied.

In so far as rights to property are concerned, the Israeli legislator does not recognize the Palestinian Arab person as a Palestinian, nor, for that matter, does he recognize him or her as a refugee. As a consequence of the 1948–49 war approximately 750,000 of the total 900,000 Palestinian Arab residents of the territories which subsequently came under Israeli rule were forcibly expelled and displaced from their homes and properties, and have since become refugees outside the borders of the newly established state. The refugees outside *and* the majority of the Palestinian Arabs who remained under Israeli rule and subsequently became Israeli citizens are classified under the terms of the Absentees' Property Law (1950) as 'absentees', and as such they are denied all rights to their properties.[7] These massive rural and urban properties, the majority of the lands inside the state of Israel, were vested following the passage of the said Absentees' Property Law with the Custodian for Absentees' Property and were moved from the Custodian to exclusive Jewish settlement and development.[8] Since 1948 the official legal status of the majority of the Palestinian Arabs under Israeli rule is that of 'present absentees'. They are present as Israeli citizens, but they are absent in so far as their rights to their properties are concerned. In order for the Jew to legally 'return', the Palestinian Arab has to be legislated out of existence as 'absent'.

Yet no Israeli Zionist opposition can accept the Palestinian Arab presence inside the Jewish state. It can accept the Arab presence alongside the state of Israel (Peace Now). It can accept the Palestinian Arab presence alongside the state of Israel (the Israeli Council for Israeli Palestinian Peace). But it cannot accept the reconstitution of Palestinian Arab individual and collective social, political and national rights inside the state of Israel, since this, it would be correctly argued, is tantamount to the dismantling of the state of Israel as a Jewish state and the transformation of Israel back into Palestine.

The essence of the Palestinian resistance movement, its driving force and the fountain of its morality, is the struggle to re-establish Palestinian presence in those parts of Palestine from which the Palestinian Arab is expelled. The justice of the Palestinian resistance is rooted in its commitment to implement the return of the Palestinian Arab refugees and the rehabilitation of their individual and collective national life in all parts of their homeland Palestine out of which they are excluded as 'absentees'. The majority of the Palestinian Arab refugees cannot return to their original homes and lands. These homes no longer exist, and where they do exist they are inhabited by Jewish families.

The Palestinian Arab village of Sheikh Muannas has been levelled under the car parks and buildings of the University of Tel Aviv. The Palestinian struggle for national liberation does not aim to pull down the University of Tel Aviv and reconstruct the pre-1948 Palestinian Arab village of Sheikh Muannas. The Palestinian struggle rightly aims to alter the regional and international balance of power in order to secure that the Palestinian Arab refugees of Sheikh Muannas are able to rehabilitate their lives as close as possible to their original homes. In the case of Sheikh Muannas, this is likely to be in the very attractive residential quarters of Ramat Aviv and Afeqah near Tel Aviv University. And indeed, that is how it should be.

The Israeli-Palestinian conflict is in its fundamental aspects a conflict between a settler-colonial state and the national native resistance. As such it is polarized very much like similar conflicts that have developed since World War I throughout the colonial periphery of the Western world. Given the priorities of settler-colonial societies, and given the individual and corporate motivation which led to their formation in the first instance, all settler-colonial societies are structured around, and predicated upon, the necessity to exclude the native population from equal participation in the colonial domain. Since the colonial project is inconsistent with the universal principle of equality of rights for all, the native population as a whole cannot, by the definition of the elementary terms of the colonial project, be given equal rights in the colonial realm. The granting of equality of rights to all, both the settler *and* the excluded native, must therefore invariably entail, as it has in fact historically done, the dismantling of the colonial legal and political structures.

In the framework of Zionist political perceptions all Zionist parties are aligned in their support, either by deliberate design or *post factum*, by way of endorsing the *faits accomplis* established in the course of the 1948–49 war, for the expulsion, evacuation and transfer of the mass of the Palestinian Arab society out of the territories of pre-1967 Israel. This Zionist consensus is expressed lucidly by one of the persons central to the organization of the Zionist colonization project, the late Joseph Weitz, deputy chairman of the Board of Directors of the Jewish National Fund, in his *Diaries*, published in Hebrew in Israel in 1965. On 19 December 1940 he wrote:

> After the [Second World] war the question of the land of Israel and the question of the Jews would be raised beyond the framework of 'development'. Amongst ourselves, *it must be clear that there is no room for both peoples in this country*. No 'development' will bring us closer to our aim, to be an independent people in this small country.

> If the Arabs leave the country, it will be broad and wide-open for us. And if the Arabs stay, the country will remain narrow and miserable. When the War is over and the English have won, and when the judges sit on the throne of Law, our people must bring their petitions and their claim before them; and the only solution is Eretz Israel [the land of Israel], or at least Western Eretz Israel, *without Arabs. There is no room for compromise on this point*! The Zionist enterprise so far, in terms of preparing the ground and paving the way for the creation of the Hebrew State in the land of Israel, has been fine and good in its own time, and could do with 'land-buying' – but this will not bring about the State of Israel; that must come all at once, in the manner of a Salvation (this is the secret of the Messianic idea); and there is no way besides transferring the Arabs from here to the neighbouring countries, *to transfer them all*, except maybe for Bethlehem, Nazareth and Old Jerusalem, *we must not leave a single village, not a single tribe*. And the transfer must be directed to Iraq, to Syria, and even to Transjordan. For that purpose we'll find money, and a lot of money. And only with such a transfer will the country be able to absorb millions of our brothers, and the Jewish question shall be solved, once and for all. There is no other way out. (Emphasis added)[9]

Eight years later, in the framework of the 1948–49 war, Weitz and his colleagues at the top echelons of the Zionist and subsequently Israeli political hierarchy had the opportunity to put this design into effect. Thus on 18 May 1948 Weitz enters the following report of his conversation with Moshe Shertok (later Sharett), Israel's first Minister of Foreign Affairs:

> Transfer – *post factum*; should we do something so as to transform the exodus of the Arabs from the country into a fact, so that they return no more? . . . His [Shertok's] answer: he blesses any initiative in this matter. His opinion is also that we must act in such a way as to transform the exodus of the Arabs into an established fact.[10]

And later that year, he records his reflections following a visit to an Arab village in the process of being razed to the ground by tractors:

> I went to visit the village of Mi'ar. Three tractors are completing its destruction. I was surprised; nothing in me moved at the sight of the destruction. No regret and no hate, as though this was the way the world goes. So we want to feel good in this world, and not in some world to come. We simply want to live, and the inhabitants of those mud-houses did not want us to exist here. They not only aspire to dominate us, they also wanted to exterminate us. And what is interesting – this is the opinion of all our boys, from one end to the other.[11]

In consequence of this Zionist consensus, when, following the 1967 war, the remaining parts of Palestine, namely, the West Bank and the Gaza strip, came under Israeli occupation, the critical discussion inside the World Zionist Organization and among the various Zionist parties inside the state of Israel concentrated on the question of how much, if any, of the newly acquired occupied territories could be incorporated into the Jewish state given the regional and international balance of power at any given stage. The main division in this discussion is familiar and well documented.[12]

It is important to underline, however, that the critical subject of Zionist consensus, the area where the continued existence of the state of Israel is critically tested, is not the post-1967 occupied territories of the Sinai peninsula, the Gaza strip, the West Bank, the Golan Heights and southern Lebanon, but rather the pre-1967 occupied territories conventionally referred to as the state of Israel proper.

It cannot be sufficiently emphasized that it is possible to remain inside, though very much at the margin of, the Zionist realm as opposition calling for unconditional withdrawal from all post-1967 occupied territories, including East Jerusalem. There have been, and there are, Zionist individuals and political parties who argue that given the regional and international balance of power the only rational prospects for the consolidation and continued existence of Israel as a Jewish state are on the basis of Israel's pre-1967 borders. Furthermore, it is possible to remain inside, though very much at the margin of, the Zionist realm, as opposition calling for unconditional recognition of the PLO as sole legitimate representative of the Palestinian Arab people and the right of self-determination of the Palestinian Arab people in a sovereign independent PLO-administered state *alongside* the state of Israel in its pre-1967 borders. In the view of this Zionist opposition, given the regional and international balance of power, including the emergence of the Palestine Liberation Organization and the mobilization of the Palestinian people in armed resistance against Israel since 1965, such an alternative political programme is the only long-term guarantee for the continued existence of the state of Israel as a Jewish state. Prominent among these individual Zionist opposition members are Professor Yeshaayahu Leibowitz, an orthodox religious Zionist, and Uri Avneri, a secular Zionist and former member of the pre-1948 Zionist underground, the National Military Organization (Irgun) led at the time by Menachem Begin, subsequently Prime Minister of the state of Israel.

In order to understand the full significance of all this for Israel's internal opposition it is important to recognize the impact of the 1982 Lebanon war on the Israeli Jewish public.

In many ways, Lebanon is Israel's Vietnam, and indeed, the mass opposition inside Israeli Jewish society to the continued involvement of Israel in Lebanon has developed, very much like the mass opposition in the US to the continued American involvement in Vietnam in the late 1960s and early 1970s, in the wake of the public recognition that the Lebanon war has failed to achieve its stated political objects; that the Israeli army in Lebanon is sinking into a quagmire; and that Israeli casualties are being sacrificed 'in vain' for a war that must be lost and cannot be redeemed.

There is no doubt that mass Israeli Jewish opposition to the war mounted some four weeks after the commencement of the war when it became evident that the Israeli army would be unable to destroy the PLO, and that the joint resistance of the PLO and the Lebanese national forces achieved what was thought in Israel to be virtually impossible, namely, successful armed confrontation over a protracted period of time against the Israeli army, the strongest military machine in the Middle East and the sixth most powerful army in the world.

The important distinction between Israel's Lebanon and America's Vietnam, however, is that the political aim and just cause of the Vietcong were to secure the withdrawal of all US troops from Vietnam - not to introduce the Vietcong to New York. The political aim and just cause of the PLO, on the other hand, are to secure the withdrawal of all Israeli troops from Lebanon as a first step towards the liberation of Palestine and the introduction of the Palestine Liberation Organization into all parts of Palestine, including Tel Aviv.

It is elementary that so long as the Palestinian Arab is excluded from his or her homeland as 'absentee', he or she is likely, and is right, to force or make space for his or her presence, if necessary with the explosive and the gun. Of the half-million people who marched in the streets of Tel Aviv against the Israeli-perpetrated and Falange-executed massacres of Sabra and Chatilla, only few would support the struggle of the survivors of the massacres and their descendants to reconstitute and rehabilitate their lives and the lives of their families in their neighbourhood in Tel Aviv.

Given the above, it must be clear to all concerned that all Zionist individuals and political organizations will unite and transcend all divisions of value judgement and political programme at one critical point: the point of the demand of the Palestinian Arab refugees of 1948 for return and repatriation in all parts of their homeland Palestine including Acre, Haifa, Jaffa and Beer Sheba. There can be marked political-programmatic divisions inside the Zionist realm as to the desired or power-politically feasible boundaries of the Jewish state. There is, however, complete consensus, uniting all Zionist individuals and parties, that inside the Jewish state, small or big, the universal principle of equality of rights for all, and specifically equality of rights between the Israeli Jewish settler and the Palestinian Arab native, cannot apply, since if applied, the state of Israel would be eliminated as a Jewish state. The Zionist claims the right of return for all Jewish communities throughout the world to the ancient Jewish homeland of Palestine after almost two millennia of dispersion and exile, but he cannot recognize the right of the Palestinian Arab communities throughout the world to the same right, after less than 50 years of the Israeli-manufactured dispersion of 1948, since if that right is recognized, there will be no part of Palestine that will remain exclusively Jewish, not even the greater metropolitan area of Tel Aviv. The late Golda Meir, as Prime Minister at the zenith of Israeli regional and international power-political achievement, reflected the logic of the Zionist colonial endeavour in Palestine in her resounding statement to the London *Sunday Times*:

> There was no such thing as Palestinians. It was not as though there was a Palestinian people in Palestine considering itself as a Palestinian people and we came and threw them out and took their country away from them. They did not exist.[13]

Almost a decade later, reflecting the questionable Israeli military performance in the 1973 war and the beginning of the decline of Israel's power position regionally and internationally, Menachem Begin, then Israel's Prime Minister, was compelled to concede in the framework of the 1978 US-negotiated Camp David Accords recognition of 'The legitimate rights of the Palestinian people and their just requirements'.[14]

The Camp David Agreements are correctly assessed as a major victory for Prime Minister Menachem Begin. Under the terms of these agreements the legitimate rights of the Palestinian people and their just requirements are translated into a political programme for a Palestinian bantustan completely consistent with Menachem Begin's conceptualization of the status of the Palestinian Arab people as the 'Arabs of the Land of Israel'. Yet, this victory was not achieved painlessly. It was achieved at the cost of two important concessions, first-time violations of the two fundamental principles underlying Zionist political perception and practice: 1) the introduction into the Zionist political discourse of a political reference to the Palestinian Arab people; 2) the acceptance that it is possible for a sovereign Israeli government to dismantle Jewish settlements not in consequence of a surrender agreement following military defeat, but as part of a political-diplomatic process, reflecting the gradual changes of Israel's regional and international power-political position.

The Palestine Liberation Organization was completely correct to reject outright and without qualification the Camp David framework. The PLO political programme of a secular democratic Palestine for all of its inhabitants, Jewish settlers and the entire Palestinian Arab people alike, is not only just, and hence winnable, but is the only programme that can, and will, lead the PLO to victory. Intelligent people such as Uri Avneri, at the margin of the Zionist consensus, recognize, and, I suspect, accept, this analysis. They therefore offer today: outright and unconditional withdrawal from all the territories occupied by Israel in 1967; outright and unconditional recognition of the PLO as the sole legitimate representative of the Palestinian people; outright and unconditional establishment of an independent sovereign Palestinian Arab state under PLO administration: this offer is an attempt to salvage for the Zionist vision what they judge can be salvaged, given the regional and international rise of the PLO and the correlative decline of the state of Israel, namely, an attempt to salvage a 'small' Jewish state in its pre-1967 boundaries on the basis of a deal with the Palestine resistance whereby the Palestine Liberation Organization will abandon its struggle to implement the right of all Palestinian Arab refugees to return and be rehabilitated in all parts of their homeland Palestine. The Zionist party that most clearly represents this line of analysis is the now virtually defunct Sheli party, whose leadership includes Ariyeh (Liyuva) Eliav, Dr General (Reserves) Matityahu Peled, as well as Uri Avneri. The Sheli political platform reads, *inter alia*, as follows:

> *A. Political Independence and the Road to Peace*
> *Israel and Zionism*
> Zionism is the national liberation movement of the Jewish people. It expresses its aspiration to live and flourish among the family of nations, to sustain its own political sovereignty in Eretz Israel and develop its own language and culture. The *Sheli* movement considers itself a full participant in the Zionist vision.
>
> The Zionism of the *Sheli* movement is identical with the striving for economic, social and political equality and with the struggle for peace with the Arab nationalist movement. This struggle is founded on the recognition that the Palestinian-Arab people have an equal right to that of the Jewish people for national self-determination in the country. The *Sheli* camp fights the nationalist conservative Zionist forces and against the forces which sustain the social gap.
>
> The *Sheli* movement rejects the slander that claims that Zionism, by its essence, aims to dominate another people, dispossess it and deny its rights. The nationalist current in Zionism feeds this slander because it is unwilling to recognize the right of the Palestinian-Arab people to self-determination as well. This current is mainly represented by the Likud parties, Gush Emunim, and circles in the Democratic Party, the National Religious Party and the Labour Party.
>
> The *Sheli* movement will struggle to realize the following principles and carry out the following tasks:
>
> *Israeli Peace Policy*
> The central objective of the Israeli foreign and security policy is the termination of the Israeli–Arab conflict and the establishment of a full and lasting peace settlement between Israel and its Arab neighbours, including the Palestinian-Arab people. In order to achieve this objective Israel must adopt a policy that does not entail extremist national positions in both the Arab and the Israeli camps. It must make use of every opening of hope in the wall of the Arab argument and respond with peace initiatives.
>
> According to the *Sheli* platform, Israel's peace initiatives must be based on the following principles:
>
> - A large Jewish majority.
> - Withdrawal from 'the territories which fell into [Israeli] hands in the Six Day War, with the exception of slight border adjustments, agreed by the parties concerned'.
> - Arab recognition of Israel.
> - Israel's recognition of the right of self-determination of the Palestinian-Arab people.

- Should the Palestinians so demand, negotiations will be held with the PLO on the basis of mutual recognition.
- The Geneva Conference could be the framework in which the peace conference will begin to act.
- All the territories out of which Israel withdraws will be demilitarized.
- *The problem of the Palestinian refugees will be solved in the main through their rehabilitation in the Palestinian state, should the Palestinian people choose to establish this state.*
- Israel will terminate immediately and unconditionally all Jewish settlement, urban and rural, 'in all the administered territories'. The existing settlements will be considered as part of the temporary reality in the territories, and Israel will not permit that they obstruct the peace process. (emphasis added)[15]

Throughout Zionist history, 'moderate' Zionist individuals and organizations, from Brit Shalom (Covenant of Peace) to Shalom Akhshav (Peace Now), from Martin Buber to Yeshaayahu Leibowitz, were invariably marginalized because of their inability to assess critically the basic Zionist political-programmatic principles; or in international legal terms, because of their predicating their morality and political-programmatic advocacy on a double standard: acceptance of UN Assembly resolution no. 181 (II) of 29 November 1947 recommending the partition of Palestine into two states, a Jewish state and an Arab state, on the one hand, and rejection of UN General Assembly resolution no. 194 (III) of 11 December 1948, recalled annually by the General Assembly, urging the return of all Palestinian refugees to their homes, on the other.

Every Israeli citizen knows, together with Moshe Dayan, that there is not one single place in this country that did not have a former Arab population. Every Israeli citizen knows, together with the leading Israeli publicist Yeshaayahu Ben Porat, that 'there is no Zionist settlement, and there is no Jewish state without displacing Arabs, and without confiscating lands and fencing them off'.[16]

Every Israeli Jew knows that the Palestinian 'absentee' is at the foundation and the centre of his or her presence in Palestine. Every Israeli Jew knows that while the Palestinian 'absentees' are excluded from any part of their homeland Palestine they are likely to place a bomb in the place from which they have been excluded, and that they will be right to do so. Hence the popular and deep-seated Zionist conviction that one can never trust the Arab; that the Arab will invariably stab his or her benefactor in the back; that given one finger the Arab will grab the entire hand; that the only good Arab is a dead Arab. Since the Palestinian Arab 'absentees' have forced their presence on the predominantly Zionist Israeli Jewish society through the process of armed struggle and the emergence of the Palestine Liberation Organization as the sole legitimate representative of the Palestinian people, mainstream Zionism is committed to attempt at any cost to pound the Palestinian back into the oblivion of 'absentee' existence.

Thus 'moderate' Zionist opposition inside the World Zionist Organization and inside Israeli Jewish society is paralysed in a double bind: as Zionists they predicate their moral and political-programmatic position on cultivated deception regarding the essential moral, political and technical terms of the Zionist colonial enterprise in Palestine. Also, as Zionists they can never align themselves with the struggle for a joint society of Jews and Arabs on the basis of complete equality of human, civil and national rights. This is the root reason why, in the final analysis, 'moderate' Zionist opposition, Labour Zionist or otherwise, will not be able to unseat the present Revisionist Zionist government.

Settler-colonial projects can be refined: note the legal distinctions between 'White', 'Coloured', 'Indian' and 'Black', and the development of the bantustans and multiple chamber parliamentary representation in the Republic of South Africa. But by its basic terms of reference, the colonial project cannot be reformed. In the face of mounting native resistance the polarization invariably leads to the dismantling of the legal settler-colonial structures. French Algeria was dismantled in 1962 and transformed into the independent Democratic and Popular Republic of Algeria. Rhodesia was dismantled in 1979 and transformed into the independent Republic of Zimbabwe and there is little doubt that analogous developments will determine the course of events in Palestine and South Africa. Confronted by the Palestinian national resistance, the Jewish state of Israel will be transformed into Palestine, and confronted with the African national resistance the white-supremacy state of South Africa will be transformed into Azania.

Settler-colonial societies can develop and consolidate in the face of native popular opposition only if aided and protected by imperial support. At the point when, in the face of native national resistance, the material and political costs of this support are pushed up to levels that are deemed by the imperial power to be no longer acceptable, the settler society or the settler state will be duly abandoned and the transformation of the disputed territory into an independent native state based on the principle of equality of rights to all of its inhabitants, the excluded native population together with the settler population, will be promptly effected and internationally sanctioned.

The conclusion of this presentation is that, given the nature of the Israeli polity as an exclusively Jewish state as it unfolds in its concrete historical context, internal reform is unlikely. Having posited the question of what made it happen, we must correlatively posit, and answer, the question of what can prevent it from happening again. Given my presentation of the question, the answer follows immediately. Internal opposition inside Israeli Jewish society cannot and will not constitute a barrier. The liberal humanist, Communist, socialist and anti-Zionist organizations and individuals inside Israeli Jewish society are increasingly marginalized over time rather than otherwise. If Mr Begin or his likely successors, Shamir, Sharon and Company are elected as Israel's future Prime Ministers it will be not in spite of but because of their role in orchestrating and organizing the Sabra and Chatilla massacres. The mainstream of the Israeli Jewish population has been systematically debilitated, through Hebrew schooling and through the extra-curricular media's political education, to the point of outright barbarity. Israeli Jewish society is subject to a process of escalating Nazification as a result of which the majority of the Israeli Jewish oriental population and much of the European Jewish population constitute the solid base of support for the Revisionist and National Religious Zionist parties. Opposition and protest are confined largely to the portion of the European Jewish population which constitutes the mainstay of Labour Zionism. It is obvious to all who have eyes to see that the Labour Zionist tradition is set on a course of irreversible decline and disintegration.

All this leads me to conclude that any hopes that reform inside Israel will be brought about by internal opposition inside the Israeli Jewish society to the present Revisionist Zionist Likud government are completely misplaced and are founded on cultivated ignorance regarding Zionist morality and Zionist history. The political situation inside Israel today is completely analogous to the political situation in Germany in the period 1933-39, after the rise to power of the National Socialist (Nazi) Party in Germany and before the outbreak of World War II. In this context I wish to make completely clear that I am not saying the Palestinian Arabs are being murdered in Israeli gas chambers. Nor am I saying that it is likely that Palestinian Arabs will be murdered in the future in Israeli gas chambers. What I am saying is that the situation of the Palestinian Arab population under Israeli rule today is completely analogous to the situation of the Jewish population under Nazi rule between the proclamation of the 1935 Nuremberg Laws and prior to the outbreak of World War II in 1939. The political climate in Israel today is determined by Prime Minister Menachem Begin's reference to the Palestinians as 'two legged animals'; he has been joined by his Minister of Defence Ariel Sharon instructing his officers to 'tear off the balls' of Palestinian Arab 'rioters' in the West Bank.[17] Almost 1.5 million Palestinian Arab people have been living under Israeli military occupation since 1967, for over 15 years. They are denied Israeli citizenship. They are denied their rights to land and property.[18] They are denied civilian rights.[19] They are subject to mass arrests in Israeli gaols and detention centres.[20] They are interned in the Ansar concentration camp, located in the most recently acquired Israeli occupied territory, South Lebanon.[21] They are massacred in Sabra and Chatilla.[22] It is these developments which led Professor Yeshaayahu Leibowitz to repeat the warning and the condemnation first voiced by one of Israel's leading anti-Zionist and human rights campaigners Professor Israel Shahak against the Nazification of the state of Israel, against Israel's 'Judeo-Nazi mentality'.[23]

There are certain conclusions that we must draw from our retrospective analysis of the third Reich. Had the Allied forces declared an international economic and political boycott of Nazi Germany in 1936 following the promulgation of the Nuremberg Laws of 1935 instead of sanctioning the Nazi regime through participation in the Olympic Games in Berlin in 1936, much bloodshed and much suffering would have been avoided. Had the

Allied forces declared war on Germany in 1938 instead of sanctioning the annexation of the Sudetenland with the Munich Peace Treaty, much bloodshed and much suffering would have been avoided.

The member-states of the Arab League are situated *vis-à-vis* Israel today very much as the majority of the European states were *vis-à-vis* Nazi Germany. Beirut is not the first Arab capital to be occupied by Israel. The first Arab capital to be occupied by Israel was Jerusalem. Beirut was the second. We should not allow Amman to become the third.

From this platform I wish to raise the call to veterans of the anti-Nazi resistance movement, some of whom play today a key role in the formation of enlightened public opinion throughout the world. From this platform I wish to raise a call to persons such as Willy Brandt and Bruno Kreisky: do not abandon your responsibility to Israeli Jewish society. Mobilize publicly, and urge every Israeli Jewish individual to follow the example you gave during World War II and declare himself or herself an ally of the PLO and a traitor to Zionist philosophy and practice. I wish to call upon all persons such as Willy Brandt and Bruno Kreisky to stand up and lend their reputation to helping the Israeli Jewish individual to face up to the only moral option available for him or her today: to join hands with the Palestinian Arab in an effort to defeat the state of Israel, and then return with the victorious Palestinian Arabs to their homeland Palestine, and assist in the reconstruction of the humanity of their own people in the framework of a new social order where all Palestinian Arabs (resident and refugees) and all Palestinian (formerly Israeli) Jews will live as equal citizens under Palestinian law.

I am a secular Jew, *kofer ba-Iqar*, an infidel, a person whose relation to his Jewish heritage is cultural and sentimental, not religious. I am not religiously Jewish in the technical sense of adhering to the 613 *mitzvot* (precepts) as a way of life. Nor am I religiously Jewish in the deistic sense of the term, in the sense of having experience or faith in the existence of God. I am Jewish in the cultural sense, in the sense of having been thrown into the world in a particular geographical and cultural location: born into Jewish society in Palestine and raised and educated under the Israeli regime. I am completely confident of my Jewish identity and the historicity of my particular point of entry into human society, in that, as far as I can judge, my hatred of hypocrisy has assisted me in always assessing critically my cultural and sentimental affiliation in the light of universal conscience.

Judaism must be contrasted with Zionism, and it is incumbent upon all of us to combat the persistent attempts by Zionists and Zionist apologists to reduce, identify or predicate Judaism and Zionism. But in this context, I join my comrade and teacher Professor Israel Shahak in condemning mainstream orthodox Judaism and calling for a radical reform of Jewish orthodoxy in the light of the universal secular values of humanism as proclaimed, for instance, by the French Revolution: freedom, equality and fraternity. Hence my commitment to the secular constitutional principle of separation of religion from the state. Hence my support for the political programme of the PLO, which aims to replace the Jewish state of Israel with a secular and democratic Palestine. It is at this point, the point of opposition to Zionism on the basis of separation of religion from the state, that the struggle of the PLO meets and provides a framework to our struggle as secular Jews, as Reform Jews or as Orthodox Jews.[24] There is little doubt in my mind that the political programme of the PLO as formalized in the concept of a secular democratic state is the most important contribution to the debate on Palestine since 1948.[25] And it is in this context that I wish to declare and share a vision. I have a vision of seeing the PLO develop further to the point where it can publish the text of its National Covenant as an advertisement in all major newspapers in the West without apology or moral sophistry. I have a vision of seeing a Palestine National Covenant reformed in terms that every decent human being could support and that would in principle allow every Jewish person in Palestine with an Israeli passport who supports the objectives of the Palestinian resistance of liberating Palestine from Zionism to become a member of the PLO. I have a vision of seeing the PLO announce its intention to guarantee constitutionally that every holder of an Israeli passport, Arab or Jew, would be entitled after the victory of the Palestinian resistance to a Palestinian passport. I have a vision of seeing the PLO become the sole legitimate representative of the Palestinian people, both the Palestinian Arab people and the Palestinian Jewish people.

Notes

1. Hannah Arendt, *Eichmann in Jerusalem: A Report on the Banality of Evil* (Faber and Faber, London, 1963).

2. Moshe Dayan, eulogy of Roy Rutenberg at Kibbutz Nahal Oz, 1956, quoted in Uri Avneri, *Israel without Zionists: A Plan for Peace in the Middle East* (Collier Books, Macmillan, New York, 1971), p. 154.

3. Moshe Dayan, address at the Israel Institute of Technology (Technion), Haifa, in response to questions from the audience as quoted in *Ha'aretz*, 4 April 1969.

4. Knesset Debates, Session 138–9, Fourth Knesset, 19 July 1960, pp. 1916, 1920.

5. For detailed exposition, see Uri Davis and Walter Lehn, 'And the Fund Still Lives: The Role of the Jewish National Fund in the Determination of Israel's Land Policies', *Journal of Palestine Studies*, vol. VII, no. 4, 1978.

6. The Israeli Law of Return, 1950, determines that 'every Jew has the right to immigrate to the country' (Article 1). The law states that:
'an *oleh* [Jewish immigrant] visa shall be granted to every Jew who has expressed his desire to settle in Israel, unless the Minister of Immigration is satisfied that the applicant (i) is engaged in an activity directed against the Jewish people, or (ii) is likely to endanger public health or the security of the state' (Article 2).
The law further stipulates that:
'a Jew who has come to Israel and subsequent to his arrival has expressed his

desire to settle in Israel may, while still in Israel, receive an *oleh* certificate' (Article 3A), and that:
'every Jew who has immigrated into this country before the coming into force of this Law, and every Jew who was born in this country, whether before or after the coming into force of this Law, shall be deemed to be a person who has come to this country as an *oleh* [Jewish immigrant] under this Law'. (Article 4)
In 1970 the law was amended in order to extend its scope to cover non-Jews married to Jews and their children and grandchildren by adding to the law Article 4A, which states that:
'the rights of a Jew under the Law, and the rights of an *oleh* under the Nationality Law, 5712–1952 as well as the rights of an *oleh* under any other enactment, are also vested in a child and a grandchild of a Jew, the spouse of a Jew, the spouse of the child of a Jew and the spouse of a grandchild of a Jew, except for a person who has been a Jew and has voluntarily changed his religion.'
As regards claiming rights by virtue of this clause:
'it shall be immaterial whether or not a Jew by whose right a right under subsection (a) is claimed is still alive and whether or not he has immigrated to Israel' (Article 4A(b)).
A Jew was defined as:
'a person who was born of a Jewish mother or who has become converted to Judaism and who is not a member of another religion' (Article 4B), thereby settling the widespread argument about 'Who is a Jew?' that had been raging in Israel for a considerable time.

This law, which enables Jews and their relatives to enter Israel even if they have no previous connection with the country, stands in sharp contrast to the treatment of Palestinians. Sabri Jiryis, 'Domination by Law', *Journal of Palestine Studies*, vol. XI, no. 1, Issue 41 (Tenth Anniversary Issue), Beirut, 1981, p. 77.

7. Absentees' Property Law (1950), Articles 1–8, 30, and Amendment No. 3 (Release and Use of Endowment Property) (1965).
1. In this Law:
(a) 'property' includes immovable and movable property, moneys, a vested or contingent right in property, goodwill and any right in a body of persons or in its management;
(b) 'absentee' means –
(1) a person who, at any time during the period between the 16th Kislev, 5708 (29 November 1947) and the day on which a declaration is published, under section 9(d) of the Law and Administration Ordinance, 5708–1948*, that the state of emergency declared by the Provisional Council of State on the 10th Iyar, 5708 (19 May 1948)† has ceased to exist,‡ was a legal owner of any property situated in the area of Israel or enjoyed or held it, whether by himself or through another, and who, at any time during the said period –

*I R No. 2 of the 12th Iyar (21 May 1948), Suppl. 1, p. 1; LSI Vol. 1, p. 7.
†I R No. 2 of the 12th Iyar (21 May 1948), p. 6.
‡Since no such declaration has been made to date, the State of Israel is legally declared to be in a state of emergency since 29 November 1947.

(i) was a national or citizen of the Lebanon, Egypt, Syria, Saudi Arabia, Trans-Jordan, Iraq or the Yemen, or
(ii) was in one of these countries or in any part of Palestine outside the area of Israel, or
(iii) was a Palestinian citizen and left his ordinary place of residence in Palestine (a) for a place outside Palestine before 1 September 1948; or (b) for a place in Palestine held at the time by forces which sought to prevent the establishment of the State of Israel or which fought against it after its establishment;
after its establishment;
(2) a body of persons which, at any time during the period specified in paragraph (1), was a legal owner of any property situated in the area of Israel or enjoyed or held such property, whether by itself or through another, and all the members, partners, shareholders, directors or managers of which are absentees within the meaning of paragraph (1), or the management of the business of which is otherwise decisively controlled by such absentees, or all the capital of which is in the hands of such absentees;
(c) 'Palestinian citizen' means a person who, on the 16th Kislev, 470 (29 November 1947) or thereafter, was a Palestinian citizen according to the provisions of the Palestinian Citizen Orders, 1925–1941, Consolidated, and includes a Palestinian resident who, on the said day or thereafter, had no nationality or citizenship or whose nationality or citizenship was undefined or unclear;
(d) 'body of persons' means a body constituted in or outside Palestine, incorporated or unincorporated, registered or unregistered and includes a company, partnership, cooperative society, society under the Law of Societies of 3 August 1909 and any other juridical person and any institution owning property
(e) 'absentees' property' means property the legal owner of which, at any time during the period between 29 November 1947 and the day on which a declaration is published under section 9 (d) of the Law and Administration Ordinance, 5708–1948, that the state of emergency declared by the Provisional Council of State on 19 May 1948 has ceased to exist, was an absentee, or which at any time as aforesaid, an absentee held or enjoyed, whether by himself or through another; but it does include movable property held by an absentee and exempt from attachment or seizure under section 3 of the Civil Procedure Ordinance, 1938;
(f) 'vested property' means property vested in the Custodian under this Law;
(g) 'held property' means vested property actually held by the Custodian, and includes property acquired in exchange for vested property;
(h) 'released property' means property released under section 28:
(i) 'area of Israel' means the area in which the law of the State of Israel applies;
(j) 'bill' means a bill of exchange, a cheque, a promissory note or any other negotiable instrument.

Item (i) means that although East Jerusalem has been officially annexed to Israel and its population made subject to the law of the State of Israel, the

the status of its Palestinian Arab residents is that of 'absentees'. They are 'absentees' in so far as their rights in properties in Palestine are concerned. They are very much present for all other matters such as taxation, conformity to Israeli civil and criminal codes, etc.

Articles 2–8 of the Law define the office of the Custodian of Absentees' Property and the terms of the vesting of absentees' property in the Custodian:

2. (a) The Minister of Finance shall appoint, by order published in *Reshumot*, a Custodianship Council for Absentees' Property, and shall designate one of its members to be the Chairman of the Council. The Chairman of the Council shall be called the Custodian.
   (b) The Custodian may bring an action and institute any other legal proceeding against any person and be a plaintiff, defendant or otherwise a party in any legal proceeding.
   (c) The Custodian is entitled to be represented in any legal proceeding by the Attorney-General or his representative.
   (d) When the Custodian ceases to hold office, his functions, powers, rights and duties shall automatically pass to the Minister of Finance; when another person is appointed Custodian, the said functions, powers, rights and duties shall automatically pass to him, and so on from Cutstodian to Custodian.
3. (a) The Custodian may, with the written approval of the Minister of Finance, appoint inspectors of absentees' property and delegate to any of them any of his powers, except the power to appoint inspectors. A notice of the appointment and scope of powers of every inspector shall be published by the Custodian in *Reshumot*.
   (b) The Custodian may appoint agents for the management of held property on his behalf and may fix and pay his remuneration.
   (c) The Custodian may appoint officials and other employees, whose status shall be the same as that of other State employees.
4. (a) Subject to the provisions of this Law –
   (1) all absentees' property is hereby vested in the Custodian as from the day of publication of his appointment or the day on which it became absentees' property, whichever is the later date.
   (2) every right an absentee had in any property shall pass automatically to the Custodian at the time of the vesting of the property; and the status of the Custodian shall be the same as was that of the owner of the property.
   (b) The proceeds of vested property shall be dealt with like the vested property yielding the proceeds.
   (c) Vested property –
   (1) shall remain vested property so long as it has not become released property under section 28 or ceased to be absentees' property under section 27;
   (2) may be taken over by the Custodian wherever he may find it.
   (d) Where the Custodian has acquired any property which was not absentees' property at the time of the acquisition, in exchange for vested property, the acquired property shall become held property and shall be dealt with as was the property in exchange for which it was acquired.
5. The fact that the identity of an absentee is unknown shall not prevent his

property from being absentees' property, vested property, held property or released property.

6. (a) A person who has in his possession any absentees' property is bound to hand it over to the Custodian.
(b) A person who has a debt to, or any other obligation towards an absentee shall pay such debt or discharge such obligation to the Custodian.

7. (a) The Custodian shall take care of held property, either himself or through others having his consent.
(b) The Custodian may, himself or through others having his written consent, incur any expense and make any investments necessary for the care, maintenance, repair or development of held property or for other similar purposes.

8. (a) The Custodian may carry on the management of a business on behalf of an absentee, whether or not he indicates that the business is managed by the Custodian, but he shall always have the right to sell or lease the whole or a part of the business, and –
(1) if it is the business of an individual – to liquidate it;
(2) if it is the business of a partnership all the partners of which are absentees, or of a company all the directors or shareholders of which are absentees, or of a cooperative society all the members of which are absentees – to wind up the partnership, company or cooperative society by order published in *Reshumot*.
(b) Where the Custodian has published a winding up order under sub-section (a) (2), the winding up shall be conducted –
(1) in the case of a partnership or company – as if the winding up order had been made by a competent court in accordance with part V of the Partnership Ordinance or in accordance with part VI of the Companies Ordinance, as the case may be;
(2) in the case of a cooperative society – as if the winding-up order had been made by the Registrar of Cooperative Societies in accordance with section 47 of the Cooperative Societies Ordinance,
and in every case as if the Custodian had been appointed as a liquidator not replaceable by another liquidator.

Article 30 of the Law sets out the rules of evidence applicable to the Custodian's transactions in absentees' property:

30. (a) Where the Custodian has certified in writing that a person or body of persons is an absentee, that person or body of persons shall, so long as the contrary has not been proved, be regarded as an absentee.
(b) Where the Custodian has certified in writing that some property is absentees' property, that property shall, so long as the contrary has not been proved, be regarded as absentees' property.
(c) A certificate of the Minister of Defence that a place in Palestine was at a particular time held by forces which sought to prevent the establishment of the State of Israel or which fought against it after its establishment shall be conclusive evidence of its contents.
(d) A copy certified by the Custodian of an entry in his books or official files or of another document in his possession shall, in any action or other legal proceeding, be accepted as *prima facie* evidence of the correctness of its contents.
(e) A written confirmation by the Custodian as to matters within the

scope of his functions shall, unless the Court has otherwise directed be accepted in any action or other legal proceeding as *prima facie* evidence of the facts stated in the confirmation.

(f) The Custodian and his inspectors, agents and officials are not bound to produce in any action or other legal proceeding any book, file or other document the contents of which can be proved in accordance with this section, and are not bound to testify on matters which can be proved through a confirmation of the Custodian as specified in this section, unless the Court has otherwise directed.

(h) A certificate, a confirmation, a permit or any other document which purports to have been signed, issued, given or delivered by the Minister of Defence, the Minister of Finance or the Custodian shall, as long as the contrary has not been proved, be considered to have been so signed, issued, given or delivered.

(i) The plea that a particular person is not an absentee, within the meaning of section 1(b) (1) (iii), by reason only that he had no control over the causes for which he left his place of residence as specified in that section shall not be heard.

It seems that the 1950 formulation of the Absentees' Property Law was inadequate in so far as seizing Muslim *Waqf* property was concerned. The Knesset therefore introduced in 1965 the following Amendment to the Law: Absentee's Property (Amendment No. 3) (Release and Use of Endowment Property) Law, 5725–1965

1. (a) In section 4 of the Absentees' Property law, 5710–1950 (hereinafter referred to as 'the principal law'), the following subsection shall be inserted after subsection (a):

1A (1) Where any property is an endowment under any law, the ownership thereof shall vest in the Custodian free from any restriction, qualification or other similar limitation prescribed, whether before or after the vesting, by or under any law or document relating to the endowment if the owner of the property, or the person having possession or the right of management of the property, or the beneficiary of the endowment, is an absentee. The vesting shall be as from 12 December 1948 or from the day on which one of the aforementioned becomes an absentee, whichever is the later date.

(2) The provisions of this subsection shall not void any restriction, qualification or other similar limitation prescribed by or under this Law or imposed by the Custodian and shall not void any transactions effected by him.

(b) This section shall have effect retroactively as from the date of the coming into force of the principle law . . . .

(Quoted in Hasan Amun, Uri Davis *et al.*, *Palestinian Arabs in Israel: Two Case Studies* (Ithaca Press, London, 1977), Appendix III, pp. 83–90.)

8. The Palestinian Arab population of some 150,000 which remained under Israeli rule after the 1948–49 war has over the past three and a half decades increased through a natural growth rate of over 4% per annum to approximately 700,000 at present, constituting 17% of the total population of the state of Israel in its pre-1967 boundaries. With the exception of Nazareth and Safa'amr, the majority of the Palestinian Arab population of all major cities in Palestine (Tiberias, Beisan, Safad, Acre, Haifa, Jaffa,

Lydda, Ramleh, Beer Sheba, Jerusalem (West)) have been expelled. Most of the surviving urban population are concentrated in Arab ghettos inside these, now predominantly Jewish, cities. The majority of these urban ghetto residents are not native inhabitants, but refugees from neighbouring Palestinian Arab villages who sought shelter from the 1948–49 hostilities in the city and were subsequently classified under the Absentees' Property Law, 1950, as 'present absentees'. Their lands were handed over to exclusive Jewish cultivation and development, and their villages destroyed. Of the 500 Palestinian Arab villages in the territories that fell under Israeli rule following the 1948–49 war, 400 were forcibly evacuated and subsequently razed to the ground. 100 remained under Israeli rule concentrated in Galilee and the Triangle. The majority of the Palestinian Arab population inside pre-1967 Israel lives in these 100 villages. The villages survived, but their lands were confiscated for exclusively Jewish settlement. See, for instance, Sabri Jiryis, *The Arabs in Israel* (Monthly Review Press, New York, 1976) and Ian Lustick, *Arabs in the Jewish State* (University of Texas Press, Austin, 1980).

9. Joseph Weitz, *My Diary and Letters to the Children* (Massad, Tel Aviv, 1965), vol. II, pp. 181–2.

10. Ibid., vol. III, p. 293.

11. Ibid., p. 302. For details of the overall Israeli military evacuation plan, see Walid Khalidi (ed.), *From Haven to Conquest*, notably Netanel Lorch, 'Plan Dalet', and 'Appendix VII: Zionist Military Operations 1 April 1949–15 May 1948, With the Framework of Plan Dalet' (Institute of Palestine Studies, Beirut, 1971), pp. 755–60, 856–7.

12. See, for instance, Michael Brecher, *Decision in Crisis: Israel 1967 and 1973* (University of California Press, Berkeley and Los Angeles, 1980), Rael Jean Isaac, *Party and Politics in Israel: Three Visions of a Jewish State* (Longman, New York, 1981), Hani Abdallah, *Al-Ahzab al-Siyasiyya fi Israil* ('The Political Parties in Israel'), (Institute of Palestine Studies, Beirut, 1981).

13. *Sunday Times*, 15 June 1969.

14. Camp David Agreements, West Bank and Gaza, Article C, 17 September 1978.

15. Sheli's most veteran MP is Uri Avneri, and a political biographical outline of his career in this context is in order:

Uri Avneri was born in 1923 in Beckum, Germany, as Helmut Ostermann. In 1933 his family settled in Palestine and in the period 1938–41 he was a member of the IZL (Irgun) under the command of Menachem Begin who in 1977 became Israel's fifth Prime Minister. Between 1941 and 1946 Uri Avneri was a regular contributor to the Fascist Hebrew periodicals *Ha-Hevrah* ('Society') and *Ba-Maavak* ('In the Struggle'). In the 1948–49 war he was a company commander of the motorized commando unit known as 'Samson's Foxes' whose political commissar was the writer and poet Abba Kobner. In 1951 he co-founded with Shalom Cohen the photographic news weekly *Haolam Hazeh* ('This World') of which he has ever since been editor-in-chief. In 1958 he became the founding member of the anti-French Israel Committee for Free Algeria. In the mid-1960s he became a founding member of the League against Religious Coercion and the Committee against the Military Government. From 1965 to 1973, he was Member of Parliament for the Haolam Hazeh (New Force) movment. From 1979 to 1980, he was Member of Parliament for Sheli.

Throughout his life, Uri Avneri has presented his membership of the IZL and the Givati brigade commando unit 'Samson's Foxes' as most positive credentials testifying to his credibility as an Israeli patriot. He has never made any public self-critical re-evaluation of his membership in the IZL and fighting in the 1948 war, nor of the official criminal 'order of the day' issued in the daily battle sheets by the political commissar of the Givati battalion Abba Kobner. This failure is striking in the light of the nature of the material in question. For instance, the following is extracted from the battle sheet of 12 July 1948, entitled 'Aju al-Yahud (The Jews Have Come): The Night of Raid and Purge':
'Indeed we broke the spirit of the enemy and also rent their bodies open. But the enemy strength is still there. It is an enemy. It is an army. Though we are confident that the dung of the corpses of the invaders [will fertilize] our fields into blossom. . . .'

The following extract is from the battle sheet of 14 July 1948, entitled 'The Dogs of Anglo-Faruq Under our Wheels':
'The defenders of Negbah stand like walls of red hot iron, and the waves of dogs attack and smash their heads against the walls of defence. . . . At the time of the attack our units were held down by a strong enemy fire, which was there at the strength of a full battalion. In a long and fierce face to face battle the enemy army was defeated and 'Samson's Foxes' broke through forward. And suddenly the ground became soft: corpses! Tens of corpses under their wheels. The driver recoiled: human beings are under his wheels! He halted for a moment. He then remembered Negbah and Beit Daras – and he ran them down! Do not recoil sons: the dogs of murder should be judged in blood! The more you excel in running down the dogs of blood, the deeper you will learn to love the beautiful, the good, freedom. That is not enough. Gird up your loins, boys. Here, our jeeps will tomorrow be amphibian. We will march in a river, in the river of blood of the invaders. From Beit Afa to Iraq Suweidan. From Isdud – until they drown to their necks! Until the dogs never return to the edge of their den. Run them down! Ready.'

The following extract is taken from the battle sheet of 17 July 1948, entitled 'Moon Nights':
Deep are our skies in the nights of Tamuz. A full moon overflows and a light breeze flutters over the southern hills. And man longs for home, and the heart longs for the woman and the mothers and the distant songs of children. But around you the debilitated eyes of the dogs of the Nile glitter. Dogs into the Nile! Into the Nile! No: cursing, praying, loving – press the trigger! Slaughter. Slaughter. Let there be no hope for the invader . . . .

These quotes are from *Prozah* ('Prose') August-September 1977, p. 28. I am indebted to Dr Israel Shahak for the reference.

The implications of presenting participation in the war crimes committed in 1948 as glorious patriotism are far reaching and affect Avneri's entire political career.

Haolam Hazeh weekly under Avneri's and Cohen's leadership quickly became Israel's best muck-raking independent Israeli newspaper exposing corruption and attacking both foreign and home policies of the Israeli government. Throughout the 1950s and 1960s the paper led the struggle against the violation of human and political rights of Arabs under Israel Jewish rule, against the notorious Defence (Emergency) Regulations (1945), against the military regime, religious coercion, corruption, etc.

Uri Avneri was first elected to the Israeli Parliament in 1965. During the 1967 war as editor-in-chief of *Haolam Hazeh* he issued a daily news sheet *Daf* ('Page') which came out with an issue carrying a huge headline 'On Damascus!' advocating the Israeli occupation of the Syrian capital. When the annexation of East Jerusalem came to a vote in the Israeli Parliament shortly after the war (27 June 1967) Uri Avneri joined the national coalition government and voted for the annexation of the city. This is the only political act which he has publicly regretted throughout his entire political career.

16. 'The Mistake, the Naivety and the Hypocrisy', by Yeshaayahu Ben-Porat, *Yediot Aharonot*, 14 July 1972. The affair of the Rafah Approaches is essentially the fencing of lands in that area by a military authority for the consideration of needs described as being of 'security'. Security, in the language of the Israeli Establishment, and of the Establishment in the Land of Israel since way back, meant and still means, not only to erect an artillery position or a gun in a given spot so as to defend it, but also – and at particular times maybe essentially – the creation of Jewish territorial continuity in order to establish a pure Zionist fact. In other words: the redemption of the country by way of land appropriation by various means, Jewish settlement on the same lands, and its fortification by military and security means.

This is what took place in the Rafah Approaches, and is not different in essence from that which has taken place in other locations in the Land of Israel and the state of Israel, since the day Zionism started to accomplish itself. This includes displacing of Arab residents, in this case Bedouin, from the areas that were fenced, and preventing them from returning to their lands.

When Katyusha shells land on Kiryat-Shmoneh or in its surroundings, isn't there almost always an announcement made by the IDF spokesman, saying that 'our forces shot back in the direction of the sources of fire'? And what does it mean, if not counter-shelling, almost automatic, directed at the Lebanese village nearest to the 'sources of fire' and in which – in the shelled village – there may be saboteurs, but there are certainly peaceful toilers of the land.

One truth is that there is no Zionist settlement, and there is no Jewish state without displacing Arabs and without confiscating lands and fencing them off. A second truth is that in the war against the Arabs, including the terrorists, Israel never committed herself, and cannot commit herself to harm only regular or irregular warriors. And a third truth is that within the framework of the assumptions developed above, Israel has tried in the past and will try in the future to do its best not to kill innocent civilians and not to displace Arab inhabitants by methods not approved of and sanctioned by law and order.

Overt and courageous talk, and clarification of the Zionist conception of the world upon which the state was founded may indeed expose the government to strong criticism at home and to vicious attacks in the world. In spite of that, open-heartedness, both at home and abroad, will dissipate misunderstandings and tear apart the envelope of hypocrisy which covers many of our actions and failures . . .

(Quoted in Uri Davis and Norton Mezvinsky, *Documents from Israel 1967–*

1973: Readings for a Critique of Zionism (Ithaca Press, London, 1975), pp. 74–5.)

17. 'Deputy Commander of the Judea District in Testimony Before the Military Court: "Sharon Said in Instructions Regarding Treatment of Arab Rioters in the West Bank: Tear Their Balls Off",' *Ha'aretz*, 29 December 1982.

18. Meron Benvenisti, *West Bank and Gaza Data Base Project: Pilot Study Report* (unpublished MS); see also David Shipler's reference to the Benvenisti paper quoting the lands made available by the Begin government for Israeli settlements as being 55 to 65% of the total area of the West Bank, *New York Times*, 12 September 1982.

19. Raja Shehada and Jonathan Kuttab, *The West Bank and the Rule of Law* (International Commission of Jurists and its West Bank Affiliate, Law in the Service of Man, Geneva, 1980).

20. Dr General (Reserves) Matityahu Peled estimates that by 1980 20% of the Palestinian Arab population of the West Bank and the Gaza strip, over 200,000 persons in all, had been gaoled for varying periods by the Israeli occupation authorities since 1967. (See Matityahu Peled, 'The Problem of the Security Prisoners: the Disliked Comparison', *Ha'aretz*, 7 August 1980.)

21. The International Commission to Enquire into Reported Violations of International Law by Israel during its Invasion of the Lebanon, *Israel in Lebanon* (Ithaca Press, London, 1983).

22. Ibid.

23. 'Professor Leibowitz Called for Counter Terror: "Had I Been Younger I Would Have Done It Myself", *Yediot Aharonot*, 13 February 1983. The title of this press report refers to statements made by Professor Leibowitz at a press conference in Jerusalem, to the effect that without counter-terror against right-wing Jewish terrorism in Israel, the opposition in Israel would be destroyed. In this context Leibowitz repeated again his condemnation of the 'Judeo-Nazi mentality' in Israel:

'The big crisis of the Jewish people is that the overwhelming majority of the Jews genuinely desire to be Jewish – but they have no content for their Judaism other than a piece of coloured rag attached to the end of a pole and military uniform. The consciousness and the desire to be Jewish did not vanish, rather they are transformed today into a Judeo-Nazi mentality'.

See also his *Haolam Hazeh* interview by Sarit Yishai following the Sabra and Chatilla massacres:

'This is the necessary and natural continuation of our political line in the last fifteen years. If we must rule over another people, then it is impossible to avoid the existence of Nazi methods. The massacre was done by us. The Phalange are our mercenaries, exactly as the Ukrainians and the Croatians and the Slovakians were the mercenaries of Hitler, who organized them as soldiers to do the work for him. Even so we have organized the assassins in Lebanon in order to murder the Palestinians.

What has happened in Lebanon, the terrible massacre committed in the refugee camps is an additional step in the process of suicide of the State of Israel. Humanity will have no other choice but to destroy the State of Israel!'

(*Haolam Hazeh*, 22 September 1982)

24. It is on the basis of this principle that I can stand here with confidence

and declare my enormous admiration for Neturei Karta, the only Orthodox Jewish tradition that commands my respect, not because of its Jewish values but because of its opposition to Zionism. Neturei Karta opposes Zionism as the worst expression of Jewish apostasy in that it attempts to bring about through human political action a sequence of events that according to orthodox Jewish tradition can be brought about only through direct divine and messianic intervention: the ingathering of Jewish exiles and the reconstruction of Jewish political sovereignty. They are, from an orthodox Jewish point of view, completely committed to the separation of religion from the state until the time of messianic redemption, which for me as a secular Jew is definitely good enough.

25. The continued and repeated criticism of the Palestine National Covenant, Articles 5 and 6, on the grounds that under the terms of these articles the status of the majority of the Israeli Jewish society is reduced to statelessness is basically correct. There is a discrepancy between the official programme of a democratic state as officially established by the Palestine National Council since its Eighth Session (1971) on the one hand, and the Palestine National Covenant, Articles 5 and 6, which together determine that only those Jews who had normally resided in Palestine until the beginning of the Zionist invasion will be considered Palestinians. It is necessary to amend the Covenant in order to make it consistent with the Palestine Liberation Organization official political programme. Such an amendment could perhaps read as follows:

Article 6 (unaltered)

The Jews who had normally resided in Palestine until the beginning of the Zionist invasion will be considered Palestinians.

Article 6A

All Israeli Jewish citizens, who became Israeli citizens by force of Israel Nationality Law 1952 as amended in 1958 and 1968, are entitled to Palestinian citizenship.

Article 6B

Liberated Palestine will be a secular democratic state and will constitutionally guarantee equality under law to all its citizens without distinction or discrimination by religion, culture, nationality, language, race or sex.

I wish to indicate to all those Zionist apologists who point to the Palestine National Covenant in condemnation while, of course, lending justification and support to Israeli apartheid legislation, that the fact that the Palestine National Covenant on this matter is to be condemned does not reduce in any way the justice of the Palestinian cause or the rightness of the Palestine resistance.

Appendix: 'About the Soft and the Delicate' by Amos Oz (from *Davar*, 17 December 1982) (emphases added)

'You can call me anything you like. Call me a monster or a murderer. Just note that I don't hate Arabs. On the contrary. Personally, I am much more at ease with them, and especially with the Beduin, than with Jews. Those Arabs we haven't yet spoilt are proud people, they are irrational, cruel and generous. It's the Yids that are all twisted. In order to straighten them out you have to first bend them sharply the other way. That, in brief, is my whole ideology.

'Call Israel by any name you like, call it a Judeo-Nazi state as does Leibowitz. Why not? Better a live Judeo-Nazi than a dead saint. I don't care whether I am like Ghadafi. I am not after the admiration of the gentiles. I don't need their love. I don't need to be loved by Jews like you either. I have to live, and I intend to ensure that my children will live as well. With or without the blessing of the Pope and the other religious leaders from the New York Times. I will destroy anyone who will raise a hand against my children, I will destroy him and his children, with or without our famous purity of arms. I don't care if he is Christian, Muslim, Jewish or pagan. History teaches us that he who won't kill will be killed by others. That is an iron law.

'Even if you'll prove to me by mathematical means that the present war in Lebanon is a dirty immoral war, I don't care. Moreover, even if you will prove to me that we have not achieved and will not achieve any of our aims in Lebanon, that we will neither create a friendly regime in Lebanon nor destroy the Syrians or even the PLO, even then I don't care. It was still worth it. Even if Galilee is shelled again by Katyushas in a year's time, I don't really care. We shall start another war, kill and destroy more and more, until they will have had enough. And do you know why it is all worth it? Because it seems that this war has made us more unpopular among the so-called civilised world.

'*We'll hear no more of that nonsense about the unique Jewish morality*, the moral lessons of the holocaust or about the Jews who were supposed to have emerged from the gas chambers pure and virtuous. No more of that. The destruction of Eyn Hilwe (and it's a pity we did not wipe out that hornets' nest completely!), the healthy bombardment of Beirut and that tiny massacre (can you call 500 Arabs a massacre?) in their camps which we should have committed with our own delicate hands rather than let the Phalangists do it, all these good deeds finally killed the bullshit talk about a unique people and of being a light upon the nations. No more uniqueness and no more sweetness and light. Good riddance.

'I personally don't want to be any better than Khomeini or Brezhnev or Ghadafi or Assad or Mrs Thatcher, or even Harry Truman who killed half a million Japanese with two fine bombs. I only want to be smarter than they are, quicker and more efficient, not better or more beautiful than they are. Tell me, do the baddies of this world have a bad time? If anyone tries to touch them, the evil men cut his hands and legs off. They hunt and catch whatever they feel like eating. They don't suffer from indigestion and are not punished by Heaven. I want Israel to join that club. Maybe the world will then at last begin to fear me instead of feeling sorry for me. Maybe they will start to tremble, to fear my madness instead of admiring my nobility. Thank god for that. Let them tremble, let them call us a mad state. Let them understand that we are a wild country, dangerous to our surroundings, not normal, that we might go crazy if one of our children is murdered – just one! That we might go wild and burn all the oil fields in the Middle East! If anything would happen to your child, god forbid, you would talk like I do. Let them be aware in Washington, Moscow, Damascus and China that if one of our ambassadors is shot, or even a consul or the most junior embassy official, *we might start World War Three just like that*!'

. . . We are talking while sitting on the balcony of the pretty country house belonging to C. which is situated in a prosperous *Moshav*. To the west we see a burning sunset and there is a scent of fruit trees in the air. We are being served iced coffee in tall glasses. C. is about fifty years old. He is a man well known for his (military) actions. He is a strong, heavy figure wearing shorts but no shirt. His body is tanned a metallic bronze shade, the colour of a blond man living in the sun. He puts his hairy legs on the table and his hands on the chair. There is a scar on his neck. His eyes wander over his plantations. He spells out his ideology in a voice made hoarse by too much smoking:

'Let me tell me [sic] what is the most important thing, the sweetest fruit of the war in Lebanon: It is that now they don't just hate Israel. *Thanks to us, they now also hate all those Feinschmecker Jews in Paris, London, New York, Frankfurt and Montreal*, in all their holes. At last they hate all these nice Yids, who say they are different *from us, that they are not Israeli thugs, that they are different Jews, clean and decent*. Just like the assimilated Jew in Vienna and Berlin begged the anti-semite not to confuse him with the screaming, stinking Ostjude, who had smuggled himself into that cultural environment out of the dirty ghettos of Ukraine or Poland. It won't help them, those clean Yids, just as it did not help them in Vienna and Berlin. Let them shout that they condemn Israel, that they are all right, that they did not want and don't want to hurt a fly, that they always prefer being slaughtered to fighting, that they have taken it upon themselves to teach the gentiles how to be good Christians by always turning the other cheek. It won't do them any good. Now they are getting it there because of us, and I am telling you, it is a pleasure to watch.

'*They are the same Yids who persuaded the gentiles to capitulate to the bastards in Vietnam*, to give in to Khomeini, to Brezhnev, to feel sorry for Sheikh Yamani because of his tough childhood, to make love not war. Or rather, to do neither, and instead write a thesis on love and war. We are through with all that. The Yid has been rejected, not only did he crucify Jesus, but he also crucified Arafat in Sabra and Chatilla. *They are being identified with us and that's a good thing*! Their cemeteries are being desecrated, their synagogues are set on fire, all their old nicknames are being revived, they are being expelled from the best clubs, people shoot into their ethnic restaurants murdering small children, forcing them to remove any sign showing them to be Jews, forcing them to move and change their profession.

'Soon their palaces will be smeared with the slogan: Yids, go to Palestine! And you know what? *They will go to Palestine because they will have no other choice! All this is a bonus we received from the Lebanese war. Tell me, wasn't it worth it?* Soon we will hit on good times. The Jews will start arriving, the Israelis will stop emigrating and those who already emigrated will return. Those who had chosen assimilation will finally understand that it won't help them to try and be the conscience of the world. The "conscience of the world" will have to understand through its arse what it could not get into its head. The gentiles have always felt sick of the Yids and their conscience, and now the Yids will have only one option: to come home, all of them, fast, to install thick steel doors, to build a strong fence, to have submachine guns positioned at every corner of their fence here and to fight like devils against anyone who dares to make a sound in this region. And *if anyone even raises his hand against us we'll take away half his land and burn the other half, including the oil. We might use nuclear arms.* We'll go on until he no longer feels like it. . . .

'. . . You probably want to know whether I am not afraid of the masses of Yids coming here to escape anti-semitism smearing us with their olive oil until we go all soft like them. Listen, history is funny in that way, there is a dialectic here, irony. Who was it who expanded the state of Israel almost up to the boundaries of the kingdom of King David? Who expanded the state until it covered the area from Mount Hermon to Raz Muhammad? Levi Eshkol. Of all people, it was that follower of Gordon, that softie, that old woman. Who, on the other hand, is about to push us back into the walls of the ghetto? Who gave up all of Sinai in order to retain a civilised image? Beitar's governor in Poland, that proud man Menachem Begin. So you can never tell. I only know one thing for sure: *as long as you are fighting for your life all is permitted, even to drive out all the Arabs from the West Bank, everything.*

'Leibowitz is right, we are Judeo-Nazis, and why not? Listen, a people that gave itself up to be slaughtered, a people that let soap to be made of its children and lamp shades from the skin of its women is a worse criminal than its murderers. Worse than the Nazis . . . *If your nice civilised parents had come here in time instead of writing books about the love for humanity and singing Hear O Israel on the way to the gas chambers, now don't be shocked, if they instead had killed six million Arabs here or even one million, what would have happened? Sure, two or three nasty pages would have been written in the history books, we would have been called all sorts of names, but we would be here today as a people of 25 million!*

'*Even today I am willing to volunteer to do the dirty work for Israel, to kill as many Arabs as necessary, to deport them, to expel and burn them, to have everyone hate us, to pull the rug from underneath the feet of the diaspora Jews, so that they will be forced to run to us crying. Even if it means blowing up one or two synagogues here and there*, I don't care. And I don't mind if after the job is done you put me in front of a Nuremberg Trial and then jail me for life. Hang me if you want, as a war criminal. Then you can spruce up your Jewish conscience and enter the respectable club of civilised nations, nations that are large and healthy. What you lot don't understand is that *the dirty work of Zionism is not finished yet*, far from it. True, it could have been finished in 1948, but you interfered, you stopped it. And all this because of the Jewishness in your souls, because of your diaspora mentality. For the Jews don't grasp things quickly. If you open your eyes and look around the world you will see that darkness is falling again. And we know what happens to a Jew who stays out in the dark. So *I am glad that this small war in Lebanon frightened the Yids. Let them be afraid, let them suffer.* They should hurry home before it gets really dark. So I am an anti-semite? Fine. So don't quote me, quote Lilienblum instead [an early Russian Zionist – ed.]. There is no need to quote an anti-semite. Quote Lilienblum, and he is definitely not an anti-semite, there is even a street in Tel Aviv named after him. (C. quotes from a small notebook that was lying on his table when I arrived:) 'Is all that is happening not a clear sign that our forefathers and ourselves . . . wanted and still want to be disgraced? That we enjoy living like gypsies.' That's Lilienblum. Not me. Believe me, I went through the Zionist literature, I can prove what I say.

'And you can write that I am a disgrace to humanity, I don't mind. On the contrary. Let's make a deal: *I will do all I can to expel the Arabs from here, I will do all I can to increase anti-semitism, and you will write poems and essays about the misery of the Arabs and be prepared to absorb the Yids I will force to flee to this country* and teach them to be a light unto the gentiles. How about it?'

It was there that I stopped C.'s monologue for a moment and expressed the thought passing through my mind, perhaps more for myself than for my host. Was it possible that Hitler had not only hurt the Jews but also poisoned their minds? Had that poison sunk in and was still active? But not even that idea could cause C. to protest or to raise his voice. After all, *he is said to have never shouted under stress, even during the famous operations his name is associated with . . . .*

Part IV: Zionism: Help or Hindrance to US Foreign Policy?

15. Time to Speak Peace and Understanding

Hon. Paul N. McCloskey Jr

I want to tell you the truth so I first have to tell you that the reason that I have spent some part of my time seeking peace – not only in the Far East and Southeast Asia but in the Middle East – is that, if in your youth you were privileged to be shot at and were close to the explosion of grenades and artillery shells, you gain such an intense fear that quite often you don't want to see anybody else ever hurt again. It is amusing to me, sometimes, that those who want war as a means of settlement of disputes have very rarely seen war, and those who have, have generally formed a conscious desire to try to avoid it.

I want to thank EAFORD and AJAZ for holding this conference. As Chairman Arafat has recognized, it comes at a crucial time because it represents a discussion of ideas many of which, through decades of training and media presentation in the American press, radio and television, are believed to be unacceptable in our political arena. I come to you today not so much to discuss these ideas as to tell you about the political arena. When scholars meet to debate ideas, I think the first thing to recognize is that it is generally many years before those ideas, discussed in the freedom, the sanctity and the opportunity for study of a college campus, are enacted into law or become new public policy.

Scholars may have their ideas accepted 20 or 50 or 1,000 years after their death but not very often in their lifetime are they privileged to see those concepts recognized by politicians. To understand politics you have to understand that to be politic means not to offend. The people that I respect at this conference today are those who, if necessary for truth, are willing to offend.

The American Jew who is willing to suggest that Israel is wrong, that Palestinians are human beings and have rights, that there ought to be a Palestinian state, offends his peers. The American Jew who speaks out for these ideas is viciously condemned in much of the American Jewish community.

The moderate Arab leader who suggests that perhaps we should recognize Israel's right to exist may be marked for assassination. As Dr Davis pointed out, no Arab leader can accept Israel's right to exist and speak out for it without risking overthrow or assassination.

The secret of American politics is that political leaders reflect and represent public opinion in the United States. They are not leaders but representatives of public opinion.

The battle for peace will be won or lost in the battle for American public opinion.

I have realized from every country I have visited in the Middle East, from every person of every persuasion that I have talked to about peace and understanding, that the bottom line is that American public opinion must be changed if we are ever to achieve peace in the Middle East.

I suggest at the outset that we recognize that the path to peace passes through the rejection of hatred and fear. If there are two elements, two human emotions, that we're all subject to and that will cause us to do the combative thing, the assault rather than compromise, they are fear and hatred. Fear on the part of the Jews who for 2,000 years have suffered anti-Semitism; in his lifetime a Jew might have been silent or his parents may have been silent while Jews were executed in fearful numbers. There is also the desire to be proud as Jews of something that Israelis have shown they can do that even Americans cannot: the raid on Entebbe, for example, as compared with the American attempt to get our hostages back from Iran. Is it not understandable to every American that Jews are often motivated by a deep fear, remembering the anti-Semitism in their lifetime, the execution of six million Jews, the warning in their youth to be quiet, 'don't make waves or you will attract anti-Semitism'? It should be understandable that among Jews today, even though many disagree with Begin and Sharon, even though many think that Begin and Sharon are as dangerous as Hitler was in his time, they will remain silent. The persecuted have indeed become the persecutors.

My Jewish colleagues in the Congress have quite often told me privately, 'The trouble with Begin is that he believes Arabs are less than human.' But they can't say that publicly. You can't be elected from New York or Beverly Hills or St Louis or Las Vegas, Nevada, if you speak the truth about the Middle East. To be politic is not to offend and it's understandable that American politicians do not often wish to speak the truth. The truth will offend nearly everyone. I hope to offend you all in one way or another, to provoke your thought. Because quite often I have found the single voice that changed my opinion was a voice which offended me, that on re-examination of why I was offended I was forced to rethink the position I once held and, because I was offended, to re-examine a view or a set of facts.

I worry that we are, so many of us here, from Churches. The separation of Church and state to me is the most significant accomplishment of the American ethic. If you note what happens when religious power is connected with governmental power, you always, nearly always, have a disaster, whether it is the Ayatollah or any other religious leader.

I can recall in the heat of the war in Vietnam the greatest single support for the Vietnam war in Congress was among the prayer breakfast group. 'God is on our side. Pray to God and extinguish Laos and their villages:

they're Communists.'

So we have a great advantage, sitting here representing different faiths, Christianity, Judaism, Zionism. We can discuss the merits of those religious views and thank God that none of our religious views govern us. We can accommodate the religious views of others. I'm anti-Zionist but not anti-Jewish. Hitler's greatest sin – among many – was his decree that non-Aryans should be executed. It's very similar today. The concept that the right to Eretz Israel means some people must be excluded and, to exclude them, you must treat them as less than human is intolerable.

But we, as Americans, cannot be too condescending towards that point of view. We've seen that type of idea in our own time. You will recall that within our lifetime, the lifetime of many of us, we were once mesmerized as Hitler mesmerized the German people into first condemning Jews as less than human, and then accepting their incarceration and finally their execution. We were mesmerized by Pearl Harbor into uncritical acceptance of unfairness to Japanese-Americans. The then Attorney-General, later Governor, ultimately Chief Justice of the United States Supreme Court, Earl Warren, led the effort to put Japanese-Americans in concentration camps after Pearl Harbor. My first job was in Earl Warren's District Attorney's office in California. There was no kinder or more compassionate man. In later life he was to say that his single greatest error, of all the decisions and opinions he made, was that passionate early condemnation of the Japanese-Americans, their imprisonment for years until we discovered that the 442nd Regimental Combat Team had earned more purple hearts than any other American fighting regiment in World War II. The Japanese-Americans were loyal to this country.

So let's not condemn the Arabs and the Israelis for their passions. We Irish, Mr Kelly, have been killing each other in Belfast for 300 years because of a Catholic–Protestant difference. If there is any people in the world prone to violence and unreason, senseless violence, the bombing of women and children, it's we Irish. So perhaps we owe a greater duty than most to try to mediate between Arabs and Jews.

The danger today is that public debate in this country is being stifled. There is not one among you who does not face the danger of being held up as either anti-Semitic or pro-PLO in communities that for 30 years have been led to believe that anti-Semitism is terrible and that the PLO are assassins or terrorists or worse. And the most dedicated to the Palestinian cause cannot take great pride in the use of assassination or the bombing of school buses or the machine-gunning of Olympic athletes as a means to demonstrate dedication to a cause. If we're going to turn away from fear and hatred, it's got to be on both sides of the fence.

But I would like to turn now to the political side of trying to achieve justice for the Palestinians. I suppose the question most often asked, and it's been asked in this conference in these first two days, is: why does America behave as it does, giving unquestioned, unqualified and ever-increasing support to Israel, despite the fact that Israel has violated our laws, flouted our agreements, and slapped our President in the face. Let me refer to the specifics.

Under US law, when US-supplied weapons are used to invade a neighbouring country, other than in self-defence, we are to cut off those supplies of weapons. When we gave Israel the cluster bomb in 1974, we specified the bomb would be used only when Israel was attacked by the regular forces of at least two nations. The CBU was not to be used against irregular troops and never to be used in civilian areas.

The cluster bomb, as you know, comes in a canister about 15 feet long. It is dropped out of an aircraft, timed to explode at 1,000 feet. It scatters little bombs over perhaps 25 acres. Those little bombs spinning through the air are timed to go off at five-minute intervals up to 30 minutes. Some go off at 5, 10, and 15 minutes. The planes depart. The bomblets lie around. The soldiers know what they are and avoid them. Little children come out, old people come out to go shopping, the children pick them up and are blown up. Somebody walks by and one may go off. They're devastating against civilians which is why we specified, by contract with the Israelis, that they would not be used in civilian areas.

I found cluster bombs all over West Beirut in July 1982, even in the courtyard of an Islamic hospital. No PLO installations or defenders were anywhere near. The Israelis violated their agreement with the United States, yet we did nothing.

Our Arms Control Law specifies that if a foreign country violates an agreement on the supply of arms, we will cut off arms deliveries.

When the President proposed his peace plan, when Philip Habib negotiated in Lebanon, the provision we asked the PLO to accept was that if they left their women, children and old people behind, we would obtain the assurance from the Israelis they would not go into West Beirut. Israel violated that agreement. As a result of that violation, with Israel taking in the Christian militia to, in their own words, 'purge' the camps, everybody in the Middle East knew the massacre could and would happen.

But the most important agreement of all with the United States, was violated by Israel's response to President Reagan's recommendation that Israel stop the settlements on the West Bank. The response was, 'We are going to build more of them and we are going to build them more rapidly and we're going to accelerate the pace of West Bank settlement, in violation of Camp David.' There is no way you can read the Camp David Agreement, whether you're for or against it, and sanction those West Bank settlements. In three specific places the Camp David Accords recite that the agreement is based on 'Resolution 242 and all of its parts'. What are those parts?

Recognition of Israel is one, essentially within its pre-1967 borders. The second is that when Israel is safe from force or threat of force, it will give up the West Bank and Gaza. When Begin signed that agreement, he knew he did not intend to give up the West Bank and Gaza. As early as 1974, he'd been saying publicly to his own party, 'We intend to annex the West Bank and Gaza.' Begin was deliberately misleading the President of the

United States, when he signed Camp David. Even after those violations of agreements in summer and autumn 1982, the United States Congress, with scarcely a voice raised in protest, voted *more* aid to Israel.

It's no wonder that in the Arab world they say, 'What are you doing? Why do you do it?'

My purpose today is to tell you. It is a secret in American politics: it is not known to most of the American people. It's widely believed that politicians are responsive to public opinion, the majority view of their constituents. The secret is that this is absolutely untrue. The politician is *most* responsive to a small minority of political opinion, public opinion, under certain conditions. The minority has to be a group of people whose views are so deeply held, generally backed by a religious reasoning, that it is motivated to participate actively in political effort to support those views.

That's what the American politician is responsive to. It's not known. It's not discussed by politicians any more than academicians discuss publicly the private politics as to who is going to get tenure and who is not, or who is going to be dean and who is not; any more than doctors discuss publicly which of their colleagues are guilty of malpractice; or any more than the Jewish community wants to discuss publicly the divisions that they have over Begin.

The conditions to which a politician responds require these elements: that the minority view be deeply held, that it be held by a strongly organized, cohesive group, that this group is active in supporting or opposing political candidates, and the fourth condition is that there is no counter-lobby. Now, when those four conditions exist in American politics, the politician will be far more responsive to that minority view than he will be to general public opinion. I ask you to take that as a given and I will cite you the two lobbies that are the most powerful in the United States as a result.

Number one – far above any other lobby – is the 'Jewish community' lobby in the United States, AIPAC (American Israel Public Affairs Committee). Many Jews don't even know it exists. But the 33 major Jewish organizations support AIPAC and its operations here in Washington to the hilt. It is tightly organized. It has the ability to communicate with its members. Within 24 hours AIPAC can relay to every major city in the United States and every Jewish community in the United States precisely what it wants that community the next day to say to its newspapers, to its radio talk shows, to its television call-in shows and to its members of Congress.

There are six million Jews in America. Perhaps half of them do not know that AIPAC exists. But all of them know Israel exists. All of them know about the Holocaust. All of them have experienced anti-Semitism in their lives and in their communities. All of them want to see Israel survive and prosper. Well, I won't say all of them want Israel to survive and prosper. The Jewish community is as deeply divided as, say, the Arab community. But, in any event, the cohesiveness of AIPAC has made it the most feared lobby in America.

The second-rank lobby is the National Rifle Association. If you think it isn't a religious view that your right hand has a born extension of a pistol you do not know the National Rifle Association. It is founded on the Second Amendment. But the National Rifle Association members deeply believe that the Constitution comes from God and the right for man to carry arms is virtually God-given. That Association has been effective and they've been effective in the same manner as the Jewish community. If they know that there are ten congressional races out of the 435 in the United States where a man or a woman may be elected who is for gun control, and if they also know that in a community the election is going to be close, they will pour all of the resources of the two million NRA members across the nation into those ten districts. If they defeat five of those candidates, the word goes out to the other 430 members of Congress, 'Don't take on the National Rifle Association.'

The majority of the American people have said they'd like gun control in some form. Congress routinely votes 90 to 10 against gun control. The majority of the American people would cut off aid to Israel tomorrow, if the Israelis don't get out of Lebanon and the West Bank, and yet that issue isn't even framed. There isn't a politician that dares raise the issue even to discuss it, let alone support it.

Politicians are not responsive to public opinion unless it is translated into action. Apathy is the greatest enemy of a democratic system.

When I was in Israel in summer 1982 a Jewish Israeli taxi driver said, 'Mr McCloskey, the problem with a democracy like ours is that our government must be responsive to the most outrageous elements, to the people who care most deeply.' In Israel it is the religious party, which electorially constitutes a small minority, that believes they own the West Bank and Gaza. Consequently, in an election where one party got 48% and the other got 48%, if you wanted to govern Israel, you had to appeal to the 4%. So the government of Israel is irresistibly motivated by the people who care, who care deeply enough to involve themselves in the political process. This is the second given of democracy. But I find, strangely enough, that many people who care most deeply, scholars who will give a weekend to gathering in Washington to discuss an issue of this kind, will often be the very last to involve themselves in the political process. We would rather discuss ideas than contribute to campaigns or walk precincts or insist that the candidates answer 'yes' or 'no' questions.

Now, no politician wants to answer 'yes' or 'no'. You can't be politic and give a 'yes' or 'no' answer. You'd offend one side or the other. When in doubt, straddle.

I have thought that someone ought to run for the presidency of the United States in the Republican primary against Ronald Reagan merely to force him to answer the questions: why, Mr President, have you not asked the Congress to invoke the law of the United States to cut off aid to Israel? Why are you afraid to do so?

I can tell you why he hasn't done so. He knows he could not get it through the Congress. If you're elected every two years and the only lobby in your district is AIPAC and there is no Arab-American lobby or no Peace in the Middle East lobby, then why pay any attention to what is right? If you can be defeated in the next election by 2% of your people who are backed up by 100% of the money from around the country the political result is a very great diversion from what is right or even what is law.

Let me tell you precisely why Congress cast that vote in December 1982 in our lame-duck session to forgive Israel $750 million of debts it owed to the United States. Why? Because in the preceding June, AIPAC had had two leading citizens from every one of the congressional districts of the United States call on their congressman. When they called on me, these two very fine people from Los Altos made their position unmistakably clear, coached by AIPAC. Let me say this. In every community, in every profession, in every business, let's acknowledge it, our Jewish fellow-citizens have attained excellence. Whether it is due to close family ties or the desire to study, I cannot think of a profession, a law firm, a business, an art colony, a music colony and, most of all, a communications medium, in which Jews have not excelled. If I have one piece of advice to Arab American mothers and fathers, it's send your child to media school.

We've got enough engineers, doctors and lawyers in the Arab community. What we need are some television commentators, some Arab American newspaper editors and reporters, and we'll finally get a fair shake in the press.

I asked these two people from Los Altos, marvellous people, reputable citizens, great human beings, what's on your agenda this time?

Was it to talk about the traditional Jewish sense of justice that prevailed before Begin, the Jewish concept of values that, perhaps because of oppression against Jews, is as highly developed as any there is in the world? All of the great faiths have value. The Islamic faith, to me, is just as beautiful as the Christian faith. I have rarely met an Islamic moderate who didn't teach me something about the beauties of the faith of Islam.

When we went to Beirut in 1982 at the height of the bombing, we were told by a member of our embassy, 'You're going to be surprised, you members of Congress, to find that the people here in Beirut who are cruel are the Christians, that the Islamic people are the people of tolerance here. This of course is not the prevailing view in the United States.'

But let me tell you what happened when I asked these two Jewish citizens whom I respect and for whom I have a great deal of affection, 'What's on your agenda this year?' They said, 'Well, Congressman, AIPAC's position this year is (1) that we don't want you to give any anti-aircraft weaponry to Jordan, and (2) we want you to forgive Israel's debts to the United States.'

Now, they can't say that publicly. No Zionist leader will urge on public television today that Israel's debts to the United States should be forgiven. You can't make those arguments stand up. You can't argue that Israel ought to have the right to renege on Camp David, to abandon UN resolution 242. You can't argue that they have a right to deprive Palestinian prisoners of war of any rights at all or to treat Palestinians as they're treating them. You can't argue those matters publicly. But you can privately tell your congressman you want him to forgive Israel's debts to the United States.

Can you imagine the public outcry, at a time when our budget is $200 billion in deficit, at the idea that we ought to give Israel $2.5 billion this year? You might have argued it when they needed it, when they were weak and surrounded by hostile Arab military forces which far exceeded their own. Today, however, I think Syria is absolutely terrified of a war with Israel. They know Damascus would be levelled in about 20 minutes. Whatever the rhetoric may be, the last thing the Syrians want is to go to war with Israel.

And yet we give Israel $2.5 billion. And Alan Cranston, a candidate of the Democratic Party for the presidency of the United States, a fine man in every other way, is saying, 'If I'm elected president we'll forgive Israel its debts.' Why? If you're a Democrat and you want to run for the presidency, not to have Zionist money in your campaign is tantamount to defeat. As you rose to your feet this morning in response to an emotional appeal, the 'Jewish community' will rise to its feet almost *en masse* to give that money to the man who will protect Israel to the last degree.

But, in any event, in addition to the secret lobbying that occurred last June to forgive Israel its debts, a very interesting thing happened to two candidates for the Congress. One is Paul Findley, who had the courage to meet with Yassir Arafat and, like myself, to say, 'Hey, Arafat's a moderate.' That is the worst crime you can commit because the Zionist ethic requires you to treat Palestinians as terrorists. They must not be considered as human beings. Even the thought that there is such a thing as a Palestinian moderate defeats the whole Zionist programme today.

An interesting anecdote is relevant here. When I was in Jerusalem, having just come from Beirut, I was in anguish. I had walked through the streets of West Beirut with Mary Rose Oakar, a Syrian-ancestry American congresswoman. We'd stopped a lady who was going through some rubble of a 19-storey apartment building that had collapsed on the street, and Mary Rose asked her in Arabic, 'What are you looking for?' She responded, 'I'm looking for the body of my daughter.' Then her 12-year-old son pointed his finger at me and said, 'You Americans have killed my little sister.' That is the belief in the entire Arab world. And they are right. The Israelis would not be taking the position they are today without Begin's absolute assurance that the Congress of the United States will back him up.

You ask, 'Why does the Congress back him up?' Let me tell you what happened in November 1982. Paul Findley was a 20-year Republican veteran, one of the most decent Republicans in the Congress, a moderate, who had met with Arafat, who had urged recognition of the PLO. Over $500,000 were sent by the Zionists across the United States in 1980 into his little cornbelt district in downstate Illinois to try to defeat him. They did it again in 1982 and they did defeat him by 2,000 votes.

If you heard Ted Koppel on television that night you have a classic example of why we do not get a fair picture in the American media. If Arab money goes into a political campaign, it is front-page news. If Zionist money goes into a campaign, it may not even be reported. Ted Koppel, looking at that result, looked down and said, 'Here's an interesting result, in downstate Illinois 20-year Republican veteran Paul Findley is losing by 2,000 votes. That's significant because of the heavy influx of – and he paused and he said – '*out-of-state* money into the campaign.' He could not bring himself to say 'Jewish' money because the Zionist machine has dropped an iron curtain so that for a non-Jew to use the words 'Jewish community' or 'Jewish lobby' or 'Jewish control' of Congress on these issues is to be anti-Semitic and in the liberal community, in the moderate community, none of us want to be called anti-Semitic.

There was a second example in the November 1982 election. A US congressman, Tom Lantos, of California said to the Jewish community, 'We need another voice for Israel in the Congress. I am threatened, support me.' And the Jews in Las Vegas and St Louis, Fort Lauderdale, Palm Beach and New York sent nearly a million dollars into this little district in California, twice the money that his opponent raised, to defeat one candidate and to support another who supported Israel.

Now, what impact do you think those two elections had on a candidate who might privately feel that Israel is wrong? He would like to speak out against Israel and in favour of Palestinian rights but knows there is a lobby on one side that is dedicated to his defeat if he does so. There is no lobby on the other side to support the moderate who will debate ideas, who will deplore the actions of Israel and the United States government. The Arab nations recognize that the battle is going to be won or lost in the battle for American opinion. But the Arab nations have been unwilling to put money into public relations efforts in this country. If the battle is to be won or lost in American public opinion, it can only be won with the education of the American people to reject an idea that has religiously been drummed into their ears for 30 years, that Palestinians are less than human, that there should not be a Palestinian state, that Arafat is a terrorist.

You know, Begin's book, *The Revolt*, which I commend to everyone as good reading, shows that Begin was an absolute terrorist. There is nothing like the condemnation of a terrorist by one who has been a terrorist himself.

What Begin did between 1943 and 1947 against the occupying British power was terrorism. There's no way you can look favourably at what the Irgun was doing from 1943 to 1947 and then say that what the Palestinians are attempting to do now is somehow evil. But, having understood the process, Begin of course is competent to speak out.

But let me close. Let me just say this, that for peace, understanding by the American people of the Middle East is absolutely essential. The courage for American leaders to speak out, the pressure, must come from the American community. It will not come from politicians. Politicians who speak out will be defeated. It is not politic to tell the truth. I thought today we had the second coming from Nazareth. Reverend Al-Assal is one of the finest men, and he gave one of the finest speeches I've heard. The man from Nazareth.

Remember what happened to the first man from Nazareth when he tried to tell the truth. It was years after his death before his philosophy became accepted.

So I suppose that, like Dr Davis, but with a slightly different bias, I would say this is the time to seek peace and understanding. This is the time to speak for peace and understanding to the American people. But rather than deplore the actions of politicians, we must try to affect public opinion and then force these politicians to be representative of American public opinion. Any person who speaks as I have is going to be condemned, as you have all been. The reason I came, really, was out of respect for Rabbi Berger and those who have tried to be moderates. It is not easy to be a moderate leader.

But I would like to suggest that, as the Jewish community has become actively involved in recent years, it is time for those who seek peace to get actively involved. Ordinarily it takes years. The effort that started in opposition to the Vietnam war in the mid-1960s didn't really reach fruition on the college campuses or in the churches. It reached fruition finally when the business community leaders, the opinion leaders of America, got involved in the 1970s. *Then* we ended the war. We ended the war by vote of Congress seven years after efforts started to end the war.

What I fear most of all is that the lack of an American peace movement for the Middle East, the lack of a Middle East peace movement that spreads across the broad spectrum of American society could lead us into nuclear war. The danger of nuclear war is not so much between us and the Soviets. Our institutions and theirs have a built-in bias against sudden action. There's an inertia in the bureaucracy that may some day cause the Soviets to collapse just as it could collapse our country. But I don't think the danger of nuclear war stems from US–Soviet confrontation. The danger of nuclear war stems from a religious belief on the part of Begin, a religious justification that, if any other country in the Islamic world develops a bomb or even a civilian reactor, Begin has the right to destroy it as he did the Iraqi reactor.

I think most people would say the Pakistanis today are developing a nuclear capacity. They face the Indians. The Indians have the bomb. Pakistanis will never feel secure unless they have it. When the Pakistanis have the bomb or even start to develop a nuclear capacity, I think it fair to assume that Israel will try to destroy that capacity.

So you have a tinderbox in that part of the world which might result in an exchange of nuclear weapons. There is no way, in my judgement, to prevent Arab leaders from obtaining nuclear weapons within the next decade and possibly in much less time. Anyone can design a nuclear weapon today. It's common knowledge. It takes money, it takes craftsmanship, the engineering skill to craft the bomb, but the diagram of the bomb is known, the materials that go into the bomb are available and, if I were an Arab leader and wanted to be the next Muhammad or the next prophet, I might want to have an atomic bomb and destroy Israel. So it is clearly going to happen and, if there is an atomic war between the Israelis and the Arabs in the next decade and the United States and the Soviets go on the kind of nuclear alert that they must, any of you who have served in the military know the danger. Some skipper of a submarine, some sergeant, some pair of lieutenants in a silo in Montana or North Dakota, the danger of an accidental discharge of a nuclear weapon, and the war that could destroy the United States is here.

This is my motivation. It's not a hatred of Israel. I support Israel's right to exist. I support the Palestinian right to statehood. But the fear of an atomic war is something that ought to galvanize Americans into a peace movement to force justice in the Middle East, if only to avoid nuclear war. I suggest to you that the peace movement, the anti-nuclear movement that saw people in 19 states vote for a freeze, despite the admonition of the President of the United States; that the Alliance for a Middle East Peace ought to reach out to those that are opposed to nuclear war because this is the real danger.

I urge all of you to try to get involved in asking that 'yes' or 'no' question, 'Well, Congressman, when you run next year, are you going to vote to cut off aid to Israel unless they get out of Lebanon, unless they stop those West Bank settlements, and unless they negotiate fairly for Palestinian autonomy on the West Bank and Gaza? If not, we're going out to work against you and we've got 6,000 people in your district that are going out to work against you and we have a newsletter just like AIPAC's and we're going to change the policy of the United States by demanding it of our elected representatives.'

16. The Zionist Organization/Jewish Agency in International and United States Law

Sally V. Mallison
Research Associate, International & Comparative Law Program, George Washington University

W. Thomas Mallison
Professor of Law and Director, International & Comparative Law Program, George Washington University

see p.250 for copyright notice.

I. The 'Jewish People' Concept and the Creation of the Zionist Organization/Jewish Agency in International Law

A. The Context of the 'Jewish People' Claims

The 'Jewish people' nationality claims are the core of Zionist public law.[1] They have the same importance to Zionists as the First Amendment rights have to Americans.

Shortly after the then newly elected Prime Minister Begin returned to Israel following his July, 1977 visit to the United States, the *Israel Digest* (American Edition) published an article which included some of his views. It stated:

> Replying to American questioners [concerning the settlement policy] Israel's Prime Minister had told them that there are several dozen Bethlehems, Hebrons, Shilohs and Beth-els in the United States. 'Imagine if the Governors of some states were to ban Jews from settling in these towns. What an outcry there would be against such racial discrimination!
>
> 'How can we, a Jewish government, prevent the Jews of Eretz Yisrael from buying land or building their homes in the original Bethlehem, Hebron, Shiloh and Beth-el?'[2]

The analogy Mr. Begin draws between 'Jews' moving into towns in the United States and into towns in the occupied territories is a false one. 'Jews' moving into any town in the United States do so as individuals with the same domestic law rights and obligations as any other Americans.[3] In contrast, 'Jews' moving into any place in the occupied territories do so as members of 'the Jewish people' with claimed national rights to establish exclusivist 'Jewish' settlements and later to make the claim to sovereignty on behalf of Israel. The meaning of 'Jew' is entirely different in the United States law from the meaning of the same word in Israeli law. In United States law a Jew is a private individual who, like the adherent of any other religion, is entitled to practise his religion and is protected from the imposition of a state religion. In Israeli law a Jew is a member of a legally defined nationality group who is entitled to special rights and benefits which are denied to other Israelis.[4]

Although the term 'the Jewish people' does not appear in Holy Writ, it was given an almost exclusively religious meaning until the founding of Zionism. Its most usual use was as a synonym for 'Jews,' 'Israelites,' and 'the Children of Israel.' The Zionist movement has captured the term for its own juridical-political purposes. However, even though a specific nationalistic meaning is given to the words, the Zionists have not rejected whatever political advantages accrue to them from the ambiguities involved. Thus they accept the support of those who have found humanitarian or religious meanings in 'the Jewish people.'

In a fundamental sense, political Zionism is the reaction of Jews to ghetto life and the consequent denial to them of an opportunity to participate meaningfully in the secular life of the states of their regular nationalities.[5] Zionism is based upon an acceptance of anti-Semitism now and has been so based since its inception in 1897. Illustration may be provided from the words of Dr. Theodor Herzl in his Zionist classic, *The Jewish State*: 'We naturally move to those places where we are not persecuted, and there our presence produces persecution. This is the case in every country, and will remain so, . . . till the Jewish question finds a solution on a political basis.'[6]

Thus Zionism and its 'Jewish State' act upon the postulate that anti-Semitism is fundamental and ineradicable. The Zionist juridical objectives that 'the Jewish people' be constituted as an additional nationality entity, membership in which is to be conferred upon all Jews, are based upon this postulate.[7] The 'Jewish people' concept is used to recruit Jewish immigration to Israel and to achieve other Zionist political objectives. The alleged 'solution' to anti-Semitism is to 'ingather' all Jews into the State of Israel.

A contemporary illustration of the importance of anti-Semitism as a guide to Zionist action is provided by Arthur Hertzberg, a leading proponent of Zionism in the United States:

> The assumption that anti-Semitism 'makes sense' and that it can be put to constructive uses – this is at once the subtlest, most daring, and most optimistic conception to be found in political Zionism. . . . What is new in Herzl is that, assuming, as the heir of assimilation, that anti-Semitism is rational, he boldly turned this idea outward into the international arena.[8]

The 'Jewish people' concept is consistently advanced as a juridical claim in international law decision-making contexts. A particularly well known example involved the exploitation of the claim in the *Eichmann Case*.[9] The Nazi murder of millions of innocent men, women and children is one of the most tragic events of the present century. All moral individuals of whatever national or religious identification share revulsion at these crimes. A large group of victims was designated by the Nazis as 'Jews.' Other designated groups included, *inter alia*, 'Poles,' 'Gypsies,' and 'Slavs.' Many other civilians throughout Europe were also murdered by the Nazis even though they could not be included properly in even the most extended definitions of the specified victim groups. These crimes have been established by overwhelming evidence, including documents prepared by the Nazis themselves, in the forty-two volumes of *The Trial of the Major War Criminals Before the International Military Tribunal* at Nuremberg,[10] as well as in other post-war trials.

The juridical concept of crimes against humanity (as opposed to a concept of crimes against the victims and their co-religionists alone) was firmly established in international law by the principal *Nuremberg Trial* and other post-World War II trials.[11] The jurisdictional authority derived from crimes against humanity is a very extensive one which is usually termed universality of jurisdiction. 'Universality,' in this jurisdictional sense, authorizes any state having custody of the accused to try him without regard to the geographic location and time elements of the acts alleged to constitute the crime against humanity. In addition, the national state trying the accused may not discriminate upon the basis of the national identity of the accused or that of the victim.[12]

The evidence produced before the Israeli trial court in the case against Adolf Eichmann appears to be ample to establish his guilt for crimes against humanity. If this had been the principal charge against Eichmann, it seems probable that Israel would have been entitled to invoke universality of jurisdiction. It is particularly significant that the Israeli court in the *Eichmann Case*[13] paid only lip service to the concept of crimes against humanity. Instead, the court placed reliance upon the Zionist concept of 'crimes against the Jewish people' nationality status of Eichmann's victims. Similarly, the court preferred to base its jurisdictional claim to try Eichmann principally upon the alleged link between the State of Israel and 'the Jewish people' rather than upon the recognized authority of universality of jurisdiction.

A sense of reality concerning the *Eichmann Case* can be achieved by examination of the following excerpt from it:

> In view of the recognition by the United Nations of the right of the Jewish people to establish their State, and in the light of the recognition of the established Jewish State by the family of nations, the connection between the Jewish people and the State of Israel constitutes an integral part of the law of nations.[14]

It is significant that the claim of juridical connection between 'the Jewish people' and the State of Israel is set forth not as a claim, but as though it were already established as 'an integral part of the law of nations.' The Zionist objection to basing the claim to jurisdictional authority upon the established concepts of crimes against humanity and ensuing universality of jurisdiction is that the established concepts recognize the membership of Jews in the common humanity of all. Such recognition is inconsistent with a purpose of 'the Jewish people' nationality claims which is to separate Jews from other individuals in public law. Thus, in the Zionist public law conception of the *Eichmann Case*, the regular nationality status of Jewish victims of the Nazis was ignored or minimized in favor of their alleged nationality status as members of 'the Jewish people.' The Zionist objective was to show that only the Zionist State of Israel seeks to protect the Jewish victims of the Nazis.[15] In contrast, the principal *Nuremberg Trial* and the subsequent war crimes trials employed the concepts of crimes against humanity and universality of jurisdiction without discrimination based upon the religious or national identity of the victims or the accused.

The United States Department of State has responded to the 'Jewish people' concept as follows:

> The Department of State recognizes the State of Israel as a sovereign State and citizenship of the State of Israel. It recognizes no other sovereignty or citizenship in connection therewith. It does not recognize a legal-political relationship based upon the religious identification of American citizens. It does not in any way discriminate among American citizens upon the basis of their religion.
>
> Accordingly, it should be clear that the Department of State does not regard the 'Jewish people' concept as a concept of international law.[16]

Although this indicates official rejection of the 'Jewish people' claim as 'a concept of international law,' there are interesting questions which remain concerning the efforts to implement the concept.

It is an error to regard the establishment of the State of Israel as the end of Zionism and its 'Jewish people' concept. The establishment of the State is regarded by the Government of Israel and the Zionist Organization as only one step in obtaining assent to the 'Jewish people' claims in law.[17] Another key step, consisting of a wide range of subordinate public law measures including municipal statutes, involving imposing 'Jewish people' nationality law obligations upon Jews who are nationals of states other than Israel. Former Prime Minister Ben-Gurion has stated this in specific terms:

> First of all there is the collective duty of the Zionist Organization and of the Zionist Movement to assist the State of Israel in all conditions and under any circumstances, towards accomplishment of 4 central matters – the Ingathering of the Exiles, the building up of the country, security and absorption and fusion of the Dispersions within the State.
>
> This signifies assisting the State whether the government to which the Jews in question owe allegiance desires it or not. . . .[18]

Mr. Berl Locker, speaking as chairman of the Zionist Executive at a Session of the Zionist General Council, stated as one of 'the basic doctrines of Zionism in the present day': 'Jews as a community do possess a collective loyalty to the State of Israel, as Israel is the national home of the entire Jewish people.'[19]

B. The Claims to Constitute the Zionist Organization/Jewish Agency as a Public Body

Since the Zionist Organization has claimed status as a public body, a brief consideration of the subjects of international law is essential. It is widely recognized that the subjects of international law are no longer limited to national states and now include international public bodies or organizations.[20]

Public bodies are usually constituted as subjects of international law through the explicit multilateral agreement of states (conventional law), and there is no authority for a state to constitute a public body unilaterally. Such bodies may, on occasion, be constituted by necessary implication drawn from an appraisal of their substantive powers. The United Nations, in spite of its preeminent position as the principal general function public body, is not explicitly constituted as a public body by its Charter. The International Court of Justice in its opinion concerning *Reparation for Injuries suffered in the Service of the United Nations* ('Count Bernadotte's Case'),[21] however, determined that the United Nations enjoys international juridical status or 'personality' as a necessary implication from the substantive powers which are granted to it by the Charter. It would have been unsound to allow the substantive grants of power to be frustrated through the failure to find the ancillary status or personality. The Court found the United Nations to be a 'subject of international law and [a body] capable of possessing international rights and duties . . . .' The present significance of the opinion is that it illustrates the empirical analysis which must be made in an inquiry concerning status as a public body-subject of international law. In answering the question as to whether or not the Zionist Organization has been constituted as a public body the same empirical test must be employed.

The principal juridical consequence of status as a public body, of course, is subjection to the law.[22] There can be no grant of powers and status as a public body without the accompanying legal obligations of a subject of the law. These obligations include, at the minimum, both the specific legal limitations imposed upon the public body and the general legal limitations which apply to all subjects of international law.

It is clear that in Zionist conception the Zionist Organization was claimed to be a public body representing all Jews from its inception in 1897.[23] Such a claim standing alone is, however, not the equivalent of authoritative international decision. The Balfour Declaration of 1917 necessarily involved the implicit recognition by the British Government of the public body status of the Zionist Organization because Dr. Weizmann and his associates claimed to act on behalf of organized Zionism and not as private individuals.[24] The Declaration manifested the British view that the Organization had the juridical status to receive the precatory clause as well as to be subjected to the legal limitations embodied in the safeguards. Although this still did not amount to the according of public body status by the community of states, it was a significant step toward this objective. The political 'alliance' between the Zionist Organization and the British Government allowed the former to participate in the Paris Peace Conference of 1919 and also allowed it to participate in the drafting of the Mandate for Palestine.[25] Although the Zionists did not achieve all of their political objectives, a number were incorporated in the terms of the Mandate concerning the functions and status of the Organization. The preamble to the Mandate[26] incorporated the substance of the Balfour Declaration and spelled out its safeguard clauses in full. Article 4 is the most important provision concerning the Zionist Organization. It provides in part:

> An appropriate Jewish agency shall be recognized as a public body for the purpose of advising and co-operating with the Administration of Palestine. . . . The Zionist organisation, so long as its organisation and constitution are in the opinion of the Mandatory appropriate, shall be recognized as such agency.

Thus the League of Nations, acting in behalf of the world community of the time, constituted the Zionist Organization as a public body.

The issue of the juridical status of the Zionist Organization/Jewish Agency was considered by the Permanent Court of International Justice in the three cases which are collectively termed the *Mavrommatis Palestine Concessions Cases*.[27] The Court determined authoritatively that the Organization/Agency was an international public body under article 4 of the League of Nations Mandate.

The provisions of the Mandate, and particularly those concerning the close relationship of the Zionist Organization/Jewish Agency to the Palestine Administration, could lead to the conclusion that the Zionist Organization was an integral part of the governmental administration of Palestine. The British Government, nevertheless, took a different position shortly before the Mandate became effective. In the Churchill White Paper of July 1, 1922 the British Government stated:

> That special position relates to the measures to be taken in Palestine affecting the Jewish population, and contemplates that the Organisation may assist in the general development of the country, but does not entitle it to share in any degree in its Government.[28]

The White Paper included a paragraph barring the Organization from possessing 'any share in the general administration of the country.'

For a short time the Organization/Agency observed these limitations. Thereafter, as its political and military power increased, it violated the express limitations in the Mandate and its undertakings to the British Government whenever the political objectives of Zionist nationalism and its claimed constituency of 'the Jewish people' made this desirable. The 1946 report of a non-partisan and respected fact-finding committee, the Anglo-American Committee of Inquiry, provided a careful analysis of the activities of the Jewish Agency in Palestine, stating in part: 'This Jewish shadow Government has ceased to cooperate with the Administration in the maintenance of law and order, and in the suppression of terrorism.'[29]

Thus the Zionist Organization exercised the public body powers accorded to it by the Mandate, but the limitations imposed upon it by the same authority were violated. It advanced the 'Jewish people' claims in opposition to the British Government before the Permanent Mandates Commission of the League of Nations.[30] In 1947–1948 it transferred its political pressure activities to the United Nations and advanced them there under the 'Jewish Agency' name until it was formally replaced by the name of the State of Israel.

The Zionist Organization also conducted its public body activities within national states including the United Kingdom, and diplomatic negotiations took place between the Organization and the British Government. A basic negotiating objective of the Organization was to impose upon the Government the principle that its primary legal obligation under the Mandate was not to the native inhabitants of Palestine but to the Zionist claimed constituency of 'the Jewish people.'[31]

The principal focus of Zionist Organization public body activities shifted from the United Kingdom to the United States in the early part of the Second World War. The Biltmore Declaration of May 11, 1942 provides illustration of these pressure group activities there. That Declaration demanded the establishment of a 'Jewish Commonwealth' in Palestine without any reference to or regard for the safeguard clauses of the Balfour Declaration which were embodied in the Mandate for Palestine then in force.

The Zionist Organization/Jewish Agency, and not the Government of Israel, undertook to negotiate a reparations agreement with the Federal Republic of Germany on behalf of 'the Jewish people.' The result was the Luxemburg Agreement of 1953[32] in which Germany agreed to pay to the Government of Israel a sum estimated at two billion dollars in reparations for Nazi confiscation of property belonging to Jews, whether or not the particular Jews subsequently became Israeli nationals.

The end of the British Mandate and the establishment of the State of Israel on May 14, 1948 terminated the legal authority for the public body status of the Zionist Organization/Jewish Agency and no action taken by the United Nations provided a continuing juridical basis for the Organization. Since one of its principal political objectives had been the creation of the State of Israel, one might conclude that the Organization was now dissolved, but the facts indicate that it continued to function.

The Executive Reports submitted to the 23rd Zionist Congress at Jerusalem (1951) indicate in considerable detail the continuing functions of the Zionist Organization after the termination of the Palestine Mandate. The function of diplomatic negotiations, which had been done by the Organization alone before 1948, was now to be shared with the Government. The recruitment of Jewish immigrants into Israel, however, remained a pre-eminent function of the Organization.[33] In addition, the Zionist national funds continued their fund-raising efforts, and according to these Executive Reports the Jewish Agency financed the war effort against the Arab states 'during the early months of fighting as well as in the period preceding it.'[34]

Problems remained, nevertheless, in terms of the allocation of public or governmental functions between the Government of Israel and the Organization. The concern of the Government lest the Organization perform a role for the State of Israel analogous to that which it had performed for the Mandatory Government was expressed by the Prime Minister. *The Jewish Agency's Digest* reported in 1949 that Mr. Ben-Gurion said, 'This would not be tolerated under the State of Israel.'[35]

It is clear that the functions performed by the Organization and the working relationships between it and the Government constituted a *de facto* status for the Organization and a juridical relation between it and the Government. Its continuing purpose was to organize 'the Jewish people' to support the state and to provide Jewish immigration for it.[36]

A recent example of the use of the 'Jewish people' claims is the statement made by Ambassador Blum in the Security Council on June 6, 1982[37] when he attempted to justify the Israeli attack on the Palestine Liberation Organization (P.L.O.) and invasion of Lebanon.[38] He stated that 17 Jews had been killed by the P.L.O. since July 1981 and provided 15 specific examples which included eight Israeli Jews, seven of whom were apparently killed in Israel, and an Israeli diplomat killed in France.[39] He also referred to seven Jews killed in foreign countries including Austria, Belgium, and West Berlin, none of whom were stated to be Israeli citizens.[40] The inclusion by Mr. Blum of attacks on non-Israeli Jews outside the state of Israel is consistent with 'the Jewish people' nationality claims. Mr. Maksoud, the permanent observer of the League of Arab States, was the only speaker in the Security Council on June 6 who responded specifically to these claims by Mr. Blum. He stated:

> I am sure that the Jews of the United States, of the United Kingdom, of France, of the Soviet Union, of all the countries in the world reject Israel's claim to be the spokesman for all the Jews in the world and the protector of their rights.[41]

But the 'Jewish people' claims continue to be advanced, and this is one of the primary purposes of the Zionist Organization/Jewish Agency and the Government of Israel.

II. The Implementation of the Claims to Public Body Status through the Government of Israel Status Law and the Covenant Between the Government of Israel and the Zionist Organization

A. The Legislative History

The 23rd Congress of the World Zionist Organization met in Jerusalem during August, 1951. The most significant item on the agenda concerned the juridical status of the Zionist Organization. The Congress produced an important resolution entitled 'Status for the Zionist Organization' which provided, *inter alia*:

> The Congress considers it essential that the State of Israel shall grant, through appropriate legislative act, status to the World Zionist Organization as the representative of the Jewish people in all matters relating to organized participation of the Jews of the Diaspora in the development and upbuilding of the country and the rapid absorption of the immigrants.
>
> * * * *
>
> The following spheres of activity [for the Zionist Organization/ Jewish Agency] shall be fixed among others, for the forthcoming period:
>
> (a) The organization of immigration, the transfer of immigrants and their property to Eretz Israel;
> (b) Participation in the absorption of immigrants;
> (c) Youth Aliyah;
> (d) Development of agricultural settlements;
> (e) Acquisition and amelioration of land by the Jewish National Fund;
> (f) Participation in development projects.[42]

The Government of Israel was also interested in providing a formal juridical status for the Zionist Organization in view of the termination of the Mandate. In 1952 Prime Minister Ben-Gurion stated in the Knesset concerning the proposed status legislation:

> This Bill differs generally from other laws not only in form but also in content. Usually a law is intended to change or improve something. This enactment is intended to maintain, to confirm, and to give legal force and State recognition, to a basic fact – the experience of the Jewish people, its historic continuity, unity, and aspiration. It will give the impress of the State and the law to the fact that the State of Israel is the creation of the Jewish people, indelible proof and faithful base of its existence, and primary instrument for its liberation.[43]

This official statement is particularly important in demonstrating that the Status Bill was intended to confirm or ratify the existing state of affairs. It also provides further indication of the centrality of the 'Jewish people' concept. In the same statement, the Prime Minister also said:

> The State of Israel cannot intervene in the internal life of the Jewish communities abroad, cannot direct them or make demands upon them. However unique is the State of Israel in the manner of its emergence and in its task, it is obliged to operate like every other state, and its capacity outside its borders is restricted. It is the Zionist Organization . . . which is able to achieve what is beyond the power and competence of the State, and that is the advantage of the Zionist Organization over the State.[44]

The Status Law was enacted on November 24, 1952 and a statement of its 'constitutional' importance appeared in the *Israel Government Year-Book*:

> The World Zionist Organization-Jewish Agency for Eretz Israel Law 5713–1952 was of great constitutional importance. The Prime Minister, in submitting the Law to the Knesset, defined it as 'one of the foremost basic laws.' This Law completes the Law of the Return in determining the Zionist character of the State of Israel. The Law of the Return established the right of every Jew to settle in Israel, and the new Law established the bond between the State of Israel and the entire Jewish people and its authorized institutions in matters of immigration into and settlement in Israel.[45]

The State of Israel has no constitution, but its 'basic laws' possess predominant constitutional characteristics including having considerably more importance than routine legislation.

B. The Provisions of the Status Law

The first three sections of the Status Law provide introduction and background to the entire statute. The first section sets forth the consistent Zionist-Israel juridical claim of factual and legal connections between the State of Israel and the entire 'Jewish people.' The second section refers to the historic public body functions of the Zionist Organization in behalf of the claimed constituency of 'the Jewish people.' It also accurately recognizes the central role of the Organization in creating the State. This historical section is important in showing State recognition of the past functions of the Organization. Such deference is probably politic in view of the somewhat changed role of the Organization since the establishment of the State. Section 3 is recognition of the fact that the Zionist Organization and Jewish Agency are simply different names for the same institution. It includes the phrase that the Organization 'takes care as before of immigration', which indicates the consistent performance of the immigration function before and after the establishment of the State of Israel in 1948.

The purview directly concerning status provides in section 4:

> The State of Israel recognises the World Zionist Organization as the authorised agency which will continue to operate in the State of Israel for the development and settlement of the country, the absorption of immigrants from the Disapora and the coordination of the activities in Israel of Jewish institutions and organisations active in those fields.

Section 6 indicates that the Organization is the instrument to achieve the political unity of Jews. The provision in it concerning an 'enlarged' Organization/Agency is a planned arrangement whereby non-Zionists may be involved more directly in Zionist activities at some future time. This same type of arrangement was previously effectuated through the 'enlarged Jewish Agency' which was recognized in 1930 as the 'public body' under the Mandate.

Section 11 states that the Organization's Executive is 'a juristic body.' This is analogous to article 4 of the Palestine Mandate which constituted the Organization as 'a public body.' Tax exemption is a typical attribute of governmental status, and section 12 establishes the principle of exemption of the Zionist Organization/Jewish Agency and its subordinate bodies. This is probably done because the Executive and its branches and fronts are performing public functions which would otherwise be performed by the Government itself. In this respect, the Executive is simply treated as a part of the Government.

The Law (in section 7) authorizes the Organization to enter into what is called a 'Covenant' or agreement with the State to arrange the more specific details of the status of the Organization 'and the juridical form of its co-operation with the Government.'

C. The Provisions of the Covenant

The use of the word 'Covenant',[46] which has religious implications, to establish or recognize a political-legal relationship is an interesting reflection of the importance which it is given. The preamble to the Covenant states that it is entered into in accordance with the Status Law. It is clear that without the Status Law as enabling legislation the Organization would not have the authority to make an agreement with the State. The question which must be raised, however, is the extent to which an agreement where one of the two parties participates by authorization of the other amounts to an actual negotiated agreement as opposed to a unilateral Government of Israel public law allocation of functions within a single sovereignty.

The first section of the Covenant sets forth and accepts each of 'the fields of activity' enumerated in the Status Resolution of the 23rd Zionist Congress. By emphasizing functions concerning Jewish immigration and settlement, it gives appropriate recognition in Zionist public law to what section 5 of the Status Law describes as 'the central task of the State of Israel and the Zionist Movement in our days.' In addition, the latter part of the section specifies further functions to be performed. The adding of functions beyond those requested demonstrates the confidence of the Government in the Organization as an efficient tool for implementing the 'Jewish people' concept. The characterization in the first section of the Keren Kayemeth Leisrael (the Jewish National Fund) and the Keren Hayesod (the United Israel Appeal) as 'institutions of the Zionist Organization' is of considerable legal significance. It means that the analysis concerning the juridical status of the Zionist Organization applies equally to the Jewish National Fund and the United Israel Appeal.

The last clause of section 1, consistent with section 4 of the Status Law, states that the Executive shall coordinate 'the activities in Israel of Jewish institutions and organizations' which act within the scope of the functions carried out by the Zionist Organization. It adds that this is to be done 'by means of public funds.' The conclusion which follows is that coordination employing public funds is governmental coordination.[47]

Section 2 of the Covenant requires that the activities of the Organization within Israel be carried out consistently with law. At first glance this appears to be a routine provision but it also adds that such activities must be consistent with subordinate administrative orders which are applicable to governmental authorities. The result is another example of treatment of the Organization as a part of the Government.

The Coordination Board, which according to section 8 of the Covenant 'shall be established,' is the same one which has been in existence since 1951. The Covenant, therefore, merely formalizes it. The Coordination Board deals with the central Zionist task of the recruitment of Zionist immigrants from 'the Jewish people' outside of Israel under the Law of Return. Mr. Moshe Sharett served on the Board first as Prime Minister and later as Chairman of the Zionist Executive, and he stated its importance:

> I should like to place on record here the serious attitude of the Prime Minister towards the Coordinating Committee, at least in the period in which I have been participating in its meetings. Not only does he always respond to any demand to call a meeting of the Committee, but on his own initiative he calls meetings and places questions on the agenda for joint consideration.
>
> Resolutions are faithfully respected and when there is any matter liable to cause complications such as a clash of appeals or of financial projects, the Government always calls upon us to study the question. When we call upon the Government, there is always a response. A network of sub-committees of the Coordinating Committee has proliferated dealing with all sorts of questions.[48]

Section 11 of the Covenant provides for a 'special arrangement' to be added to it as another annex concerning tax exemption for the Zionist Organization and 'any of its institutions,' giving them the benefit of governmental status within the State of Israel. In a significant contrast, the same Zionist institutions are treated as private charitable funds for tax purposes by the United States Government. The result is substantial tax benefits to these institutions in both cases but upon opposite juridical bases. It must be doubted that the same fund-raising institutions can be public and governmental in Israel and private and philanthropic in the United States.

Annex A of the Covenant consists of a note to the Zionist Executive from the Government. The first paragraph indicates that the Zionist Executive 'and its institutions' are to be treated as parts of the Government of Israel in terms of administrative orders concerning 'investigations, searches and detentions in Government offices.' The second paragraph states that the Executive will not maintain, within Israel, 'judicial or investigative machinery of its own' except consistent with Israel law. In Annex B the Government establishes an 'order of precedence at official ceremonies' which includes both Zionist Organization and Government officials. This does not refer to diplomatic precedence extended to officials of a foreign state by the Government of Israel, but is based on 'the Government's decision' concerning internal Government of Israel ceremonies. Although this may be accurately termed a matter of ceremonial precedence, it is, nevertheless, a matter of substantive importance because it means that the Zionist Organization officials are recognized in the most direct manner as being a part of the structure of the Government.

Zionist juridical ideology has been accurately described by Mr Moses Lasky, a distinguished California lawyer:

> All Jews of the world form one Nation, the State of Israel is the lawful representative of that portion of the Nation dwelling in Zion [Israel], and the Zionist Organization is the authorized representative of the Nation dwelling elsewhere throughout the world. The two are co-ordinate representatives of one nation and thus may make covenants and treaties and cooperate with each other to a common end.[49]

At the Zionist General Council meeting in Israel in 1954, at the time of the effectuation of the Covenant, the chairman of the committee on the 'Status of the Zionist Organization' stated concerning the juridical status provided for the Organization by the Covenant:

> From the letters attached to the Covenant you will see that the Government has granted the Jewish Agency and its institutions the status of Government institutions. In addition it has consented to give the Chairman and Members of the Zionist General Council official status in its official ceremonies.[50]

While the Covenant appears to be an agreement in form, it is a unilateral public law instrument in substance, with the Zionist political elite represented on each side of the supposed negotiations. Apparently, the covenant or agreement form was highly desirable as a matter of appearance since it seems to show in both the title and the text that the Government of Israel and the Zionist Executive are two separate bodies. Although the Zionist Organization/Jewish Agency has a different name and other superficial indications of separate identity from the Government, it is subject to the overriding control of the Government of Israel. There are two alternative conclusions which may be drawn from the evidence. The first is that there is only one Zionist-Israel sovereignty in fact and in law. In its internal separation of powers, provision may be made for the performance of particular governmental functions by the Zionist Organization as is done presently through the Coordination Board pursuant to the Status Law and the Covenant. In the same way, the substance of the present separation of powers may be provided for *de facto* as was done prior to the Covenant. The separation of powers may also be changed in any way including a performance of the Organization's governmental functions by another part of the Government which is given a name suggesting a separate identity. Further, any existing separation of powers may be abolished with the result that all functions are performed directly by the Government as such. In the event of any such changes, there could be no substitute for a juridical analysis which examines the governmental functions performed rather than the names employed.[51]

An alternate conclusion which is also supported by both the primary and secondary public law sources is that the Organization/Agency is a public body closely linked in law to the Government and controlled by it. Even though section 11 of the Status Law designates the Zionist Executive as a 'juristic body,' this falls short of the multilateral state authority which is required to constitute a public body in international law. However, when section 11 is combined with the other provisions of the Status Law and Covenant and the actual public body functions performed since 1948, it does provide some indication of the intent to continue public body status under Israeli domestic law. If the conclusion of the public body status of the Organization/Agency should be appraised as more persuasive than the conclusion of its status as part of the Government of Israel, the same juridical effects would follow. It would then be clear that the public body is subject to all relevant legal limitations including those which bind its creator state. The Organization/Agency would still have to be recognized as an integral part of a single Zionist-Israel sovereignty because of the effective control the Government exerts over it.

The most compelling conclusion is that the Zionist-Israel sovereignty contains an Organization/Agency component which is in some aspects part of the Government and in others its captive public body. Whichever aspects predominate at a particular time and for a particular purpose, the component is nevertheless subject to effective control by the Government of Israel. The juridical effects are not varied whether the Organization/Agency be appraised as government, public body, or both. In any or all three of these appraisals of status it remains a component of the single Zionist-Israel sovereignty.

III The Zionist Organization/Jewish Agency under United States Law

A. The Requirements of the Foreign Agents Registration Act (F.A.R.A.)

The purpose of the Foreign Agents Registration Act (F.A.R.A.)[52] is not to prevent the political activities, including propaganda, in the United States of the non-diplomatic agents of foreign governments, public bodies, and other principals. It is, in contrast, to describe completely the identity and characteristics of the foreign principal for which the agent acts and the particular political activities. To accomplish this purpose, such agents are required to register with the Department of Justice, to provide detailed information, and to file supplementary registration information every six months. Section 2 (a) (2) of the F.A.R.A. requires each registrant to provide, *inter alia*:

> a true and complete copy of its charter, articles of incorporation, association, constitution, and bylaws, and amendments thereto; a copy of every other instrument or document and a statement of the

terms and conditions of every oral agreement relating to its organization, powers, and purposes; and a statement of its ownership and control.

Until 1971 the Zionist registrant under the F.A.R.A. was the 'American Section of the Jewish Agency for Israel,' Registrant No. 208. Its initial and supplementary registration statements did not meet the requirements of section 2 (a) (2) quoted above. During the period 1968–1970 administrative proceedings were instituted before the Department of Justice to compel compliance. This was done initially on behalf of the American Council for Judaism, then the principal anti-Zionist Jewish organization in the United States, and subsequently on behalf of American Jewish Alternatives to Zionism.[53] In spite of the strenuous Zionist opposing arguments, Registrant No. 208 was compelled to file the World Zionist Organization–Jewish Agency Status Law (1952)[54] on October 25, 1968, and the Covenant Between the Government of Israel and the Zionist Executive Called Also the Executive of the Jewish Agency (1954)[55] on August 28, 1969. These two constitutive documents of the agent and its foreign principal (the Government of Israel or the Zionist Organization/Jewish Agency or both) created serious potential damage to each in that the documents demonstrated that neither the registrant nor its foreign principal were the voluntary private organizations which they claimed to be.

An even greater blow was dealt to the registrant and its foreign principal on June 9, 1970 when the Department of Justice required the filing of the tax annex to the Covenant. It is formally titled 'Appendix to the Covenant Between the Government and the Executive of the Jewish Agency' and dated July 19, 1957.[56] Its first section provides in full: 'In this Appendix – "The Executive" – includes the Jewish National Fund and Karen Hayesod -- United Israel Appeal.' The balance of the Tax Appendix provides comprehensive tax immunity for the funds on this premise that they are an integral part of the Zionist Executive. The juridical effect is that they are either a part of the Government of Israel or of its created and controlled public body.

Subsequent actions demonstrated the concern of the Zionist Organization/Jewish Agency. In 1971 there was an alleged and highly publicized 'reorganization' of the Zionist Organization/Jewish Agency which resulted in changing its name for some purposes to the 'Reconstituted Jewish Agency.'[57] The apparent purpose of the 'reorganization' was to put the Zionist political and the non-Zionist philanthropic operations on a plane of nominal equality with each of them having one-half of the control of the Jewish Agency as it was reconstituted.[58] This would result in the appearance of equal control of the disposition of the funds raised by the Jewish Agency and its subordinate institutions. One of the interesting aspects of this 1971 'reorganization' is that it was modeled upon the earlier 'reorganization' which took place under the auspices of Dr. Chaim Weizmann, then the President of the Zionist Organization/Jewish Agency, in 1929.[59] Dr. Weizmann's stated purpose in creating the 'enlarged Jewish Agency' in 1929 was to bring non-

Zionist philanthropists into the work of the Zionist Organization/Jewish Agency by creating the impression that they had a share of control of the use of the funds raised. It was important then as in 1971 that the funds not appear to be under political control because of the domestic laws which grant tax deductions for charitable purposes in the United States.

During the same year 1971, the American Section of the Jewish Agency, Registrant No. 208, de-registered under the F.A.R.A. on the alleged grounds that it was no longer engaged in political activities. In the same year the Zionist Organization/Jewish Agency registered under the name, 'World Zionist Organization–American Section, Inc.' as Registrant No. 2278. Registrant No. 208 had consistently listed its foreign principal as 'The Executive of the Jewish Agency for Israel, Jerusalem, Israel,' whereas Registrant No. 2278 has consistently listed its foreign principal as 'The Executive of the World Zionist Organization, Jerusalem, Israel.' In short, the foreign principal of the past and present registrants is identical although the wording is different. The striking change in the new registration is that neither the Status Law (1952), nor the Covenant (1954), nor the Tax Appendix (1957) has been filed initially or subsequently although the foreign principal is the same as that of the prior registrant and the specifics of the registration statements of the past and present registrants provide persuasive evidence that the foreign agents (the registrants) are the same or substantially the same.

B. The 1975 Israeli 'Amendment' to the Status Law

In 1975 the Israeli Knesset enacted a law[60] which prescribed certain amendments to the Status Law (1952). One of its features included a new section 2A to be added to the earlier law (termed 'the principal Law' in the amendment). This section provides in full: 'The Jewish Agency for Israel is an independent voluntary association consisting of the World Zionist Organisation and other organisations and bodies. It operates in the State of Israel in fields chosen by it with the consent of the Government.'[61] The juridical effect of this declaration that the Jewish Agency is 'an independent voluntary association' amounts to no change at all in the existing basic Government of Israel control of the single Zionist Organization/Jewish Agency. The lack of change is emphasized by the provision that the Jewish Agency contains the Zionist Organization within it.

Section 3 of the principal law which stressed the identity of the Jewish Agency and the Zionist Organization is replaced by an amendment which states that they (identified separately by name) 'take care of immigration as before.' The 'replaced' wording in section 3 of the principal law read that the single organization 'takes care as before of immigration.' Section 4 of the amendment changes section 4 of the principal law by making each of the separately named bodies 'authorised agencies' for operation within the State of Israel by authority of its government. This, like the 'change' in section 3, is not a change in substance since the added section 2A which makes the Zionist Organization part of the Jewish Agency remains in effect.

In the same way, other provisions of the supposed amendments appear to be designed to produce changes in appearance without change in substance.

Sections 6, 7, and 8 of the amended law provide, *inter alia*, for two covenants to be entered into – one with the Agency and one with the Organization. Section 6 of the amendments provides that a new subsection shall be added to section 8 of the principal law and this subsection states in full: 'The Covenant with the Jewish Agency for Israel shall provide for full cooperation and coordination on its part with the State of Israel and its Government in accordance with the laws of the State.'[62] This significant section provides for continuing control of the Jewish Agency (and its stated sub-division the Zionist Organization) by 'the laws of the State' and this is a specific enactment resulting in no change in the prior constitutive authority and documents of the Organization/Agency. Sections 8, 9 and 10 of the amended law provide some appearance of a separation between Organization and Agency but without change in meaning.

The name of the principal law is 'World Zionist Organization–Jewish Agency (Status) Law', and section 11 of the amended law solemnly proclaims that the principal law shall be 'renamed' the 'World Zionist Organisation and Jewish Agency for Israel (Status) Law.'

In many ways the most interesting part of the 1975 amendments is section 12 (the last section)[63] which states that the amendments shall be effective *ex post facto* from June 21, 1971 which is the date when the Jewish Agency was 'reconstituted.' As Israeli municipal law, the 1975 amendments are designed to give a semblance of reality to the alleged changes made by the 'reconstitution' of the Jewish Agency at that time. It is probable that the *ex post facto* aspect is also designed to lend credibility to the de-registration of a Zionist agent and the registration of a supposedly different Zionist agent in 1971. There is, however, no lawful method by which an Israeli law can be given *ex post facto* effect in so far as it has an impact on events in the United States. Even if the 1975 law could be given such effect, it would be without legal significance because of the lack of substantive change in it.

Careful searches of the initial and supplementary registration statements of the World Zionist Organization–American Section, Inc., Registrant No. 2278, do not reveal the filing of the 1975 amendments or of the two 'covenants' referred to in section 5 of the amendments. Consequently, Registrant No. 2278 has not complied with the requirements of the F.A.R.A. and, thus far, the United States Department of Justice has not compelled it to do so. The 1975 amendments, its 'covenants,' if in existence, the 1952 'principal law,' the Covenant of 1954, and its annexes including the Tax Appendix of 1957 remain its constitutive authority and their filing is required by section 2 (a) (2). Among other sections of the F.A.R.A. which are violated in section 2 (a) (3) which requires, *inter alia*, full information concerning:

> the extent, if any, to which each such foreign principal is supervised, directed, owned, controlled, financed, or subsidized, in whole or in

part, by any government of a foreign country or foreign political party, or by any other foreign principal.

C. Conclusion

The conclusion of juridical status which follows from this evaluation of the 1975 'amendments' and the failure of the current Zionist Registrant No. 2278 to comply with the F.A.R.A. is the same as that based upon the pre-existing constitutive documents. It is that the Zionist Organization/Jewish Agency and its fund raising institutions in the United States, including the Jewish National Fund, the United Israel Appeal, and its subsidiary the United Jewish Appeal, are either parts of the Government of Israel or they comprise a public body created and controlled by that government. The fund raising components of the Organization/Agency do not exercise effective domestic control over the allocation and use of funds raised in the United States and cannot do so under the constitutive authority which controls them. More specifically, the funds raised are disbursed under the direct control of the Government of Israel or under its indirect control through the Organization/Agency. This results in the mingling of the supposed philanthropic contributions with the other financial resources of the Government of Israel. Consequently, the funds do not meet the requirements of United States law[64] for tax exempt status and for the tax deductibility of contributions made to them. This conclusion is well known and was stated as long ago as 1963 by the authoritative Zionist scholar, Professor Nadav Safran: 'Moreover, the American government never seriously attempted to question the classification of the billion dollars of donations made by American Jews as tax-exempt "charity", though this money went, in effect, into the general development budget of Israel.'[65]

In making a legal analysis of the Zionist Organization/Jewish Agency and its political and financial activities, it is helpful to rely upon the wisdom of John Locke written almost three centuries ago: 'For it is not Names, that Constitute Governments, but the use and exercise of those Powers that were intended to accompany them. . . .'[66]

Notes

1. Mallison, 'The Zionist-Israel Juridical Claims to Constitute "The Jewish People" Nationality Entity and to Confer Membership in It: Appraisal in Public International Law,' 32 *Geo. Wash. L. Rev.* 983–1075 (1964).

2. 20 *Israel Digest* (Amer. Ed.) No. 16, p. 5, col. 2 (Aug. 12, 1977) [published by the World Zionist Organization-Amer. Sec.].

3. Amendment I to the U.S. Constitution prohibits the government from making distinctions between individuals on the basis of religious identification. Concerning the settlements, see Mallison & Mallison, *Settlements and the Law: A Juridical Analysis of the Israeli Settlements*

in the Occupied Territories (Amer. Educational Trust, Wash., D.C., 1982).

4. *E.g.*, The Law of Return, as amended, 4 Israel Laws (auth. transl.) 114 (1950). *Rufeisen v. Minister of Interior* ('Brother Daniel Case'), 16 P.D. 2428 (1962), Selected Judgments of Sup. Ct. Israel: Spec. Vol. p. 1 (1971) and *Shalit v. Minister of Interior*, 23 P.D. (II) 477 (1969), *id.* at p. 35 apply the statute to determine membership in 'the Jewish people.'

5. The same conclusion is reached in Taylor, *Prelude to Israel: An Analysis of Zionist Diplomacy, 1897-1947*, v, vi (1959).

6. Herzl, *The Jewish State: An Attempt at a Modern Solution of the Jewish Question* 19, 20 (D'Avigdor & Cohen transl., 1943).

7. *Supra* note 1.

8. Hertzberg (ed.), *The Zionist Idea: A Historical Analysis and Reader*, Introduction at 49 (1966).

9. *The Attorney-General of the Government of Israel v. Adolf Eichmann*, 36 Int'l L. Reps. 18–276 (Dist. Ct. of Jerusalem, Israel, Dec. 11–12, 1961), aff'd 36 *id.* 277–342 (Sup. Ct. of Israel, May 29, 1962).

10. Official Text of the International Military Tribunal, Nuremberg (1947) [cited hereafter as I.M.T.]. See the Judgment of the Tribunal, 1 I.M.T. 171.

11. See *e.g. United States v. Ohlendorf* ('The Einsatzgruppen Case'), 4 Trials of War Criminals Before the Nuernberg Military Tribunals 1, 496–500 (1948).

12. The requirements of universality of jurisdiction stated in the text are based upon the decisions of the post-World War II trials conducted by the United States and its allies. The judicial formulation is reflected in McDougal & Feliciano, *Law and Minimum World Public Order: The Legal Regulation of International Coercion* 717–18 (1961). See also 1 Oppenheim-Lauterpacht, *International Law* 753 (8th ed. 1955).

13. *Supra* note 9.

14. *Id.* at 52–53.

15. The same conclusion is reached in Rogat, *The Eichmann Trial and the Rule of Law* 15–17 and *passim* (1961).

16. Letter from Assistant Secretary of State Talbot to Dr. Elmer Berger, Executive Vice President of the American Council for Judaism, April 20, 1964 in 8 Whiteman, *Digest of International Law* 35 (1967).

17. The continuing claims after the establishment of the State of Israel are examined in *supra* note 1, at 1036–49. The continuing use of the 'Jewish people' claim is illustrated by Israeli representatives at the United Nations. See, *e.g.*, the statement of Ambassador Yehuda Blum, the Permanent Representative of Israel, on the floor of the General Assembly when the agenda item 'Question of Palestine' was being considered on 2 Dec. 1980 in which he advanced the 'Jewish people' claim five times. 35 *G.A. Provisional Verbatim Record*, A/35/PV. 77 at 46.

18. Article entitled 'Tasks and Character of a Modern Zionist,' based on a speech delivered at the World Conference of Haichud Haolami on Aug. 8, 1951. Jerusalem Post, Aug. 17, 1951 at 5, cols. 3–8 at cols. 4–5.

19. Organization Dept. of the Zionist Executive, *Session of the Zionist General Council* 44 (July 21–29, 1954).

20. 'Practice has abandoned the doctrine that States are the exclusive subjects of international rights and duties.' Memorandum of the Secretary-

General of the United Nations, *Survey of International Law in Relation to the Work of Codification of the International Law Commission*, A/cn. 4/Rev. 1, p. 19 (Feb. 10, 1949).

21 *Advisory Opinion*, [1949] I.C.J. Reps. 174.

22. *E.g.*, the *Mavrommatis Palestine Concessions Cases* cited in *infra* note 27 which held that the Zionist Organization was a public body limited by law.

23. At Basle, Herzl described the Zionist Organization as 'an agency for the Jewish people' intended to negotiate with governments. First Zionist Congress Address of Aug. 29, 1897 in Hertzberg, *supra* note 8 at 226.

24. See Mallison, 'The Balfour Declaration: An Appraisal in International Law,' in I. Abu Lughod (ed.), *The Transformation of Palestine* 61 (1971).

25. 1 Esco Foundation for Palestine, *Palestine: A Study of Jewish, Arab, and British Policies* 151–77 (1947); Taylor, *Prelude to Israel: An Analysis of Zionist Diplomacy 1897–1947* at 6–7 (1959).

26. The entire Mandate is set forth as the preamble to the Anglo-American Convention on Palestine, 44 U.S. Stat. 2184 (1925). It also appears in 2 UNSCOP, *Report to the General Assembly, 2 U.N. GAOR, Supp. 11*, pp. 18–22, U.N. Doc. A/364 Add. 1 (9 Sept. 1947), and in Stoyanovsky, *The Mandate for Palestine* 355 (1928).

27. [1924] P.C.I.J. ser. A, No. 2; [1925] P.C.I.J. ser. A, No. 5; [1927] P.C.I.J. ser. A, No. 11.

28. Jewish Agency for Palestine, *Book of Documents Submitted to the General Assembly of the United Nations Relating to the Establishment of the National Home for the Jewish People*, 28, 29 (Tulin, ed. 1947).

29. Anglo-American Committee of Inquiry, *Report to the United States Government and His Majesty's Government in the United Kingdom* 39 (1946).

30. Mallison, 'The Legal Problems Concerning the Juridical Status and Political Activities of the Zionist Organization/Jewish Agency: A Study in International and United States Law,' 9 *William & Mary Law Review* 554 at 577–78 (1968).

31. The present and following textual paragraphs are based upon *id.*, *passim*.

32. Grossman, *Germany's Moral Debt: The German-Israel Agreement* 37 (1954).

33. Zionist Organization & Jewish Agency, *Reports of the Executive Submitted to the 23rd Zionist Congress* 240–90 (Aug. 1951).

34. *Id.* at 822.

35. 2 Information Dep't of Jewish Agency and World Zionist Organization, *The Jewish Agency's Digest of Press and Events* 318 (Nov. 18, 1949).

36. *Supra* note 33, *passim*.

37. *Provisional Verbatim Record of the 2,375th Security Council Meeting*, S/PV. 2375, pp. 12–15.

38. The attack-invasion of June-Sept., 1982 is appraised in Mallison & Mallison, *Armed Conflict in Lebanon, 1982: Humanitarian Law in a Real World Setting* 1–33 (Amer. Educational Trust, Wash. D.C., 1983).

39. *Supra* note 37 at 9–11.

40. *Id.* Mr. Blum did not produce any evidence of P.L.O. responsibility for any of the alleged attacks.

41. *Id.* at 61.

42. Organization Dep't of the Zionist Executive, *Fundamental Issues of Zionism at the 23rd Zionist Congress* 135–36 (1952). The term 'Youth Aliyah' refers to youth immigration to Israel.

43. *Supra* note 35 at 1060–61 (May 16, 1952).

44. *Id.* at 1069–70.

45. State of Israel, *Government Year-Book* 57 (1953–54). The Status Law is in 7 Israel Laws (auth. transl.) 3.

46. The text of the Covenant is in Organization Dept. of the Zionist Executive, *Session of the Zionist General Council* 106–09 (July 21–29, 1954).

47. The same conclusion is reached by M. Lasky, *Between Truth and Repose* 41 (Amer. Council for Judaism, 1956).

48. *Supra* note 46 at 210–11 (March 18–26, 1963).

49. *Supra* note 47 at 49.

50. *Supra* note 46 at 105.

51. See *infra* note 66 and accompanying text.

52. 52 U.S. Stat. 63 (1938) as amended, 22 U.S. Code Sec. 611 (1964). Injunctive remedies were added to the F.A.R.A. in the 1966 amendments, sec. 8 (f). These amendments greatly facilitated the administrative proceedings before the Department of Justice during 1968–1970. See the text accompanying *infra* notes 53–56. The amendments were the main result of the Senate Hearings on Zionist activities conducted under the chairmanship of Senator J.W. Fulbright in 1963.

53. A charitable organization dedicated to maintaining Judaism as a religion of universal moral values and exposing the basic inconsistency between Judaism and Zionism.

54. 7 Israel Laws 3, in Appendix A.

55. Appendix B.

56. Appendix C.

57. A comprehensive description and analysis of the 'reorganization' is in the semi-official Jerusalem Post, 'Special Supplement – Founding Assembly: The Reconstituted Jewish Agency,' June 21, 1971.

58. The 'Pincus Plan' (named for Mr. Arye Louis Pincus, the Chairman of the Zionist Organization/Jewish Agency Executive) providing for an equal number of non-Zionist and Zionist delegates to the Zionist Organization/Jewish Agency Assembly was implemented. *Id.* at 3 and 16. A large number of the named 'non-Zionist' delegates are apparently committed Zionists. *Id.* at 16.

59. *Trial and Error: The Autobiography of Chaim Weizmann*, 376–89 (Chap. 27 entitled 'The Jewish Agency') (East and West Library, London, 1950).

60. World Zionist Organisation-Jewish Agency for Israel (Status) (Amendment) Law, 30 Israel Laws 43 (1975), in Appendix D.

61. 30 Israel Laws 43 at 44.

62. *Id.*

63. *Id.* at 45.

64. Internal Revenue Code, 26 U.S. Code Secs. 170 and 501 (c) (3) concerning the immunity from taxation of charitable organizations and the tax deductibility of gifts to them.

65. *The United States and Israel* 278 (Harvard, 1963).

66. John Locke, *The Second Treatise of Government: an Essay Concerning the True Original, Extent, and End of Civil Government* sec. 215 (1698) in *John Locke: Two Treatises of Government* 427 (Laslett ed. 1960).

Appendix A: World Zionist Organization–Jewish Agency (Status) Law, 5713–1952, Passed by the Knesset on the 6th Kislev, 5713 (24 November 1952)

1. The State of Israel regards itself as the creation of the entire Jewish people, and its gates are open, in accordance with its laws, to every Jew wishing to immigrate to it.

2. The World Zionist Organization, from its foundation five decades ago, headed the movement and efforts of the Jewish people to realize the age-old vision of the return to its homeland and, with the assistance of other Jewish circles and bodies, carried the main responsibility for establishing the State of Israel.

3. The World Zionist Organization, which is also the Jewish Agency, takes care as before of immigration and directs absorption and settlement projects in the State.

4. The State of Israel recognizes the World Zionist Organization as the authorized agency which will continue to operate in the State of Israel for the development and settlement of the country, the absorption of immigrants from the Diaspora and the coordination of the activities in Israel of Jewish institutions and organizations active in those fields.

5. The mission of gathering in the exiles, which is the central task of the State of Israel and the Zionist Movement in our days, requires constant efforts by the Jewish people in the Diaspora; the State of Israel, therefore, expects the cooperation of all Jews, as individuals and groups, in building up the State and assisting the immigration to it of the masses of the people, and regards the unity of all sections of Jewry as necessary for this purpose.

6. The State of Israel expects efforts on the part of the World Zionist Organization for achieving this unity; if, to this end, the Zionist Organization, with the consent of the Government and the approval of the Knesset, should decide to broaden its basis, the enlarged body will enjoy the status conferred upon the World Zionist Organization in the State of Israel.

7. Details of the status of the World Zionist Organization – whose representation is the Zionist Executive, also known as the Executive of the Jewish Agency – and the form of its cooperation with the Government shall be determined by a Covenant to be made in Israel between the Government and the Zionist Executive.

8. The Covenant shall be based on the declaration of the 23rd Zionist Congress in Jerusalem that the practical work of the World Zionist Organization and its various bodies for the fulfillment of their historic tasks in Eretz Israel requires full cooperation and coordination on its part with the State of Israel and its Government, in accordance with the laws of the State.

9. There shall be set up a committee for the coordination of the activities of the Government and Executive in the spheres in which the Executive shall operate according to the Covenant; the tasks of the Committee shall be determined by the Covenant.

10. The Covenant and any variation or amendment thereof made with the consent of the two parties shall be published in 'Reshumot' and shall come into force on the day of publication, unless they provide for an earlier or later day for this purpose.

11. The Executive is a juristic body and may enter into contracts, acquire,

hold and relinquish property and be a party to any legal or other proceeding.
12. The Executive and its funds and other institutions shall be exempt from taxes and other compulsory Government charges, subject to such restrictions and conditions as may be laid down by the Covenant; the exemption shall come into force on the coming into force of the Covenant.

DAVID BEN-GURION
Prime Minister

YOSEPH SPRINZAK
Chairman of the Knesset
Interim President of the State

Appendix B: Covenant between the Government of Israel (hereafter the Government) and the Zionist Executive Called also the Executive of the Jewish Agency (hereafter the Executive)

Entered into this day, in accordance with the Zionist Organization-Jewish Agency Status Law, 1952.

Functions of Executive

1. The functions of the Zionist Executive which are governed by this Covenant are: The organizing of immigration abroad and the transfer of immigrants and their property to Israel; participation in the absorption of immigrants in Israel; Youth Immigration; agricultural settlement in Israel; the acquisition and amelioration of land in Israel by institutions of the Zionist Organization, the Keren Kayemeth Le Israel and the Keren Hayesod; participation in the establishment and the expansion of development enterprises in Israel; the encouragement of private capital investments in Israel; assistance to cultural enterprises and institutions of higher learning in Israel; the mobilization of resources for financing these functions; the coordination of the activities in Israel of Jewish institutions and organizations acting within the sphere of these functions with the aid of public funds.

Activities under the Law

2. Any function carried out in Israel by the Executive or on its behalf hereunder shall be executed in accordance with the laws of Israel and such administrative regulations in force from time to time as govern activities of governmental authorities whose functions cover or are affected by the activity in question.

Immigration

3. In organizing immigration and in the handling of immigrants, the Executive shall act in pursuance of a programme agreed upon with the Government or authorized by the Coordinating Board (see Para. 8). Immigrants will require visas in accordance with the Law of Return 5711–1950.

Coordination Between Institutions

4. The Executive shall, with the consent of the Government, coordinate the activities in Israel of Jewish institutions and organizations which act within the sphere of the functions of the Executive.

Transfer of Functions

5. The Executive may carry out its functions alone, through its existing

institutions, or such as it may establish in future, and it may also obtain the participation of other institutions in Israel, provided that it may not transfer any of its powers or rights under this Covenant without the consent of the Government; and the Executive shall not authorize any body or institution to carry out its functions, in whole or in part, except upon prior notice to the Government.

Mobilization of Resources

6. The Executive shall be responsible for the mobilization of the financial and material resources required for the execution of its functions, by means of the Keren Hayesod, the Keren Kayemeth Le Israel and other funds.

Legislation

7. The Government shall consult the Executive in regard to legislation specially affecting the functions of the Executive before such legislation is submitted to the Knesset.

Coordination Board

8. For the purpose of coordinating activities between the Government and the Executive in all spheres to which this Covenant applies, there shall be established a Coordination Board (hereafter called the Board). The Board shall be composed of an even number of members, not less than four, half of whom shall be members of the government appointed by it, and half of whom shall be members of the Executive appointed by it. The Government and the Executive shall be entitled from time to time to replace the members of the Board by others from among their members.

Its Activities

9. The Board shall meet at least once a month. It may appoint subcommittees consisting of members of the Board or also non-members. The Board shall from time to time submit to the Government and the Executive reports of its deliberations and recommendations. Subject as aforesaid, the Board shall make its own rules of procedure.

Permits and Facilities

10. The Government will see to it that its duly authorized agencies shall issue to the Executive and its institutions all permits and facilities required by law for activities carried out in accordance with this Covenant so as to facilitate the Executive's functions.

Relief from Taxes

11. Gifts and legacies to the Executive or to any of its institutions shall be exempt from Inheritance Tax. All other problems connected with the exemption of the Executive, its Funds and its other institutions from payment of taxes, customs duties and other governmental levies, shall be the subject of a special arrangement between the Executive and the Government. This arrangement shall be formulated in an annex to this Covenant within eight months, as an integral part thereof, and shall be effective as from the date of signature of this Covenant.

Alterations

12. All proposals for alterations or amendments to this Covenant, or any addition thereto, must be made in writing and no alteration or amendment of this Covenant, or addition thereto, shall be made except in writing.

Notifications
13. Any notice to be sent to the Government shall be sent to the Prime Minister, and any notice to be sent to the Executive shall be sent to the Chairman of the Executive in Jerusalem.

Date of Coming into Force
14. This Covenant shall come into force on the date of signature.

IN WITNESS WHEREOF, etc.
SIGNED – Jerusalem
July 26, 1954

FOR THE GOVERNMENT
MOSHE SHARITT,
Prime Minister

FOR THE ZIONIST EXECUTIVE
BERL LOCKER
DR. NAHUM GOLDMANN
Chairmen

Annex A

Jerusalem, July 26, 1954

The Chairman
Zionist Executive
The Jewish Agency
Jerusalem

Dear Mr. Chairman,

I have the honour to inform you of the Government's decision that any administrative order that may be in force from time to time in regard to investigations, searches and detentions in Government offices shall apply also to the Executive and its institutions as defined in the Covenant entered into this day between the Government of Israel and the Zionist Executive.

You have agreed, and the Government has taken note, that the Zionist Executive will not maintain in Israel judicial or investigative machinery of its own, except in compliance with the laws of the State and in constant coordination with the Attorney-General of the Government of Israel.

Yours sincerely,
(sgd.)
Prime Minister

Annex B

Jeruslem, July 26, 1954

The Chairman
Zionist Executive
The Jewish Agency
Jerusalem

Dear Mr. Chairman,

I have the honour to inform you of the Government's decision that in the order of precedence at official ceremonies the Chairmen of the Zionist Executive and the Chairman of the Zionist General Council will immediately follow the Members of the Government; Members of the Zionist Executive will be equal in precedence to Members of the Knesset, and Members of the

Zionist General Council will immediately follow Members of the Knesset.

Yours sincerely
(Sgd.)
Prime Minister

Annex C

The Jewish Agency,
P.O.B. 92.
Jerusalem
July 26, 1954

The Prime Minister
Jerusalem

Dear Mr. Prime Minister,

We have the honour to acknowledge the receipt of your letter in which you inform us of the Government's decision that any administrative order that may be in force from time to time in regard to investigations, searches and detentions in Government offices shall apply also to the Executive and its institutions as defined in the Covenant entered into this day between the Government of Israel and the Zionist Executive.

We hereby confirm that the Zionist Executive has agreed not to maintain in Israel judicial or criminal investigative machinery of its own, unless approved by the Government, and that any such machinery will function in constant co-ordination with the Attorney-General of the Government of Israel.

Yours sincerely
(sgd.)
Chairmen of the Executive

Appendix C: Appendix to the Covenant Between the Government and the Executive of the Jewish Agency[1]

In accordance with section 11 of the Covenant between the Government of Israel (hereinafter 'the Government') and between the Executive of the Jewish Agency for Israel (hereinafter 'the Executive') made on 25 Tammuz 5714 (26 July, 1954), as amended, this Appendix was signed this day:

1. In this Appendix – 'The Executive' – includes the Jewish National Fund and Keren Hayesod – United Israel Appeal.

2. The Executive shall be exempt from taxes and the other government mandatory payments that are specified hereafter subject to such limitations and conditions as follows:

(a) From municipal property tax under the Municipal Property Tax Ordinance 1940, and from agricultural property tax under the Agricultural Property Tax Ordinance, 1942, for all property that is not leased thereby and was not given to another party in any manner whatsoever.

(b) From fees under the Land Transfer (Fees) Regulation 5716–1956 and under the Cooperative Houses Regulations, 5713–1953.

(c) From land appreciation tax under the Land Appreciation Tax Law, 5709–1949.

(d) From the tax under the War Damage Compensation Tax Law, 5711–1951, with respect to those properties of the Executive that were not leased and not given to another party in any manner whatsoever, and in respect whereof the Executive requests the exemption thereof from the tax. If the Executive requests an exemption for any property as aforesaid, it will not be entitled to compensation in respect of such property from the fund under the War Damage Compensation Law, as is set out in the War Damage Compensation Tax (Payment of Damages) Regulations 5713–1953.

(e) From compulsory loans under the Compulsory Loan Law, 5713–1953.

(f) From registration fees and capital fees under sections 1 (1), 1 (2), 1 (3), 1 (8), 1 (9) and 1 (10) of the Companies (Fees) Order 5713–1953, provided:

(i) that the exemption from the fee as aforesaid in respect of a company having a share capital shall apply only with respect to that portion of the fee which bears the same ratio to the total fee as is the ratio of the fraction of the share capital attributable to the Executive in respect whereof such fee is paid to the entire sum of the said share capital.

(ii) that the aforesaid exemption from the fee in respect of a company that does not have a share capital shall apply only to that portion of the fee the amount whereof is equal to the amount of the fee divided by the number of members for whom the fee is paid and multiplied by the number of members who are entitled to the exemption under this Appendix.

(g) (i) From purchase tax under the Purchase Tax Law, 5712–1952 – in respect of merchandise to the Executive the tax rate wherefor exceeds 10%, and in respect of the importation of all merchandise, provided that the merchandise is designated for the execution of its duties;

1 Yalkut Pirsumim 549, 5717 (1. 8. 1957), p. 1204.

(ii) From customs duties under the Customs Tariff and Exemptions Ordinance, 1937 – in respect of all merchandise imported by the Executive for development purposes and in respect whereof the Executive has notified the Director of Customs at the time of application for a licence to import the said merchandise, or if the merchandise does not require an import licence – prior to the order, of the import of the merchandise.

(iii) With reference to merchandise in respect whereof an exemption has been given under this section and which the Executive has transferred to another party or which has been transferred for a different use or purpose other than that wherefor an exemption was granted, the Executive shall be liable for payment of the tax commencing from the time of the transfer.

(h) From income tax and company profits tax, under the Income Tax Ordinance, 1947, and from any other tax imposed on income –with respect to all income of the Executive; provided that the exemption shall not apply to income from dividends or interest on debentures paid to the Executive by a company which deals in trade, works or any enterprise unless such company deals in trade, works or any enterprise designed for settling the land or absorption of immigrants.

(i) From stamp duty under the Stamp Duty Ordnance – with respect to the following documents:

(1) Debentures issued by the Executive in respect whereof stamp duty applies under item 26 of the Schedule to the Stamp Duty Ordinance, when a guarantee for their redemption is secured by guarantee of the State of Israel;

(2) The transfer of all stocks and shares in respect whereof stamp duty applies under item 37 (c) of the Schedule to the Stamp Duty Ordinance and in respect whereof the Executive is transferee;

(3) Receipts given by the Executive;

(4) Guarantees under item 27 of the said Schedule when the guaranteed party is the Executive or guarantees given by the Executive when the guaranteed party is a body supported by the Executive.

(j) From licence fees under the Transport Ordinance in respect of all vehicles of the Executive which are not private motor vehicles as defined in the Transport Ordinance.

3. (a) The exemptions granted to the Executive under sections 2 (a), 2 (b), 2 (c), 2 (d), 2 (e) and 2 (i) (1) shall also be granted to Himanutah Company Ltd.

(b) Himanutah Company Ltd., will be exempt from income tax, company profits tax, and from other taxes imposed upon income, with respect to income received by it from its real estate transactions.

4. The exemptions under this Appendix are supplementary to exemptions under any other law and do not detract therefrom.

IN WITNESS WHEREOF the parties have signed in Jerusalem on this day of 20 of Tammuz 5717 (19 July, 1957).

Nahum Goldman
The Zionist Executive

David Ben-Gurion
The Government of Israel

Appendix D: 30 Israel Laws 43 (1975)

World Zionist Organisation - Jewish Agency for Israel (Status) (Amendment) Law, 5736-1975*

Addition of section 2A.

1. In the World Zionist Organisation - Jewish Agency for Israel (Status) Law, 5713-1953 (hereinafter referred to as 'the principal Law'), the following section shall be inserted after section 2:

> '2A. The Jewish Agency for Israel is an independent voluntary association consisting of the World Zionist Organisation and other organisations and bodies. It operates in the State of Israel in fields chosen by it with the consent of the Government.'.

Replacement of section 3.

2. Section 3 of the principal Law shall be replaced by the following section:

> '3. The World Zionist Organisation and the Jewish Agency for Israel take care of immigration as before and conduct absorption and settlement projects in the State.'.

Amendment of section 4.

3. In section 4 of the principal Law, the words 'the World Zionist Organisation as the authorised agency which will continue to operate' shall be replaced by the words 'the World Zionist Organisation and the Jewish Agency for Israel as the authorised agencies which will continue to operate'.

Addition of section 6A.

4. The following section shall be inserted after section 6 of the principal Law:

> '6A. The provisions of sections 5 and 6 shall apply *mutatis mutandis* to the Jewish Agency for Israel.'.

Replacement of section 7.

5. Section 7 of the principal Law shall be replaced by the following section:

> '7. Details of the status of the World Zionist Organisation and the Jewish Agency for Israel and the form of their cooperation with the Government shall be determined by Covenants to be made in Israel between the Government and each of these two bodies.'.

Amendment of section 8.

6. In section 8 of the principal Law –

> (1) the words 'with the World Zionist Organisation' shall be inserted after the words 'the Covenant';
>
> (2) the subsection mark '(a)' shall be inserted after the '8' and the following subsection shall be added after subsection (a):
>
> > '(b) The Covenant with the Jewish Agency for Israel

* Passed by the Knesset on the 19th Tevet, 5736 (23rd December, 1975) and published in *Sefer Ha-Chukkim* No. 790 of the 28th Tevet, 5736 (1st January, 1976), p.49; the Bill and an Explanatory Note were published in *Hatza'ot Chok* No. 1115 of 5734, p. 162.

shall provide for full cooperation and coordination on its part with the State of Israel and its Government in accordance with the laws of the State.'.

Replacement of section 9. 7. Section 9 of the Law shall be replaced by the following section:

'9. Two committees shall be set up for the coordination of activities between the Government and the World Zionist Organization and the Jewish Agency for Israel in the spheres in which each of them is to operate according to the Covenant made with it. The tasks of the committees shall be determined by the Covenants.'.

Amendment of section 10. 8. In section 10 of the principal Law, the words 'The Covenant and any variation or amendment thereof' shall be replaced by the words 'The Covenants and any variation or amendment thereof'.

Replacement of section 11. 9. Section 11 of the principal Law shall be replaced by the following section:

'11. The World Zionist Organisation and the Jewish Agency for Israel are juristic persons and may enter into contracts, acquire, hold and relinquish property and be parties to any legal or other proceedings.'.

Amendment of section 12. 10. In section 12 of the principal Law, the words 'The Executive and its funds and other institutions' shall be replaced by the words 'The World Zionist Organisation and the Jewish Agency for Israel and their respective funds and other institutions'.

Change of title. 11. The principal Law shall be renamed the World Zionist Organisation and Jewish Agency for Israel (Status) Law, 5713–1952.

Commencement. 12. This Law shall have effect from the 28th Sivan, 5731 (21st June, 1971).

Yitzchak Rabin
Prime Minister

Efrayim Katzir
President of the State

Paper presented at 'A Conference for Understanding and Peace. Judaism or Zionism: What Difference for the Middle East?' 6-7 May 1983, in Washington DC.

 Portions of this paper are based on portions of Mallison, 'The Zionist-Israel Juridical Claims to Constitute "The Jewish People" Nationality Entity and to Confer Membership in It: Appraisal in Public International Law', *George Washington Law Review* (June, 1964) and on Mallison, 'The Legal Problems Concerning the Juridicial Status and Political Activities of the Zionist Organization/Jewish Agency: A Study in International and United States Law', *William & Mary Law Review* (Spring, 1968). Both Law Reviews have granted permission for the use of this material. An expanded version of this study will appear in Mallison & Mallison, *The Palestine Problem in International Law and World Order* to be published by Longman Group, London, in 1985.

17. The Press and the Middle East: A Passage through the Looking Glass

Lawrence Mosher

I chose as the title to my remarks this afternoon 'A Passage through the Looking Glass' because, when I returned to this country in late 1967, following the Arab-Israeli war of that June, I felt like an Alice in Wonderland. Americans and their press saw the Middle East very, very differently from how I did. Crossing that cultural frontier shocked me rudely and it took me a long time to come to terms with its implications.

I had been forewarned, however. While based in Beirut, I began a short-lived writing relationship with the *Reporter Magazine* in New York, a highly respected fortnightly that has since gone out of business. The first story that I both wrote and initiated described the Yemen civil war on the basis of my meetings with both the republicans and the royalists. The story was artfully edited, however, to portray Gamal Abdel Nasser as the villain, a judgement I had been careful not to make.

Later I would realize that the magazine's publisher, Max Ascoli, was an ardent Zionist who could view Nasser only through the narrow perspective of Israeli interests. If Nasser posed a threat to Israeli interests, then whatever Nasser did, whether it involved Israel or not, was bad, even in faraway little Yemen.

A few months later, the magazine asked me to do a story about Soviet involvement in Syria. I accepted that assignment but with a few reservations. In reporting that story, I visited Damascus and Jerusalem where I spent time with the United Nations Truce Supervision Organization, going over the history of the demilitarized zone that formed the Syrian-Israeli border then. It became clear that the annual spring stories filed by the press depicting Israeli farmers being bombarded by Syrian artillery had not told the whole story.

The Israeli tractors trundled farther east into the demilitarized zone every year to cultivate more land, land that legally did not belong to Israel, and the Syrians would respond by shooting at them. Arabs had originally lived in this area but they had long ago gone. Thus, the annual story of 'unprovoked Syrian hostility' was not entirely true. The sovereignty of the DMZs had never been settled because the Syrian-Israeli Armistice Commission, established in 1949, had long since stopped meeting. The Israelis had no right to attempt to use this strip and the Syrians, of course, had no right to shoot at the Israeli farmers.

But how many times have any of you heard this now well-worn Arab-Israeli news cliché reported this way? Needless to say, my story was never printed in the *Reporter Magazine* and I never attempted to write for it again.

Back in Washington, DC, I went to work for another now defunct publication, the *National Observer*, a weekly newspaper published by Dow Jones, the owner of the *Wall Street Journal*. The *Observer's* editors were remarkably unbiased concerning the Middle East and I was given a free hand to explore, among other subjects, the American Jewish scene. I had come to the realization, on passing through that crazy looking glass, that understanding the American Jewish community held the key to understanding why this country and its press had developed such a distorted perception of the Middle East and its major 20th-century dilemma, the birth of Israel.

Jack Bridge, the *Observer's* managing editor, had written an editorial in 1967 decrying the White House cover-up over the Israeli attack on the *USS Liberty*, a US spy ship that was operating off the Sinai coast at the outbreak of the Arab–Israeli war of 1967.

Parenthetically, when I went back to Israel on a trip in 1970, I met an Israeli officer who had been standing on the Sinai beach and who had observed the attack on the *USS Liberty* at first hand and who personally informed me that it was no mistake. That is not the continuing Israeli government version.

As far as I know, Bridge's protest was unique in the American press treatment of that event but it was a good harbinger. A few years later I wrote a long article about how the Jewish Agency raised money in America through the tax-exempt United Jewish Appeal to pay for such normal governmental functions in Israel as school construction and public health care. This 'charity' money, of course, allowed the Israeli government's treasury to spend otherwise obligated moneys on other items such as Phantom jets and settlements in the West Bank.

Incidentally, in pursuing that story, I initially met Tom and Sally Mallison who, through their prodigious legal research, established much of the basis for its reportage.

That story was triggered by a lawsuit brought by a sensitive and caring American Jew against the organization he had served for more than a decade, B'nai B'rith. Sol Droptese, who had run B'nai B'rith's international activities in looking after the welfare of Jews all over the world, had been fired for pointing out to his superiors that, if they continued to make their organization a tool of the Israeli government, then they should register as an agent of a foreign government.

Inherent in this story was and continues to be the very real loyalty conflict that Israel poses for so many American Jews. I don't have to tell you that my little yarn made a few waves. The late Gustave Levy, a prominent New York investment banker, who probably personally raised more money for Israel than anyone else in this country, led a delegation of leaders from

Wall Street to protest personally about my story to Warren Phillips, Dow Jones executive vice-president and now the company's president.

Phillips, a former reporter who is also Jewish, was not impressed and did not honour Levy's command to have me fired.

That story went on to be translated into Arabic, Hebrew, German and Russian. Its subhead, 'When the Blood Flows, the Money Flows', taken as a quote from a United Israel Appeal official during an interview, apparently still tickles memories. The point of its probe, however, has not been followed up much in the American press. The *Washington Post* did pursue the subject in a much flatter version later but the *New York Times*, which I knew from personal information was pursuing the same topic at the same time, never published the long story that one of its Washington-based staff had written.

Abe Rosenthal and Jim Greenfield, the *Times* managing editor and foreign editor respectively, reportedly could not decide how to handle it and so it died.

Since those days, the American press has come a long way in balancing the manner in which it portrays the Arab-Israeli conflict. My looking glass has grown less distorted and I thank God for that. I personally believe that the television coverage of the Israeli invasion of Lebanon in June 1982 marked a watershed in how the press is slowly, admittedly slowly, taking the kid gloves off its approach to matters Jewish. This transformation is probably more cultural than it is journalistic in its derivation. American Christians and Jews alike, I think, have had to deal with the feelings of guilt that arose out of the Jewish Holocaust but I think we are all getting healthier in handling this emotionally loaded hot stone as we come to terms with how properly to bury it.

I see this in the continuing but notably cooler debate these days over the Mall's Holocaust Memorial here in Washington and in the debate over Interior Secretary James G. Watt's curious attempt to compare the Holocaust to aspects of his born-again religious views.

It is not my purpose here this afternoon to present a current horrors list of press inequities in dealing with the Palestinian issue and contemporary and evolving Israel. That list can be made and I see no point in debating the conclusion, but there also is little question in my mind that the press has improved by light years since I began measuring its performance here in 1967.

As just one example of its growing sophistication, I would like to mention a Jack Anderson column that ran in the *Washington Post* on 25 April 1983. Headlined 'Terrorist Wages One-Man War Against Israel', it went on to describe Abu Nidal, the Palestinian radical whose group claimed the assassination of Dr Isam Sartawi, the PLO's European representative and a man I knew and highly respected. After listing Abu Nidal's many exploits, which included attacking a synagogue in Vienna and gunning down six persons in a Jewish-owned Paris restaurant, Anderson concluded his column:

> In the wake of the Israeli invasion of Lebanon, one secret State Department report speculated that, if Arafat were toppled from his shaky control of the PLO, the Palestinian movement . . . will probably disintegrate into radical splinter groups, which, in combination with other revolutionary forces in the region, would pose a grave threat to the moderate Arab governments.

The report added: 'Israel seems determined to vent this threat and can be expected to greatly expand its covert cooperations with revolutionary movements.' Asked what this meant, two well-placed intelligence sources explained that it was in Israel's interest to divide and conquer, to disrupt the PLO by setting one faction against the other. The sources said Israel had secretly provided funds to Abu Nidal's group.

No credible source, incidentally, suggested that Israeli leaders knowingly supported the assassination attempt on their own ambassador to provide a pretext for the Lebanon invasion. He ended the column that way.

I think this is a remarkable kind of reporting that certainly wouldn't have existed five years ago. But I also agree with my friend Elmer Berger, who has done so much to open my eyes to the hidden dynamics of the world Zionist movement, that the American press has not yet come to grips with reporting the continuing and heavy implications of this phenomenon. I hope that this conference's work in attempting to lay out clearly and dispassionately the root-cause of the Arab-Israeli dilemma, the basic contradiction in values between the principle of self-determination and the Zionist assumption of a peoplehood's superior claim to the land of Palestine, will build the basis for a more knowledgeable and less inhibited treatment of this continuing world tragedy by the American press.

18. The Rule of Principles

Dr Anis Al-Qasem

In this concluding statement, I shall not attempt to draw conclusions in the name of the participants. Such conclusions should be drawn by participants individually according to their own judgement of what they have heard. Instead, however, I am going to present for your consideration certain ideas and principles based on how EAFORD, as co-sponsor, views the problem and its solution.

It has been said that one of the main elements in the philosophy of that great Indian leader, Mahatma Gandhi, is the examination and re-examination of the criteria on which the solution of a problem has been based. The purpose of the examination is to find out whether the correct criteria have been used or whether elements foreign to the basic issue were the controlling and, consequently, a misleading factor.

The term 'criterion' is used to mean the principle taken as the standard in judging an issue or question. Being a principle, the criterion has the quality of general application to problems of the same nature. And in order to discover the criteria that should apply to any particular problem, it is essential to identify the problem correctly, and to present it as it really is, in a concise and objective manner. In this way we can find a solution, or a number of alternative solutions, as the case may merit, based on principles which are of general binding authority and application. To do otherwise would only produce solutions which leave the basic problem and its consequences unsolved.

It is in the light of these considerations that EAFORD decided to co-sponsor this Symposium. We wanted an examination of some of the assumptions and some of the criteria that have been applied or should be applied to the problem of peace in the Middle East. It has never been our intention to advocate one or more specific solutions. Our intention, however, has been and still is to provide a forum for the concerned to analyse and examine; to free the problem from irrelevant factors which have been introduced, in good or bad faith, and to reflect on the criteria that should be applied. And in all this, EAFORD is on the side of principle, in the belief that the 'rule of principles', like the 'rule of law', is ultimately the only guarantee of peace, mutual respect and understanding in the Middle East and elsewhere.

The basic principle which guides the activities of EAFORD is the principle of equality in dignity and rights for all peoples and individuals. We are with humanity as such, and to us, differences in colour or ethnic or national origin or religion are there to enrich humanity and not to degrade it. We judge peoples and individuals on their own merits and not on the basis of accidents over which they have no control. And while such accidents do not give us the right to differentiate in humanity and rights between peoples, equally they do not give the right to claim or practise superiority over those who differ from us for reasons beyond their control.

EAFORD did not invent the principle of equality in dignity and rights. That principle has been consecrated by the march of humanity through periods of suffering, victimization and discrimination, not least by the suffering of millions at the hands of the Nazi racists. It is enshrined in the Charter of the United Nations. It gave birth to the concept of war crimes and crimes against humanity for the violation of which the racist Nazi leaders were tried and convicted in the name of the international community. It inspired the most important international instruments on human rights, such as the Universal Declaration of Human Rights; the UN Declaration on the Elimination of All Forms of Racial Discrimination; the International Convention bearing the same name (see Appendix to this chapter), the International Convention on the Suppression and Punishment of the Crime of Apartheid; the International Convention on the Prevention and Punishment of the Crime of Genocide, and many other UN declarations and international conventions. It is the principle which inspires the decolonization process and resistance to foreign occupation or domination.

Thus in our approach to racism and racial discrimination as a violation of this principle of equality in dignity and rights, we apply criteria which are the birthright of man and which have been accepted by the international community as binding on all and which are applied by international and national tribunals. It has been applied by the Nuremberg Tribunal, the International Court of Justice and the European Court of Human Rights on the one hand and the Supreme Court of the United States, for example, on the other. This is not a subjective principle, nor are the criteria it establishes considerations selectively imposed by some against others. In fact, of all the international instruments on human rights, the International Convention on the Elimination of All Forms of Racial Discrimination of 1976 has received the largest number of ratifications – 115 states, including Israel, had ratified or acceded to this convention as at 1 July 1982, and most probably more states have ratified it since then. Therefore, when we judge the ideology or policies of any state, including Israel, we do not appeal to criteria invented by the Arabs or the Palestinians or the anti-Zionists. We appeal to criteria recognized and ratified by the international community, including Israel. It is true that Israel has not ratified a number of important human rights international conventions, but it is enough for our purposes that it has willingly ratified the Convention on the Elimination of Racial Discrimination and the Convention on the Crime of Genocide.

The anti-discrimination convention does not call upon signatory states only to abstain from racist policies, but also to review existing practices, policies and legislations, and to repeal those which are of discriminatory nature. The convention calls upon signatory states to prohibit and punish racist activities and organizations. It prohibits expropriation of land and property; it prohibits discriminatory legislation; it prohibits discrimination in the right to nationality and the right to return to one's country, as well as discrimination in civil or political rights; in short, it prohibits any form of discrimination based on ethnic or national belonging. We appeal to all to examine, in pursuance of the criteria which Israel itself has accepted, and determine for themselves, whether Israel is or is not in blatant and persistent violation of the human rights protected by this convention.

We in EAFORD are disturbed by the dangerous practice of the ratification of international conventions on human rights only for the record. This is particularly disturbing because one of the basic reasons for the conclusion of such conventions is to provide protection from the acts of the state itself and to involve the state directly and positively in providing such protection. When the state itself violates openly and persistently such rights in connection with a clearly definable ethnic or national group, and condones or encourages such violations by one group of the community against another, one cannot escape the conclusion that the whole system is that of racism and racial discrimination in ideology and policies.

The victims of such a system do not have any rights in the true sense. In the evening, the victim sleeps in the comfort of thinking that he owns the land he cultivates only to discover in the morning that a decision was taken in the darkness of the night to expropriate his land in favour of others. All rights become illusory: now he has them, now he has them not. And in the course of the Symposium we have heard much about these illusory rights.

When features of this kind are institutionalized in the very fabric of a state, how can such a state or its ideology be described as democratic or non-racist? Would the rule of law, which is based on equality before the law, have the meaning we normally attribute to it when discrimination forms the basis of the state and its ideology?

What kind of mentality, what kind of moral or religious values, what kind of conscience, would advocate, practise, encourage or support wholesale theft or usurpation of other people's lands, homes, orange groves, waters, livelihood, folklore, paintings, national dishes, books and research centres?

If we cannot correct the wrongs, at least let us refrain from singing their praises, or trying to force the victims to accept them as right and inevitable.

Ideologies of racial discrimination, by reason of the morals, acts and injustices they unleash, cannot but generate violence in order to attain and maintain their so-called achievements, and cannot but generate a reaction of violence on the part of the victims to protect or regain their rights, their lands, their homes and their lives. To justify and support the first and condemn the second is to confuse cause and effect, and to apply the wrong criteria. It is to condemn the children of Soweto, of Sabra and of Chatilla, instead of the murderers.

Under an ideology of racial domination there is no security for the victims or the oppressors. The security they pretend to provide to the dominant community is based on what that great American, former Senator Fulbright, has called 'the arrogance of power'. History teaches us that power has never been and will never be the eternal monopoly of any people or any country, and to rely on the rule of force instead of the 'rule of principles' is to court one tragic disaster after another.

We have seen some of the very tragic consequences of attempts at racial domination. The extermination of millions in gas chambers and concentration camps at the hands of the Nazis constitutes one of the darkest pages of human history, and the lessons of that Holocaust should never be forgotten. One lesson is that policies of racial domination are bound, sooner or later, to produce the justification for genocide and the act of genocide itself against the victims, and complete disregard for the right of others to life. During the February session of the UN Commission on Human Rights which I attended on behalf of my organization, EAFORD, I asked the representatives of Israel a question which received no answer. The question, which is recorded in the official records of the Commission, was this. Assuming that we fully accept the truth of the Israeli official statements regarding the massacre at Sabra and Chatilla, including the statement that when the Israeli authorities knew of the massacre they sent in the Israeli army to stop it, assuming all this to be true, then why did not the Israeli army arrest the culprits there and then and bring them to trial for the crime they had committed? As we all know, no one was arrested or interrogated, let alone tried, for his part in that most horrible crime. And Israel is a party to the International Convention on the Prevention and Punishment of the Crime of Genocide. No answer was given to that question and the Kahan Commission never addressed itself to it as a part of Israel's responsibility. The only answer which can be derived from the circumstances is that the right to life of the Palestinian women and children, and of all Palestinians in fact, is of no consequence and can be violated with impunity. Dealing with the responsibility of Sharon for the massacres, the Kahan Report records that 'from the Defence Minister himself we know that this consideration [i.e. humanitarian obligations] did not concern him in the least'. Another question which confirms this conclusion arises as a result of the findings of the Kahan Report: does the mere preparation of a report absolve the Israeli authorities from taking judicial action against those implicated in the massacre? The volumes prepared about the Nazi leaders were not considered a substitute for the trial of those leaders at Nuremberg. However. we sadly note that inside and outside Israel the Kahan Report seems to be considered a sufficient and final substitute for the trial of the culprits.

The conclusion of the report, that Israel's responsibility and the responsibility of its leaders for the massacre is 'indirect responsibility', is an unheard-of innovation in criminal law, international as well as municipal. In criminal law and even on the basis of the facts accepted by the Kahan Commission, Israeli leaders are accomplices in the full legal sense of the word and it is incumbent on the Israeli judicial authorities to prosecute them for the crime of genocide in accordance with the Genocide Convention to which Israel is a party. This is the only way for the Israeli judicial authorities to distinguish themselves from the Nazi judicial authorities who failed to prosecute those Nazi leaders who committed acts of genocide against the Jews and others. However, the Israeli judicial authorities failed to prosecute the murderers when they were literally in their hands, and failed, after the publication of the Kahan Report, to prosecute the accomplices who were also mentioned in it by name. The misleading and totally incorrect use of legal terminology in the report cannot but confirm the view of those like Uri Avneri,[1] who considered the commission as a part of the Establishment. The failure to prosecute cannot but lead to the same conclusion in respect of the judicial authorities in Israel.

Here in the United States, in the state of New York, a Chilean police officer who happened to be passing through was tried and convicted for torturing a Chilean boy in Chile. Former Nazi officers like Barbie are still being pursued, and rightly so, for the crimes against humanity which it is alleged they committed many years ago. The international community joined hands in a Convention on the Non-Applicability of Statutory Limitations to War Crimes and Crimes Against Humanity, and Israel is a party to that convention, so that those who committed crimes against humanity and war crimes can never feel secure, regardless of the passage of time. We have all this and yet nobody, not one person, was brought to trial in connection with the Sabra and Chatilla massacres. Not only that, but some of those who were condemned or criticized for their role are still holding very high public office and are still given red-carpet treatment by some of the governments who initiated and prosecuted at the Nuremberg Tribunal.

Surely, there is something fundamentally wrong in the criteria applied to the situation. We refuse to subscribe to the idea underlying this kind of attitude, that the value of the life of any human being depends upon the colour of his or her skin, his or her ethnic, national or religious belonging. To us, human life is sacred. It is the gift of the creator and not of the government, any government. We cannot accept the statement of Eitan, the outgoing Israeli Chief of Staff, that 'the good Arab is a dead Arab' or the dehumanization by Begin of the Palestinians when he called them 'two-legged animals'. In the light of the activities of these two Zionist leaders, these statements were not rhetorical. They expressed a definite attitude of mind dangerous in the extreme.

As a human rights organization, EAFORD cannot subscribe to a view, often expressed, that the enjoyment of human rights depends upon the realization of political solutions. Such an attitude tends to justify violations of human rights or at least to condone them. The second Article of the Universal Declaration of Human Rights reads:

> Everyone is entitled to all the rights and freedoms set forth in this Declaration, without distinction of any kind, such as race, colour, sex, language, religion, political or other opinion, national or social origin, property, birth or other status.
>
> Furthermore, no distinction shall be made on the basis of the political, jurisdictional or international status of the country or territory to which a person belongs, whether it be independent, trust, non-self-governing or under any other limitation of sovereignty.

The International Court of Justice has decided that the Universal Declaration of Human Rights forms a part of the Charter of the United Nations, which is the highest international law document. However, the Israeli Supreme Court dealt a heavy blow to the cause of human rights in Israel and the occupied territories when it decided that the declaration was not binding on the courts of Israel, and when it also decided that the Fourth Geneva Convention, which was signed and ratified by Israel, was not enforceable by Israeli courts. With decisions like these and in the absence of a constitution or bill of rights, as the case is in Israel, it is no wonder that the human rights of the Palestinians, whether in Israel or the occupied territories, are in constant jeopardy.

Respect for human rights has a permanent character which is not affected by the status of the territory. They belong to one by virtue of being a human being. The Nazis used to refer to the Jews as 'rats' and 'lice'. Now General Eitan, the outgoing Israeli Chief of Staff, has bid his farewell to the Israeli Knesset by referring to the Arabs as 'cockroaches', with only little protest from Knesset members.[2] And the Israeli Defence Minister, Mr Arens, in explaining his failure to rebuke the Chief of Staff for his statement, said 'The General is a national hero.'[3]

When misguided religious zeal is combined with fanatical nationalism there is no limit to the destructive attitudes which can be brought into play. Men of religion who should preach love, tolerance, understanding, humility, justice and brotherhood become the mouthpiece of exactly the opposite. The role of many, perhaps the majority, of the rabbis in Israel is the opposite of what we, gladly and gratefully, have seen in this Symposium. The attitude of the official Israeli rabbinate during the invasion of Lebanon could fairly be taken as a call for extermination and mass destruction. We do not and cannot accept injustices deliberately committed by human beings as the expression or fulfilment of divine justice. The Israeli religious parties and groupings have, in general, shown such fanaticism and disregard for the rights and lives of the Palestinians, and indeed of some other Jewish religious denominations, as to raise fundamental questions of belief. Since the creation of Israel, this or that religious party has held the balance whether Labour or Likud was in power, and their influence has been damaging and destructive. We, of course, respect the right of everyone and every group to have their own religious beliefs. But are we to accept a religious-nationalistic movement which preaches and practises violent intolerance of others?

What increases our concern for the future, the future of Israeli Jews and Palestinians alike, for we draw no distinction between the two as to their right to live in dignity, equality and security, what increases our concern is that none of Israel's main political parties is prepared to accept equal rights for the Palestinians. Until this very day, the birth certificate of a Palestinian child born in Israel states 'citizenship: nil' while a child of a member of the Jewish community automatically acquires the right to Israeli citizenship at birth, irrespective of his or her place of birth. The right to nationality is an inalienable right, and discrimination on the basis of national or ethnic belonging is strictly prohibited by international conventions to which Israel is a party, such as the International Convention on the Elimination of All Forms of Racial Discrimination. The Nationality Law which produced such a situation was passed while the Labour Party was in power and has been maintained ever since.

Thus we are faced with a situation where all the effective political and religious powers in Israel are committed to an ideology of racial domination which, of necessity, must pursue a policy of persistent violation of the basic rights and fundamental freedoms of the Palestinian people and which carries with it the seeds of unpleasant and perhaps dangerous reactions not only against the Israelis but also against the world Jewish community. We are very concerned about these reactions. Some in Israel may welcome such developments, though they may vehemently protest against them, in order to increase the flow of Jewish immigration into Palestine. But we are concerned. We are against anti-Semitism wherever and by whoever it is advocated or practised. We believe and support fully the right of Jews wherever they are to live in dignity and equality without any kind of discrimination.

Now, how should we approach the problem? As I said earlier, we in EAFORD do not attempt to offer solutions. We only try to strip the problem in order to expose its true nature, and then to advocate and argue for the criteria that should be applied.

In this Symposium, the distinguished speakers who preceded me threw considerable light on a number of the basic issues often associated with the problem and the manner in which it has become traditionally presented. This process is vital in the search for a solution.

However, it is not enough that the true nature of the problem should be exposed at symposia like this and by speakers like these, greatly distinguished though they are. It is essential that those who truly care about peace and justice, particularly the decision-makers, should speak out loudly and act effectively in accordance with the objective criteria applicable to the issue. In this respect, I think that no state or government whose policies directly affect the cause of world peace and the rights of others can claim immunity from analysis and criticism, where criticism is due. Israeli leaders are not famous for their restraint in their criticism and denunciation of other governments and other leaders.

One answer has never worked and will never work: appeasement. Writing in 1970 about South Africa, the great English statesman, Lord Caradon said: 'Appeasement from outside Southern Africa might put off the racial explosion but in the end it would greatly increase its devastating force.' How true, when we reflect for a moment on the situation in the Middle East. Lord Caradon outlined the first step in the process of dealing with regimes which are based on racial discrimination and the denial of the inalienable rights of the indigenous population. He said:

> First of all, the best thing we could do would be to expose, to discredit, to eliminate the hypocrites. The worst offenders are those who denounce apartheid and racial discrimination with a pharisee's pomposity, and at the same time by their actions sustain and delight those who preach and practise racial domination and injustice.[4]

The second step is that we should insist on solutions based on principles, for these are the only just and durable solutions. In this connection, it is relevant to refer to the speech of President Reagan before the British Houses of Parliament on 8 June 1982. In that speech, the President said: 'For the sake of peace and justice, let us move toward a world in which all people are at last free to determine their own destiny.'

We in EAFORD most certainly support this presidential statement which underlines two important points: the first is the direct interconnection between peace and justice on the one hand and the free determination by all people of their destiny on the other. The second point is that the right of self-determination is a right for all people with no exception. And from this presidential statement it appears to us that the President believes that no justice or peace can be realized unless all people can freely determine their own destiny. With this we also agree.

To our mind, the whole question of Palestine, with the injustices, massacres, wars and conflicts which are associated with it, has arisen from the denial to the Palestinian people of this very right advocated by the President for all people, namely the right to freely determine their own destiny. This right is still being denied, not by the international community, but only or mainly by Israel and the United States. Insistence on that right is not an obstacle to peace and justice but rather a requisite of peace and justice. It is the refusal to admit this right or the tendency to dilute it to nothingness which creates injustice and endangers peace.

Thirdly, we should insist, and we have the right to do so, on respect for the rules and principles of international law which include respect for and observance of international conventions and instruments, particularly those dealing with human rights. Human rights conventions and instruments are not concluded for the protection of states, but for the protection of individuals and groups. They give direct rights to the victims against the state, including, and particularly, their own. States which are parties to these conventions, and states who believe in the principles embodied in those conventions and instruments, have a special responsibility to ensure observance of those rights and they should use whatever leverage they have in that direction - against the perpetrators and not the victims.

We are all aware of the relentless campaigns to ensure the right of Russian Jews to leave their country and to prevent the Palestinians from returning to their country. The right to leave and the right to return are two aspects of the same right. Article 13 (2) of the Universal Declaration of Human Rights reads: 'Everyone has the right to leave any country, including his own, and to return to his country.' It is unacceptable to insist on the rights of some to leave and refuse the right of others to return to their country. Selectivity of application is harmful first to the credibility of the state concerned and secondly to the maintenance of the principle, and no state should deliberately put its credibility in question or use these principles as pawns in political games.

Fourthly, we should work hard at the creation of effective international judicial machinery which can act for the protection of human rights. This is particularly important for the victims of regimes whose basic ideology implies violation of human rights, such as the regimes whose ideology is that of racism and racial discrimination. It is significant to note that Israel, which attacks the investigative machinery of the United Nations regarding violation of human rights in the occupied territories, has made reservations on the jurisdiction of the International Court of Justice in this respect. Thus, by its own action, Israel has denied the possibility of international judicial determination of its observance of the anti-discrimination convention, and yet it attacks all those who uncover its violations.

Fifthly, international and national steps should be taken to bring to justice those accused of war crimes and crimes against humanity, regardless of who they or their victims may be. Civil rights groups in every country should remain active in this field.

In an interview published in the *Jerusalem Post* international edition the author of *The Little Drummer Girl*, John Le Carré, said:

> If you destroyed the entire PLO leadership and all the fighters you would still not scratch the surface of the Palestinian will. That's my conviction. I had the same conviction about the fighters of the Warsaw Ghetto. There are some people who simply cannot be extinguished.[5]

Let us work to protect both people from joint extinction.

Notes

1. See *Ha'olam Ha'zeh*, 16 February 1983.
2. *The Times*, London, 15 April 1983.
3. *Guardian*, London, 19 April 1983.
4. In Sir Francis Vallat (ed.), *An Introduction to the Study of Human Rights* (Europa Publications, London, 1970), p. 55.
5. 3–9 April 1983, p. 10.

Appendix: International Convention on the Elimination of All Forms of Racial Discrimination

Adopted and Opened for Signature and Ratification by General Assembly Resolution 2106 A (XX) of 21 December 1965

Entry into Force: 4 January 1969, in Accordance with Article 19.

The States Parties to this Convention,

Considering that the Charter of the United Nations is based on the principles of the dignity and equality inherent in all human beings, and that all Member States have pledged themselves to take joint and separate action, in co-operation with the Organization, for the achievement of one of the purposes of the United Nations which is to promote and encourage universal respect for and observance of human rights and fundamental freedoms for all, without distinction as to race, sex, language or religion,

Considering that the Universal Declaration of Human Rights proclaims that all human beings are born free and equal in dignity and rights and that everyone is entitled to all the rights and freedoms set out therein, without distinction of any kind, in particular as to race, colour or national origin,

Considering that all human beings are equal before the law and are entitled to equal protection of the law against any discrimination and against any incitement to discrimination,

Considering that the United Nations has condemned colonialism and all practices of segregation and discrimination associated therewith, in whatever form and wherever they exist, and that the Declaration on the Granting of Independence to Colonial Countries and Peoples of 14 December 1960 (General Assembly resolution 1514 (XV)) has affirmed and solemnly proclaimed the necessity of bringing them to a speedy and unconditional end,

Considering that the United Nations Declaration on the Elimination of All Forms of Racial Discrimination of 20 November 1963 (General Assembly resolution 1904 (XVIII)) solemnly affirms the necessity of speedily eliminating racial discrimination throughout the world in all its forms and manifestations and of securing understanding of and respect for the dignity of the human person,

Convinced that any doctrine of superiority based on racial differentiation is scientifically false, morally condemnable, socially unjust and dangerous, and that there is no justification for racial discrimination, in theory or in practice, anywhere,

Reaffirming that discrimination between human beings on the grounds of race, colour or ethnic origin is an obstacle to friendly and peaceful relations among nations and is capable of disturbing peace and security among peoples and the harmony of persons living side by side even within one and the same State,

Convinced that the existence of racial barriers is repugnant to the ideals of any human society,

Alarmed by manifestations of racial discrimination still in evidence in some areas of the world and by governmental policies based on racial superiority or hatred, such as policies of *apartheid*, segregation or separation,

Resolved to adopt all necessary measures for speedily eliminating racial discrimination in all its forms and manifestations, and to prevent and combat racist doctrines and practices in order to promote understanding between races and to build an international community free from all forms of racial segregation and racial discrimination,

Bearing in mind the Convention concerning Discrimination in respect of Employment and Occupation adopted by the International Labour Organization in 1958, and the Convention against Discrimination in Education adopted by the United Nations Educational, Scientific and Cultural Organization in 1960,

Desiring to implement the principles embodied in the United Nations Declaration on the Elimination of All Forms of Racial Discrimination and to secure the earliest adoption of practical measures to that end,

Have agreed as follows:

PART I

Article 1

1. In this Convention, the term 'racial discrimination' shall mean any distinction, exclusion, restriction or preference based on race, colour, descent, or national or ethnic origin which has the purpose or effect of nullifying or impairing the recognition, enjoyment or exercise, on an equal footing, of human rights and fundamental freedoms in the political, economic, social, cultural or any other field of public life.
2. This Convention shall not apply to distinctions, exclusions, restrictions or preferences made by a State Party to this Convention between citizens and non-citizens.
3. Nothing in this Convention may be interpreted as affecting in any way the legal provisions of States Parties concerning nationality, citizenship or naturalization, provided that such provisions do not discriminate against any particular nationality.
4. Special measures taken for the sole purpose of securing adequate advancement of certain racial or ethnic groups or individuals requiring such protection as may be necessary in order to ensure such groups or individuals equal enjoyment or exercise of human rights and fundamental freedoms shall not be deemed racial discrimination, provided, however, that such measures do not, as a consequence, lead to the maintenance of separate rights for different racial groups and that they shall not be continued after the objectives for which they were taken have been achieved.

Article 2

1. States Parties condemn racial discrimination and undertake to pursue by all appropriate means and without delay a policy of eliminating racial discrimination in all its forms and promoting understanding among all races, and, to this end:

(*a*) Each State Party undertakes to engage in no act or practice of racial discrimination against persons, groups of persons or institutions and to ensure that all public authorities and public institutions, national and local, shall act in conformity with this obligation;

(*b*) Each State Party undertakes not to sponsor, defend or support racial discrimination by any persons or organizations;

(*c*) Each State Party shall take effective measures to review governmental, national and local policies, and to amend, rescind or nullify any laws and regulations which have the effect of creating or perpetuating racial discrimination wherever it exists;

(*d*) Each State Party shall prohibit and bring to an end, by all appropriate means, including legislation as required by circumstances, racial discrimination by any persons, group or organization;

(*e*) Each State Party undertakes to encourage, where appropriate, integrationist multiracial organizations and movements and other means of eliminating barriers between races, and to discourage anything which tends to strengthen racial division.

2. States Parties shall, when the circumstances so warrant, take, in the social, economic, cultural and other fields, special and concrete measures to ensure the adequate development and protection of certain racial groups or individuals belonging to them, for the purpose of guaranteeing them the full and equal enjoyment of human rights and fundamental freedoms. These measures shall in no case entail as a consequence the maintenance of unequal or separate rights for different racial groups after the objectives for which they were taken have been achieved.

Article 3

States Parties particularly condemn racial segregation and *apartheid* and undertake to prevent, prohibit and eradicate all practices of this nature in territories under their jurisdiction.

Article 4

States Parties condemn all propaganda and all organizations which are based on ideas or theories of superiority of one race or group of persons of one colour or ethnic origin, or which attempt to justify or promote racial hatred and discrimination in any form, and undertake to adopt immediate and positive measures designed to eradicate all incitement to, or acts of, such discrimination and, to this end, with due regard to the principles embodied in the Universal Declaration of Human Rights and the rights expressly set forth in article 5 of this Convention, *inter alia*:

(*a*) Shall declare an offence punishable by law all dissemination of ideas based on racial superiority or hatred, incitement to racial discrimination, as well as all acts of violence or incitement to such acts against any race or group of persons of another colour or ethnic origin, and also the provision of any assistance to racist activities, including the financing thereof;

(*b*) Shall declare illegal and prohibit organizations, and also organized and all other propaganda activities, which promote and incite racial discrimination, and shall recognize participation in such organizations or activities as an offence punishable by law;

(*c*) Shall not permit public authorities or public institutions, national or local, to promote or incite racial discrimination.

Article 5

In compliance with the fundamental obligations laid down in article 2 of this Convention, States Parties undertake to prohibit and to eliminate racial discrimination in all its forms and to guarantee the right of everyone, without distinction as to race, colour, or national or ethnic origin, to equality before the law, notably in the enjoyment of the following rights :

(*a*) The right to equal treatment before the tribunals and all other organs administering justice;

(*b*) The right to security of person and protection by the State against violence or bodily harm, whether inflicted by government officials or by any individual group or institution;

(*c*) Political rights, in particular the rights to participate in elections—to vote and to stand for election—on the basis of universal and equal suffrage, to take part in the Government as well as in the conduct of public affairs at any level and to have equal access to public service;

(*d*) Other civil rights, in particular:

(i) The right to freedom of movement and residence within the border of the State;
(ii) The right to leave any country, including one's own, and return to one's country;
(iii) The right to nationality;
(iv) The right to marriage and choice of spouse;
(v) The right to own property alone as well as in association with others;
(vi) The right to inherit;
(vii) The right to freedom of thought, conscience and religion;
(viii) The right to freedom of opinion and expression;
(ix) The right to freedom of peaceful assembly and association;

(*e*) Economic, social and cultural rights, in particular:

(i) The rights to work, to free choice of employment, to just and favourable conditions of work, to protection against unemployment, to equal pay for equal work, to just and favourable remuneration;
(ii) The right to form and join trade unions;
(iii) The right to housing;
(iv) The right to public health, medical care, social security and social services;
(v) The right to education and training;
(vi) The right to equal participation in cultural activities;

(*f*) The right of access to any place or service intended for use by the general public, such as transport, hotels, restaurants, cafés, theatres and parks.

Article 6

States Parties shall assure to everyone within their jurisdiction effective protection and remedies, through the competent national tribunals and other State institutions, against any acts of racial discrimination which violate his human rights and fundamental freedoms contrary to this Convention, as well as the right to seek from such tribunals just and adequate reparation or satisfaction for any damage suffered as a result of such discrimination.

Article 7

States Parties undertake to adopt immediate and effective measures, particularly in the fields of teaching, education, culture and information, with a view to combating prejudices which lead to racial discrimination and to promoting understanding, tolerance and friendship among nations and racial or ethnical groups, as well as to propagating the purposes and principles of the Charter of the United Nations, the Universal Declaration of Human Rights, the United Nations Declaration on the Elimination of All Forms of Racial Discrimination, and this Convention.

PART II

Article 8

1. There shall be established a Committee on the Elimination of Racial Discrimination (hereinafter referred to as the Committee) consisting of eighteen experts of high moral standing and acknowledged impartiality

elected by States Parties from among their nationals, who shall serve in their personal capacity, consideration being given to equitable geographical distribution and to the representation of the different forms of civilization as well as of the principal legal systems.
2. The members of the Committee shall be elected by secret ballot from a list of persons nominated by the States Parties. Each State Party may nominate one person from among its own nationals.
3. The initial election shall be held six months after the date of the entry into force of this Convention. At least three months before the date of each election the Secretary-General of the United Nations shall address a letter to the States Parties inviting them to submit their nominations within two months. The Secretary-General shall prepare a list in alphabetical order of all persons thus nominated, indicating the States Parties which have nominated them, and shall submit it to the States Parties.
4. Elections of the members of the Committee shall be held at a meeting of States Parties convened by the Secretary-General at United Nations Headquarters. At that meeting, for which two thirds of the States Parties shall constitute a quorum, the persons elected to the Committee shall be those nominees who obtain the largest number of votes and an absolute majority of the votes of the representatives of States Parties present and voting.
5. (*a*) The members of the Committee shall be elected for a term of four years. However, the terms of nine of the members elected at the first election shall expire at the end of two years; immediately after the first election the names of these nine members shall be chosen by lot by the Chairman of the Committee.

(*b*) For the filling of casual vacancies, the State Party whose expert has ceased to function as a member of the Committee shall appoint another expert from among its nationals, subject to the approval of the Committee.
6. States Parties shall be responsible for the expenses of the members of the Committee while they are in performance of Committee duties.

Article 9

1. States Parties undertake to submit to the Secretary-General of the United Nations, for consideration by the Committee, a report on the legislative, judicial, administrative or other measures which they have adopted and which give effect to the provisions of this Convention:

(*a*) within one year after the entry into force of the Convention for the State concerned; and (*b*) thereafter every two years and whenever the Committee so requests. The Committee may request further information from the States Parties.
2. The Committee shall report annually, through the Secretary-General, to the General Assembly of the United Nations on its activities and may make suggestions and general recommendations based on the examination of the reports and information received from the States Parties. Such suggestions and general recommendations shall be reported to the General Assembly together with comments, if any, from States Parties.

Article 10

1. The Committee shall adopt its own rules of procedure.
2. The Committee shall elect its officers for a term of two years.
3. The secretariat of the Committee shall be provided by the Secretary-General of the United Nations.

4. The meetings of the Committee shall normally be held at United Nations Headquarters.

Article 11

1. If a State Party considers that another State Party is not giving effect to the provisions of this Convention, it may bring the matter to the attention of the Committee. The Committee shall then transmit the communication to the State Party concerned. Within three months, the receiving State shall submit to the Committee written explanations or statements clarifying the matter and the remedy, if any, that may have been taken by that State.
2. If the matter is not adjusted to the satisfaction of both parties, either by bilateral negotiations or by any other procedure open to them, within six months after the receipt by the receiving State of the initial communication, either State shall have the right to refer the matter again to the Committee by notifying the Committee and also the other State.
3. The Committee shall deal with a matter referred to it in accordance with paragraph 2 of this article after it has ascertained that all available domestic remedies have been invoked and exhausted in the case, in conformity with the generally recognized principles of international law. This shall not be the rule where the application of the remedies is unreasonably prolonged.
4. In any matter referred to it, the Committee may call upon the States Parties concerned to supply any other relevant information.
5. When any matter arising out of this article is being considered by the Committee, the States Parties concerned shall be entitled to send a representative to take part in the proceedings of the Committee, without voting rights, while the matter is under consideration.

Article 12

1. (*a*) After the Committee has obtained and collated all the information it deems necessary, the Chairman shall apppoint an *ad hoc* Conciliation Commission (hereinafter referred to as the Commission) comprising five persons who may or may not be members of the Committee. The members of the Commission shall be appointed with the unanimous consent of the parties to the dispute, and its good offices shall be made available to the States concerned with a view to an amicable solution of the matter on the basis of respect for this Convention.

(*b*) If the States parties to the dispute fail to reach agreement within three months on all or part of the composition of the Commission, the members of the Commission not agreed upon by the States parties to the dispute shall be elected by secret ballot by a two-thirds majority vote of the Committee from among its own members.

2. The members of the Commission shall serve in their personal capacity. They shall not be nationals of the States parties to the dispute or of a State not Party to this Convention.
3. The Commission shall elect its own Chairman and adopt its own rules of procedure.
4. The meetings of the Commission shall normally be held at United Nations Headquarters or at any other convenient place as determined by the Commission.
5. The secretariat provided in accordance with article 10, paragraph 3, of this Convention shall also service the Commission whenever a dispute among States Parties brings the Commission into being.

6. The States parties to the dispute shall share equally all the expenses of the members of the Commission in accordance with estimates to be provided by the Secretary-General of the United Nations.
7. The Secretary-General shall be empowered to pay the expenses of the members of the Commission, if necessary, before reimbursement by the States parties to the dispute in accordance with paragraph 6 of this article.
8. The information obtained and collated by the Committee shall be made available to the Commission, and the Commission may call upon the States concerned to supply any other relevant information.

Article 13

1. When the Commission has fully considered the matter, it shall prepare and submit to the Chairman of the Committee a report embodying its findings on all questions of fact relevant to the issue between the parties and containing such recommendations as it may think proper for the amicable solution of the dispute.
2. The Chairman of the Committee shall communicate the report of the Commission to each of the States parties to the dispute. These States shall, within three months, inform the Chairman of the Committee whether or not they accept the recommendations contained in the report of the Commission.
3. After the period provided for in paragraph 2 of this article, the Chairman of the Committee shall communicate the report of the Commission and the declarations of the States Parties concerned to the other States Parties to this Convention.

Article 14

1. A State Party may at any time declare that it recognizes the competence of the Committee to receive and consider communications from individuals or groups of individuals within its jurisdiction claiming to be victims of a violation by that State Party of any of the rights set forth in this Convention. No communication shall be received by the Committee if it concerns a State Party which has not made such a declaration.
2. Any State Party which makes a declaration as provided for in paragraph 1 of this article may establish or indicate a body within its national legal order which shall be competent to receive and consider petitions from individuals and groups of individuals within its jurisdiction who claim to be victims of a violation of any of the rights set forth in this Convention and who have exhausted other available local remedies.
3. A declaration made in accordance with paragraph 1 of this article and the name of any body established or indicated in accordance with paragraph 2 of this article shall be deposited by the State Party concerned with the Secretary-General of the United Nations, who shall transmit copies thereof to the other States Parties. A declaration may be withdrawn at any time by notification to the Secretary-General, but such a withdrawal shall not affect communications pending before the Committee.
4. A register of petitions shall be kept by the body established or indicated in accordance with paragraph 2 of this article, and certified copies of the register shall be filed annually through appropriate channels with the Secretary-General on the understanding that the contents shall not be publicly disclosed.
5. In the event of failure to obtain satisfaction from the body established

or indicated in accordance with paragraph 2 of this article, the petitioner shall have the right to communicate the matter to the Committee within six months.

6. (*a*) The Committee shall confidentially bring any communication referred to it to the attention of the State Party alleged to be violating any provision of this Convention, but the identity of the individual or groups of individuals concerned shall not be revealed without his or their express consent. The Committee shall not receive anonymous communications.

(*b*) Within three months, the receiving State shall submit to the Committee written explanations or statements clarifying the matter and the remedy, if any, that may have been taken by that State.

7. (*a*) The Committee shall consider communications in the light of all information made available to it by the State Party concerned and by the petitioner. The Committee shall not consider any communication from a petitioner unless it has ascertained that the petitioner has exhausted all available domestic remedies. However, this shall not be the rule where the application of the remedies is unreasonably prolonged.

(*b*) The Committee shall forward its suggestions and recommendations, if any, to the State Party concerned and to the petitioner.

8. The Committee shall include in its annual report a summary of such communications and, where appropriate, a summary of the explanations and statements of the States Parties concerned and of its own suggestions and recommendations.

9. The Committee shall be competent to exercise the functions provided for in this article only when at least ten States Parties to this Convention are bound by declarations in accordance with paragraph 1 of this article.

Article 15

1. Pending the achievement of the objectives of the Declaration on the Granting of Independence to Colonial Countries and Peoples, contained in General Assembly resolution 1514 (XV) of 14 December 1960, the provisions of this Convention shall in no way limit the right of petition granted to these peoples by other international instruments or by the United Nations and its specialized agencies.

2. (*a*) The Committee established under article 9, paragraph 1, of this Convention shall receive copies of the petitions from, and submit expressions of opinion and recommendations on these petitions to, the bodies of the United Nations which deal with matters directly related to the principles and objectives of this Convention in their consideration of petitions from the inhabitants of Trust and Non-Self-Governing Territories and all other territories to which General Assembly resolution 1514 (XV) applies, relating to matters covered by this Convention which are before these bodies.

(*b*) The Committee shall receive from the competent bodies of the United Nations copies of the reports concerning the legislative, judicial, administrative or other measures directly related to the principles and objectives of this Convention applied by the administering Powers within the Territories mentioned in subparagrah (*a*) of this paragraph, and shall express opinions and make recommendations to these bodies.

3. The Committee shall include in its report to the General Assembly a summary of the petitions and reports it has received from United Nations bodies, and the expressions of opinion and recommendations of the

Committee relating to the said petitions and reports.
4. The Committee shall request from the Secretary-General of the United Nations all information relevant to the objectives of this Convention and available to him regarding the Territories mentioned in paragraph 2 (*a*) of this article.

Article 16

The provisions of this Convention concerning the settlement of disputes or complaints shall be applied without prejudice to other procedures for settling disputes or complaints in the field of discrimination laid down in the constituent instruments of, or in conventions adopted by, the United Nations and its specialized agencies, and shall not prevent the States Parties from having recourse to other procedures for settling a dispute in accordance with general or special international agreements in force between them.

PART III

Article 17

1. This Convention is open for signature by any State Member of the United Nations or member of any of its specialized agencies, by any State Party to the Statute of the International Court of Justice, and by any other State which has been invited by the General Assembly of the United Nations to become a Party to this Convention.
2. This Convention is subject to ratification. Instruments of ratification shall be deposited with the Secretary-General of the United Nations.

Article 18

1. This Convention shall be open to accession by any State referred to in article 17, paragraph 1, of the Convention.
2. Accession shall be effected by the deposit of an instrument of accession with the Secretary-General of the United Nations.

Article 19

1. This Convention shall enter into force on the thirtieth day after the date of the deposit with the Secretary-General of the United Nations of the twenty-seventh instrument of ratification or instrument of accession.
2. For each State ratifying this Convention or acceding to it after the deposit of the twenty-seventh instrument of ratification or instrument of accesssion, the Convention shall enter into force on the thirtieth day after the date of the deposit of its own instrument of ratification or instrument of accession.

Article 20

1. The Secretary-General of the United Nations shall receive and circulate to all States which are or may become Parties to this Convention reservations made by States at the time of ratification or accession. Any State which objects to the reservation shall, within a period of ninety days from the date of the said communication, notify the Secretary-General that it does not accept it.
2. A reservation incompatible with the object and purpose of this Convention shall not be permitted, nor shall a reservation the effect of which would inhibit the operation of any of the bodies established by this Convention be allowed. A reservation shall be considered incompatible or inhibitive if at least two thirds of the States Parties to this Convention object to it.
3. Reservations may be withdrawn at any time by notification to this effect

addressed to the Secretary-General. Such notification shall take effect on the date on which it is received.

Article 21

A State Party may denounce this Convention by written notification to the Secretary-General of the United Nations. Denunciation shall take effect one year after the date of receipt of the notification by the Secretary-General.

Article 22

Any dispute between two or more States Parties with respect to the interpretation or application of this Convention, which is not settled by negotiation or by the procedures expressly provided for in this Convention, shall, at the request of any of the parties to the dispute, be referred to the International Court of Justice for decision, unless the disputants agree to another mode of settlement.

Article 23

1. A request for the revision of this Convention may be made at any time by any State Party by means of a notification in writing addressed to the Secretary-General of the United Nations.
2. The General Assembly of the United Nations shall decide upon the steps, if any, to be taken in respect of such a request.

Article 24

The Secretary-General of the United Nations shall inform all States referred to in article 17, paragraph 1, of this Convention of the following particulars:

(*a*) Signatures, ratifications and accessions under articles 17 and 18;
(*b*) The date of entry into force of this Convention under article 19;
(*c*) Communications and declarations received under articles 14, 20 and 23;
(*d*) Denunciations under article 21.

Article 25

1. This Convention, of which the Chinese, English, French, Russian and Spanish texts are equally authentic, shall be deposited in the archives of the United Nations.
2. The Secretary-General of the United Nations shall transmit certified copies of this Convention to all States belonging to any of the categories mentioned in article 17, paragraph 1, of the Convention.

19. Message from Habib Chatty

Secretary-General of the Islamic Conference Organization

I bring you a message of goodwill and hope, of goodwill towards this gathering of individuals whose spiritual strengths derive from the same sources as ours, of hope that this Seminar will be yet another step forward in the re-establishment of justice for a people to whom justice has too long been denied and in the creation of a better future for a city which moves the hearts of 2½ billion believers of three great faiths.

For 35 years now the problem of Palestine has lain before the conscience of the world, and the particular conscience of the United States. Two generations now have witnessed the progressive deterioration in the situation of a Palestinian people alienated from their own lands, and Jerusalem suffering from the consequences of a plan whose primary objective is the progressive modification of the cultural character of this city, sacred to the three great monotheistic religions, of making it lose its universal identity, and of erasing 24 centuries of its glorious past.

Unfortunately, attempts by the Muslim world to have its voice heard on this issue have come up against fairly insurmountable difficulties. The main reason for this lies in what we see as total American support to Israel and its policies -- a support which has in our opinion encouraged Israel to embark on an implantation and an aggressive expansionism based on a questionable 'historical right', and an equally questionable 'right to security'. Yet it continues to enjoy the unqualified support of this great country. When, may we ask, will Palestine no longer be seen through the deforming prism of electoral calculations, often linked with internal American objectives which have nothing to do with the merits of the problem?

Perhaps the fallacy lies in the continuing consideration of Israel as the key to American containment of Soviet expansionism in the Middle East. Yet the facts show that this unqualified solidarity has weakened, rather than strengthened, American positions in the Middle East, and that it continues to weaken them even further by pushing states which are least suspect of pro-Soviet leanings and loyalties into positions of 'positive neutrality' and reserve *vis-à-vis* a Western world which they see as oppressors of the Muslim people, who have committed no other crime than to have been chosen by the West to resolve its own problems of conscience.

A second reason for the deafness of the ears on which our appeal falls, lies in the unworthy stereotypes which are commonly peddled in the Western world, and which all too facilely equate Islam with fanaticism. Whoever fights against Islam is seen as fighting against fanaticism, and therefore deserving of the sympathy of the Western world, whereas the struggle of Islam itself, for respect for its sympols and for its roots, is erroneously seen as anti-Western. On the other hand, the worst demands of a Zionism which has unilaterally and questionably declared itself as the sole voice of a Jewish community, are seen as the forlorn cries of a persecuted minority. Little attempt is made to distinguish between this Zionism and a Judaism which we respect and which we feel must be distinguished from it.

Let us therefore attempt an objective analysis, in the hope that it will be judged logically and equitably on its own merits, without recourse to the stereotypes which have automatically presented a Zionist cause as full of justice, being rejected by a Muslim fanaticism full of blind obstinacy.

The tragic exterminations to which innocent Jewish populations were subjected did not as far as we know take place in any Muslim lands. Whether it be the time of the inquisition in Spain, or that of the pogroms in Russia and Poland, or of Nazism and Fascism in Germany and Italy, it is in the Western world that terror was let loose upon the Jews, and in many cases it is towards Muslim lands that they came to search for refuge. Thus the direct responsibility for the situation in the Middle East which followed the establishment of the state of Israel lies squarely at the door of the Western world. Equally, the responsibility for what we may call the re-establishment of peace in this region devolves also on this Western world and its conscience.

We in the Muslim world do not stand against Judaism, which contains a set of spiritual values which we share and believe in. The prophet Moses is as much a prophet of Islam as he is the prophet of Judaism. No, our contradiction is not with Judaism, but with a twisted Zionist philosophy which says it draws its justification from the Holocaust against the Jews, but which has turned into a holocaust against the Palestinian people. Our struggle is against racism and expansionism, against religious intolerance, against the conversion of moral and civilizational values into this political theory and practice of exclusive and arrogant expansionism.

It is altogether fitting therefore that we should be meeting here today in the capital of this country with its great and longstanding traditions of faith and decency and justice, of commitment to the principles of fundamental human rights, of the right to self-determination, of freedom of worship, of non-admissibility of territorial aggrandisement by force. It is to the standard bearers of these noble traditions that our appeal is addressed, on behalf of a people whose homes and rights have been violated, and a city which is losing its soul. More than just the Palestinians and Jerusalem, it is these principles and traditions which are at stake. We ask no more than that they be applied fairly by men of goodwill and conscience. We are happy to see that these men of goodwill and conscience today are our Jewish brothers who are just as deeply concerned by the issues at stake as we are ourselves. To them we hold out this message of hope and friendship, in admiration for their courage, their commitment to the principles of their faith, and their devotion to truth and justice.

20. Message from Yassir Arafat

Chairman of the Palestine Liberation Organization, Commander-in-Chief of the Forces of the Palestinian Revolution

In my name and on behalf of the Executive Committee of the Palestine Liberation Organization, I extend to you warm and personal greetings, wishing your conference all success.

You meet at a most critical and difficult time for the Palestinian and the Arab nation. Palestinians today suffer from a war of genocide and annihilation, directed against them by the Israeli government to totally destroy them as a people, their national and cultural identity. Thousands of Palestinians are being massacred, arrested and tortured, poisoned and expelled in the occupied Palestinian territories and in Israeli-occupied south Lebanon.

We appeal to you and to all honourable Americans to stop this genocide against the Palestinian people, to stop sending massive American weapons to Israel, and to work for a real and lasting peace in the Middle East based on the right of the Palestinian people to self-determination and national independence as well as the recognition of the PLO by the US administration, as the sole legitimate representative of our people.

You represent a humane, honourable American consciousness that opposes war, genocide and racism and seeks peace and equality for all.

I salute your noble efforts and hope we can all meet in the land of peace, the land of Palestine.

Index

Regina Sharif
NON-JEWISH ZIONISM:
Its Roots in Western History
Hb and Pb

Alain Gresh
THE PLO: THE STRUGGLE WITHIN
Towards an Independent Palestinian State
Hb and Pb

Naseer H. Aruri (Editor)
OCCUPATION:
Israel Over Palestine
Hb and Pb

B.J. Odeh
LEBANON: CLASS AND CONFESSIONALISM
A Modern Political History
Hb and Pb

Lenni Brenner
THE IRON WALL
Zionist Revisionism from Jabotinsky to Shamir
Hb and Pb

Uri Avnery
MY FRIEND, THE ENEMY
Hb and Pb

EAFORD AND AJAZ (Editors)
JUDAISM OR ZIONISM?
What Difference for the Middle East?
Hb and Pb

Richard Locke and Antony Stewart
BANTUSTAN GAZA
Hb and Pb

Leena Saraste
FOR PALESTINE
Hb and Pb

HUMAN RIGHTS

Jan Metzger, Martin Orth and Christian Sterzing
THIS LAND IS OUR LAND:
The West Bank Under Israeli Occupation
Hb and Pb

Gerard Chaliand and Yves Ternon
THE ARMENIANS:
From Genocide to Terrorism
Hb and Pb

Permanent People's Tribunal
A CRIME OF SILENCE
The Armenian Genocide
Hb and Pb

WOMEN

Asma el Dareer
WOMAN, WHY DO YOU WEEP!
Circumcision and Its Consequences
Hb and Pb

Azar Tabari and Nahid Yeganeh
IN THE SHADOW OF ISLAM:
The Women's Movement in Iran
Hb and Pb

Ingela Bendt and James Downing
WE SHALL RETURN:
Women of Palestine
Hb and Pb

Miranda Davies (Editor)
THIRD WORLD — SECOND SEX:
Women's Struggles and National Liberation
Hb and Pb

Nawal el Saadawi
THE HIDDEN FACE OF EVE:
Women in the Arab World
Hb and Pb

Raqiya Haji Dualeh Abdalla
SISTERS IN AFFLICTION: Circumcision and Infibulation of Women in Africa
Hb and Pb

Raymonda Tawil
MY HOME, MY PRISON
Pb

Juliette Minces
THE HOUSE OF OBEDIENCE: Women in Arab Society
Hb and Pb

Kumari Jayawardena
FEMINISM AND NATIONALISM IN THE THIRD WORLD
Hb and Pb

CULTURE AND SOCIETY

Hani al-Raheb
THE ZIONIST CHARACTER IN THE ENGLISH NOVEL
Hb and Pb

Fouzi el-Asmar
THROUGH THE HEBREW LOOKING GLASS
Arab Stereotypes of Children's Literature
Hb and Pb

FICTION

Nawal el Saadawi
WOMAN AT POINT ZERO
Hb and Pb

Nawal el Saadawi
GOD DIES BY THE NILE
Hb and Pb

Emile Habiby
THE SECRET LIFE OF SAEED
The Pessoptimist
Hb and Pb

Esmail Fassih
SORRAYA IN A COMA
Hb and Pb

Zed titles cover Africa, Asia, Latin America and the Middle East, as well as general issues affecting the Third World's relations with the rest of the world. Our series embrace: Imperialism, Women, Political Economy, History, Labour, Voices of Struggle, Human Rights and other areas pertinent to the Third World.